Gran
Dre

PRESENTED BY KENJI INOUE & KIMITAKE YOSHIOKA

The Colorful Cast of Grand Blue Dreaming

Diving Club Peek-a-Boo (PaB)

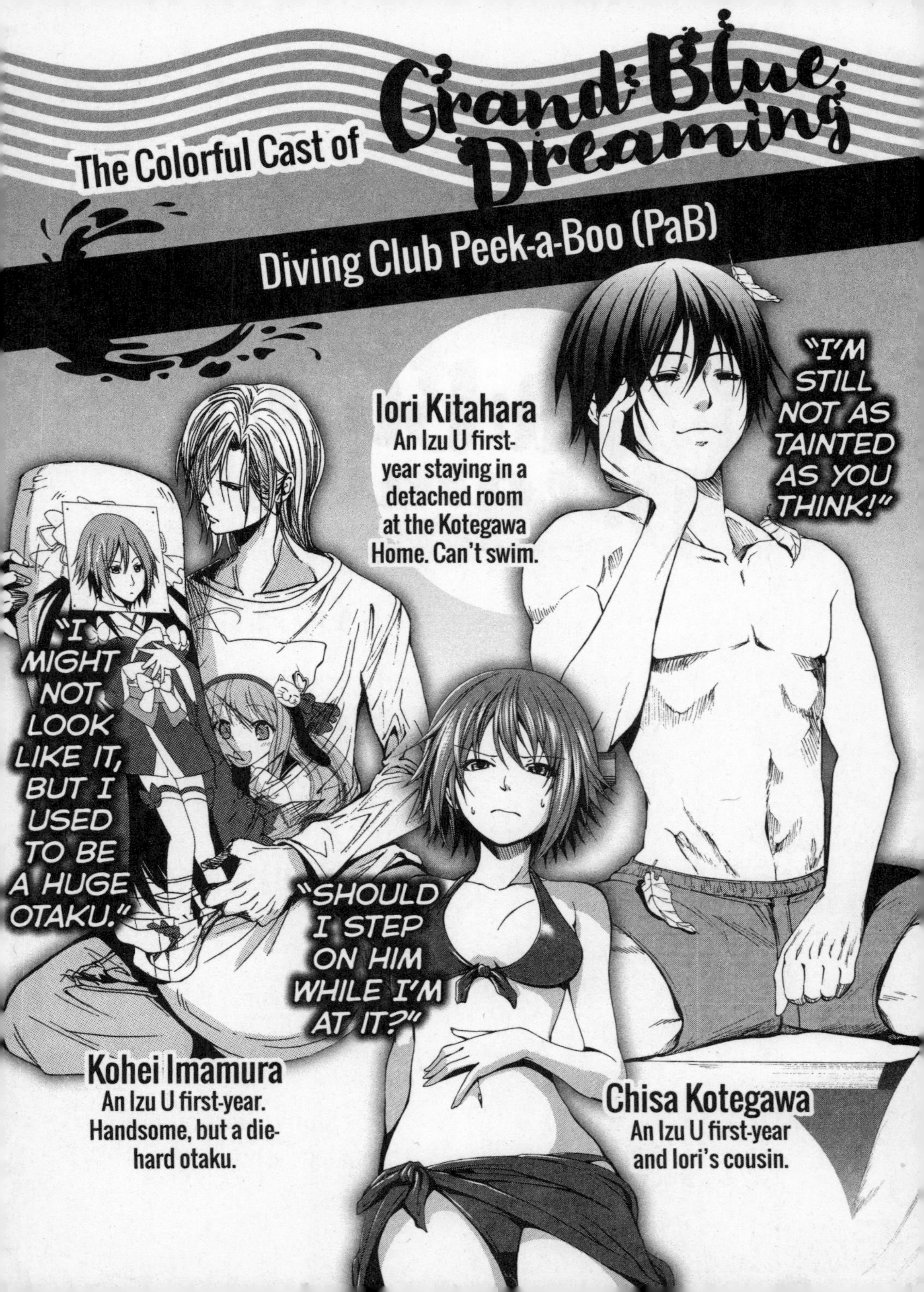
"I'M STILL NOT AS TAINTED AS YOU THINK!"
"SHOULD I STEP ON HIM WHILE I'M AT IT?"
"I MIGHT NOT LOOK LIKE IT, BUT I USED TO BE A HUGE OTAKU."

Iori Kitahara
An Izu U first-year staying in a detached room at the Kotegawa Home. Can't swim.

Chisa Kotegawa
An Izu U first-year and Iori's cousin.

Kohei Imamura
An Izu U first-year. Handsome, but a die-hard otaku.

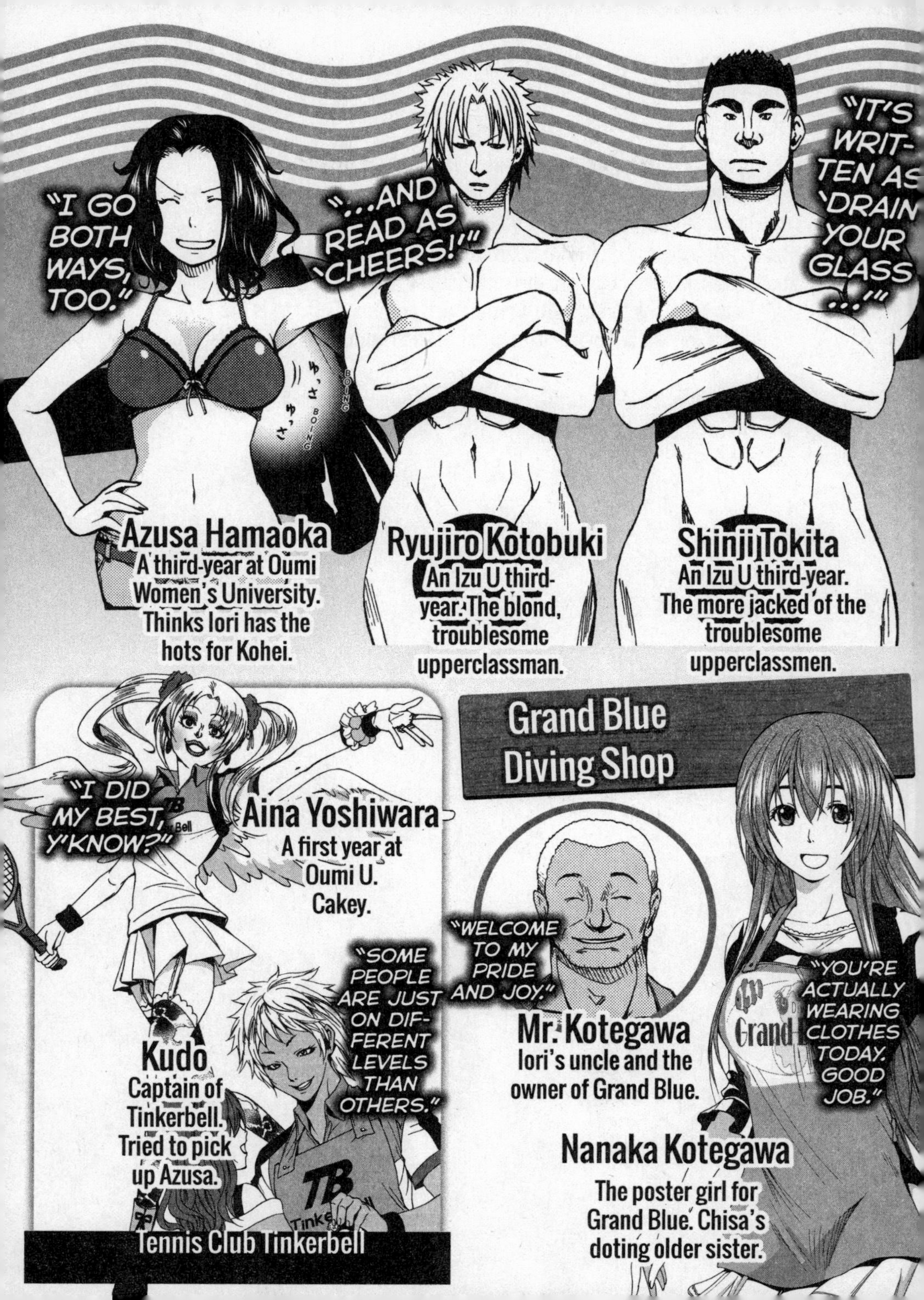

"IT'S WRITTEN AS 'DRAIN YOUR GLASS...'"
Shinji Tokita
An Izu U third-year. The more jacked of the troublesome upperclassmen.
"...AND READ AS 'CHEERS!'"
Ryujiro Kotobuki
An Izu U third-year. The blond, troublesome upperclassman.
"I GO BOTH WAYS, TOO."
ゆっさ ゆっさ
BOING BOING
Azusa Hamaoka
A third-year at Oumi Women's University. Thinks Iori has the hots for Kohei.
Grand Blue Diving Shop
"YOU'RE ACTUALLY WEARING CLOTHES TODAY. GOOD JOB."
Nanaka Kotegawa
The poster girl for Grand Blue. Chisa's doting older sister.
"WELCOME TO MY PRIDE AND JOY."
Mr. Kotegawa
Iori's uncle and the owner of Grand Blue.
"I DID MY BEST, Y'KNOW?"
Aina Yoshiwara
A first year at Oumi U. Cakey.
"SOME PEOPLE ARE JUST ON DIFFERENT LEVELS THAN OTHERS."
Kudo
Captain of Tinkerbell. Tried to pick up Azusa.
Tennis Club Tinkerbell

The Story so Far

It is Izu University's famed Spring Festival.

Aiming for the prize money, Iori shines on the stage of the "dongtest," while giving Kudo a taste of his own medicine for mocking Tinkerbell's cake-faced angel, Aina, in the process.

Meanwhile, Chisa wins the Miss Izu contest. However, despite embarrassing herself to help Iori raise money for the club, he (seemingly) went off to get cozy with another girl.. Furious, Chisa tells the crowd that Iori is her boyfriend in order to keep guys from hitting on her.

Having been wasted the entire time, Iori and Kohei are unaware that every man on campus is now out for their blood...

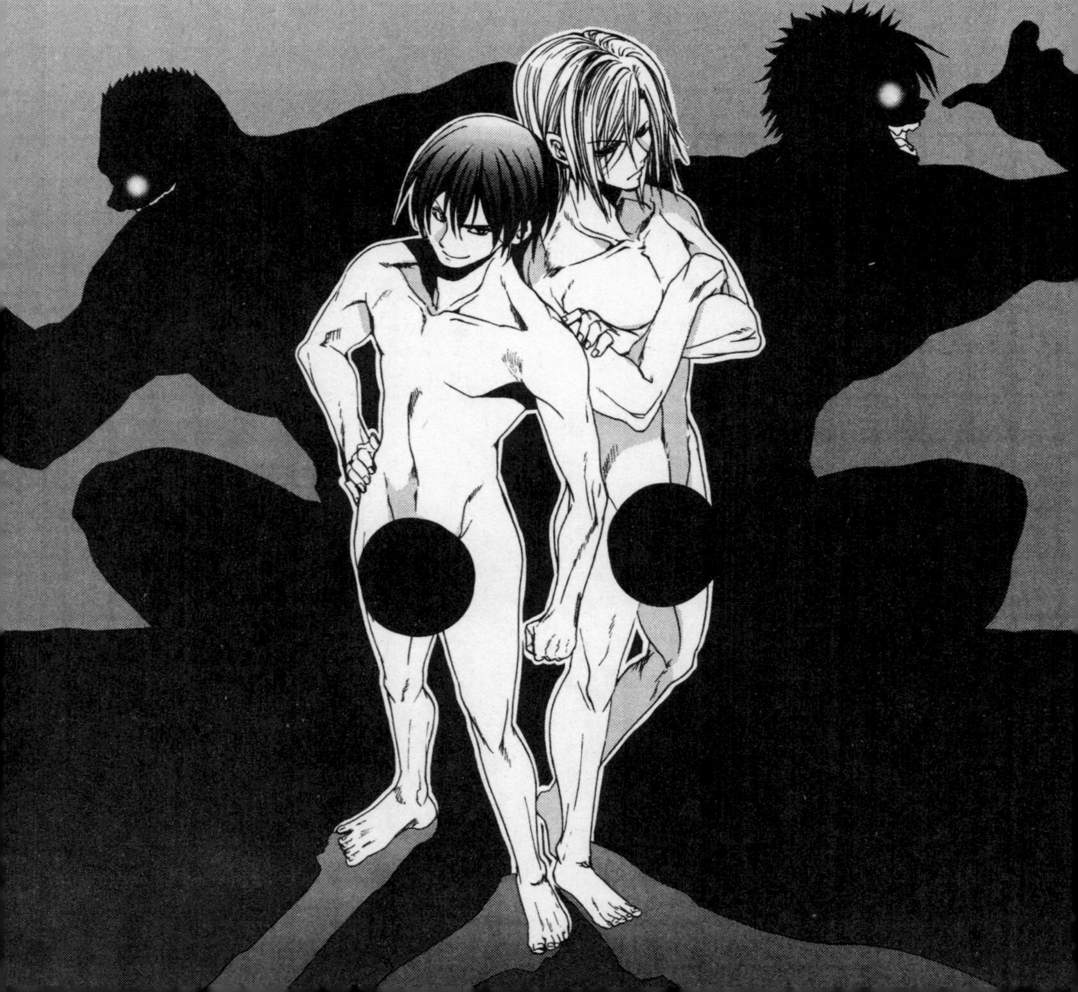

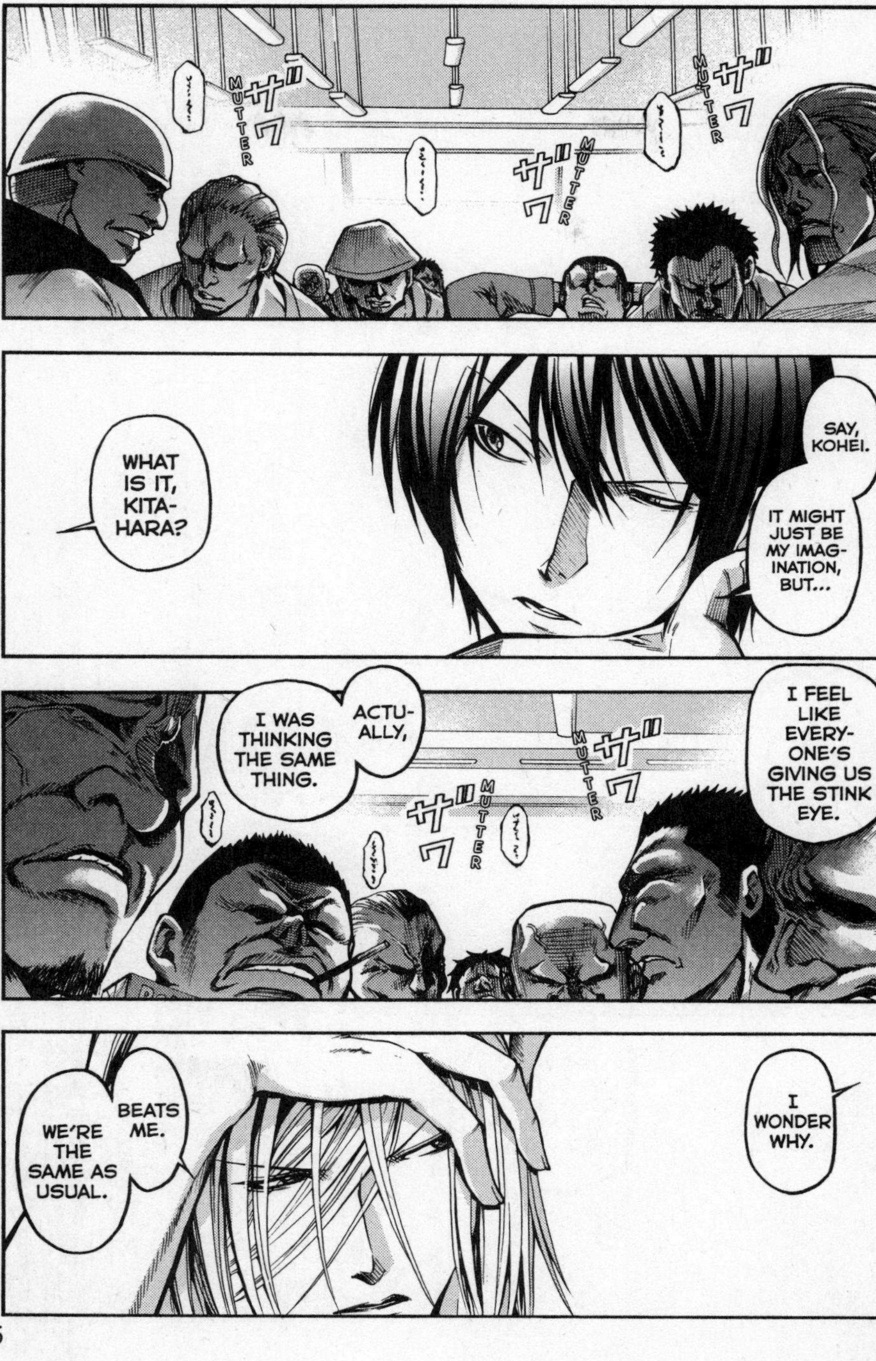
ザワ MUTTER
ザワ MUTTER
ザワ MUTTER
SAY, KOHEI.
IT MIGHT JUST BE MY IMAG-INATION, BUT...
WHAT IS IT, KITA-HARA?
I FEEL LIKE EVERY-ONE'S GIVING US THE STINK EYE.
ザワ MUTTER
ACTU-ALLY,
I WAS THINKING THE SAME THING.
ザワ MUTTER
I WONDER WHY.
BEATS ME.
WE'RE THE SAME AS USUAL.

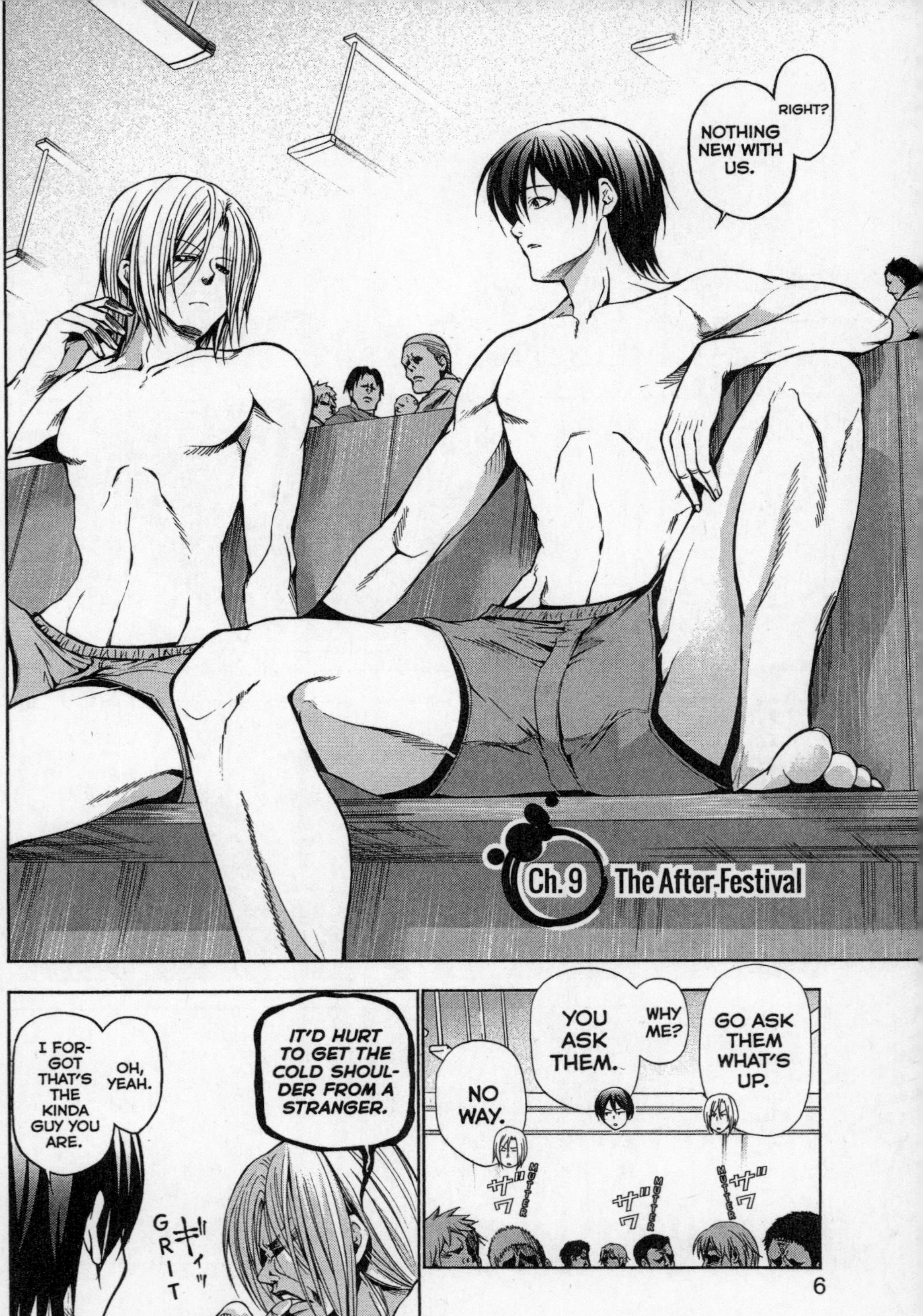
NOTHING NEW WITH US. RIGHT?
Ch. 9 The After-Festival
GO ASK THEM WHAT'S UP.
WHY ME?
YOU ASK THEM.
NO WAY.
ザワ MUTTER
ザワ MUTTER
ザワ MUTTER
IT'D HURT TO GET THE COLD SHOULDER FROM A STRANGER.
OH, YEAH.
I FOR-GOT THAT'S THE KINDA GUY YOU ARE.
ギリッ GRIT

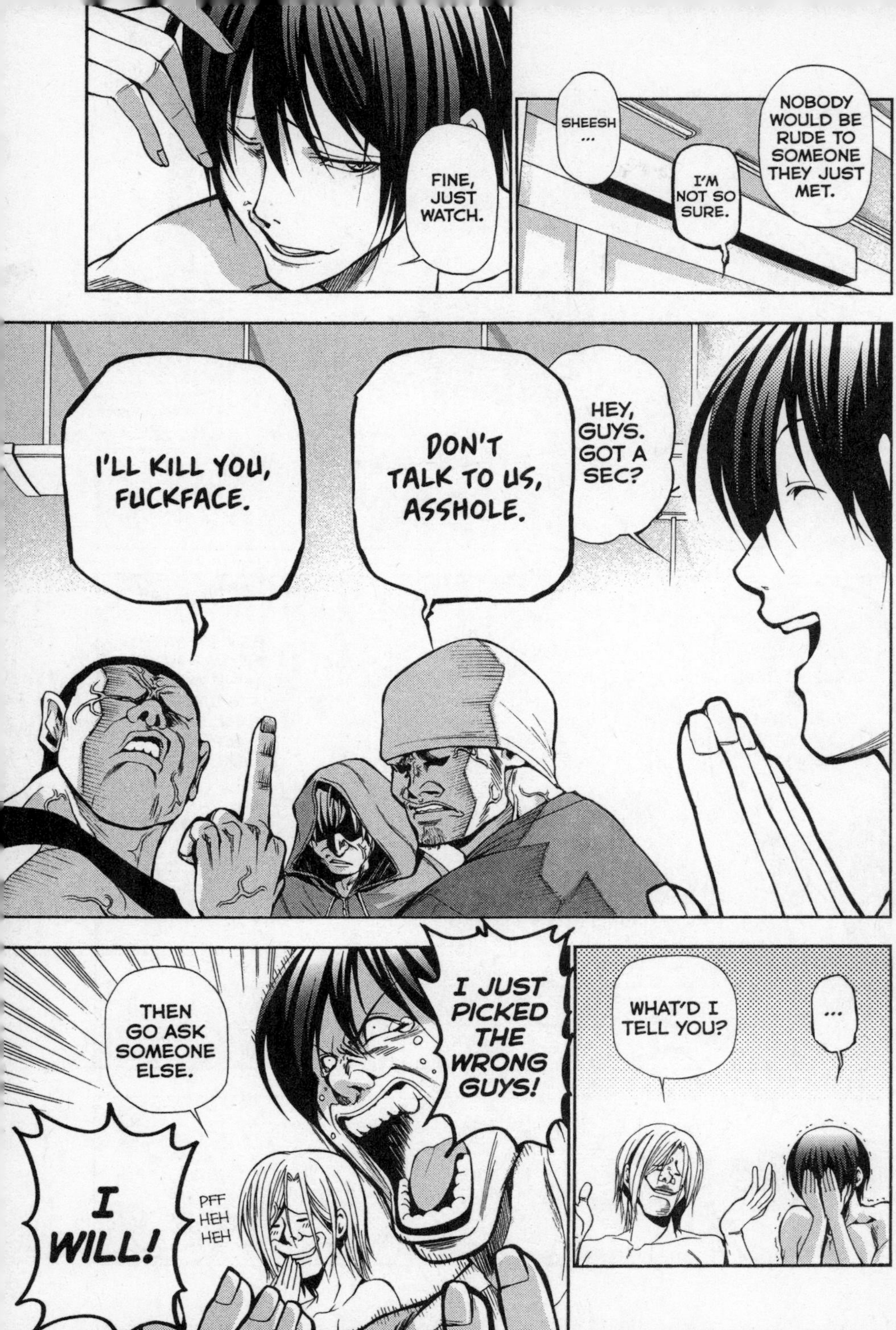
NOBODY WOULD BE RUDE TO SOMEONE THEY JUST MET.
I'M NOT SO SURE.
SHEESH ...
FINE, JUST WATCH.
HEY, GUYS. GOT A SEC?
DON'T TALK TO US, ASSHOLE.
I'LL KILL YOU, FUCKFACE.
...
WHAT'D I TELL YOU?
I JUST PICKED THE WRONG GUYS!
THEN GO ASK SOMEONE ELSE.
PFF HEH HEH
I WILL!

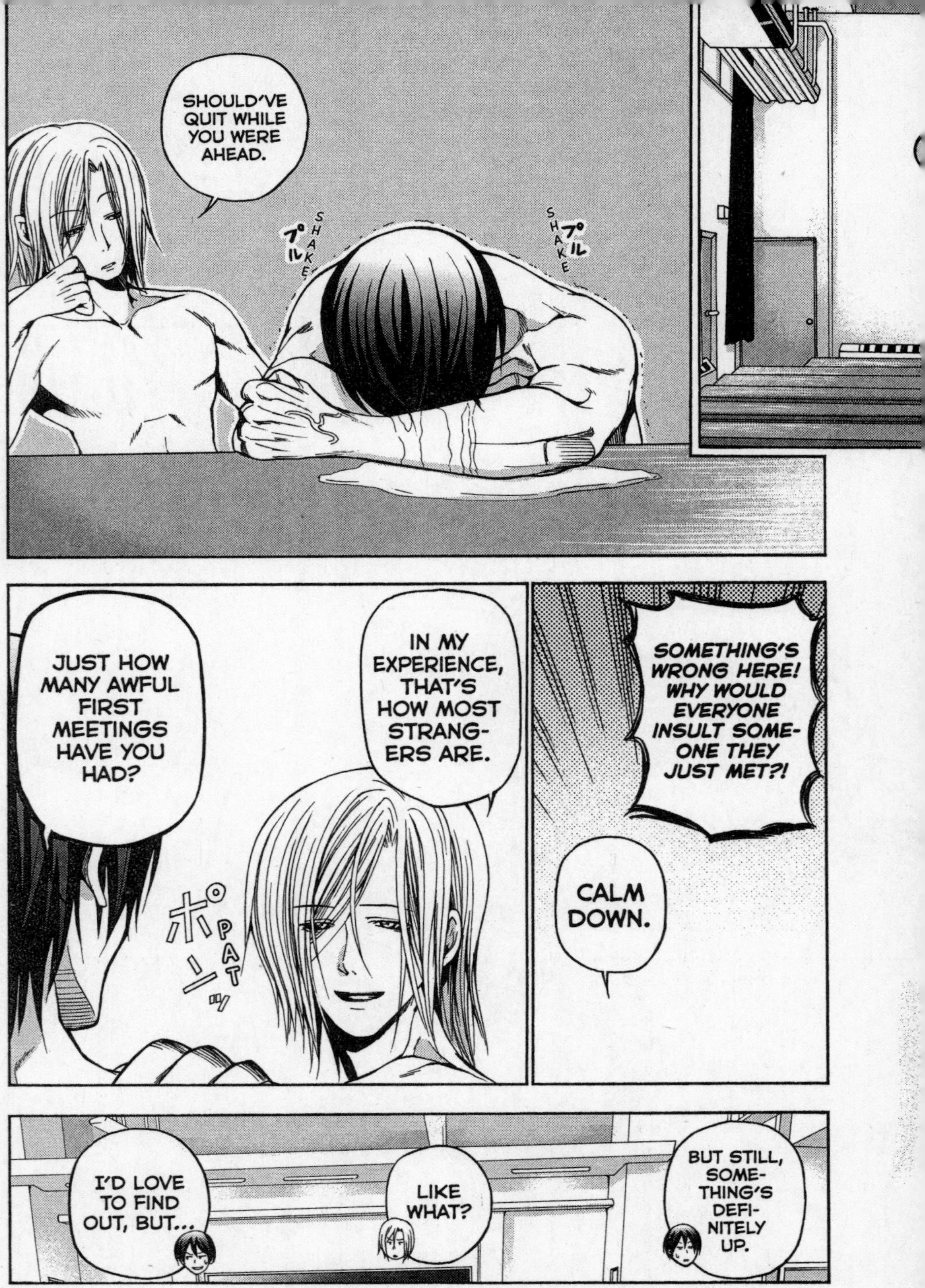
SHOULD'VE QUIT WHILE YOU WERE AHEAD.
プル SHAKE
プル SHAKE
SOMETHING'S WRONG HERE! WHY WOULD EVERYONE INSULT SOME-ONE THEY JUST MET?!
CALM DOWN.
IN MY EXPERIENCE, THAT'S HOW MOST STRANG-ERS ARE.
JUST HOW MANY AWFUL FIRST MEETINGS HAVE YOU HAD?
ポン PAT
BUT STILL, SOME-THING'S DEFI-NITELY UP.
LIKE WHAT?
I'D LOVE TO FIND OUT, BUT...

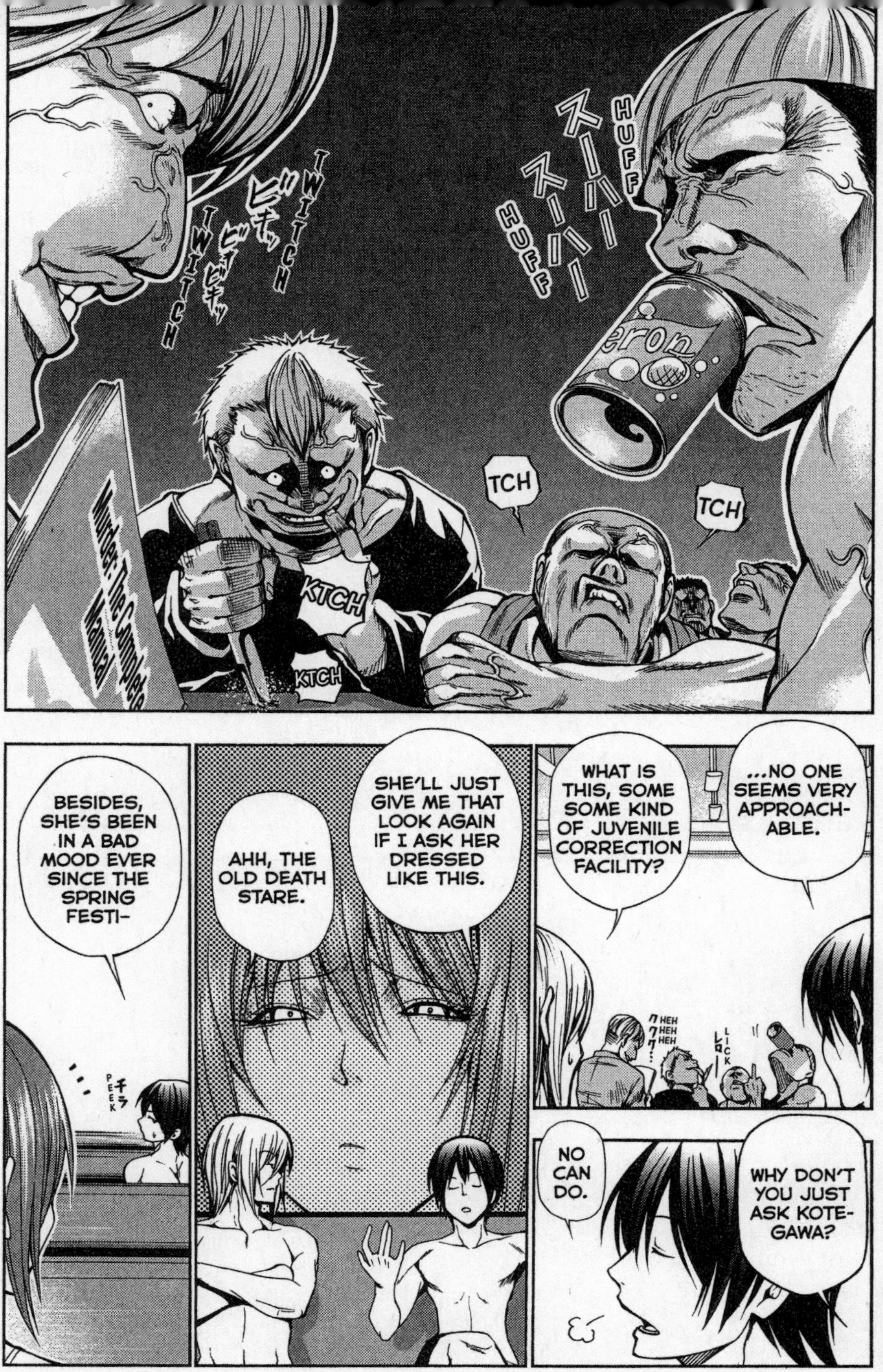

HUFF
スーハー
HUFF
スーハー
TWITCH
ビクッ
TWITCH
ビクビクッ
eron
TCH
TCH
KTCH
KTCH
Murder: The Complete Manual
...NO ONE SEEMS VERY APPROACHABLE.
WHAT IS THIS, SOME SOME KIND OF JUVENILE CORRECTION FACILITY?
LICK
レロー
HEH HEH HEH
ククク…
WHY DON'T YOU JUST ASK KOTEGAWA?
NO CAN DO.
SHE'LL JUST GIVE ME THAT LOOK AGAIN IF I ASK HER DRESSED LIKE THIS.
AHH, THE OLD DEATH STARE.
BESIDES, SHE'S BEEN IN A BAD MOOD EVER SINCE THE SPRING FESTI-
PEEK
チラ

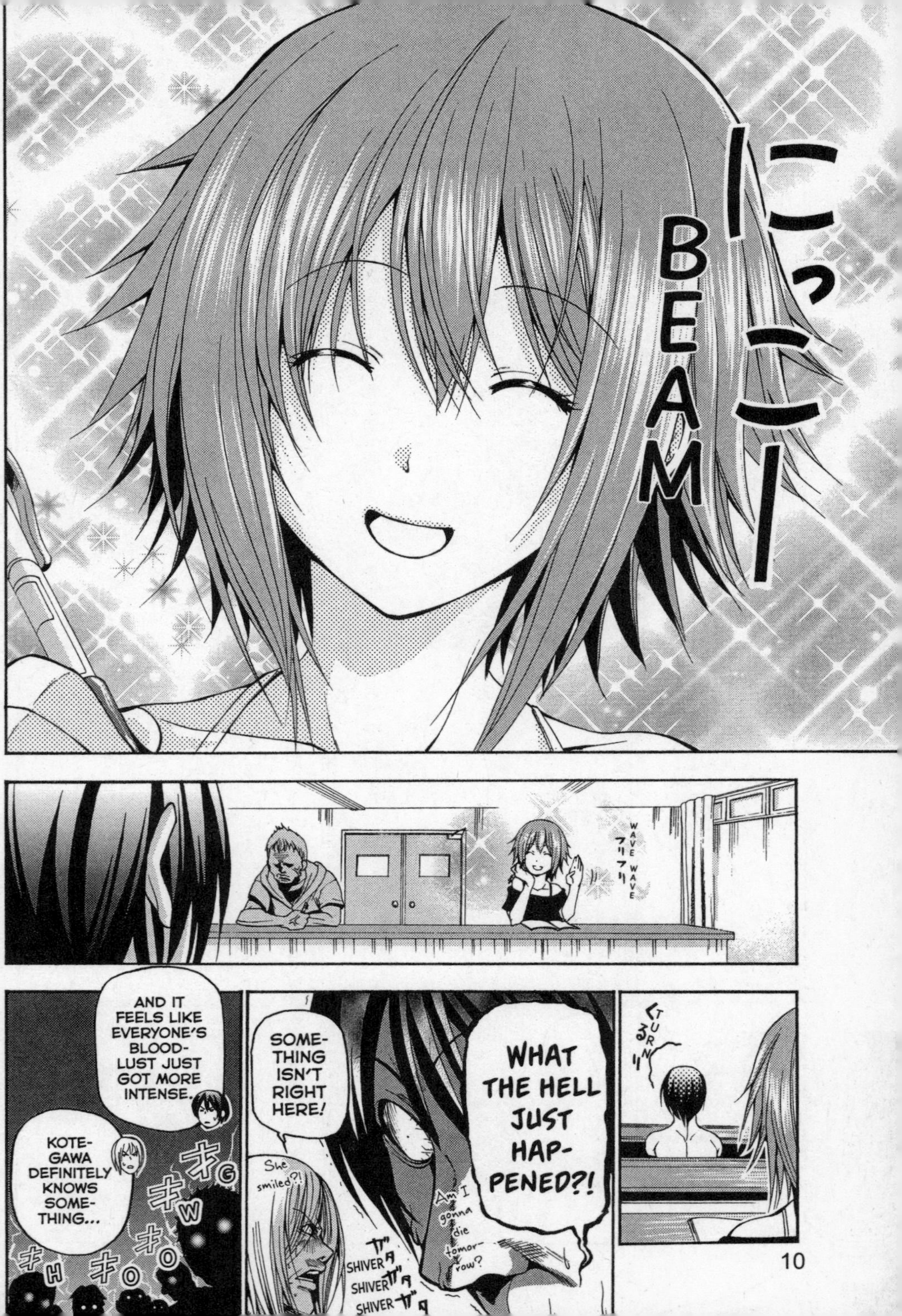

にっこー
BEAM
WAVE WAVE
フリフリ
くるり
TURN
WHAT THE HELL JUST HAPPENED?!
SOMETHING ISN'T RIGHT HERE!
She smiled?!
Am I gonna die tomorrow?
SHIVER ガタ
SHIVER ガタ
SHIVER ガタ
AND IT FEELS LIKE EVERYONE'S BLOODLUST JUST GOT MORE INTENSE.
KOTEGAWA DEFINITELY KNOWS SOMETHING...

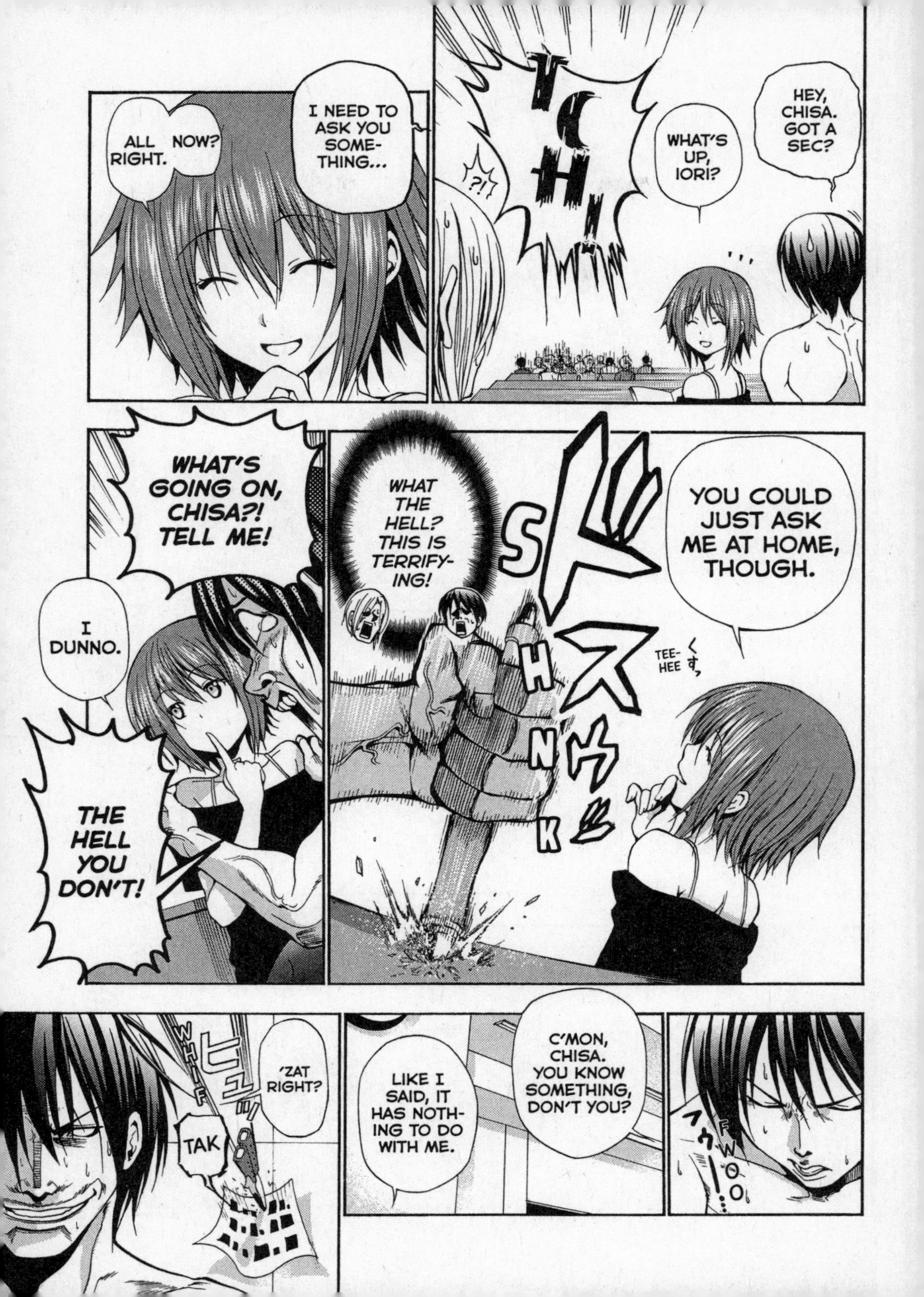
HEY, CHISA. GOT A SEC?
WHAT'S UP, IORI?
?!
I NEED TO ASK YOU SOME-THING...
NOW?
ALL RIGHT.
YOU COULD JUST ASK ME AT HOME, THOUGH.
TEE-HEE
くすっ
SHNK
ドスゥ
WHAT THE HELL? THIS IS TERRIFY-ING!
WHAT'S GOING ON, CHISA?! TELL ME!
I DUNNO.
THE HELL YOU DON'T!
FWOO
フゥ…
C'MON, CHISA. YOU KNOW SOMETHING, DON'T YOU?
LIKE I SAID, IT HAS NOTH-ING TO DO WITH ME.
'ZAT RIGHT?
WHIF
ヒュッ
TAK

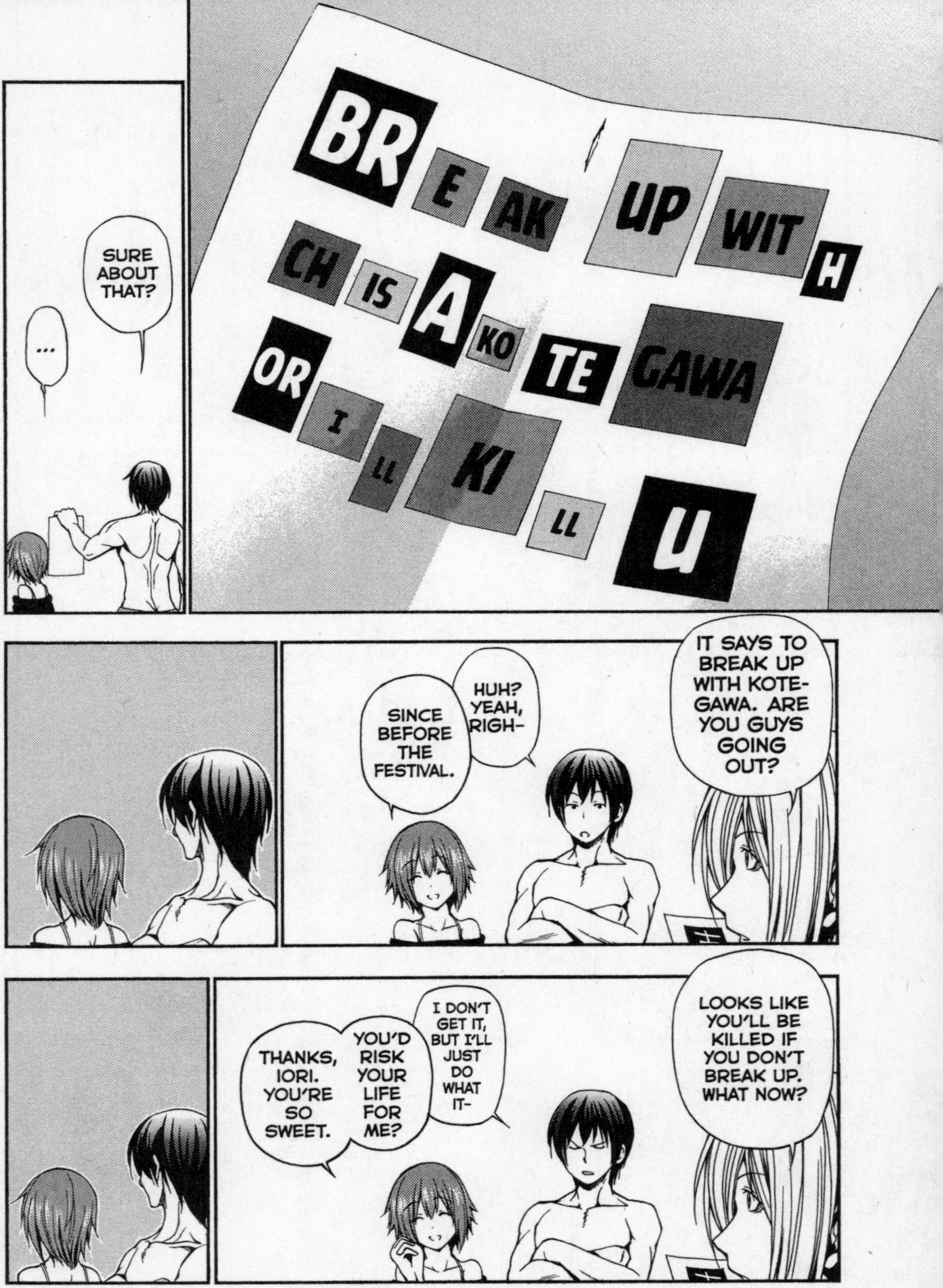
BR E AK UP WIT H
CH IS A KO TE GAWA
OR I LL KI LL U
SURE ABOUT THAT?
...
IT SAYS TO BREAK UP WITH KOTE-GAWA. ARE YOU GUYS GOING OUT?
HUH? YEAH, RIGH-
SINCE BEFORE THE FESTIVAL.
LOOKS LIKE YOU'LL BE KILLED IF YOU DON'T BREAK UP. WHAT NOW?
I DON'T GET IT, BUT I'LL JUST DO WHAT IT-
YOU'D RISK YOUR LIFE FOR ME?
THANKS, IORI. YOU'RE SO SWEET.

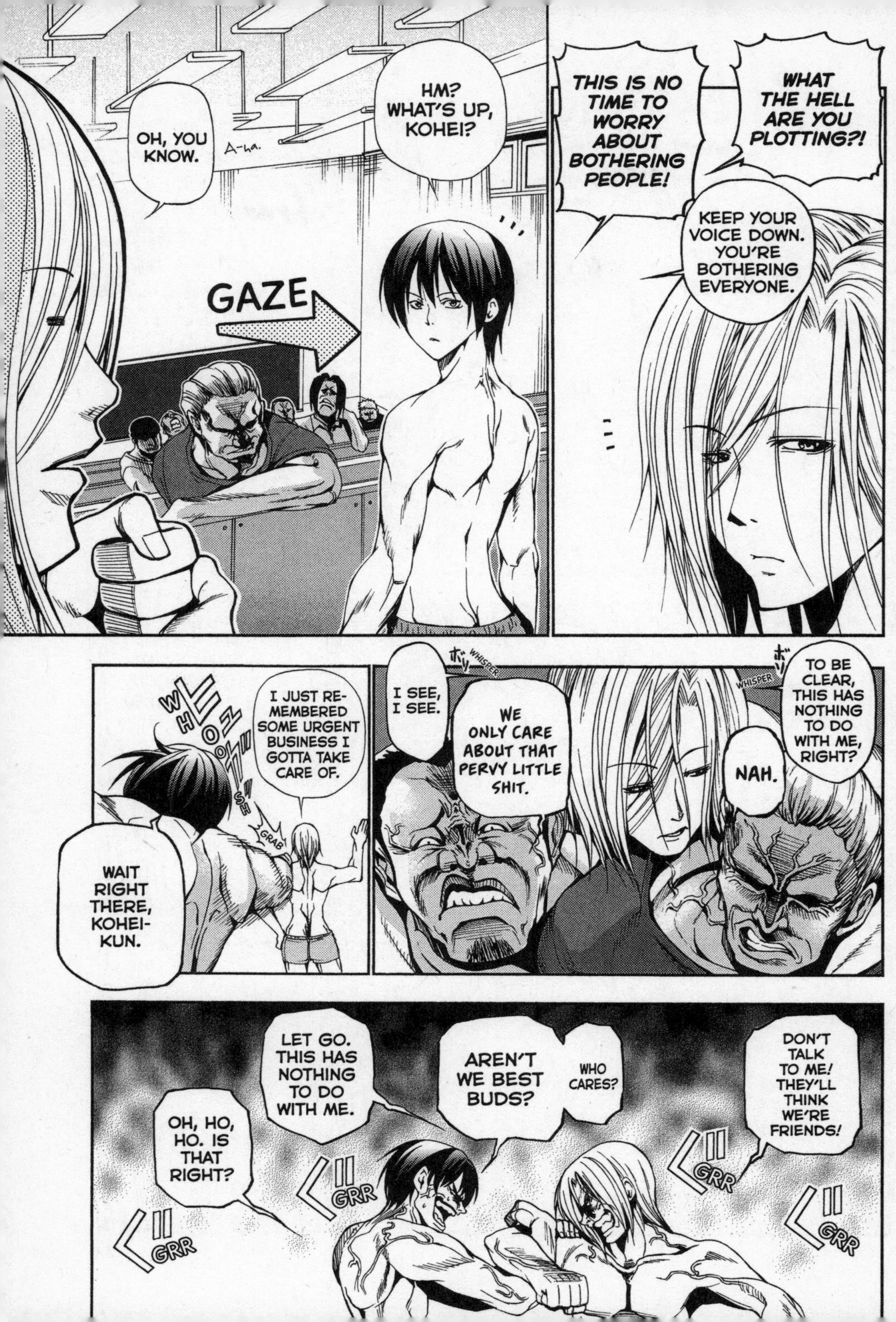
WHAT THE HELL ARE YOU PLOTTING?!
THIS IS NO TIME TO WORRY ABOUT BOTHERING PEOPLE!
KEEP YOUR VOICE DOWN. YOU'RE BOTHERING EVERYONE.
HM? WHAT'S UP, KOHEI?
OH, YOU KNOW.
A-ha.
GAZE
TO BE CLEAR, THIS HAS NOTHING TO DO WITH ME, RIGHT?
WHISPER
NAH.
I SEE, I SEE.
WHISPER
WE ONLY CARE ABOUT THAT PERVY LITTLE SHIT.
I JUST RE-MEMBERED SOME URGENT BUSINESS I GOTTA TAKE CARE OF.
WHOOOSH
GRAB
WAIT RIGHT THERE, KOHEI-KUN.
DON'T TALK TO ME! THEY'LL THINK WE'RE FRIENDS!
GRR
WHO CARES?
AREN'T WE BEST BUDS?
GRR
LET GO. THIS HAS NOTHING TO DO WITH ME.
GRR
OH, HO, HO. IS THAT RIGHT?
GRR

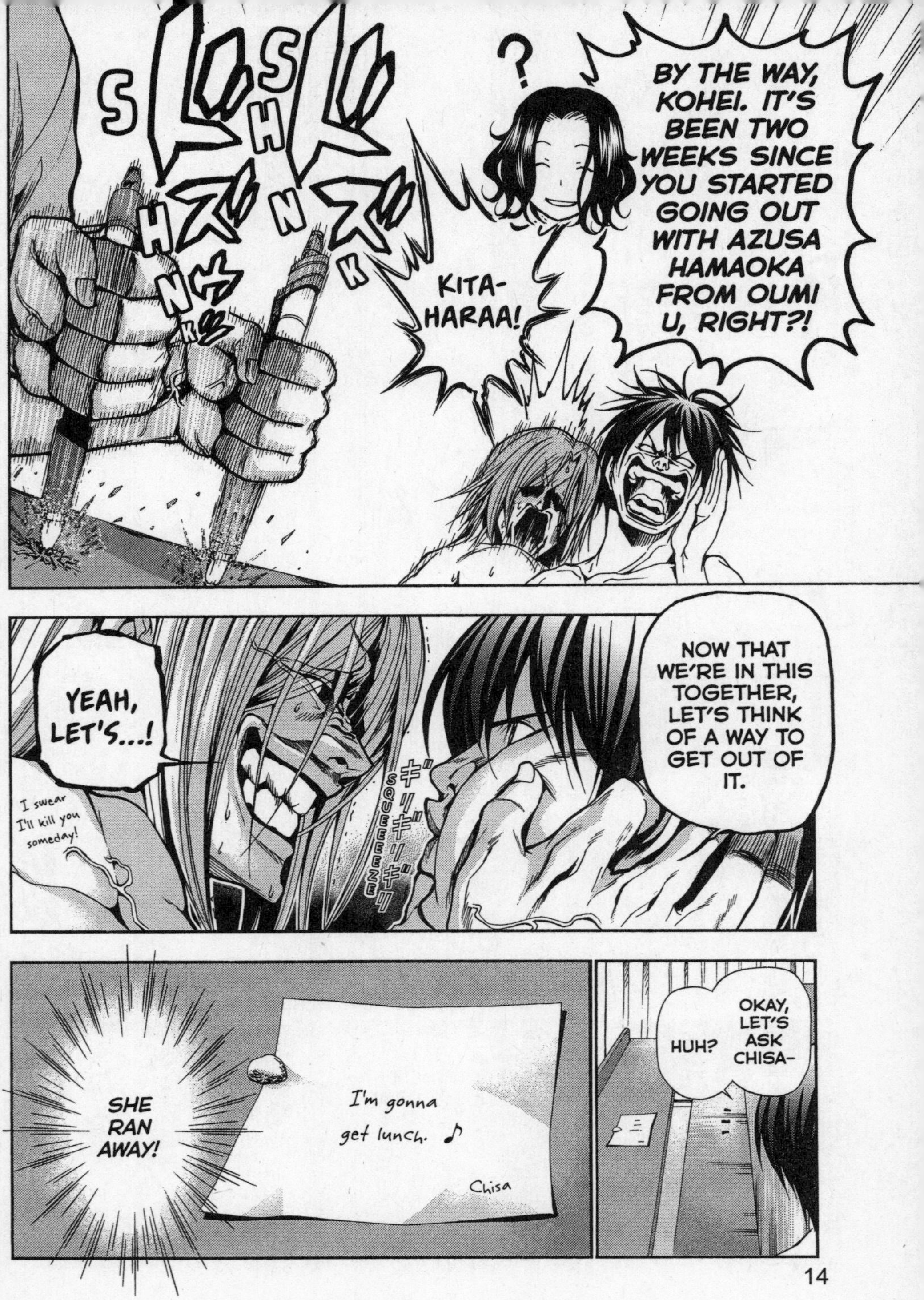
BY THE WAY, KOHEI. IT'S BEEN TWO WEEKS SINCE YOU STARTED GOING OUT WITH AZUSA HAMAOKA FROM OUMI U, RIGHT?!
?
KITA-HARAAA!
SHNK
SHNK
NOW THAT WE'RE IN THIS TOGETHER, LET'S THINK OF A WAY TO GET OUT OF IT.
SQUEEEEZE
YEAH, LET'S...!
I swear I'll kill you someday!
OKAY, LET'S ASK CHISA-
HUH?
I'm gonna get lunch. ♪
Chisa
SHE RAN AWAY!

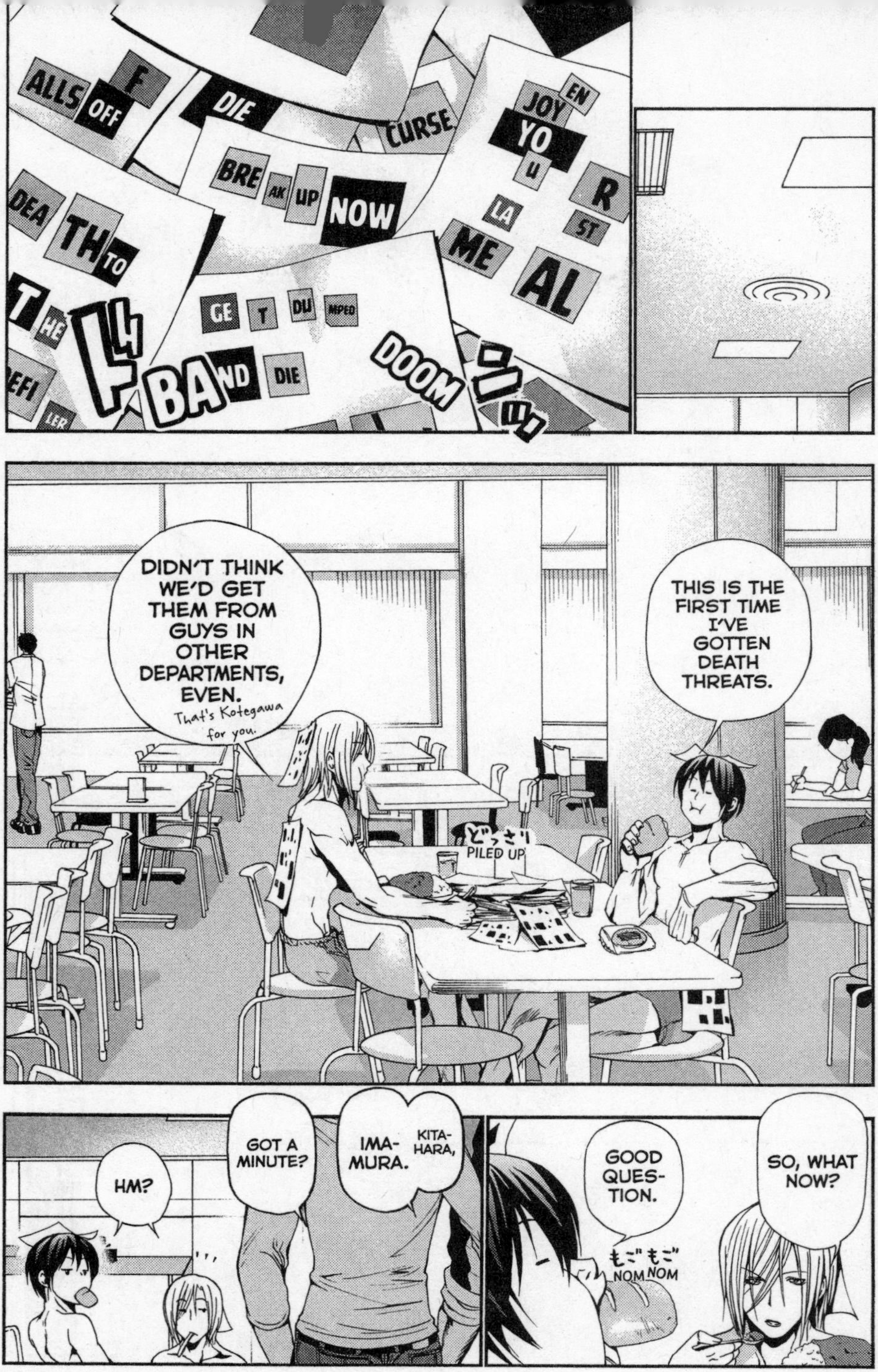

ALLS OFF F
DIE
CURSE
JOY EN
YOU
R
BRE AK UP NOW
DEA TH TO
LA ST
ME
AL
T HE
GE T DU MPED
BA ND DIE
DOOM
THIS IS THE FIRST TIME I'VE GOTTEN DEATH THREATS.
DIDN'T THINK WE'D GET THEM FROM GUYS IN OTHER DEPARTMENTS, EVEN.
That's Kotegawa for you.
どっさり PILED UP
SO, WHAT NOW?
GOOD QUESTION.
もごもご NOM NOM
KITAHARA, IMAMURA.
GOT A MINUTE?
HM?

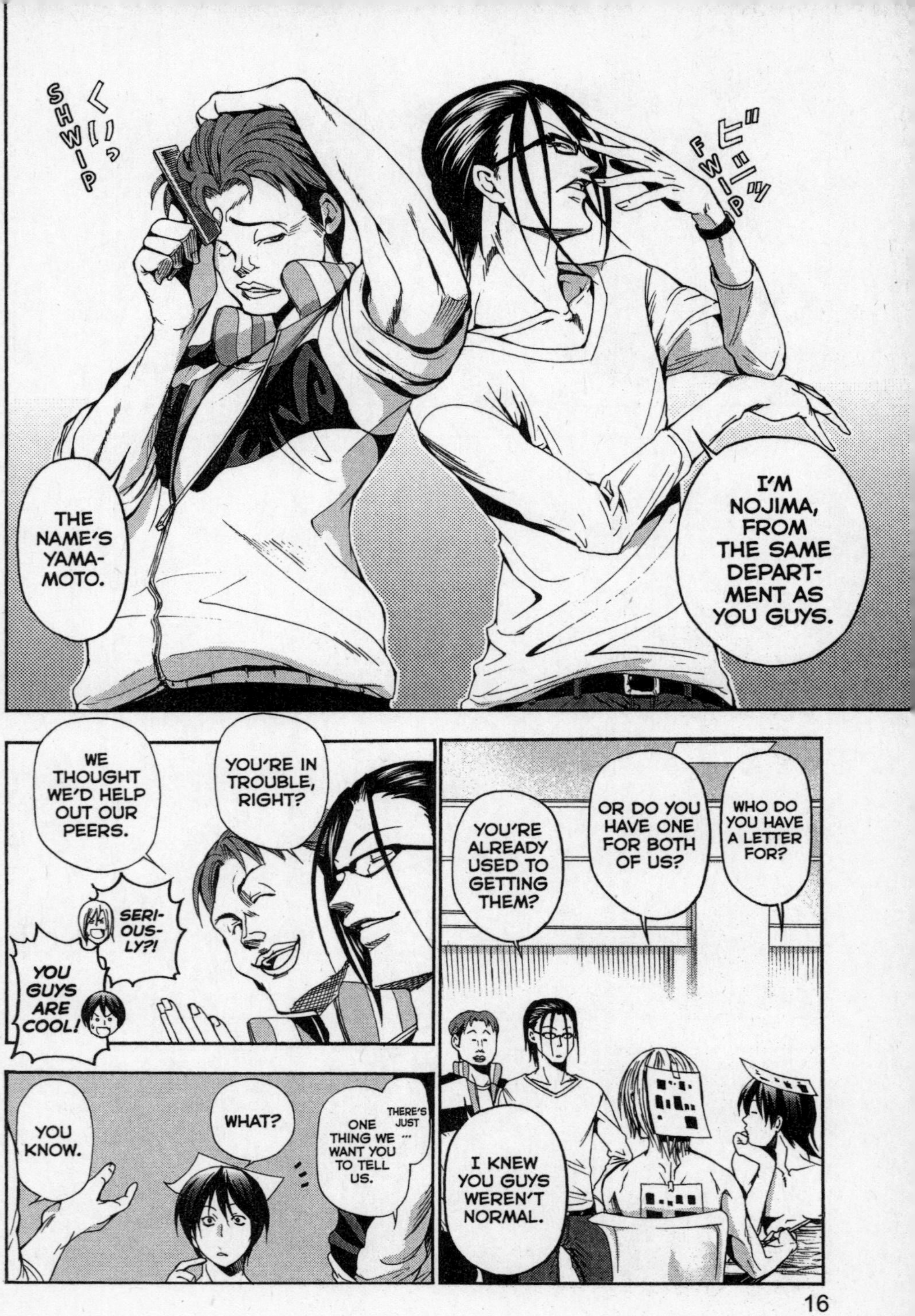
FWIP
SHWIP
I'M NOJIMA, FROM THE SAME DEPARTMENT AS YOU GUYS.
THE NAME'S YAMAMOTO.
WHO DO YOU HAVE A LETTER FOR?
OR DO YOU HAVE ONE FOR BOTH OF US?
YOU'RE ALREADY USED TO GETTING THEM?
I KNEW YOU GUYS WEREN'T NORMAL.
YOU'RE IN TROUBLE, RIGHT?
WE THOUGHT WE'D HELP OUT OUR PEERS.
SERIOUSLY?!
YOU GUYS ARE COOL!
THERE'S JUST ... ONE THING WE WANT YOU TO TELL US.
WHAT?
YOU KNOW.

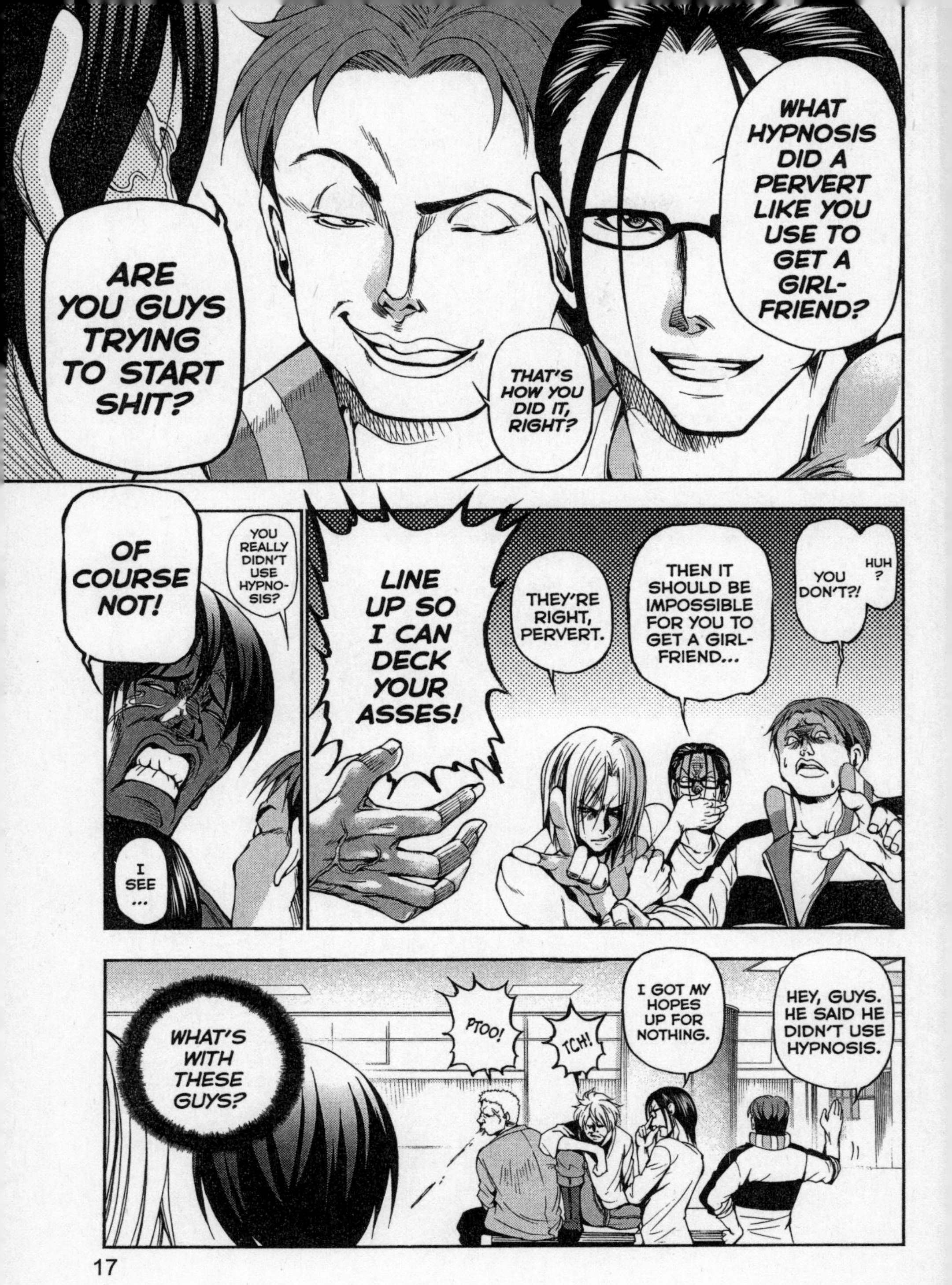
WHAT HYPNOSIS DID A PERVERT LIKE YOU USE TO GET A GIRLFRIEND?
THAT'S HOW YOU DID IT, RIGHT?
ARE YOU GUYS TRYING TO START SHIT?
HUH?
YOU DON'T?!
THEN IT SHOULD BE IMPOSSIBLE FOR YOU TO GET A GIRLFRIEND...
THEY'RE RIGHT, PERVERT.
LINE UP SO I CAN DECK YOUR ASSES!
YOU REALLY DIDN'T USE HYPNOSIS?
OF COURSE NOT!
I SEE...
HEY, GUYS. HE SAID HE DIDN'T USE HYPNOSIS.
I GOT MY HOPES UP FOR NOTHING.
TCH!
PTOO!
WHAT'S WITH THESE GUYS?

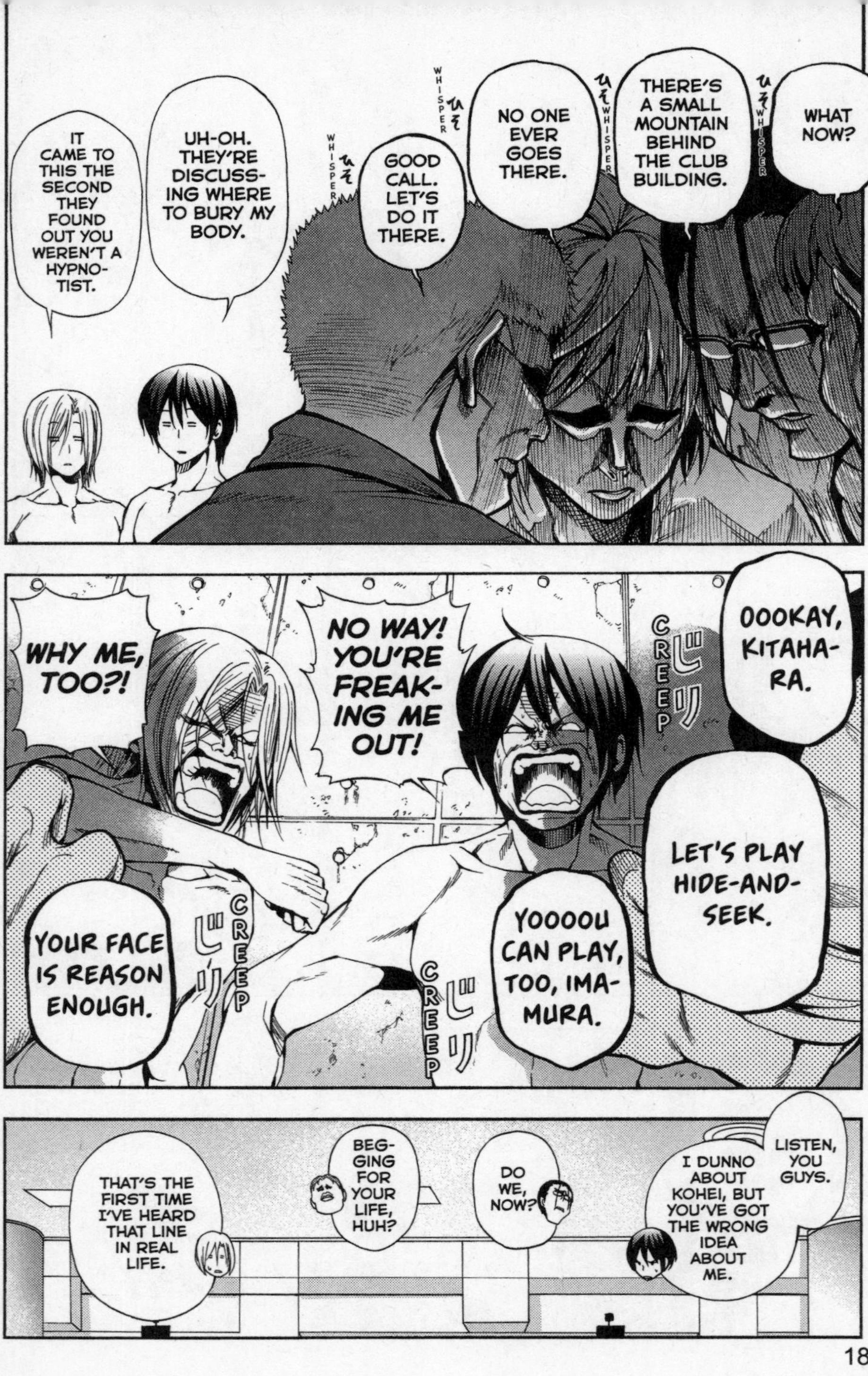
ひそ WHISPER
WHAT NOW?
ひそ WHISPER
THERE'S A SMALL MOUNTAIN BEHIND THE CLUB BUILDING.
ひそ WHISPER
NO ONE EVER GOES THERE.
ひそ WHISPER
GOOD CALL. LET'S DO IT THERE.
UH-OH. THEY'RE DISCUSSING WHERE TO BURY MY BODY.
IT CAME TO THIS THE SECOND THEY FOUND OUT YOU WEREN'T A HYPNOTIST.
OOOKAY, KITAHARA.
じり CREEP
LET'S PLAY HIDE-AND-SEEK.
NO WAY! YOU'RE FREAKING ME OUT!
YOOOOU CAN PLAY, TOO, IMAMURA.
じり CREEP
WHY ME, TOO?!
じり CREEP
YOUR FACE IS REASON ENOUGH.
LISTEN, YOU GUYS.
I DUNNO ABOUT KOHEI, BUT YOU'VE GOT THE WRONG IDEA ABOUT ME.
DO WE, NOW?
BEGGING FOR YOUR LIFE, HUH?
THAT'S THE FIRST TIME I'VE HEARD THAT LINE IN REAL LIFE.

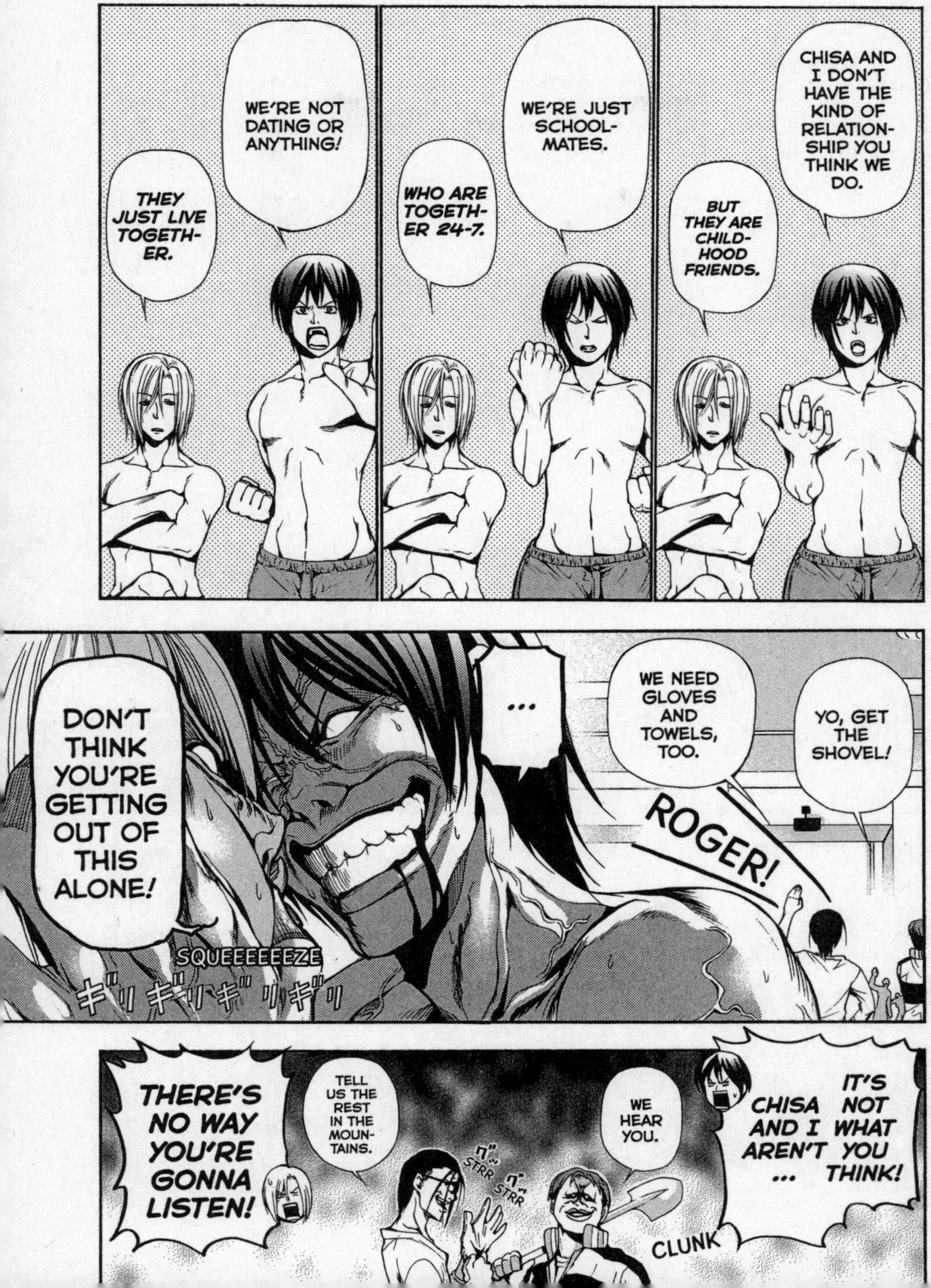
CHISA AND I DON'T HAVE THE KIND OF RELATIONSHIP YOU THINK WE DO.
BUT THEY ARE CHILDHOOD FRIENDS.
WE'RE JUST SCHOOLMATES.
WHO ARE TOGETHER 24-7.
WE'RE NOT DATING OR ANYTHING!
THEY JUST LIVE TOGETHER.
YO, GET THE SHOVEL!
WE NEED GLOVES AND TOWELS, TOO.
ROGER!
...
DON'T THINK YOU'RE GETTING OUT OF THIS ALONE!
SQUEEEEEEEZE
ギリギリギリギリ
CHISA AND I AREN'T ... IT'S NOT WHAT YOU THINK!
WE HEAR YOU.
STRR STRR
TELL US THE REST IN THE MOUNTAINS.
THERE'S NO WAY YOU'RE GONNA LISTEN!
CLUNK

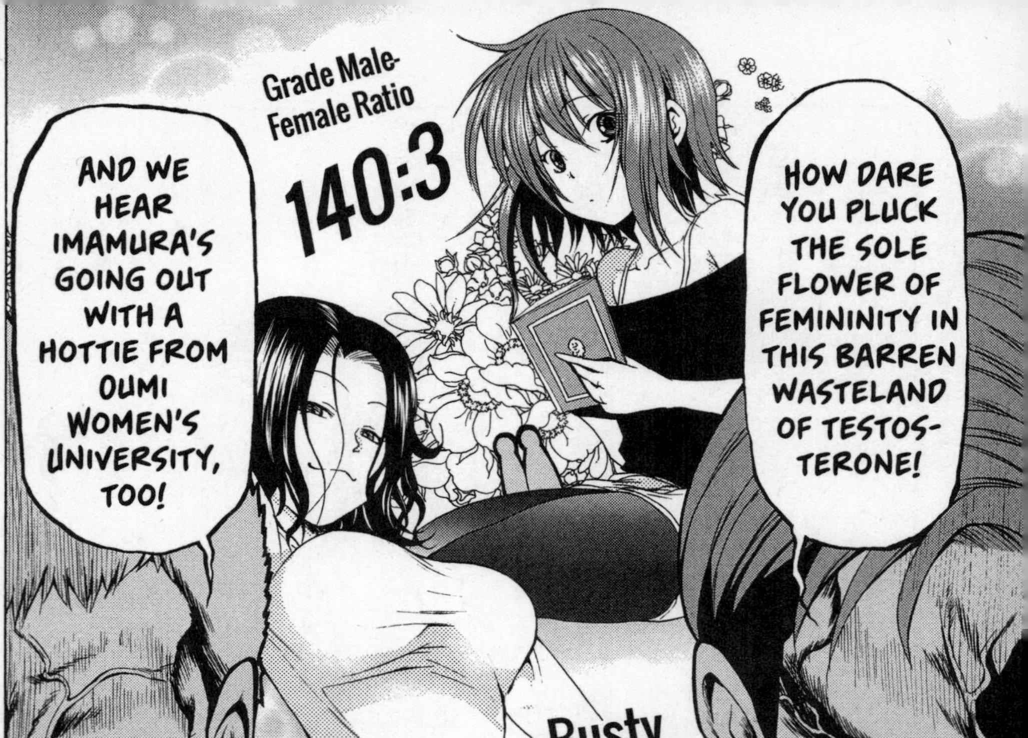
HOW DARE YOU PLUCK THE SOLE FLOWER OF FEMININITY IN THIS BARREN WASTELAND OF TESTOS-TERONE!
Grade Male-Female Ratio
140:3
AND WE HEAR IMAMURA'S GOING OUT WITH A HOTTIE FROM OUMI WOMEN'S UNIVERSITY, TOO!
Busty Older Girl

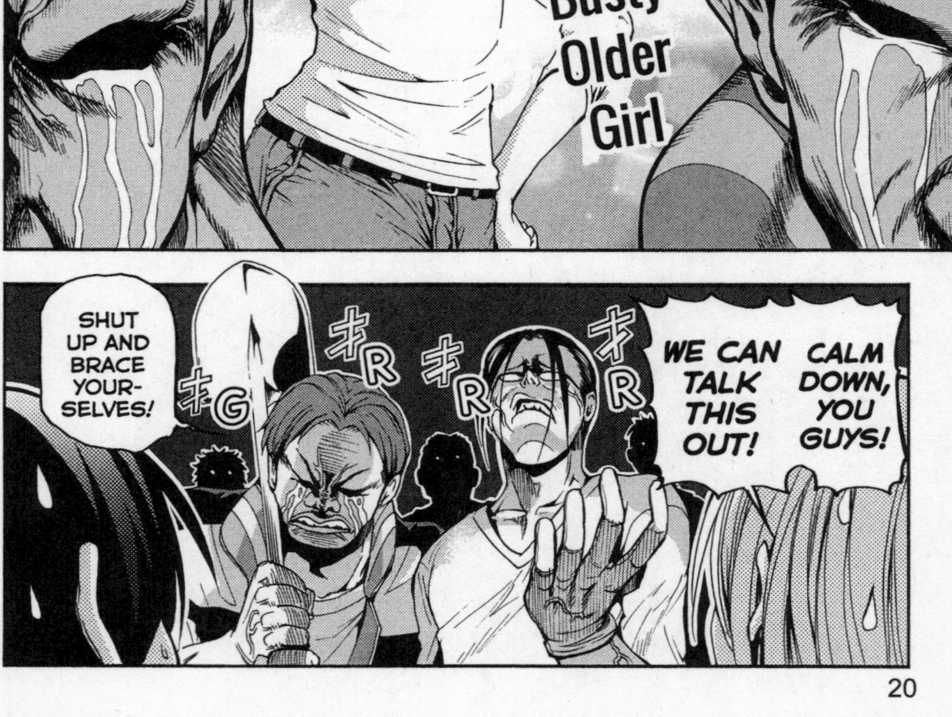
CALM DOWN, YOU GUYS!
WE CAN TALK THIS OUT!
GRRR
SHUT UP AND BRACE YOUR-SELVES!

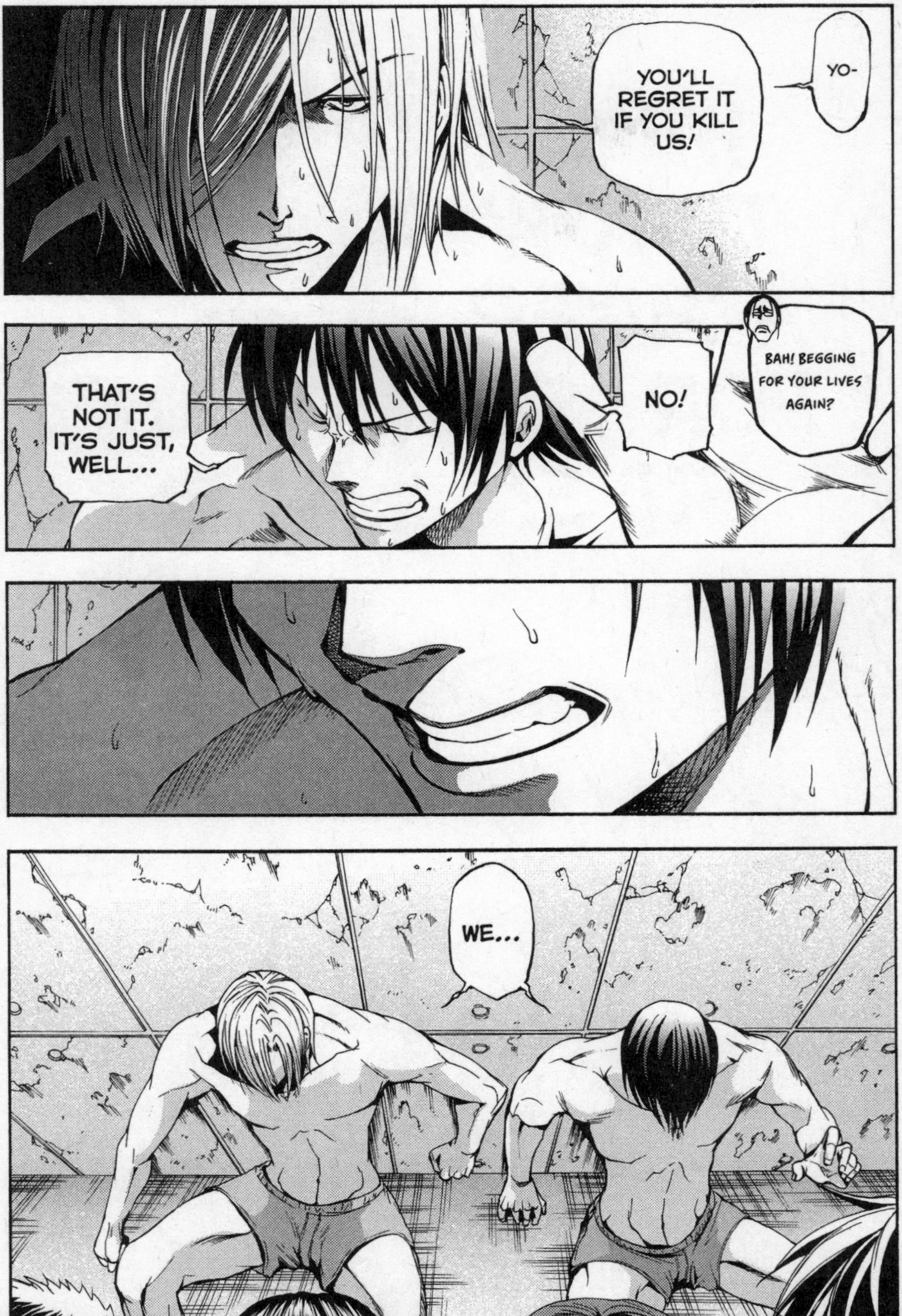
YO-
YOU'LL REGRET IT IF YOU KILL US!
BAH! BEGGING FOR YOUR LIVES AGAIN?
NO!
THAT'S NOT IT. IT'S JUST, WELL...
WE...

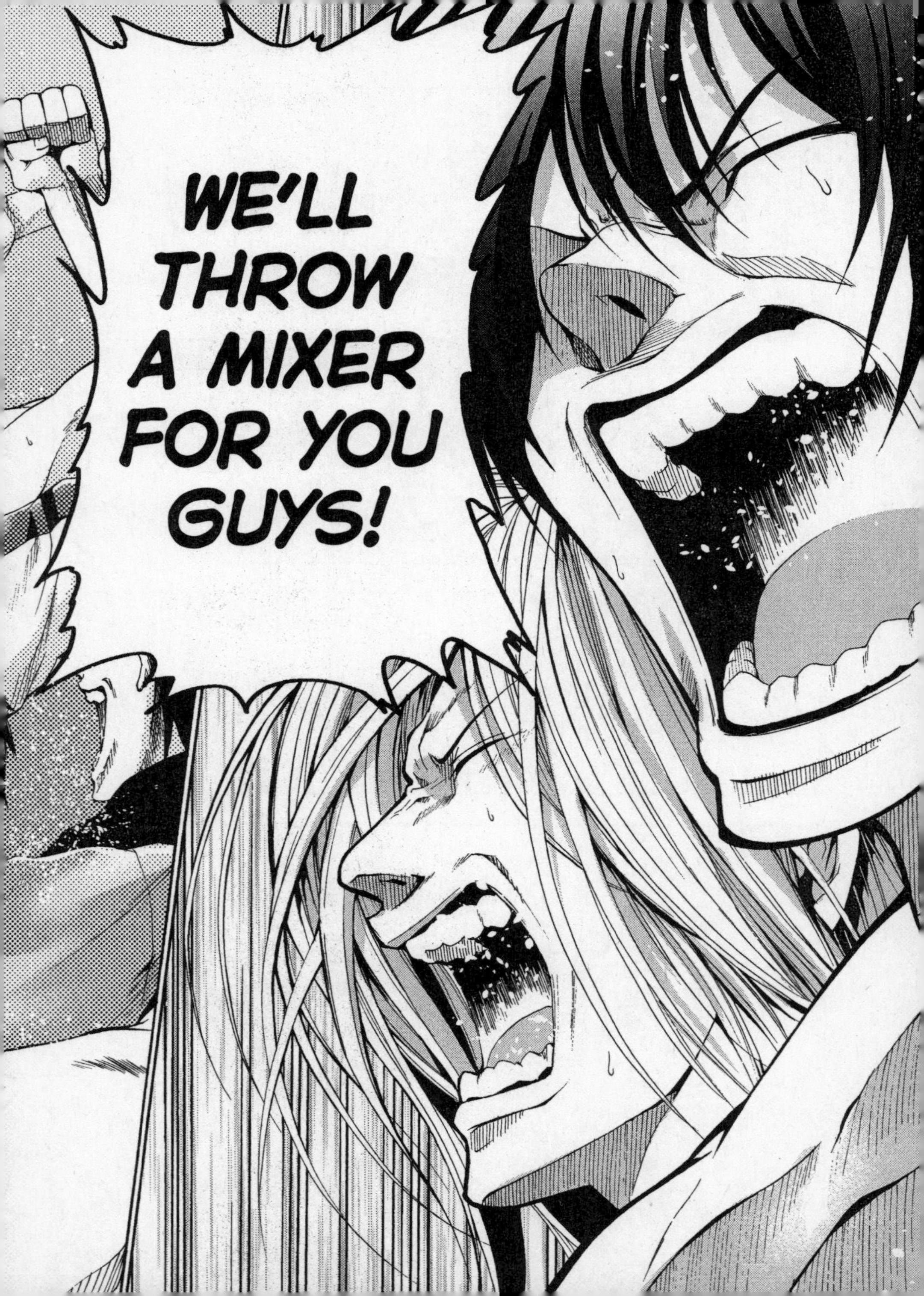
WE'LL THROW A MIXER FOR YOU GUYS!

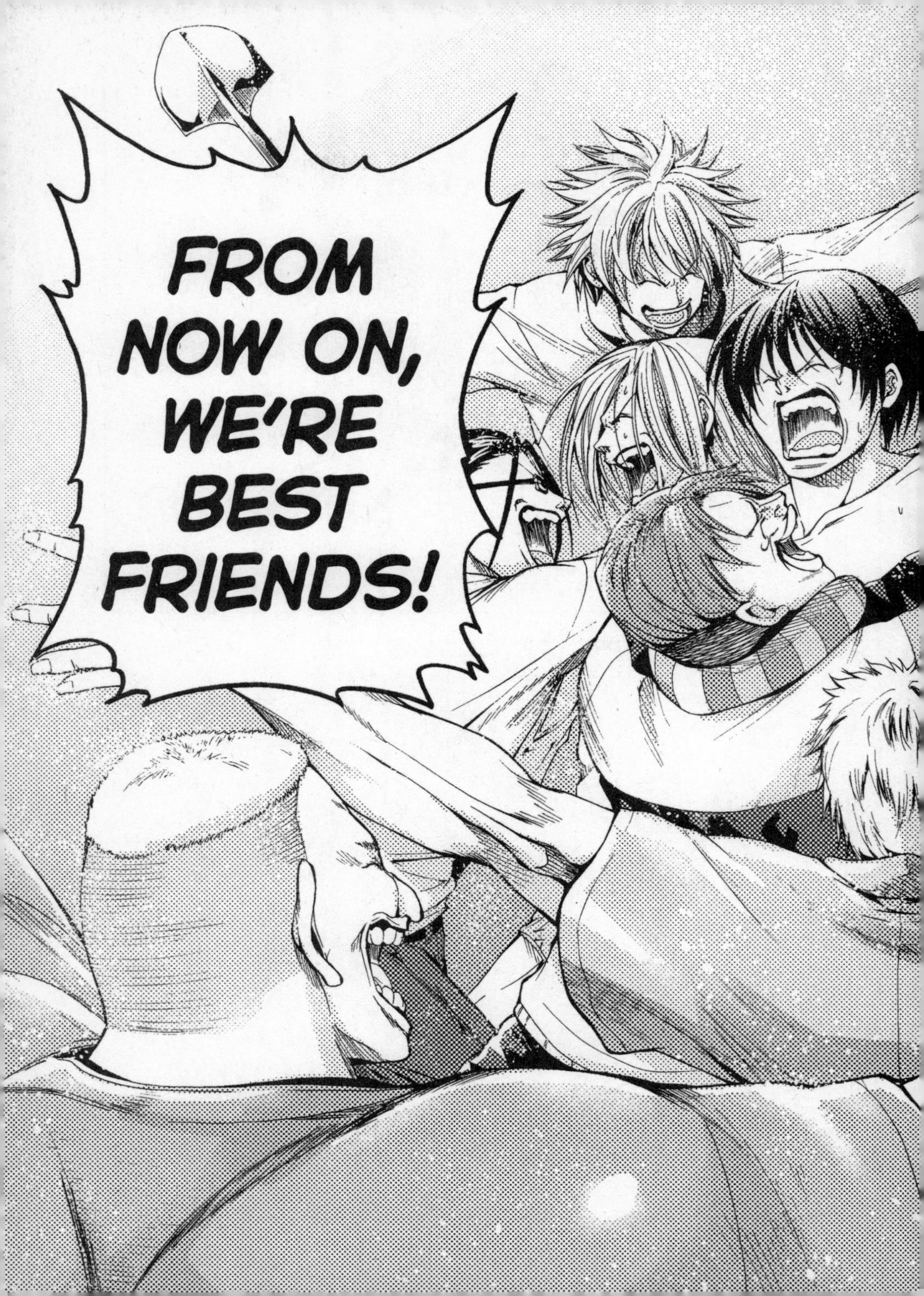
FROM NOW ON, WE'RE BEST FRIENDS!

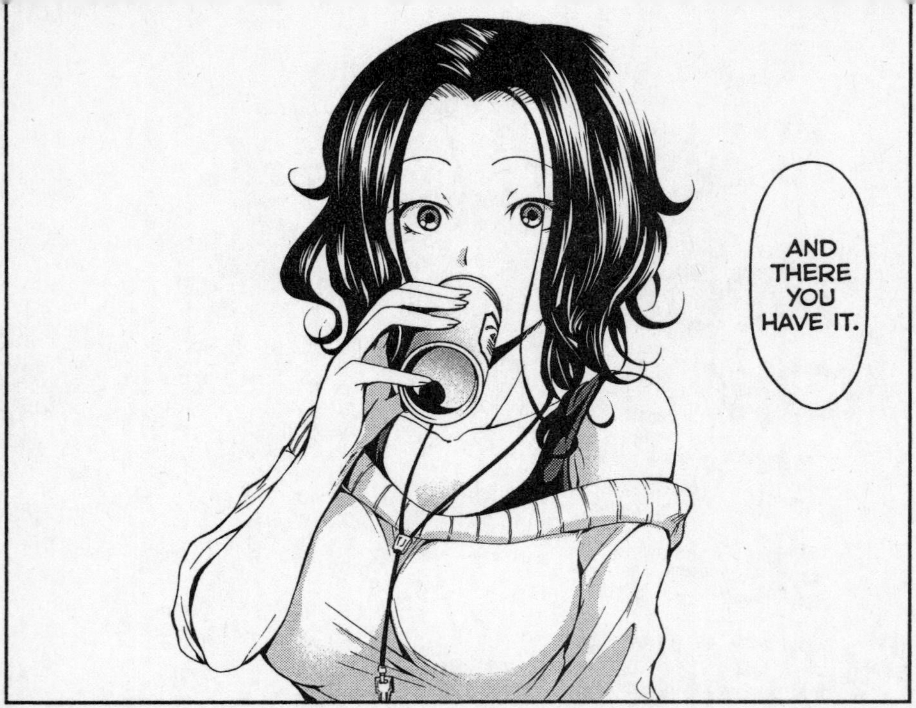
AND THERE YOU HAVE IT.

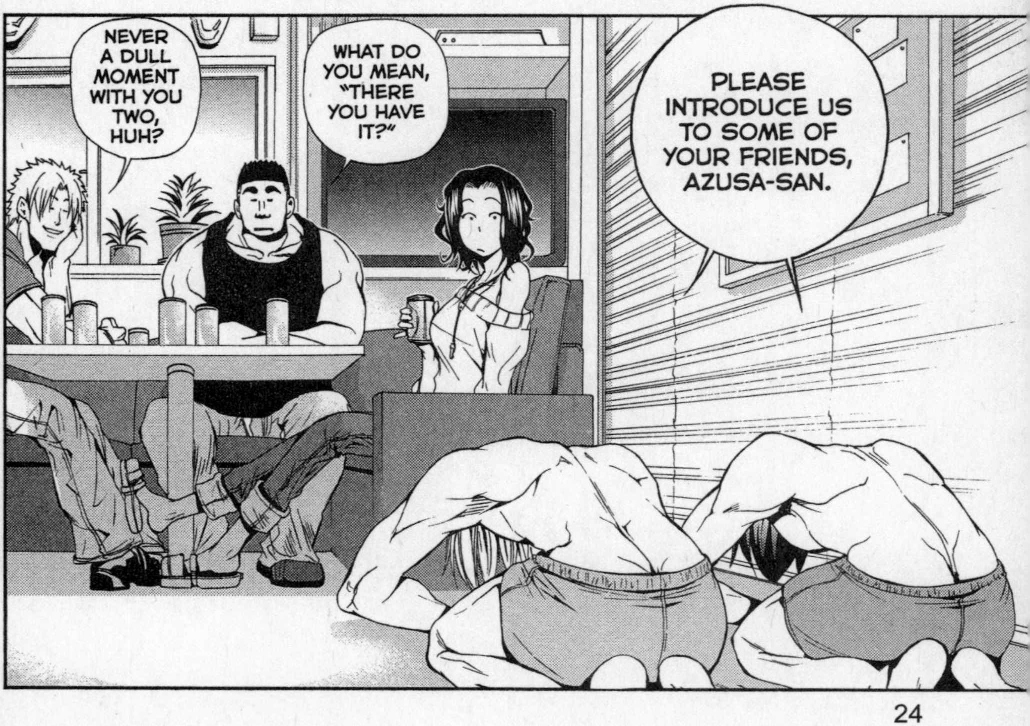
PLEASE INTRODUCE US TO SOME OF YOUR FRIENDS, AZUSA-SAN.
WHAT DO YOU MEAN, "THERE YOU HAVE IT?"
NEVER A DULL MOMENT WITH YOU TWO, HUH?

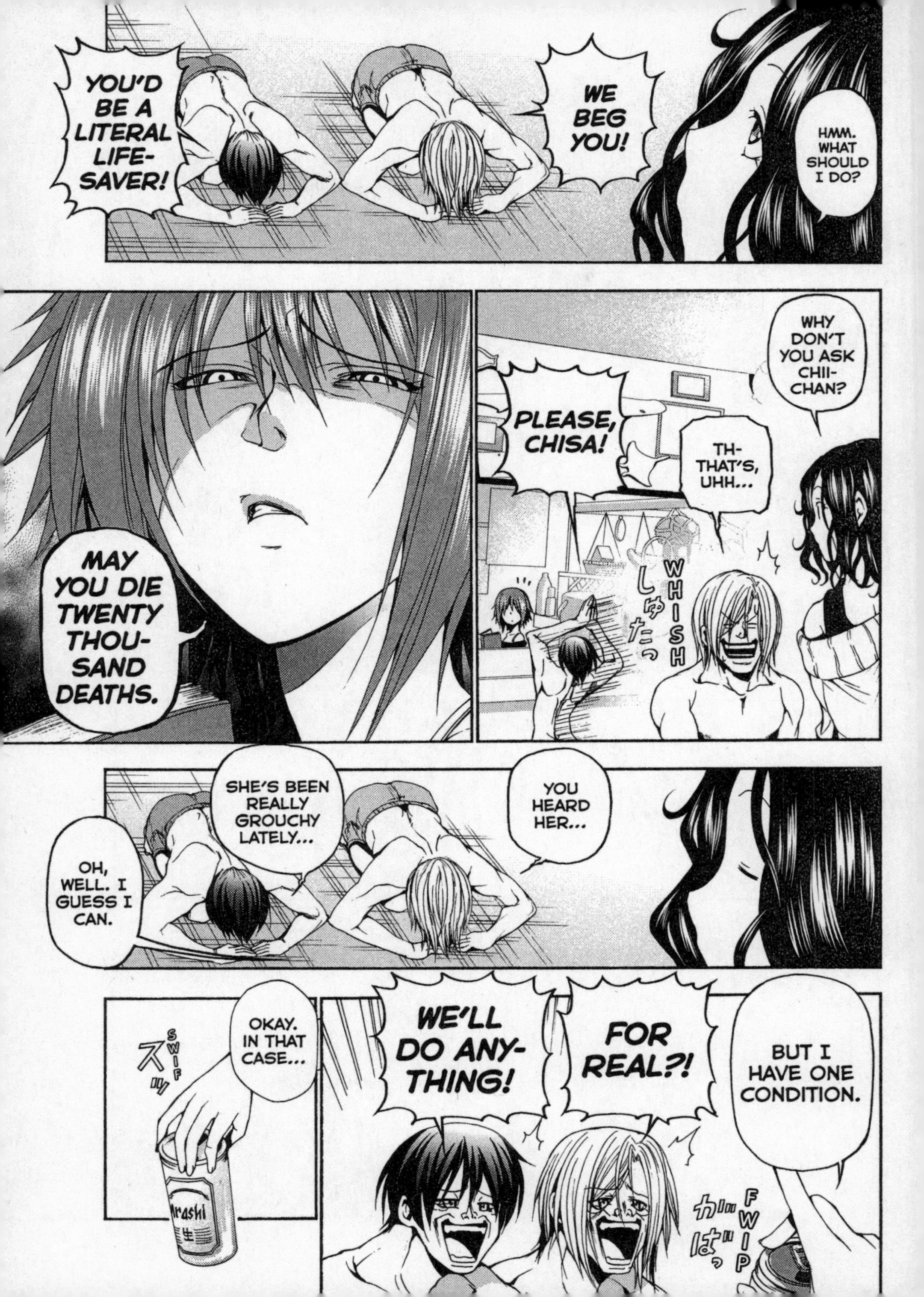
HMM. WHAT SHOULD I DO?
WE BEG YOU!
YOU'D BE A LITERAL LIFE-SAVER!
WHY DON'T YOU ASK CHII-CHAN?
TH-THAT'S, UHH...
PLEASE, CHISA!
WHISH しゅたっ
MAY YOU DIE TWENTY THOUSAND DEATHS.
YOU HEARD HER...
SHE'S BEEN REALLY GROUCHY LATELY...
OH, WELL. I GUESS I CAN.
BUT I HAVE ONE CONDITION.
FOR REAL?!
WE'LL DO ANYTHING!
FWIP かぱっ
OKAY. IN THAT CASE...
SWIF スッ
Arashi

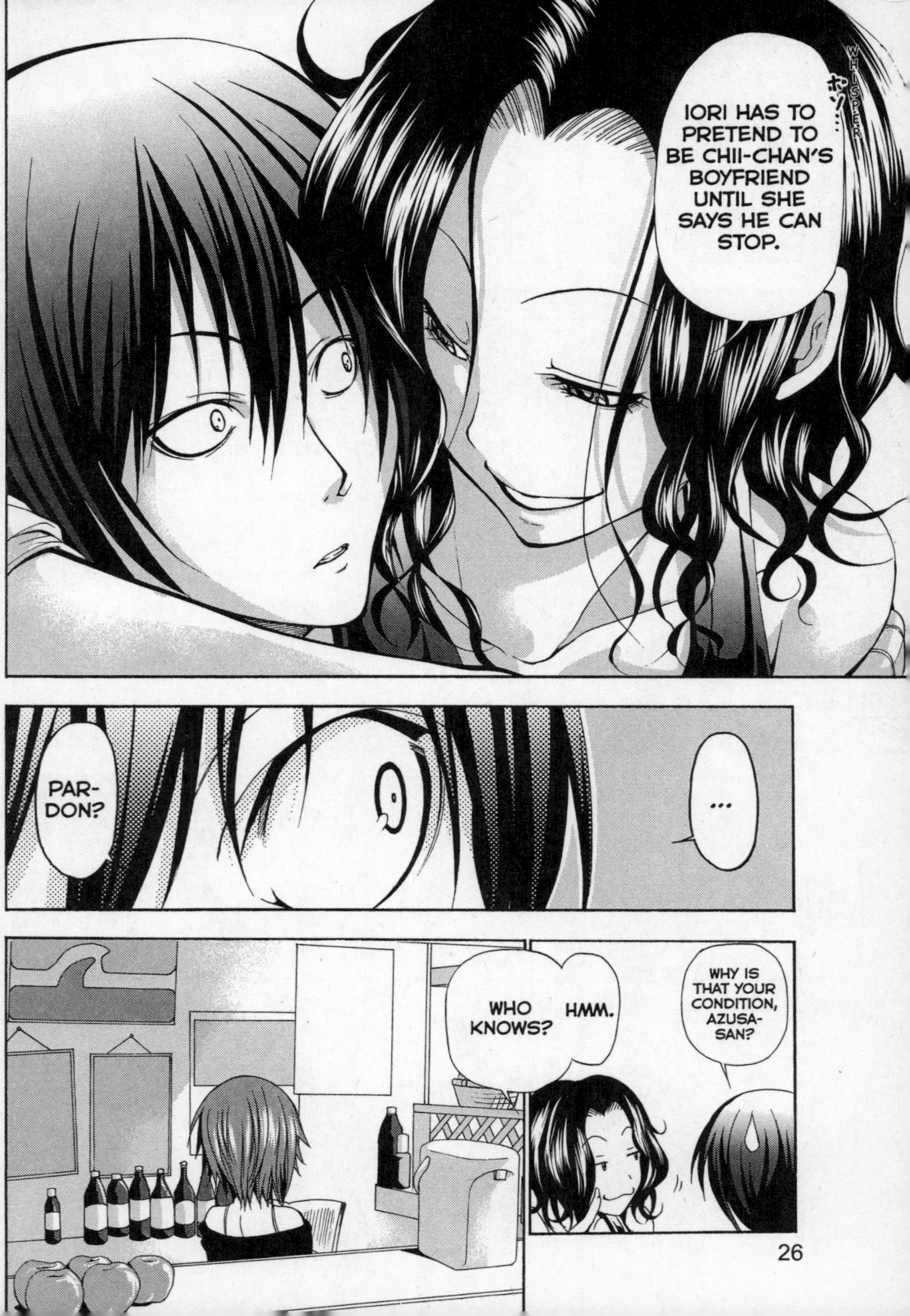
WHISPER
ボソ…
IORI HAS TO PRETEND TO BE CHII-CHAN'S BOYFRIEND UNTIL SHE SAYS HE CAN STOP.
...
PARDON?
WHY IS THAT YOUR CONDITION, AZUSA-SAN?
HMM.
WHO KNOWS?

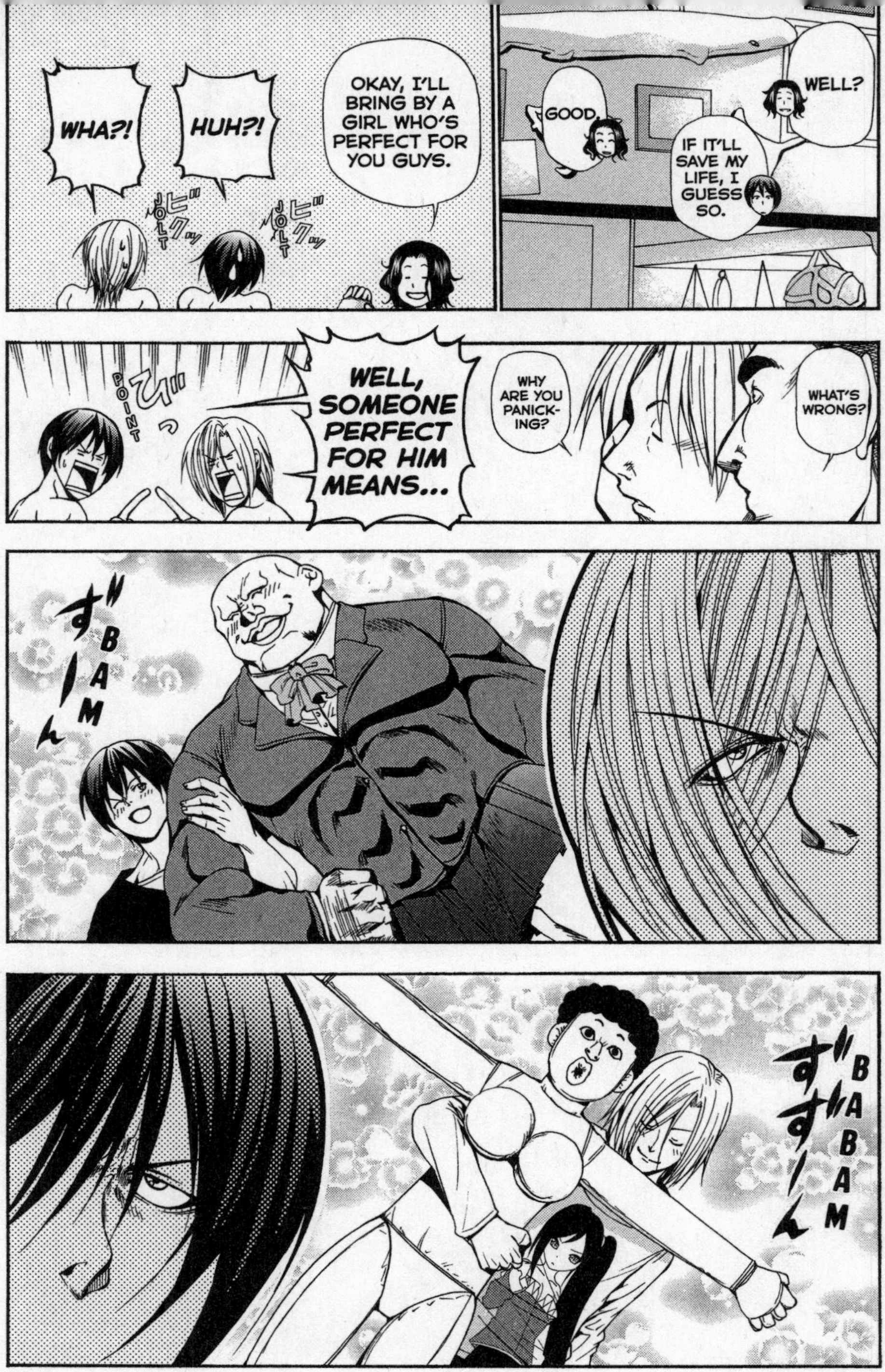
WELL?
GOOD.
IF IT'LL SAVE MY LIFE, I GUESS SO.
OKAY, I'LL BRING BY A GIRL WHO'S PERFECT FOR YOU GUYS.
HUH?!
JOLT
WHA?!
JOLT
WHAT'S WRONG?
WHY ARE YOU PANICKING?
WELL, SOMEONE PERFECT FOR HIM MEANS...
POINT
BAM
BABAM

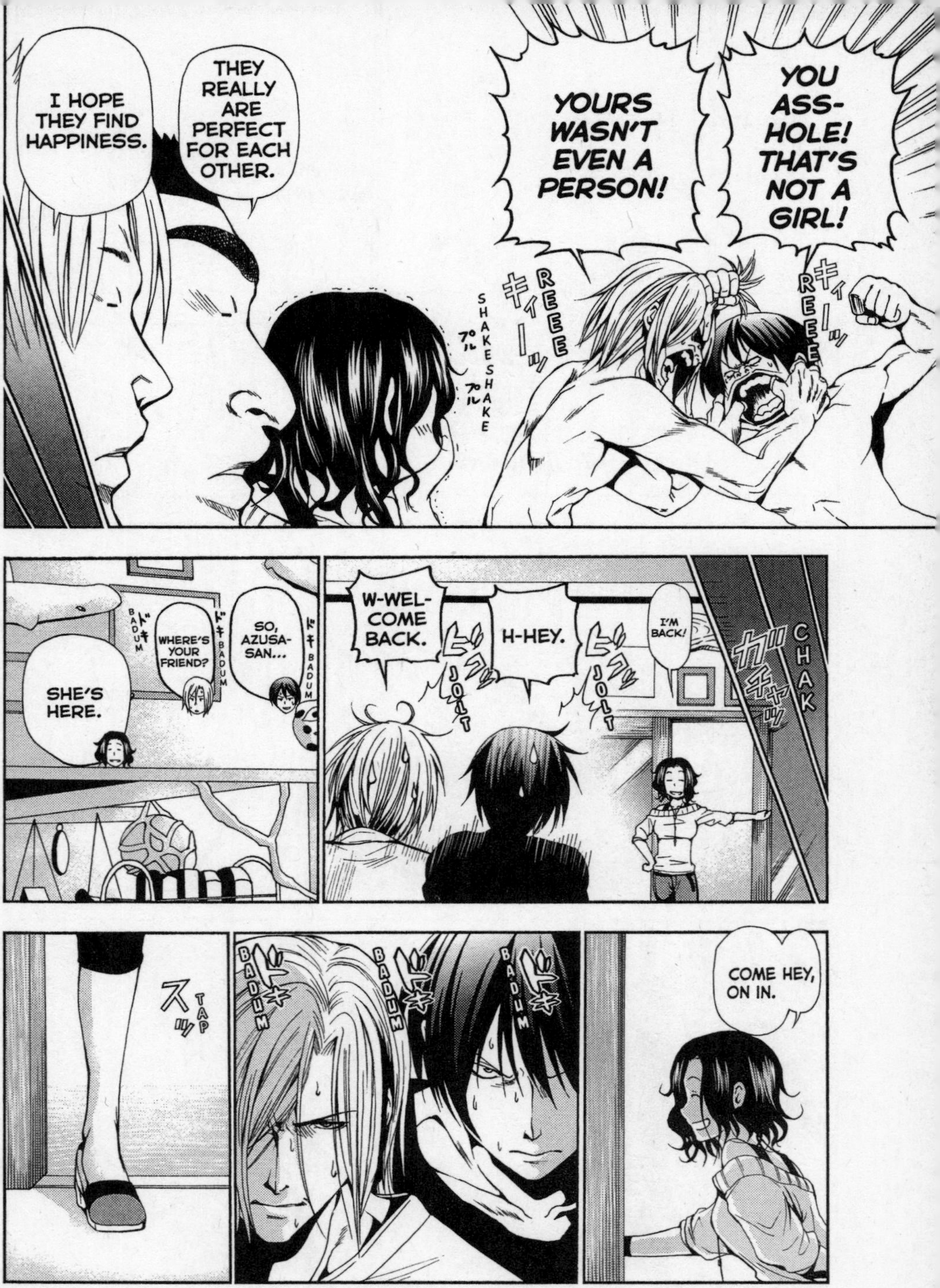
YOU ASS-HOLE! THAT'S NOT A GIRL!
REEE
YOURS WASN'T EVEN A PERSON!
REEE
SHAKE SHAKE
THEY REALLY ARE PERFECT FOR EACH OTHER.
I HOPE THEY FIND HAPPINESS.
CHAK
I'M BACK!
JOLT
H-HEY.
JOLT
W-WEL-COME BACK.
SO, AZUSA-SAN...
BADUM
WHERE'S YOUR FRIEND?
BADUM
SHE'S HERE.
COME HEY, ON IN.
BADUM
BADUM
BADUM
TAP

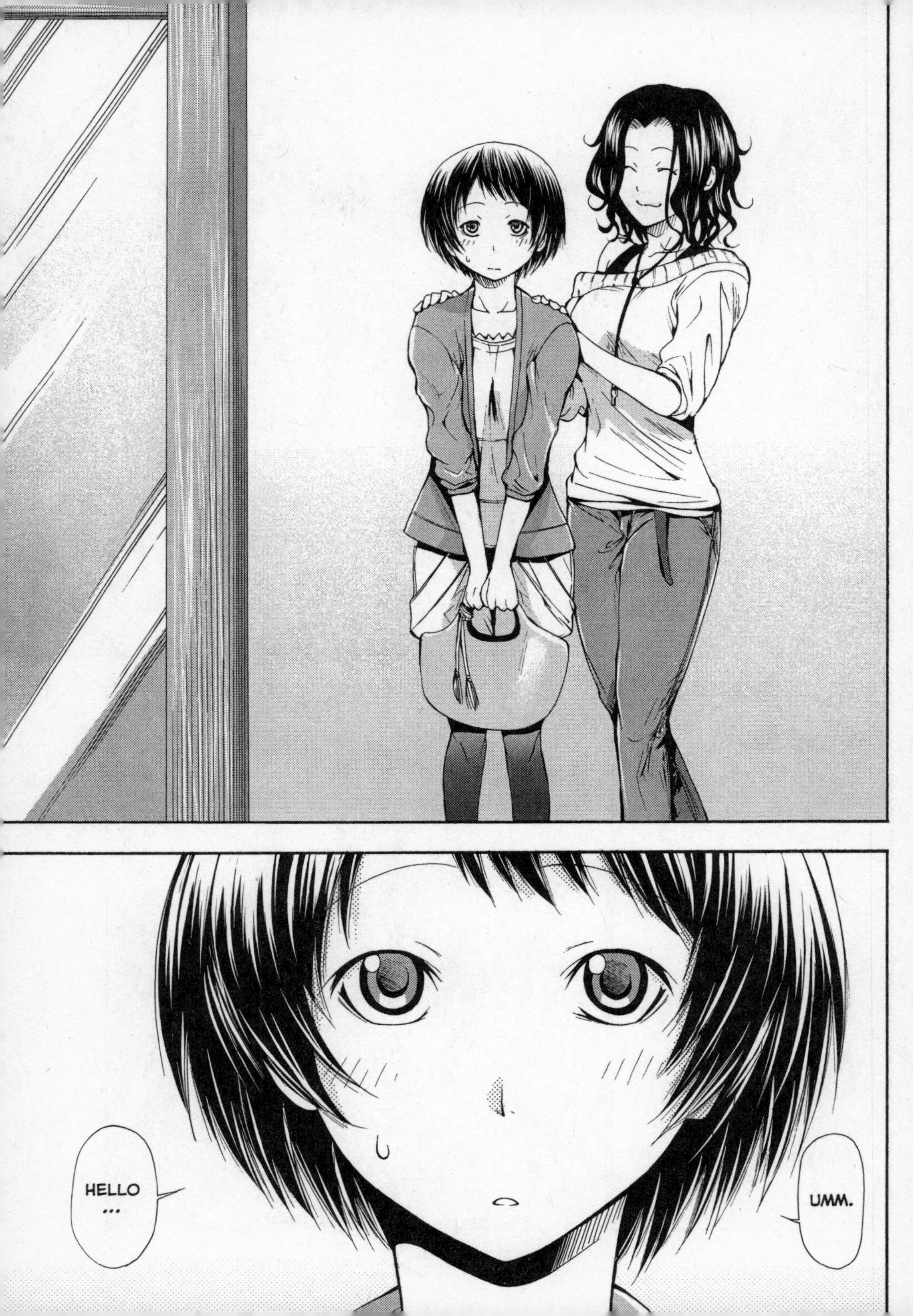
UMM.
HELLO ...

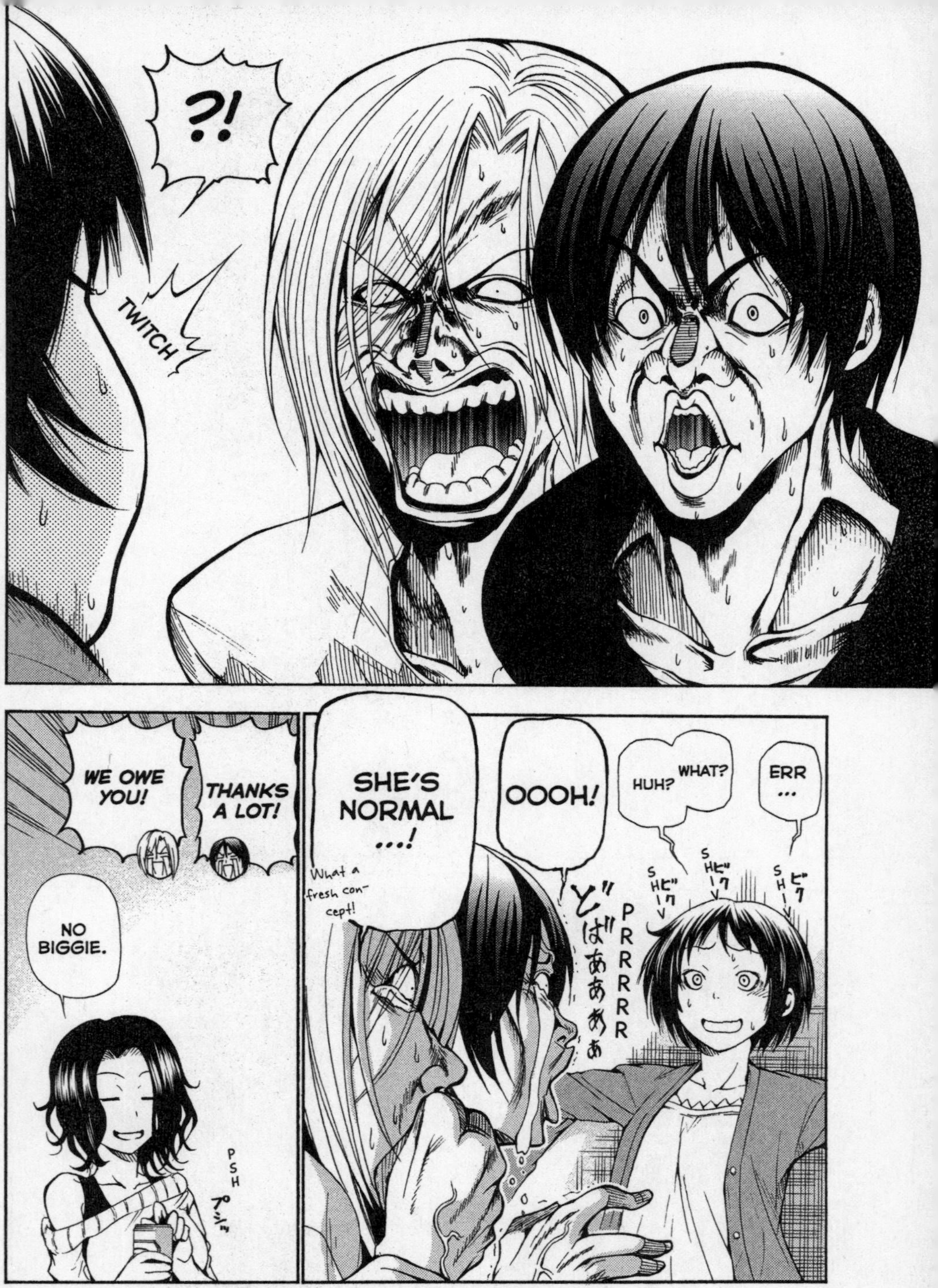
?!
TWITCH
ERR ...
HUH? WHAT?
SHIK ビク
SHIK ビク
SHIK ビク
OOOH!
PRRRRR
どばあああ
SHE'S NORMAL ...!
What a fresh concept!
THANKS A LOT!
WE OWE YOU!
NO BIGGIE.
PSH
プシュ

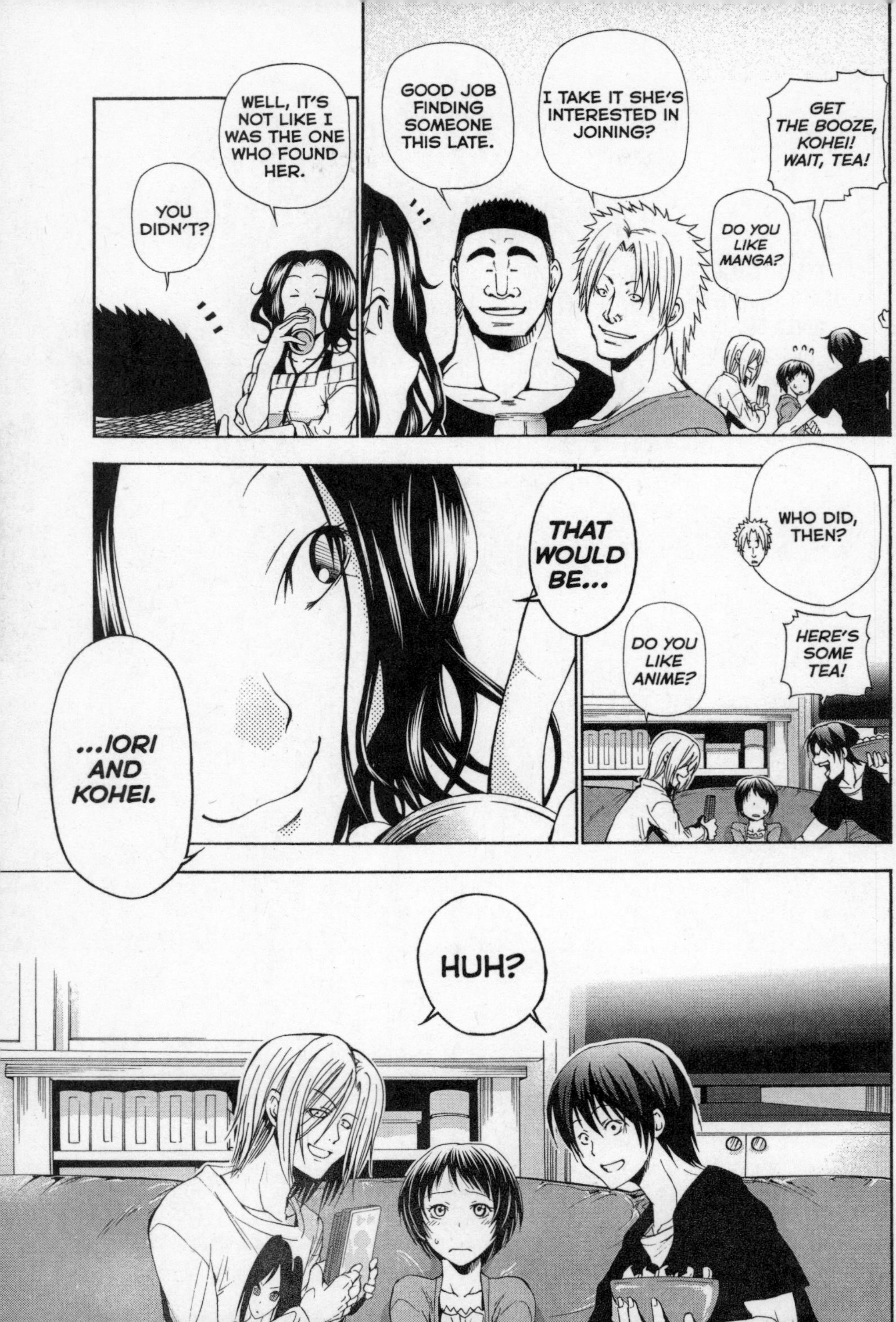
GET THE BOOZE, KOHEI! WAIT, TEA!
DO YOU LIKE MANGA?
I TAKE IT SHE'S INTERESTED IN JOINING?
GOOD JOB FINDING SOMEONE THIS LATE.
WELL, IT'S NOT LIKE I WAS THE ONE WHO FOUND HER.
YOU DIDN'T?
WHO DID, THEN?
HERE'S SOME TEA!
DO YOU LIKE ANIME?
THAT WOULD BE...
...IORI AND KOHEI.
HUH?

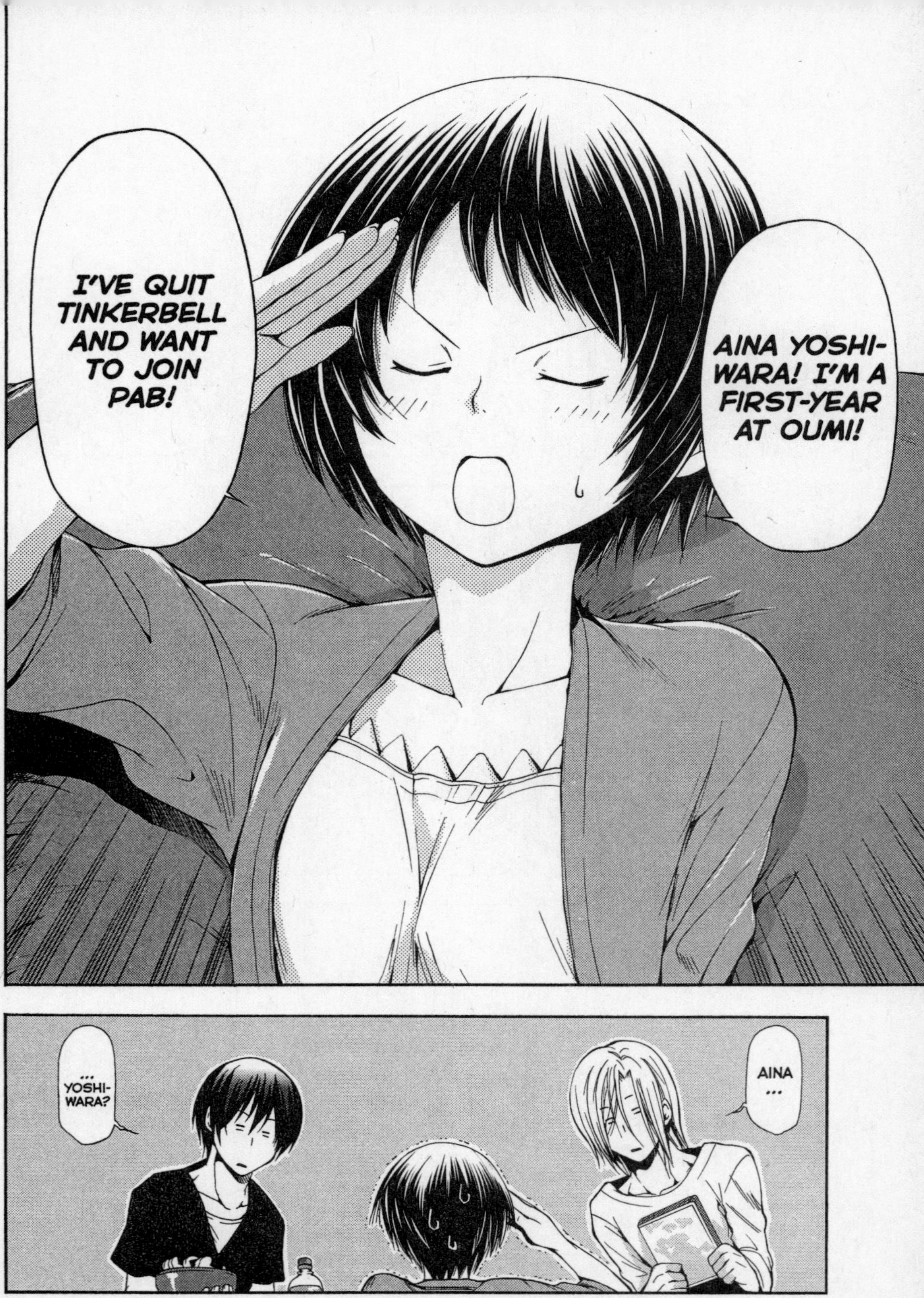
AINA YOSHI-WARA! I'M A FIRST-YEAR AT OUMI!
I'VE QUIT TINKERBELL AND WANT TO JOIN PAB!
AINA ...
... YOSHI-WARA?

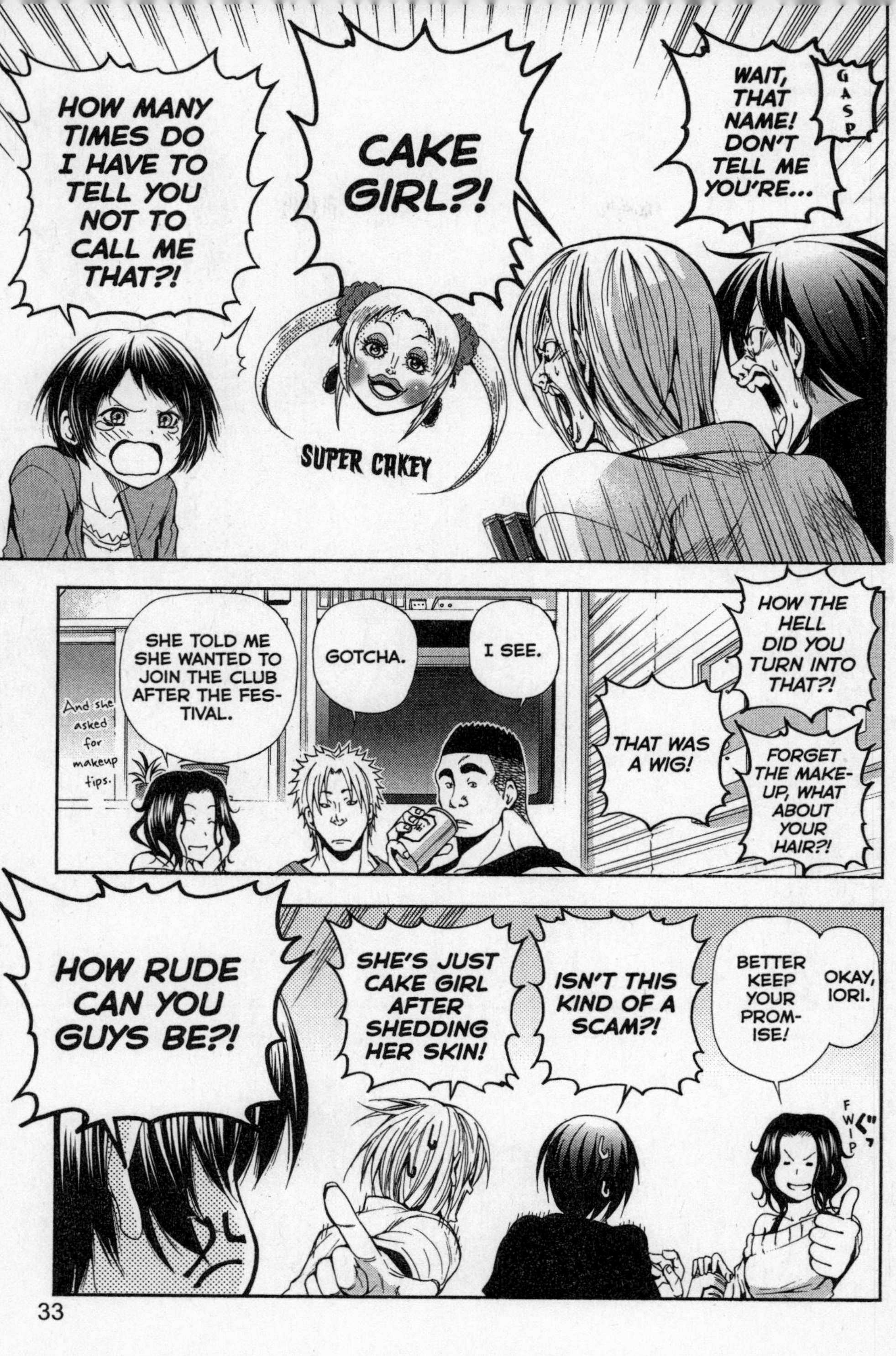

GASP
WAIT, THAT NAME! DON'T TELL ME YOU'RE...
CAKE GIRL?!
HOW MANY TIMES DO I HAVE TO TELL YOU NOT TO CALL ME THAT?!
SUPER CAKEY
HOW THE HELL DID YOU TURN INTO THAT?!
FORGET THE MAKE-UP, WHAT ABOUT YOUR HAIR?!
THAT WAS A WIG!
I SEE.
GOTCHA.
SHE TOLD ME SHE WANTED TO JOIN THE CLUB AFTER THE FES-TIVAL.
And she asked for makeup tips.
OKAY, IORI.
BETTER KEEP YOUR PROM-ISE!
FWIP
ISN'T THIS KIND OF A SCAM?!
SHE'S JUST CAKE GIRL AFTER SHEDDING HER SKIN!
HOW RUDE CAN YOU GUYS BE?!

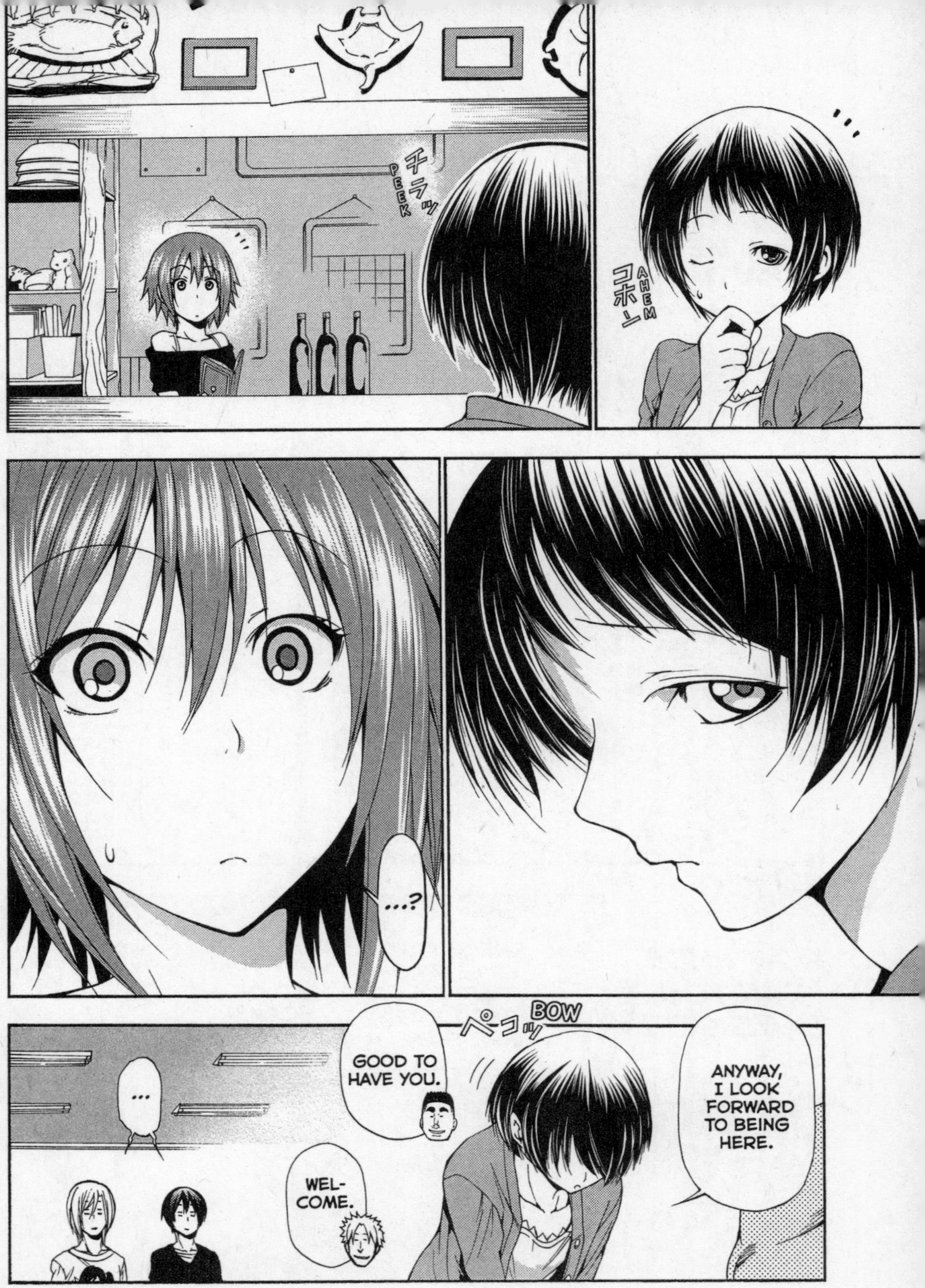
...
コホン
AHEM
チラッ
PEEK
...?
ANYWAY, I LOOK FORWARD TO BEING HERE.
ペコッ
BOW
GOOD TO HAVE YOU.
WEL-COME.
...

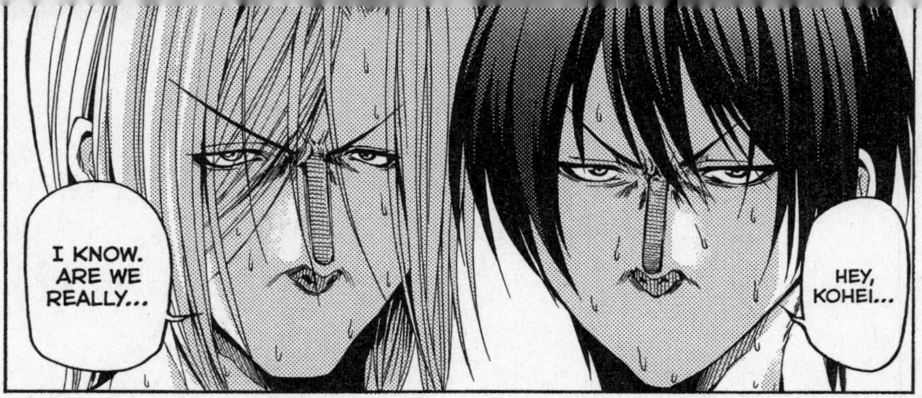
HEY, KOHEI...
I KNOW. ARE WE REALLY...

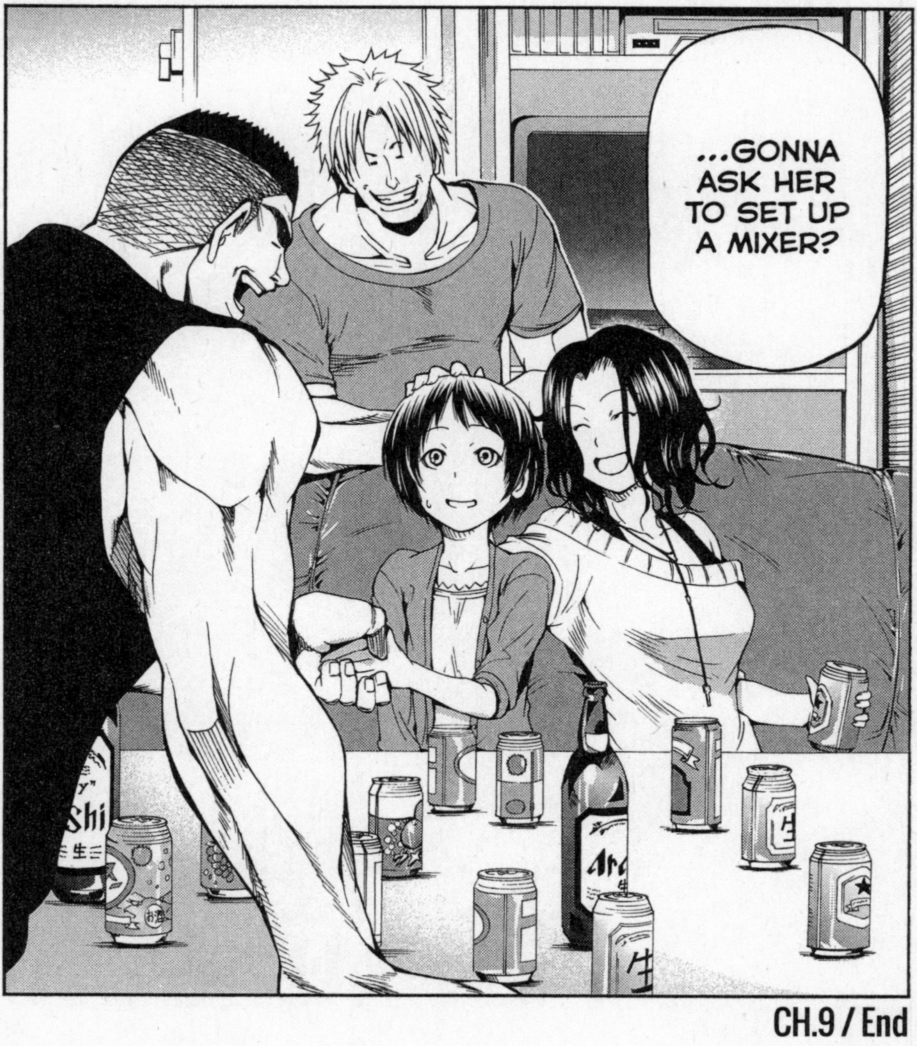
...GONNA ASK HER TO SET UP A MIXER?

CH.9 / End

Grand Blue
Dreaming

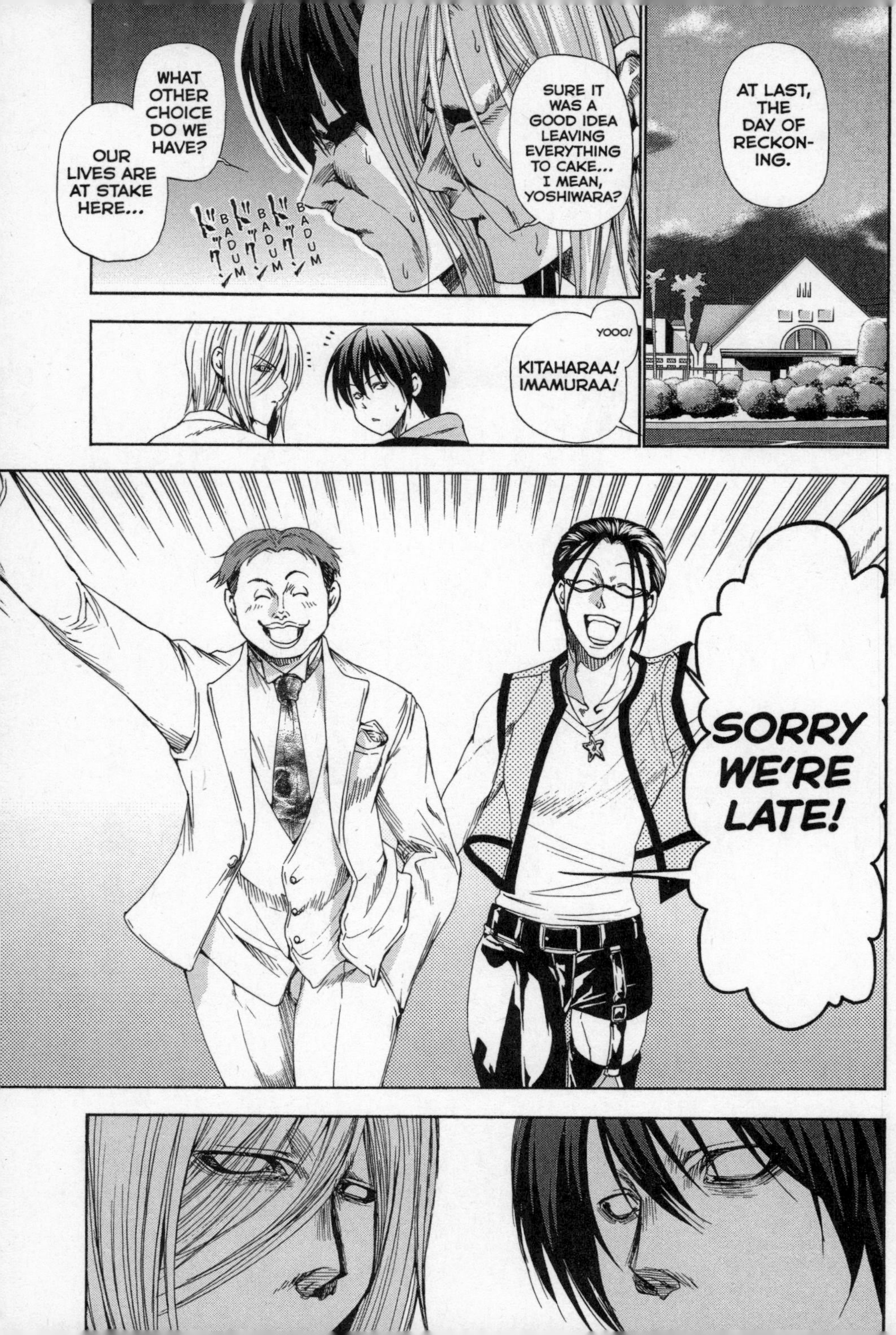
AT LAST, THE DAY OF RECKONING.
SURE IT WAS A GOOD IDEA LEAVING EVERYTHING TO CAKE... I MEAN, YOSHIWARA?
WHAT OTHER CHOICE DO WE HAVE?
OUR LIVES ARE AT STAKE HERE...
BADUM BADUM BADUM
YOOO!
KITAHARAA! IMAMURAA!
SORRY WE'RE LATE!

Ch.10 The Mixer

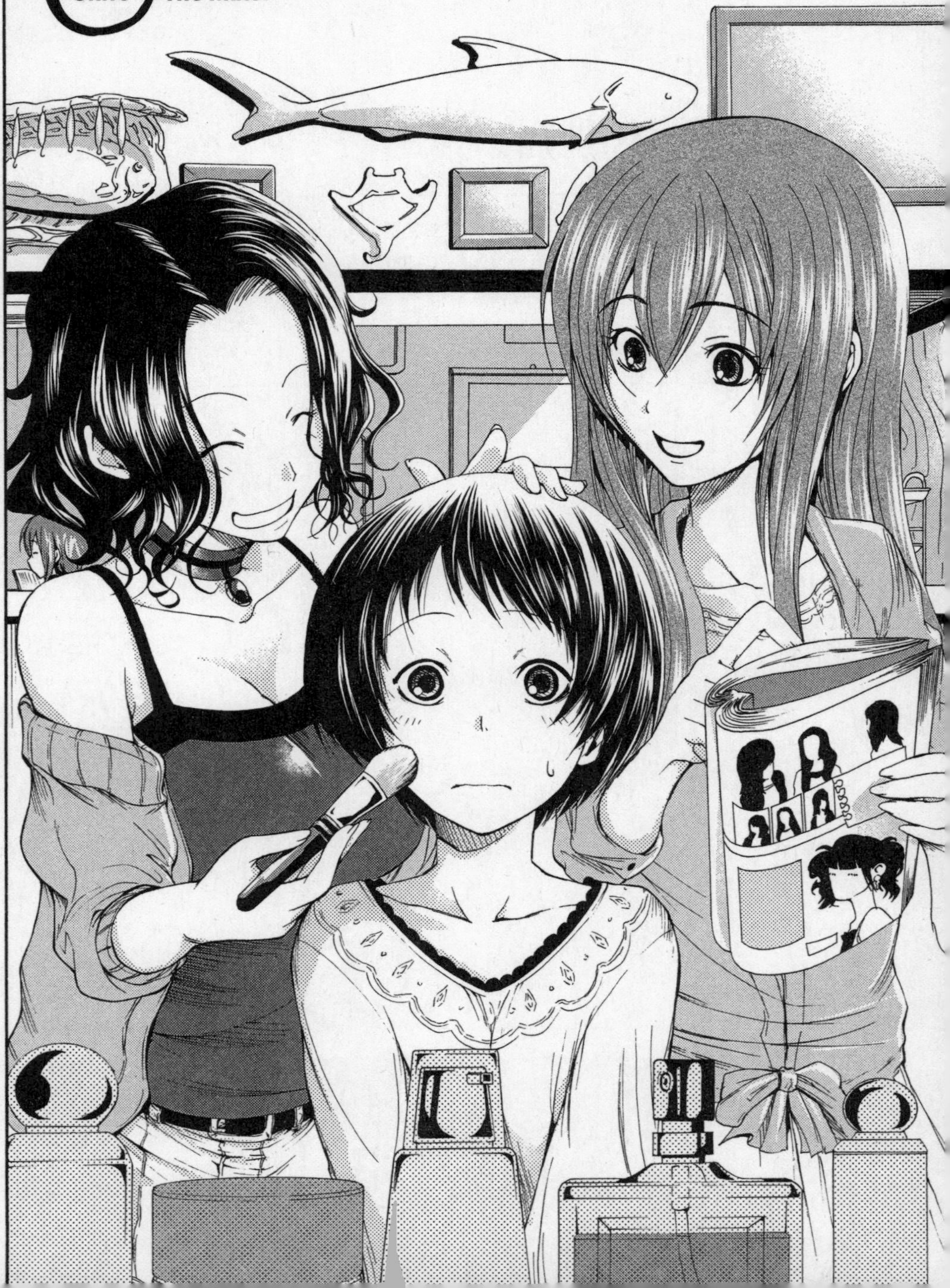

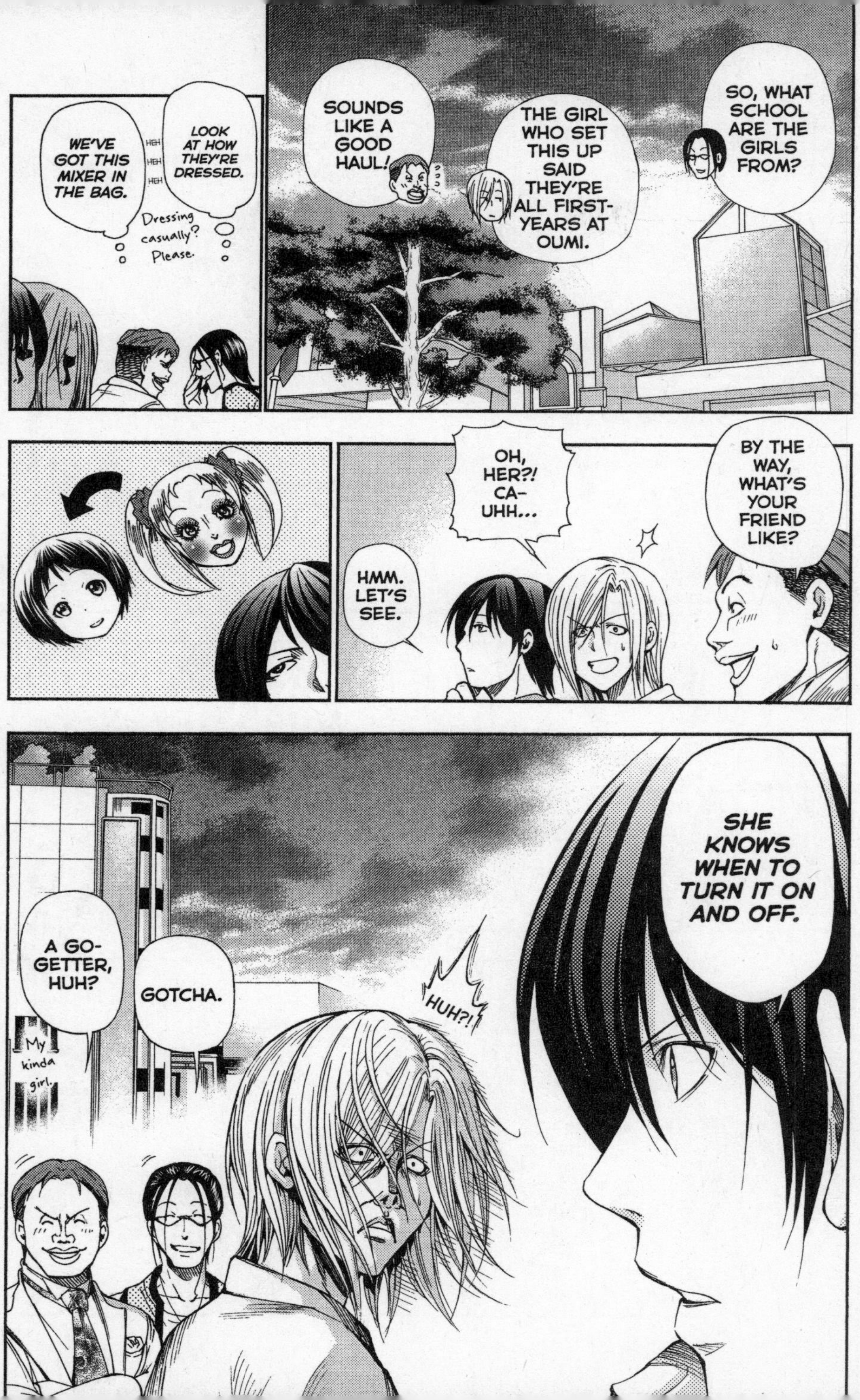
SO, WHAT SCHOOL ARE THE GIRLS FROM?
THE GIRL WHO SET THIS UP SAID THEY'RE ALL FIRST-YEARS AT OUMI.
SOUNDS LIKE A GOOD HAUL!
LOOK AT HOW THEY'RE DRESSED.
HEH HEH HEH
WE'VE GOT THIS MIXER IN THE BAG.
Dressing casually? Please.
BY THE WAY, WHAT'S YOUR FRIEND LIKE?
OH, HER?! CA— UHH...
HMM. LET'S SEE.
SHE KNOWS WHEN TO TURN IT ON AND OFF.
HUH?!
GOTCHA.
A GO-GETTER, HUH?
My kinda girl.

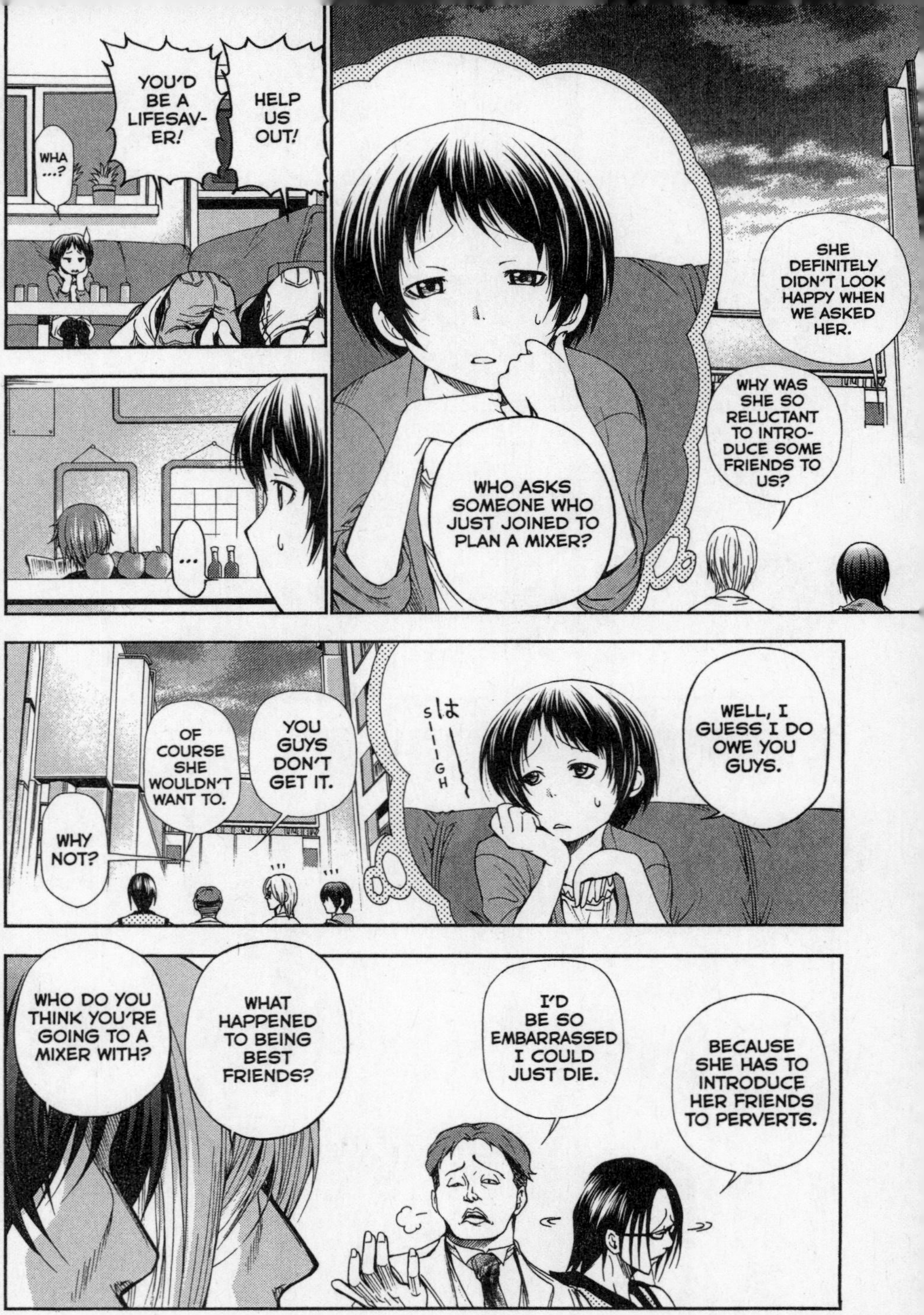
SHE DEFINITELY DIDN'T LOOK HAPPY WHEN WE ASKED HER.
WHY WAS SHE SO RELUCTANT TO INTRODUCE SOME FRIENDS TO US?
WHO ASKS SOMEONE WHO JUST JOINED TO PLAN A MIXER?
HELP US OUT!
YOU'D BE A LIFESAVER!
WHA...?
...
WELL, I GUESS I DO OWE YOU GUYS.
はぁ
SIIIGH
YOU GUYS DON'T GET IT.
OF COURSE SHE WOULDN'T WANT TO.
WHY NOT?
BECAUSE SHE HAS TO INTRODUCE HER FRIENDS TO PERVERTS.
I'D BE SO EMBARRASSED I COULD JUST DIE.
WHAT HAPPENED TO BEING BEST FRIENDS?
WHO DO YOU THINK YOU'RE GOING TO A MIXER WITH?

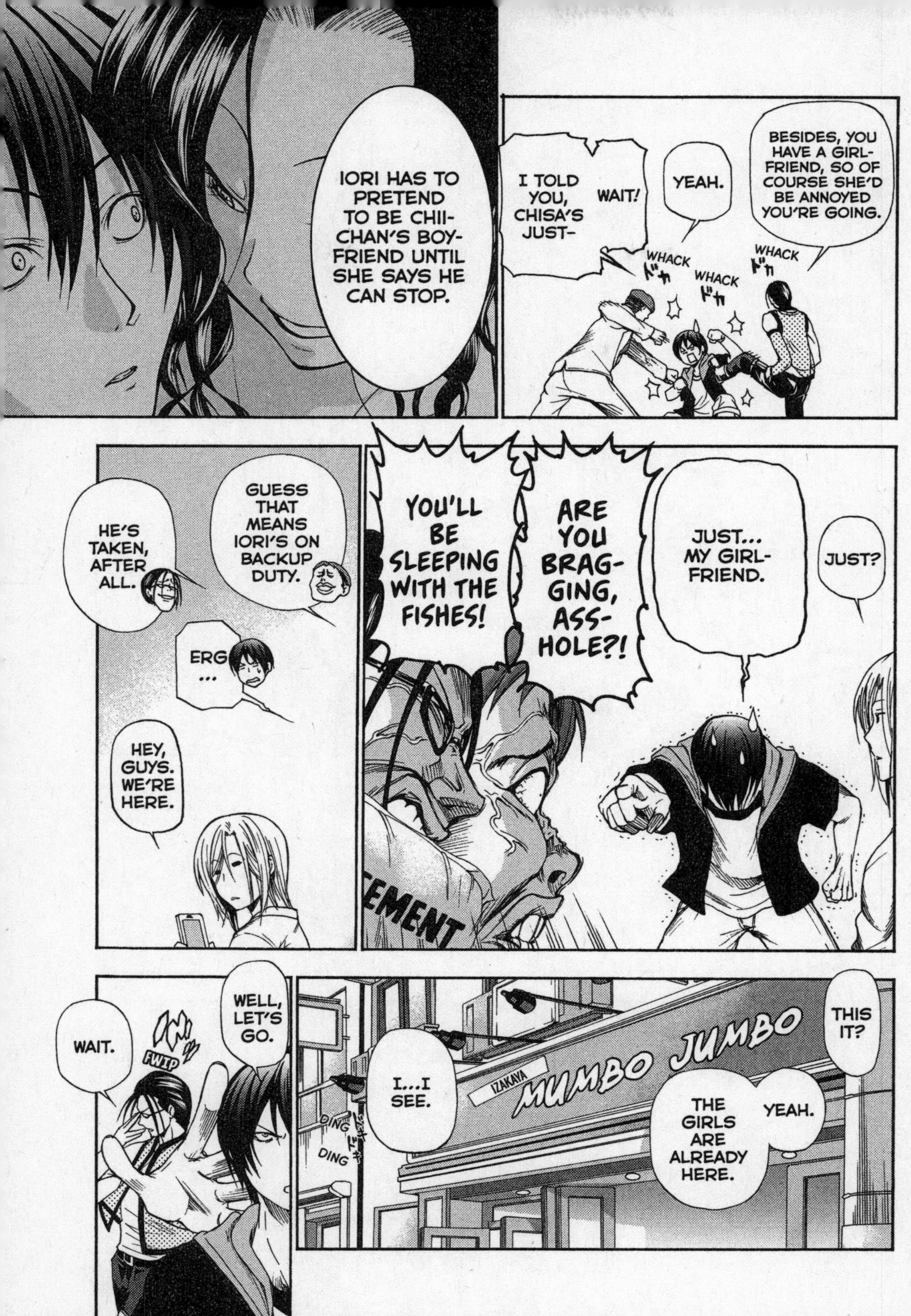
BESIDES, YOU HAVE A GIRL-FRIEND, SO OF COURSE SHE'D BE ANNOYED YOU'RE GOING.
YEAH.
WAIT!
I TOLD YOU, CHISA'S JUST-
WHACK ドカ
WHACK ドカ
WHACK ドカ
IORI HAS TO PRETEND TO BE CHII-CHAN'S BOY-FRIEND UNTIL SHE SAYS HE CAN STOP.
JUST?
JUST... MY GIRL-FRIEND.
ARE YOU BRAG-GING, ASS-HOLE?!
YOU'LL BE SLEEPING WITH THE FISHES!
CEMENT
GUESS THAT MEANS IORI'S ON BACKUP DUTY.
HE'S TAKEN, AFTER ALL.
ERG...
HEY, GUYS. WE'RE HERE.
THIS IT?
MUMBO JUMBO
IZAKAYA
YEAH.
THE GIRLS ARE ALREADY HERE.
I...I SEE.
DING
DING
WELL, LET'S GO.
WAIT.
FWIP

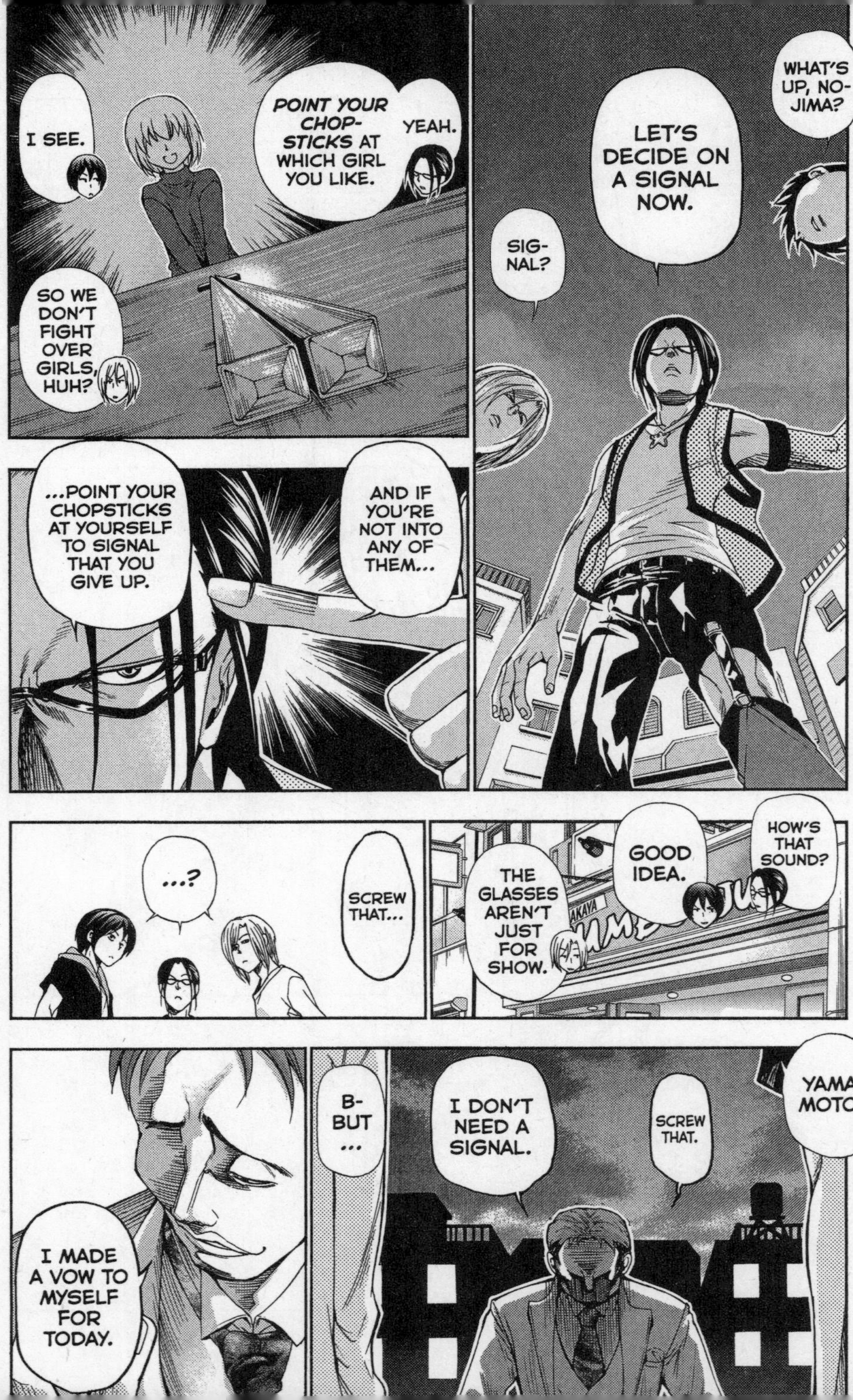
WHAT'S UP, NO-JIMA?
LET'S DECIDE ON A SIGNAL NOW.
SIG-NAL?
POINT YOUR CHOP-STICKS AT WHICH GIRL YOU LIKE.
YEAH.
I SEE.
SO WE DON'T FIGHT OVER GIRLS, HUH?
AND IF YOU'RE NOT INTO ANY OF THEM...
...POINT YOUR CHOPSTICKS AT YOURSELF TO SIGNAL THAT YOU GIVE UP.
HOW'S THAT SOUND?
GOOD IDEA.
THE GLASSES AREN'T JUST FOR SHOW.
SCREW THAT...
...?
YAMA-MOTO?
SCREW THAT.
I DON'T NEED A SIGNAL.
B-BUT...
I MADE A VOW TO MYSELF FOR TODAY.

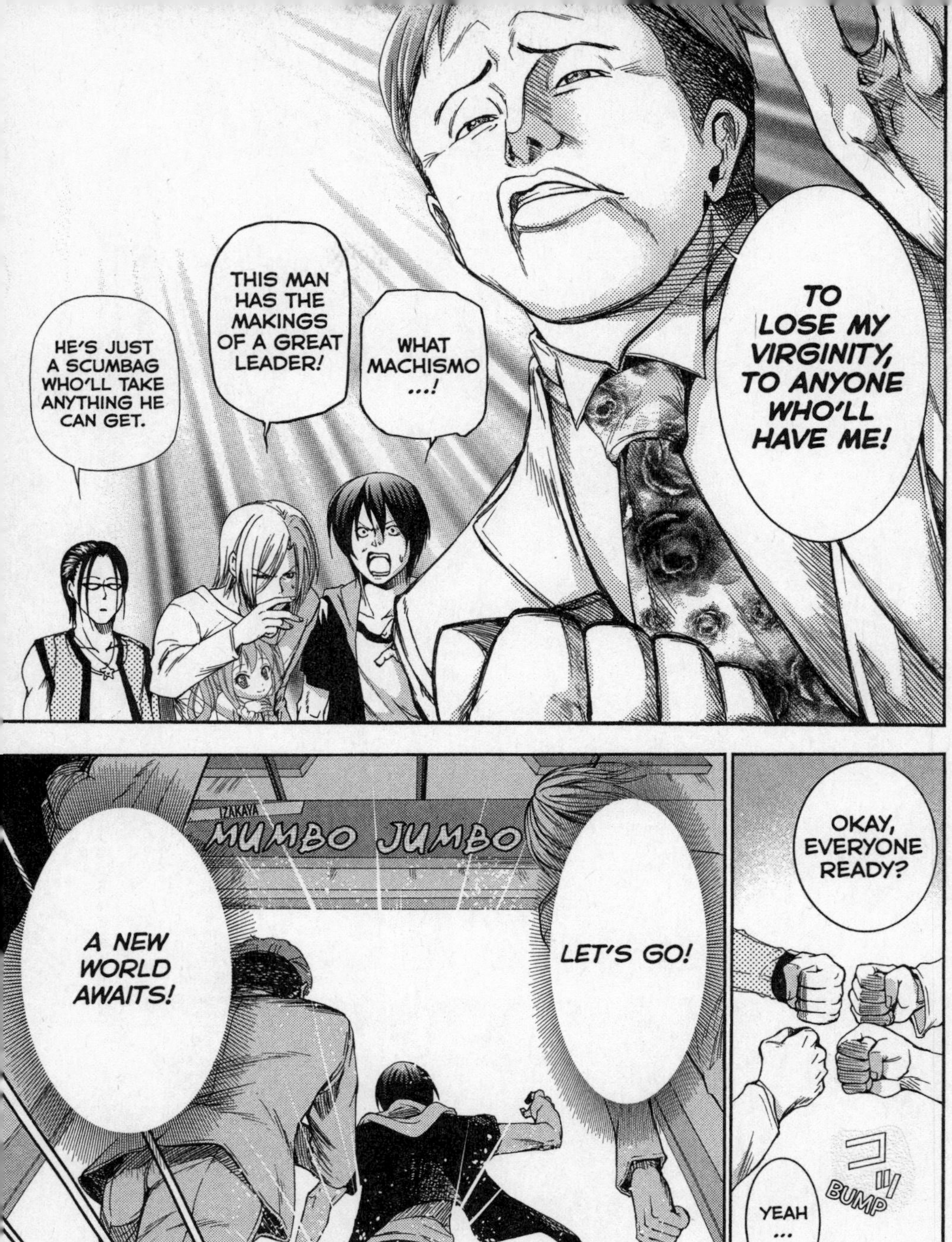
TO LOSE MY VIRGINITY, TO ANYONE WHO'LL HAVE ME!
WHAT MACHISMO ...!
THIS MAN HAS THE MAKINGS OF A GREAT LEADER!
HE'S JUST A SCUMBAG WHO'LL TAKE ANYTHING HE CAN GET.
OKAY, EVERYONE READY?
BUMP
YEAH ...
IZAKAYA
MUMBO JUMBO
LET'S GO!
A NEW WORLD AWAITS!

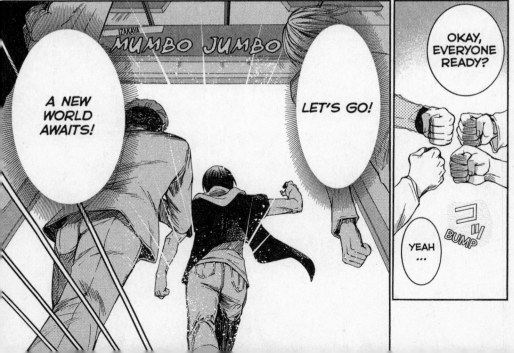

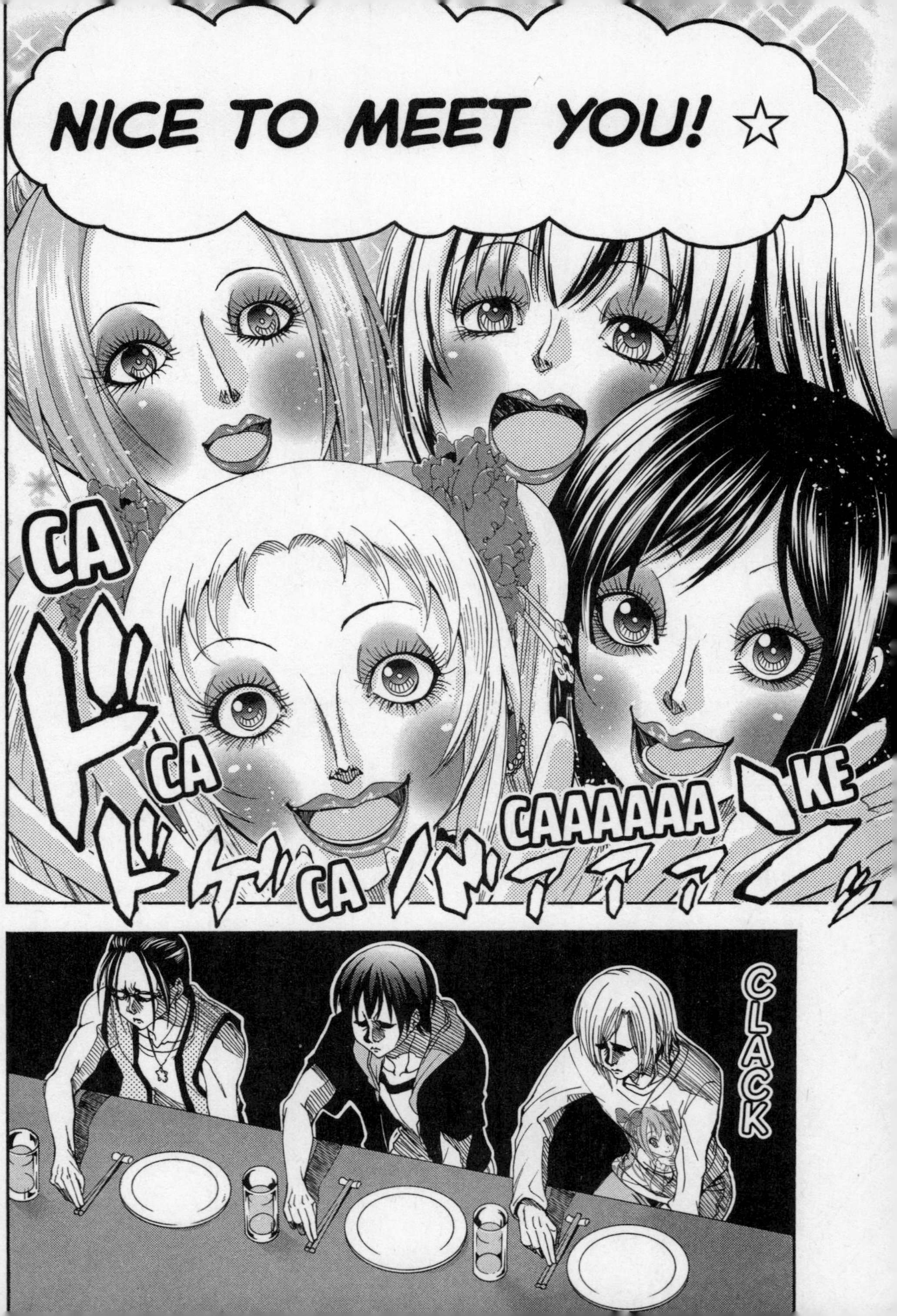
NICE TO MEET YOU! ☆
CA
CA
CA
CAAAAAA
KE
CLACK

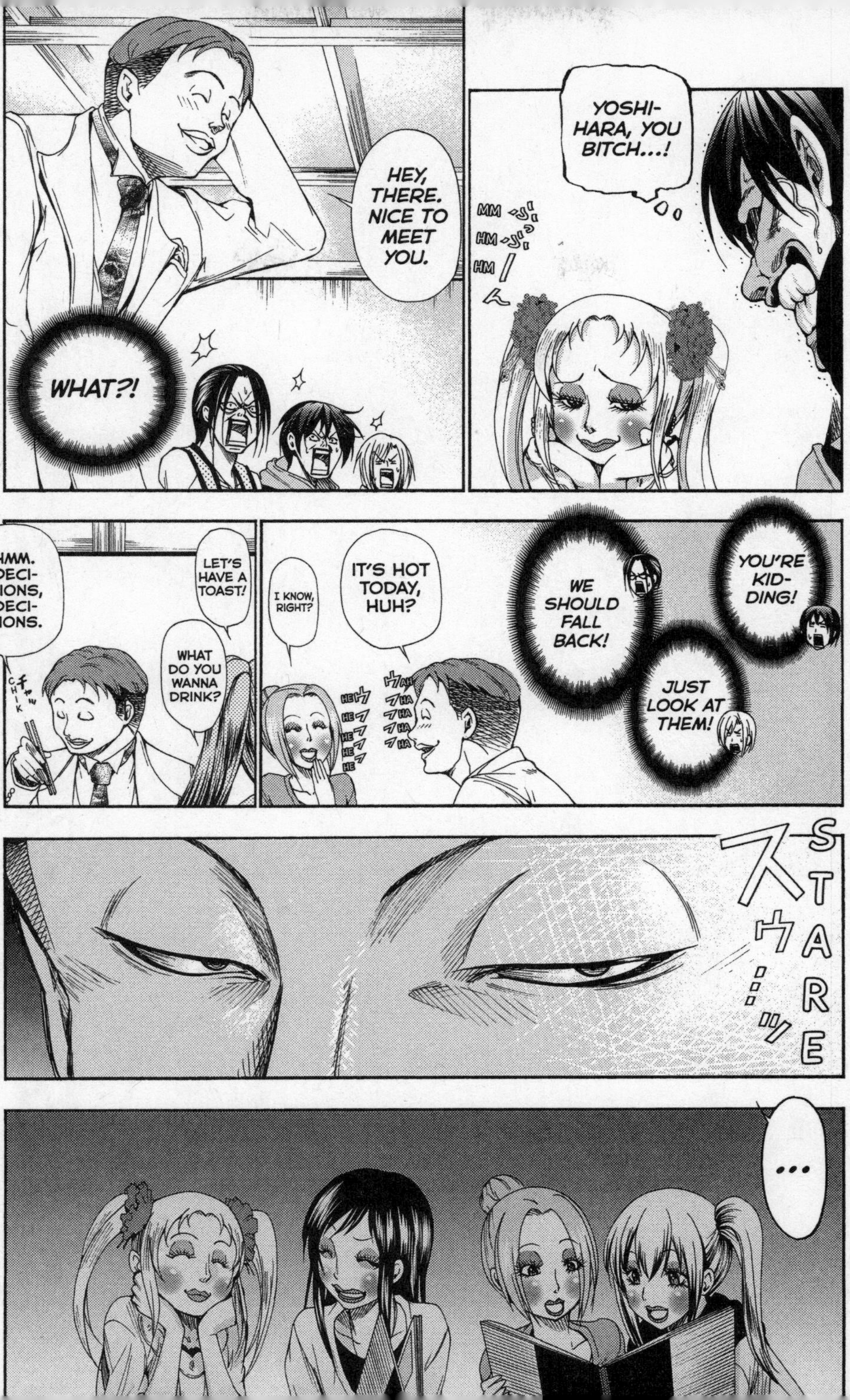
YOSHI-HARA, YOU BITCH...!
MM HM HM
HEY, THERE. NICE TO MEET YOU.
WHAT?!
YOU'RE KID-DING!
WE SHOULD FALL BACK!
JUST LOOK AT THEM!
IT'S HOT TODAY, HUH?
AH HA HA HA HA
I KNOW, RIGHT?
HE HE HE HE HE HE
LET'S HAVE A TOAST!
HMM. DECISIONS, DECISIONS.
WHAT DO YOU WANNA DRINK?
CHIK
STARE
...

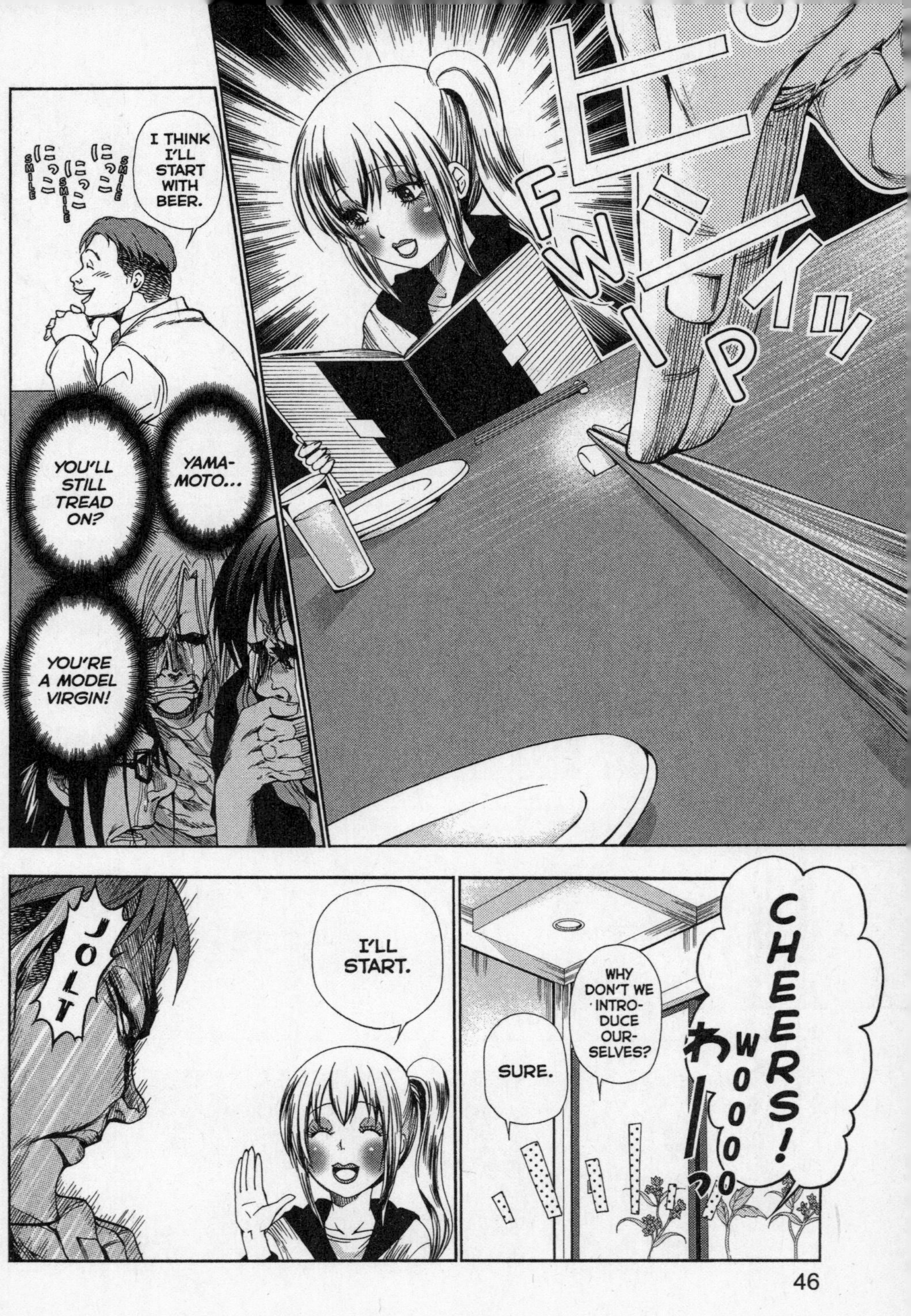
FWIP
I THINK I'LL START WITH BEER.
SMILE
SMILE
SMILE
YAMA-MOTO...
YOU'LL STILL TREAD ON?
YOU'RE A MODEL VIRGIN!
CHEERS!
WOOOOO
わーっ
WHY DON'T WE INTRO-DUCE OUR-SELVES?
SURE.
I'LL START.
JOLT

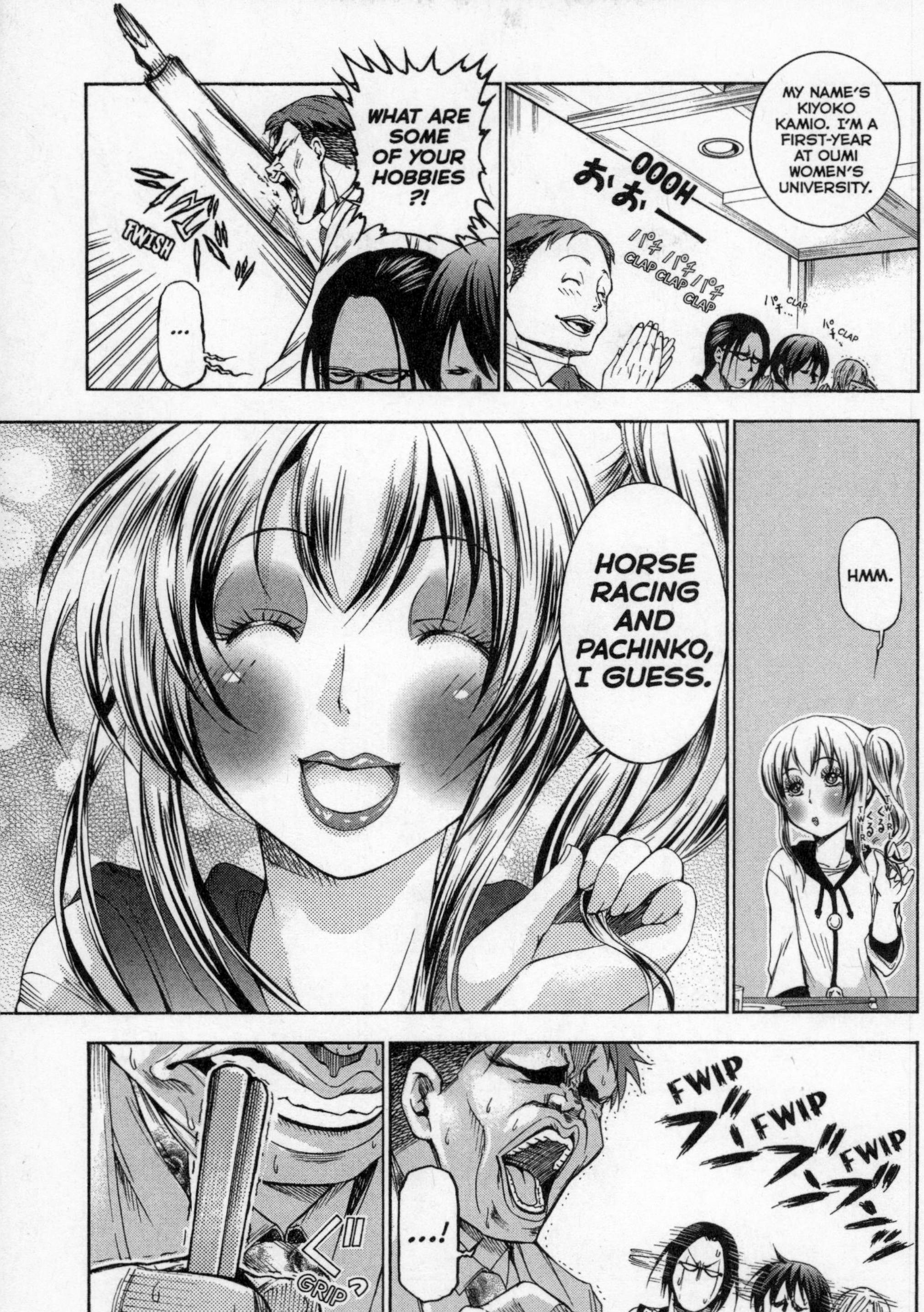
MY NAME'S KIYOKO KAMIO. I'M A FIRST-YEAR AT OUMI WOMEN'S UNIVERSITY.
OOOH
パチパチパチ
CLAP CLAP CLAP
パチ…
CLAP
パチ…
CLAP
WHAT ARE SOME OF YOUR HOBBIES ?!
FWISH
...
HMM.
TWIRL TWIRL
HORSE RACING AND PACHINKO, I GUESS.
FWIP
FWIP
FWIP
...!
GRIP

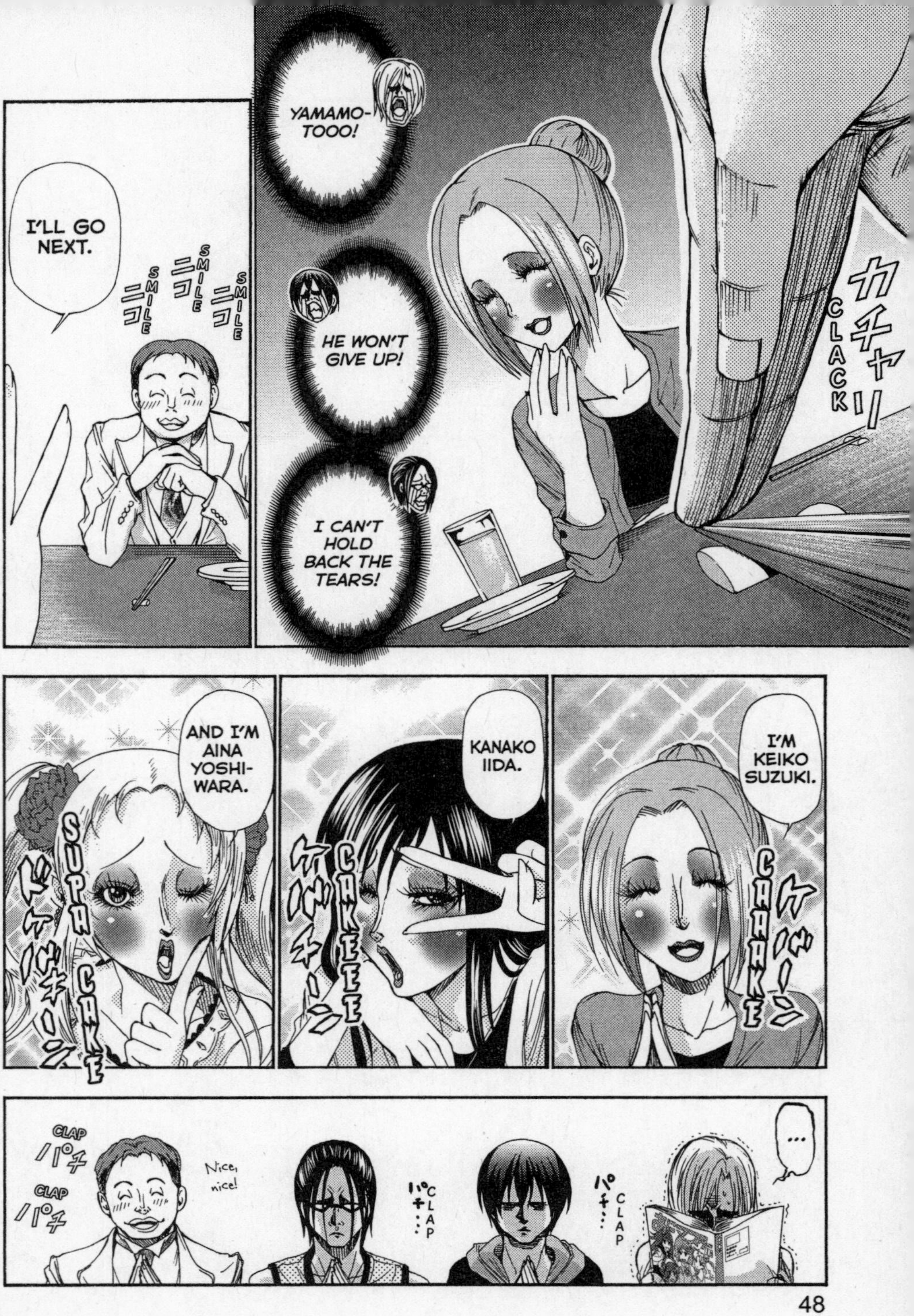
CLACK
カチャリ
YAMAMO-TOOO!
HE WON'T GIVE UP!
I CAN'T HOLD BACK THE TEARS!
I'LL GO NEXT.
SMILE ニコ
SMILE ニコ
SMILE ニコ
I'M KEIKO SUZUKI.
CAAAKE
KANAKO IIDA.
CAKEEE
AND I'M AINA YOSHI-WARA.
SUPA CAKE
...
CLAP パチ…
CLAP パチ…
Nice, nice!
CLAP パチ
CLAP パチ

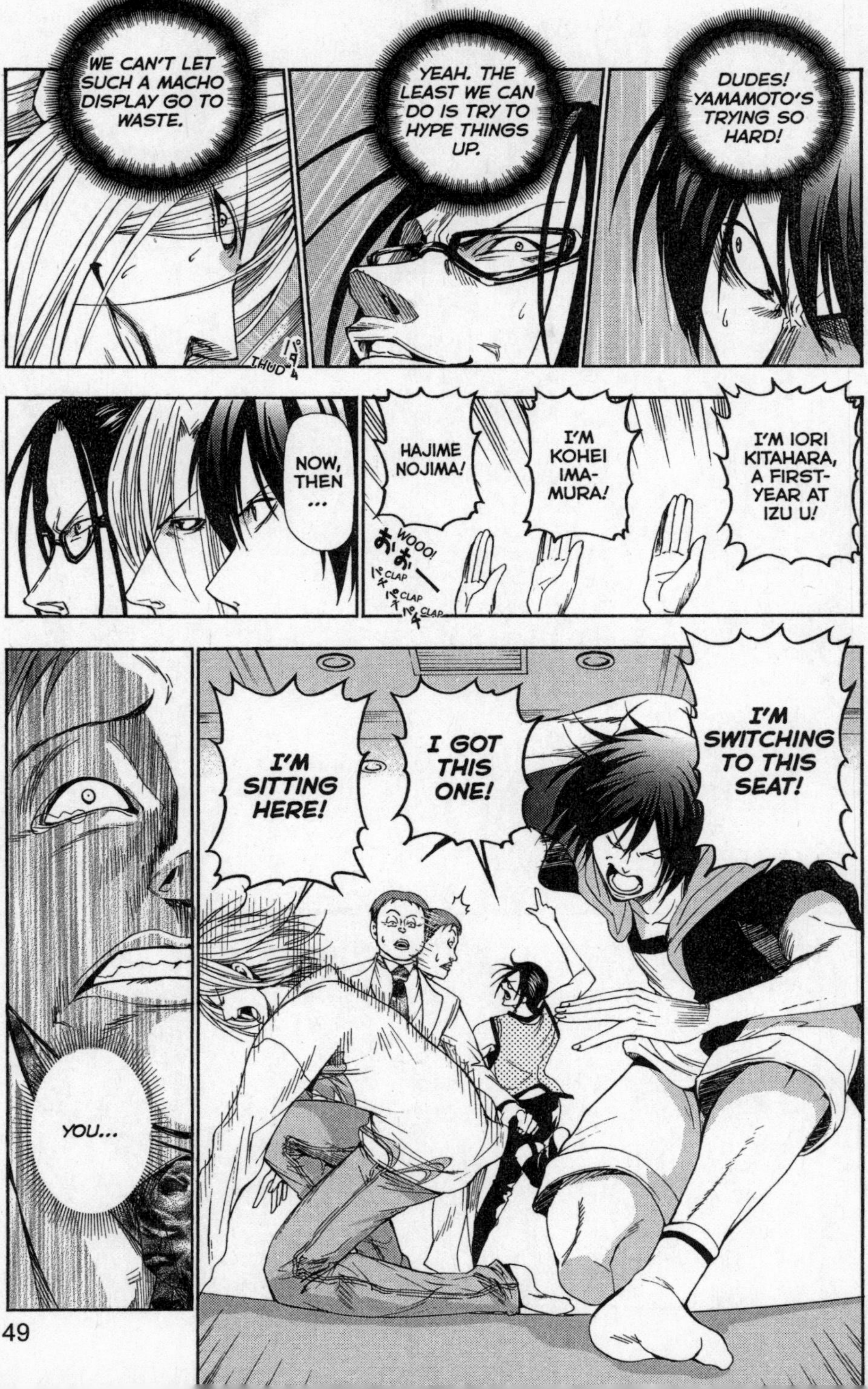
DUDES! YAMAMOTO'S TRYING SO HARD!
YEAH. THE LEAST WE CAN DO IS TRY TO HYPE THINGS UP.
WE CAN'T LET SUCH A MACHO DISPLAY GO TO WASTE.
THUD
I'M IORI KITAHARA, A FIRST-YEAR AT IZU U!
I'M KOHEI IMA-MURA!
HAJIME NOJIMA!
WOOO!
CLAP
CLAP
CLAP
NOW, THEN ...
I'M SWITCHING TO THIS SEAT!
I GOT THIS ONE!
I'M SITTING HERE!
YOU...

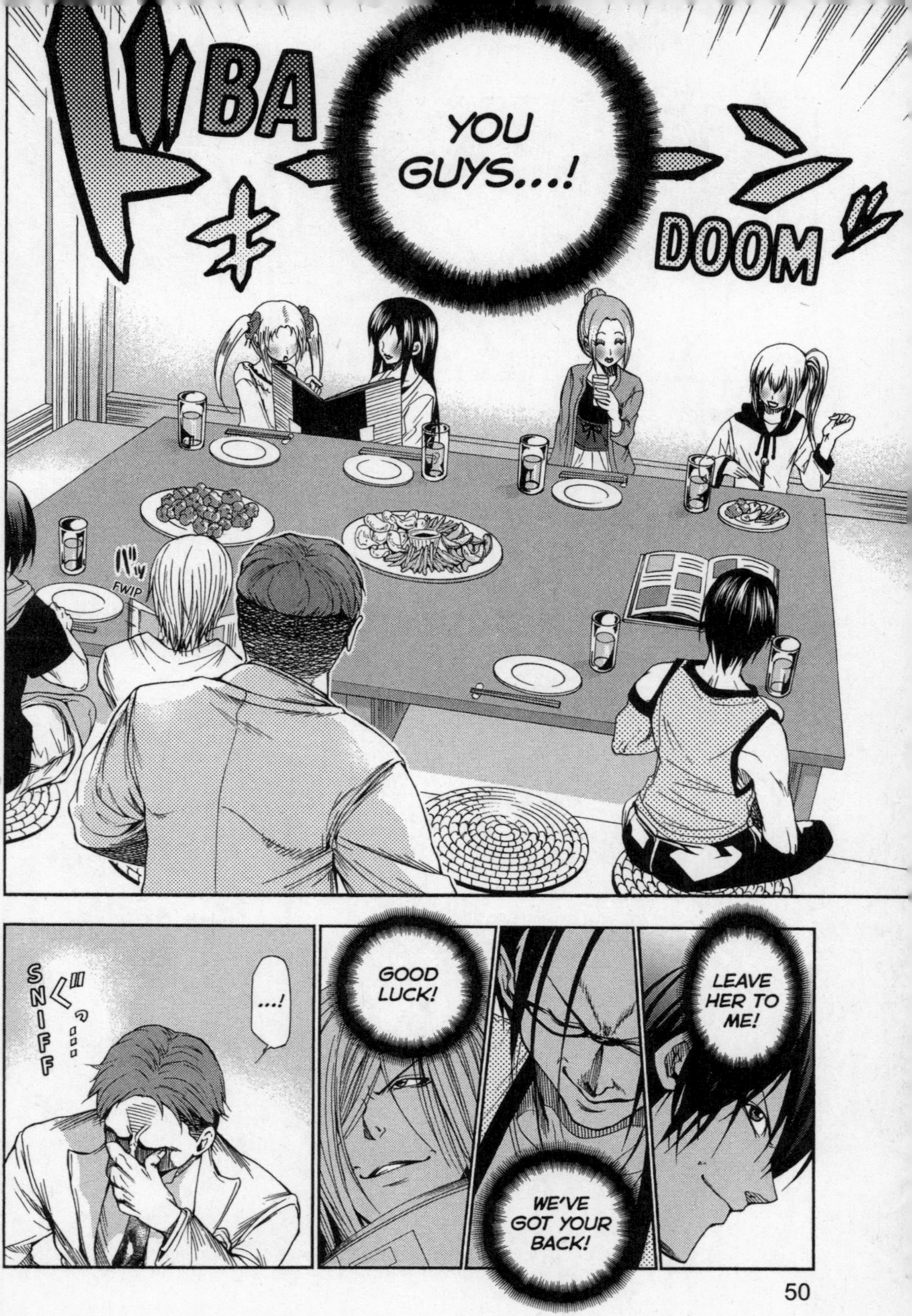
DOOM
YOU GUYS...!
BA
FWIP
LEAVE HER TO ME!
WE'VE GOT YOUR BACK!
GOOD LUCK!
...!
SNIFF

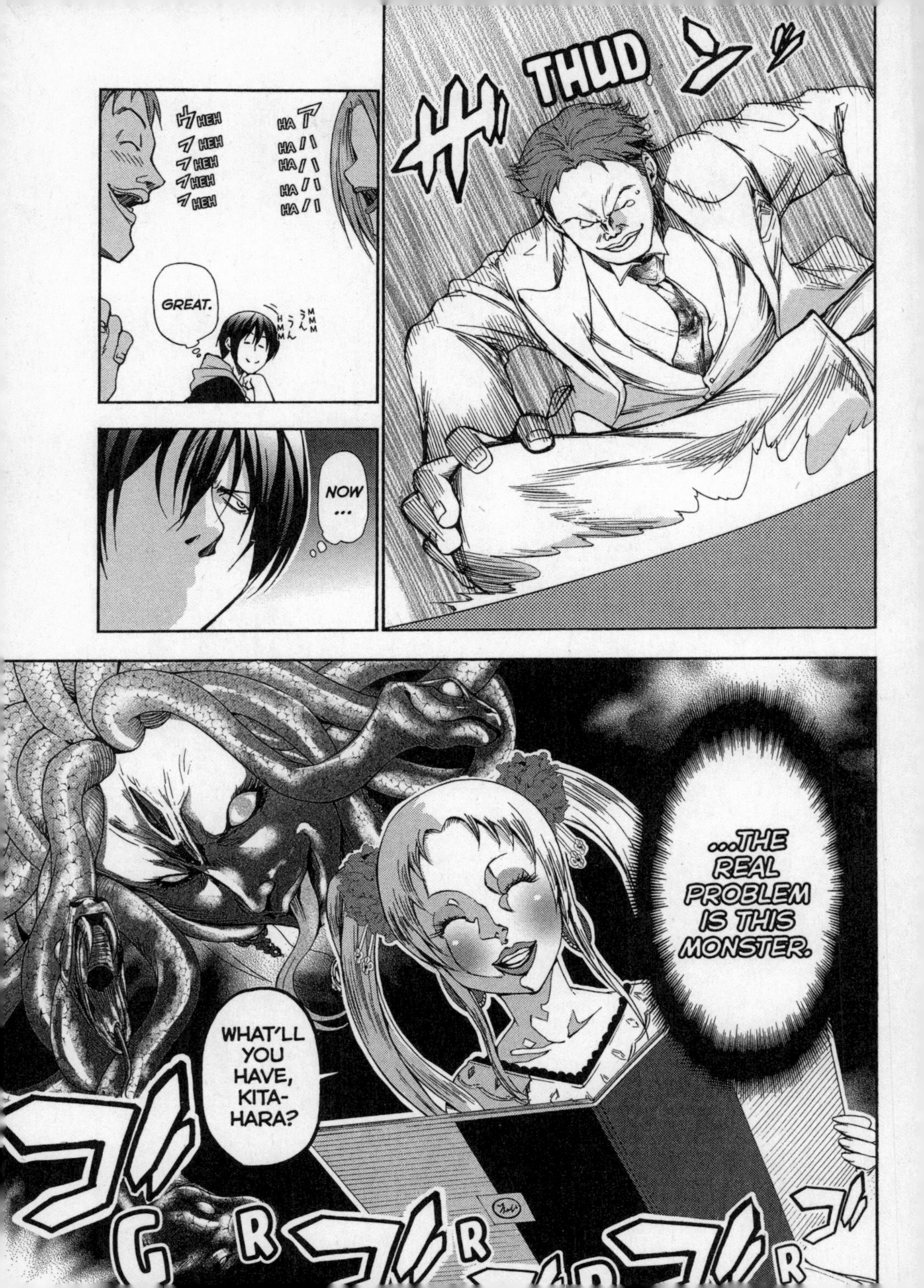
THUD
HA
HA
HA
HA
HA
HEH
HEH
HEH
HEH
HEH
GREAT.
MMM
MMM
NOW...
...THE REAL PROBLEM IS THIS MONSTER.
WHAT'LL YOU HAVE, KITA-HARA?
G
R
R
R
R

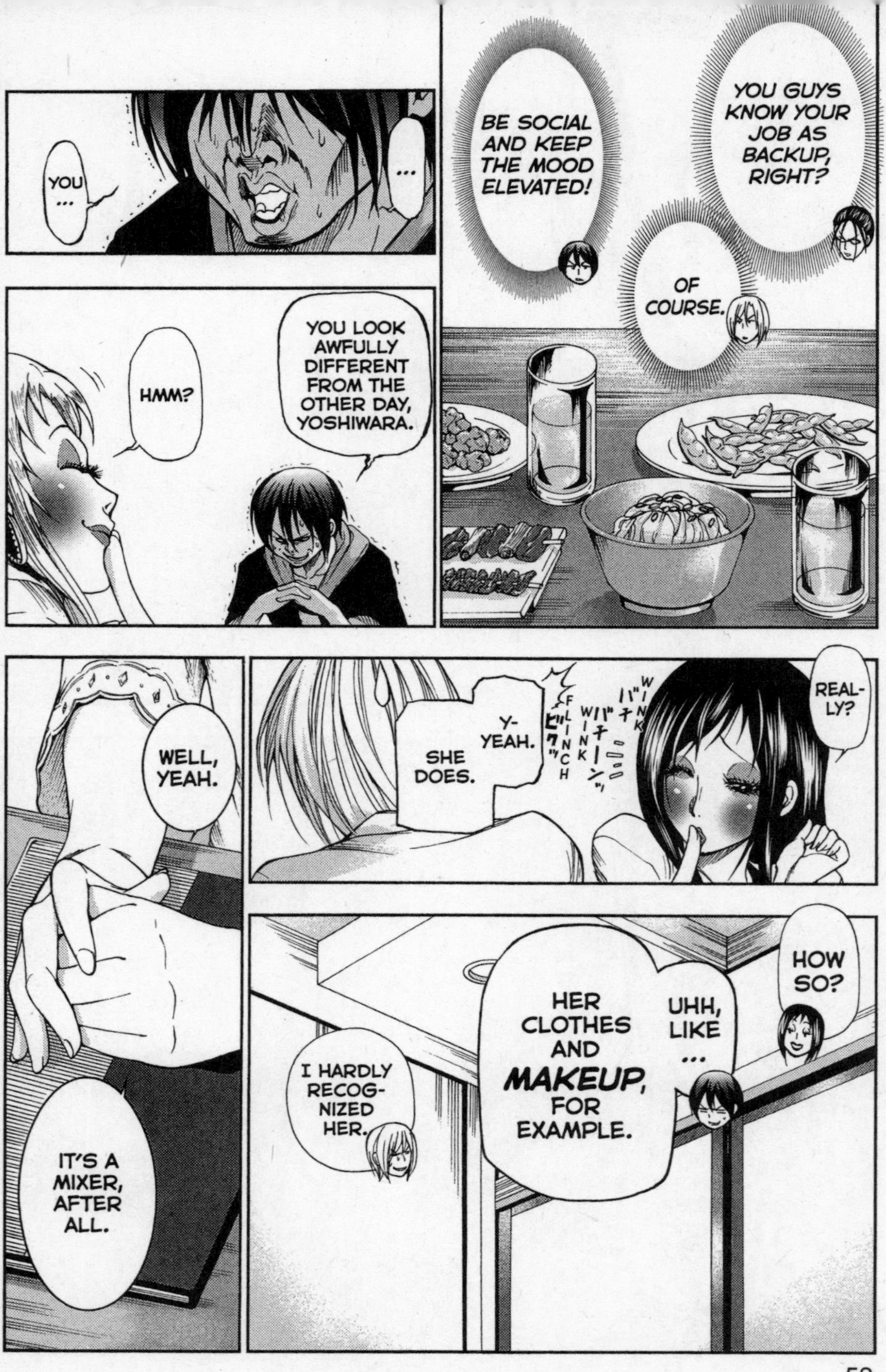
YOU GUYS KNOW YOUR JOB AS BACKUP, RIGHT?
BE SOCIAL AND KEEP THE MOOD ELEVATED!
OF COURSE.
...
YOU ...
YOU LOOK AWFULLY DIFFERENT FROM THE OTHER DAY, YOSHIWARA.
HMM?
REAL-LY?
WINK バチ
WINK バチーン
FLINCH ビクッ
Y-YEAH.
SHE DOES.
HOW SO?
UHH, LIKE ...
HER CLOTHES AND ***MAKEUP***, FOR EXAMPLE.
I HARDLY RECOG-NIZED HER.
WELL, YEAH.
IT'S A MIXER, AFTER ALL.

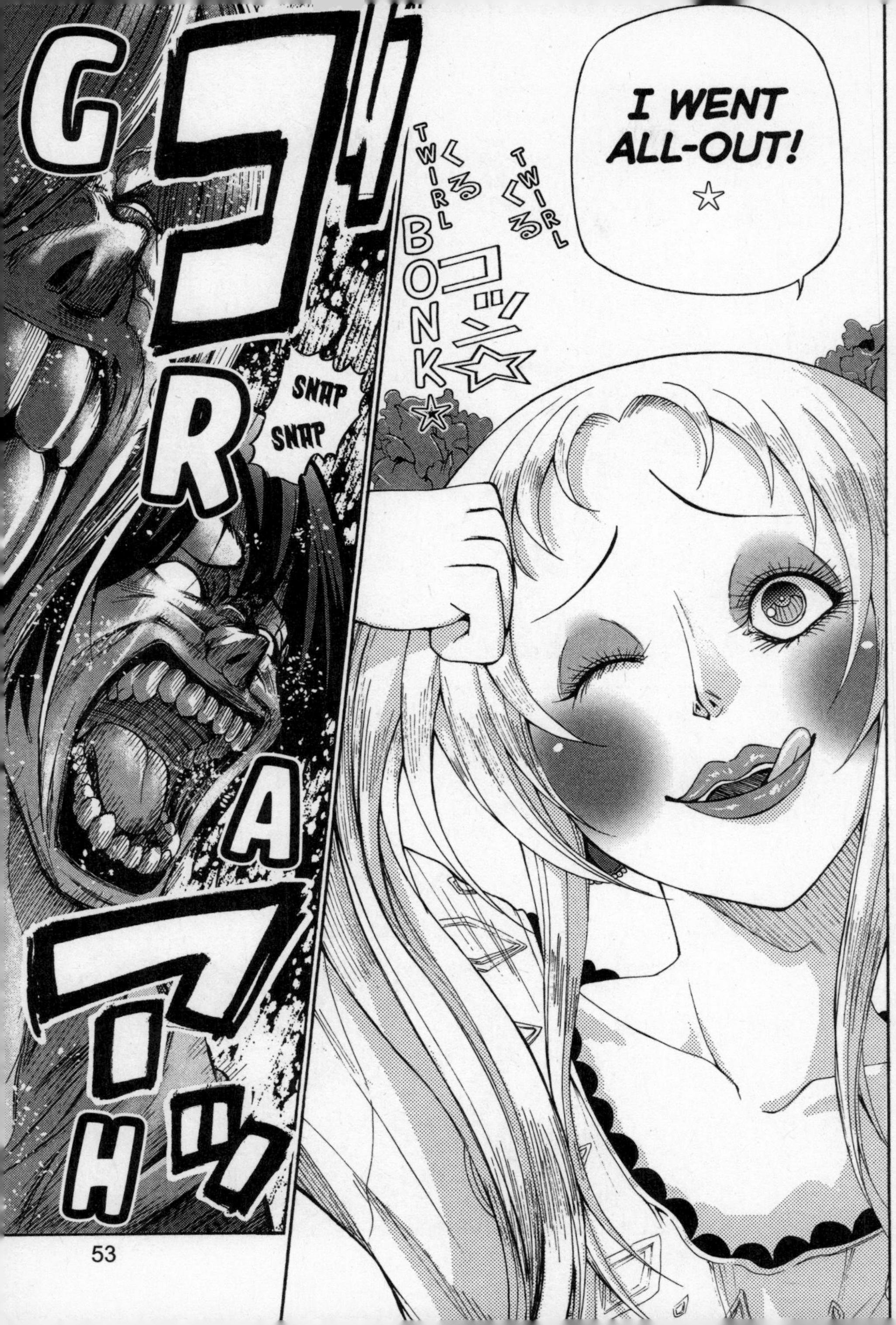
I WENT ALL-OUT! ☆
TWIRL TWIRL
BONK☆
SNAP
SNAP
GRAH

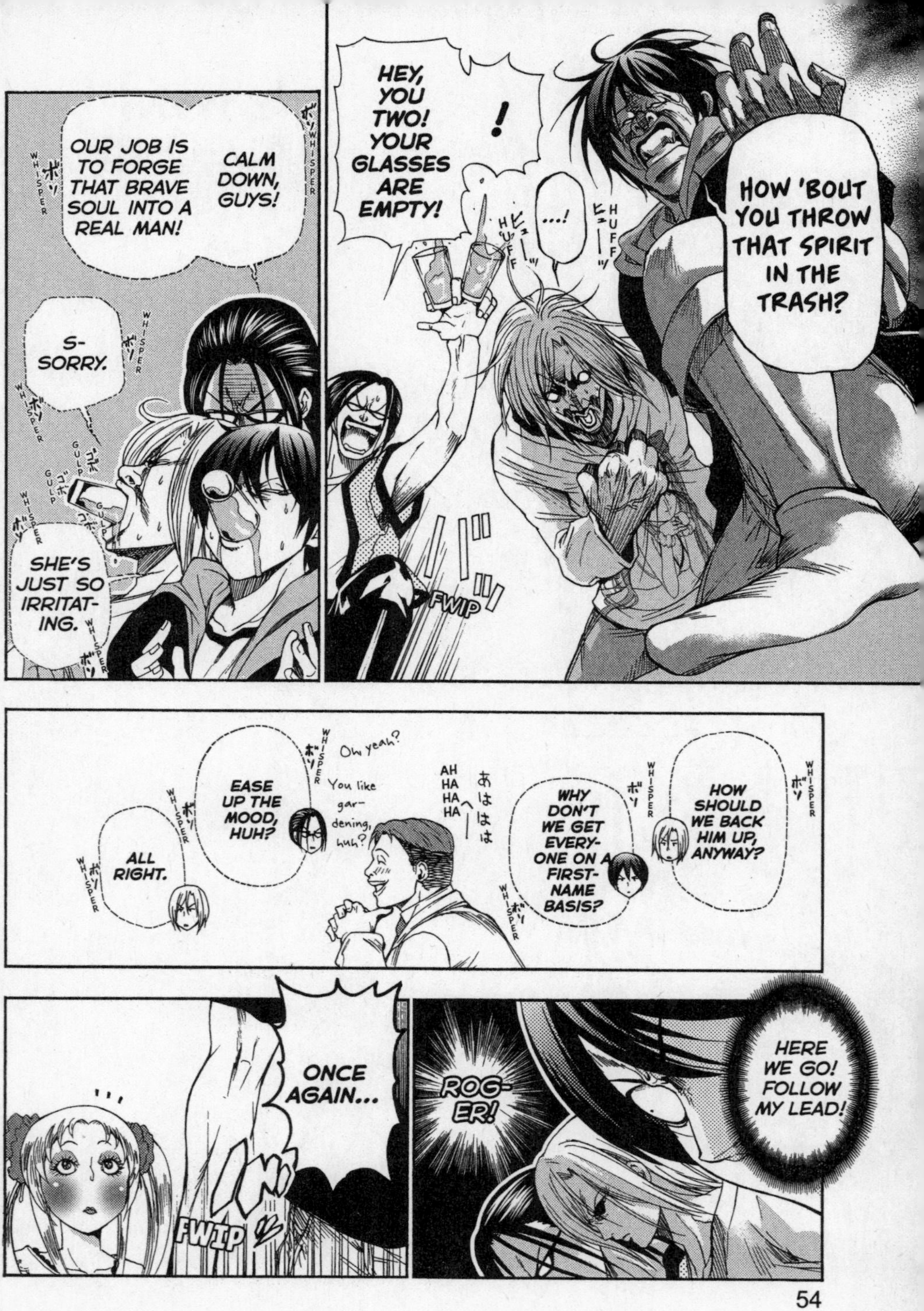
HOW 'BOUT YOU THROW THAT SPIRIT IN THE TRASH?
HUFF
HUFF
...!
!
HEY, YOU TWO! YOUR GLASSES ARE EMPTY!
FWIP
CALM DOWN, GUYS!
OUR JOB IS TO FORGE THAT BRAVE SOUL INTO A REAL MAN!
WHISPER
S-SORRY.
GULP
GULP
SHE'S JUST SO IRRITAT-ING.
WHISPER
HOW SHOULD WE BACK HIM UP, ANYWAY?
WHISPER
WHY DON'T WE GET EVERY-ONE ON A FIRST-NAME BASIS?
AH HA HA HA
あははは
Oh yeah?
You like gar-dening, huh?
WHISPER
EASE UP THE MOOD, HUH?
WHISPER
ALL RIGHT.
HERE WE GO! FOLLOW MY LEAD!
ROG-ER!
ONCE AGAIN...
FWIP

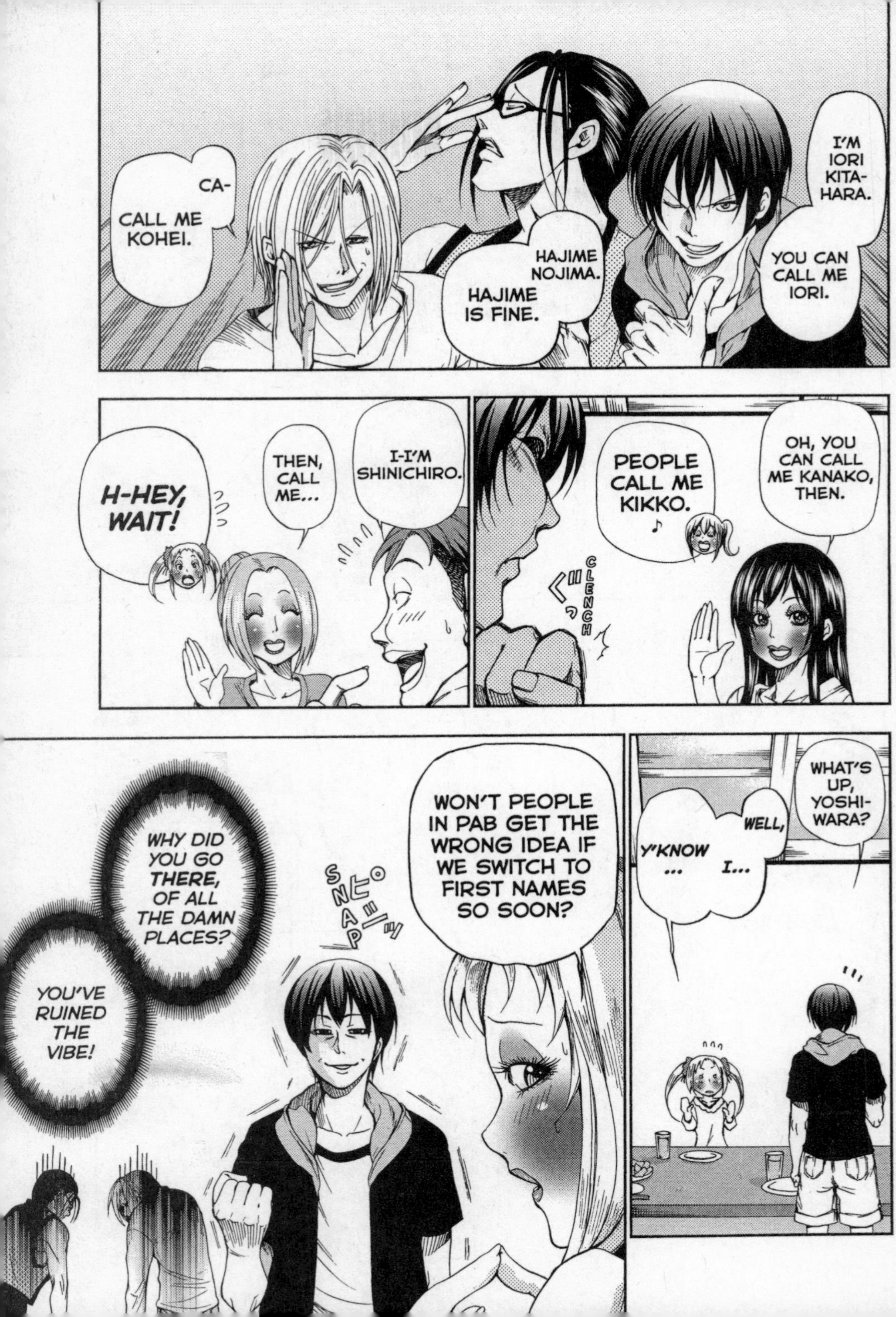
I'M IORI KITAHARA.
YOU CAN CALL ME IORI.
HAJIME NOJIMA.
HAJIME IS FINE.
CA- CALL ME KOHEI.
OH, YOU CAN CALL ME KANAKO, THEN.
PEOPLE CALL ME KIKKO. ♪
CLENCH
I-I'M SHINICHIRO.
THEN, CALL ME...
H-HEY, WAIT!
WHAT'S UP, YOSHIWARA?
WELL,
Y'KNOW ...
I...
WON'T PEOPLE IN PAB GET THE WRONG IDEA IF WE SWITCH TO FIRST NAMES SO SOON?
SNAP
WHY DID YOU GO THERE, OF ALL THE DAMN PLACES?
YOU'VE RUINED THE VIBE!

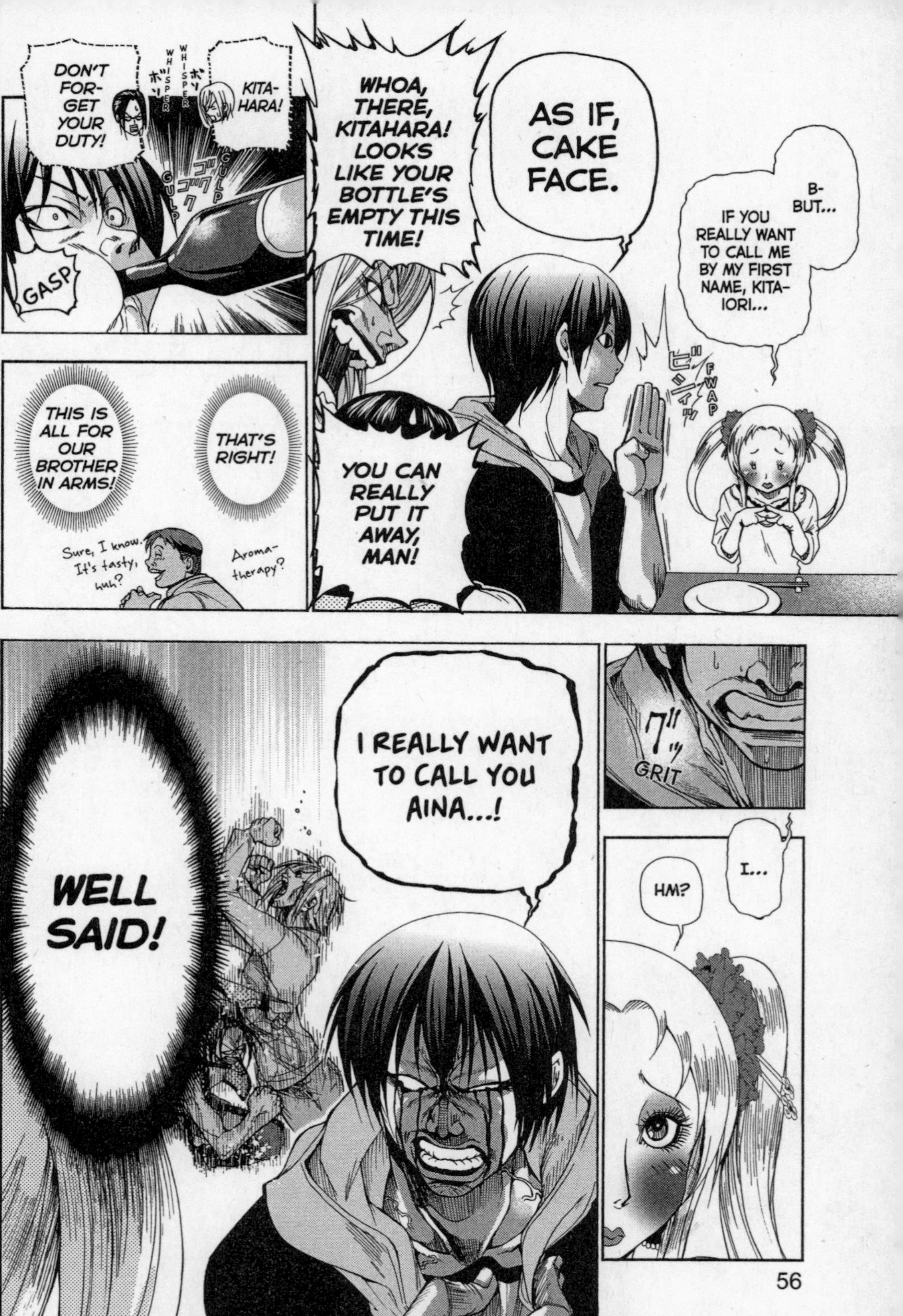
AS IF, CAKE FACE.
B-BUT... IF YOU REALLY WANT TO CALL ME BY MY FIRST NAME, KITA-IORI...
WHOA, THERE, KITAHARA! LOOKS LIKE YOUR BOTTLE'S EMPTY THIS TIME!
FWAP
YOU CAN REALLY PUT IT AWAY, MAN!
KITA-HARA!
WHISPER
WHISPER
DON'T FOR-GET YOUR DUTY!
GULP
GULP
GASP
THAT'S RIGHT!
THIS IS ALL FOR OUR BROTHER IN ARMS!
Aroma-therapy?
Sure, I know. It's tasty, huh?
GRIT
I...
HM?
I REALLY WANT TO CALL YOU AINA...!
WELL SAID!

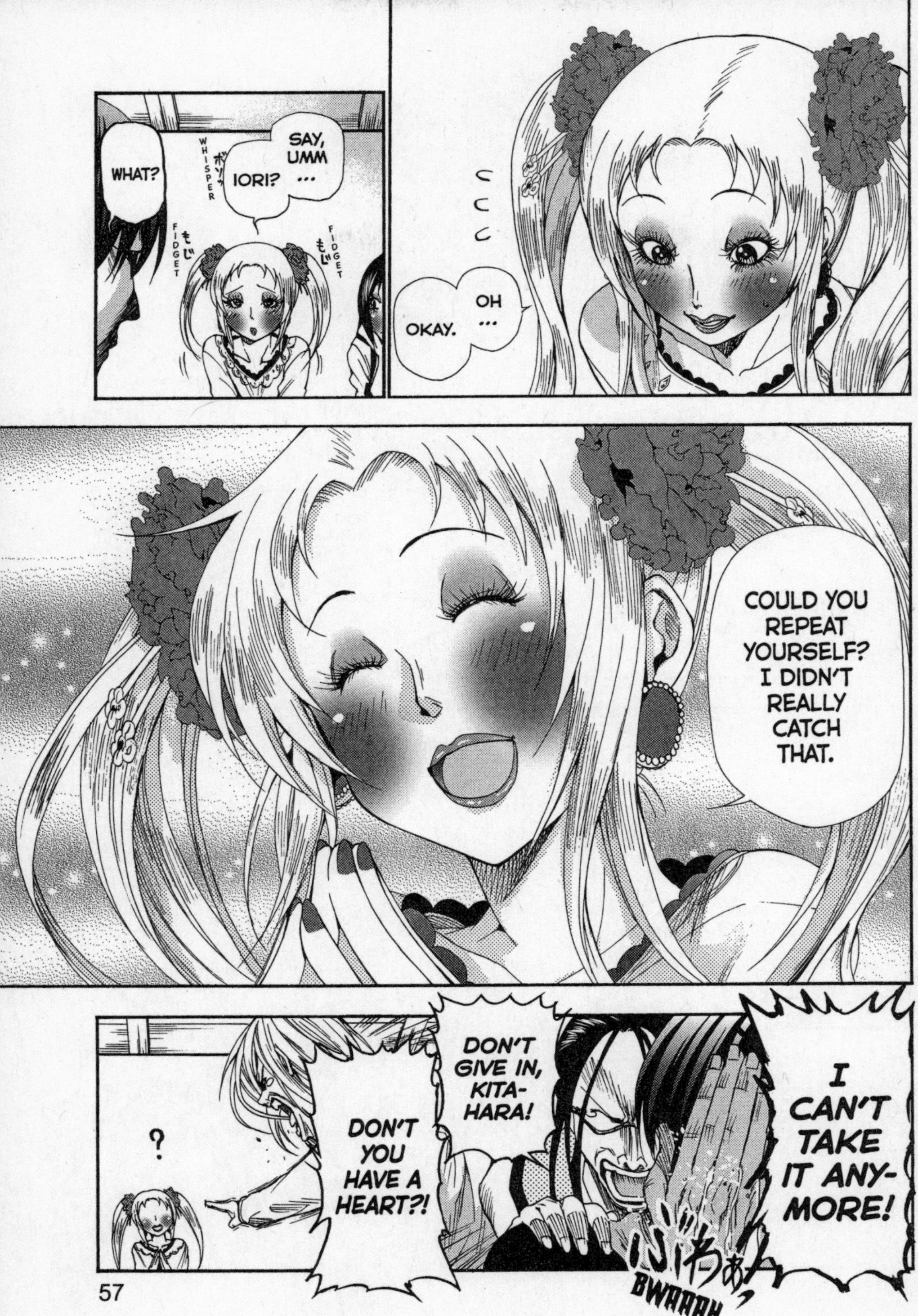
OH ... OKAY.
SAY, UMM ... IORI?
WHISPER
WHAT?
FIDGET
FIDGET
COULD YOU REPEAT YOURSELF? I DIDN'T REALLY CATCH THAT.
I CAN'T TAKE IT ANY-MORE!
BWAAAH
DON'T GIVE IN, KITA-HARA!
DON'T YOU HAVE A HEART?!
?

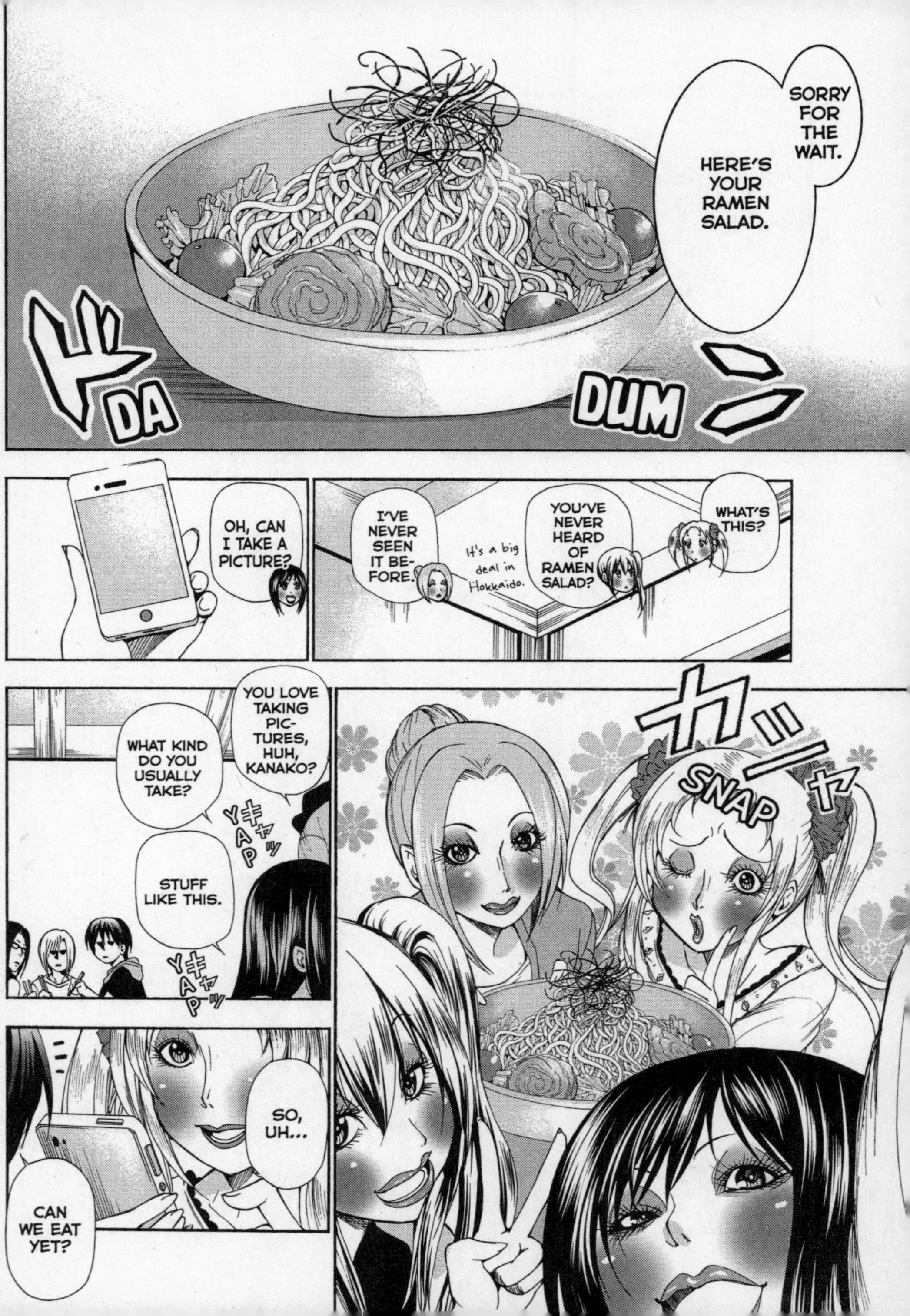
SORRY FOR THE WAIT.
HERE'S YOUR RAMEN SALAD.
DA
DUM
WHAT'S THIS?
YOU'VE NEVER HEARD OF RAMEN SALAD?
It's a big deal in Hokkaido.
I'VE NEVER SEEN IT BEFORE.
OH, CAN I TAKE A PICTURE?
SNAP
YOU LOVE TAKING PICTURES, HUH, KANAKO?
WHAT KIND DO YOU USUALLY TAKE?
YAP
STUFF LIKE THIS.
YAP
SO, UH...
CAN WE EAT YET?

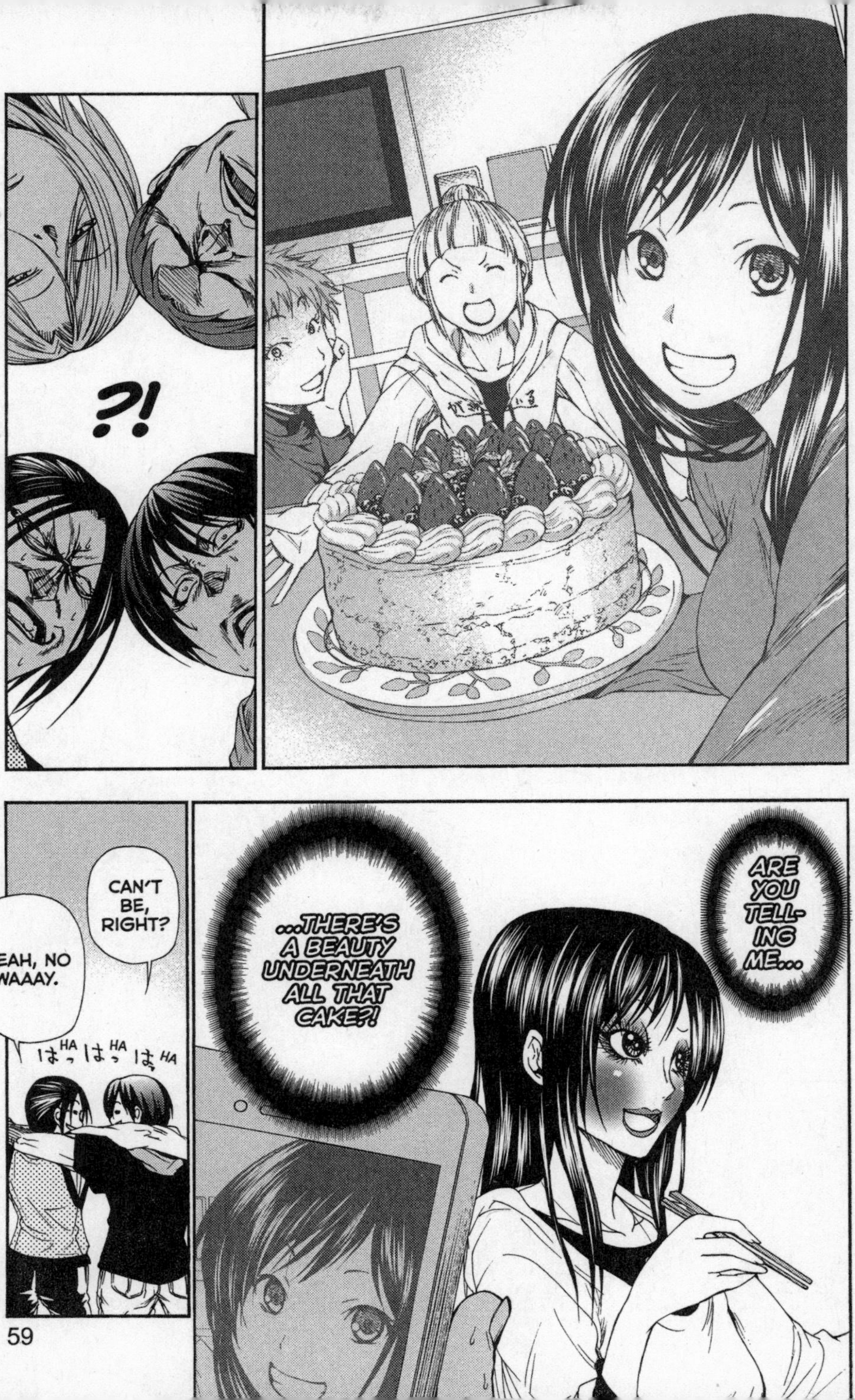
?!
ARE YOU TELLING ME...
...THERE'S A BEAUTY UNDERNEATH ALL THAT CAKE?!
CAN'T BE, RIGHT?
YEAH, NO WAAAY.
はっはっはっ HA HA HA

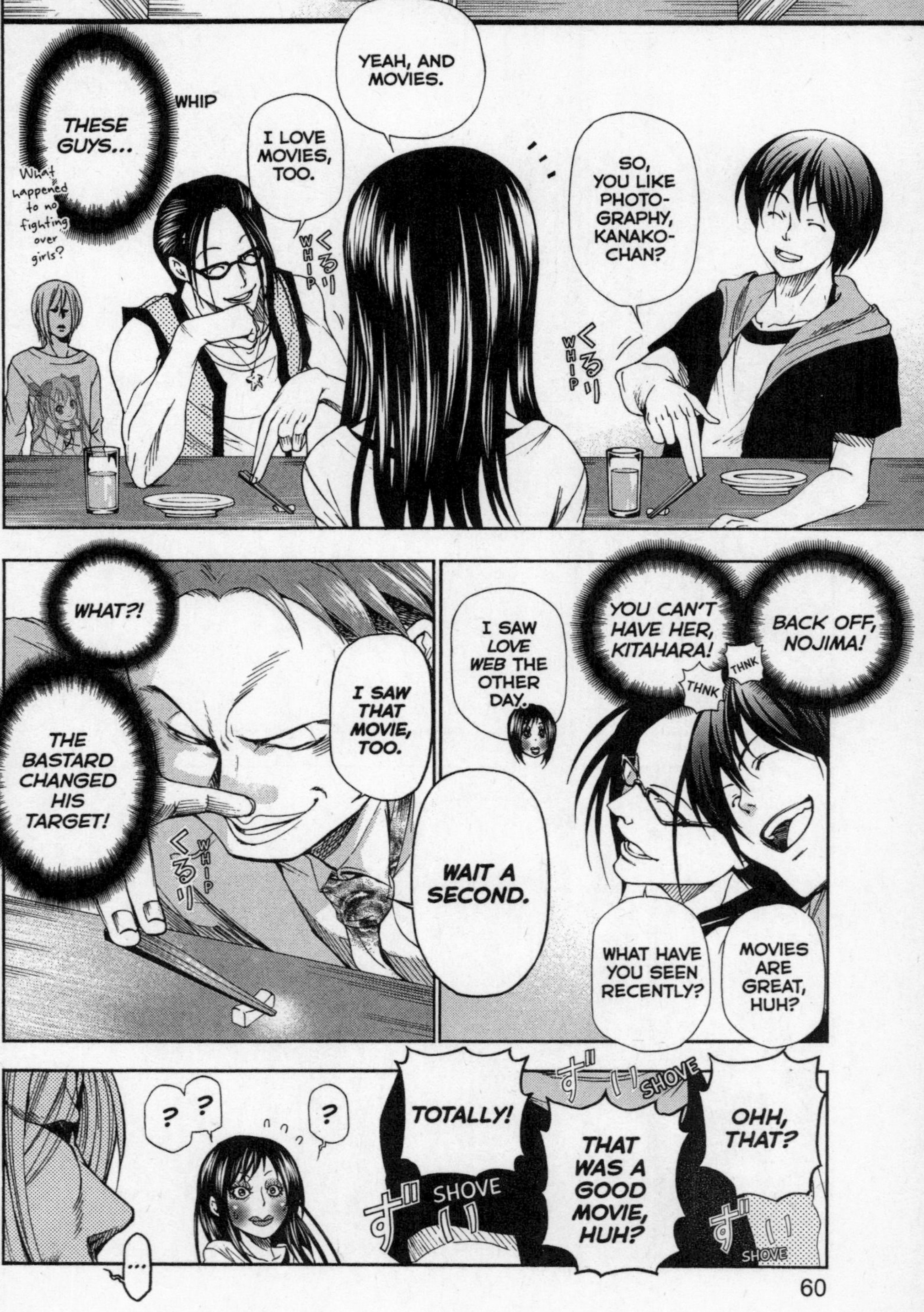
SO, YOU LIKE PHOTOGRAPHY, KANAKO-CHAN?
くるり WHIP
YEAH, AND MOVIES.
I LOVE MOVIES, TOO.
くるり WHIP
WHIP
THESE GUYS...
What happened to no fighting over girls?
BACK OFF, NOJIMA!
YOU CAN'T HAVE HER, KITAHARA!
THNK
THNK
I SAW LOVE WEB THE OTHER DAY.
MOVIES ARE GREAT, HUH?
WHAT HAVE YOU SEEN RECENTLY?
WHAT?!
I SAW THAT MOVIE, TOO.
THE BASTARD CHANGED HIS TARGET!
WAIT A SECOND.
くるり WHIP
OHH, THAT?
ずい SHOVE
ずい SHOVE
THAT WAS A GOOD MOVIE, HUH?
TOTALLY!
ずい SHOVE
?
? ?
...

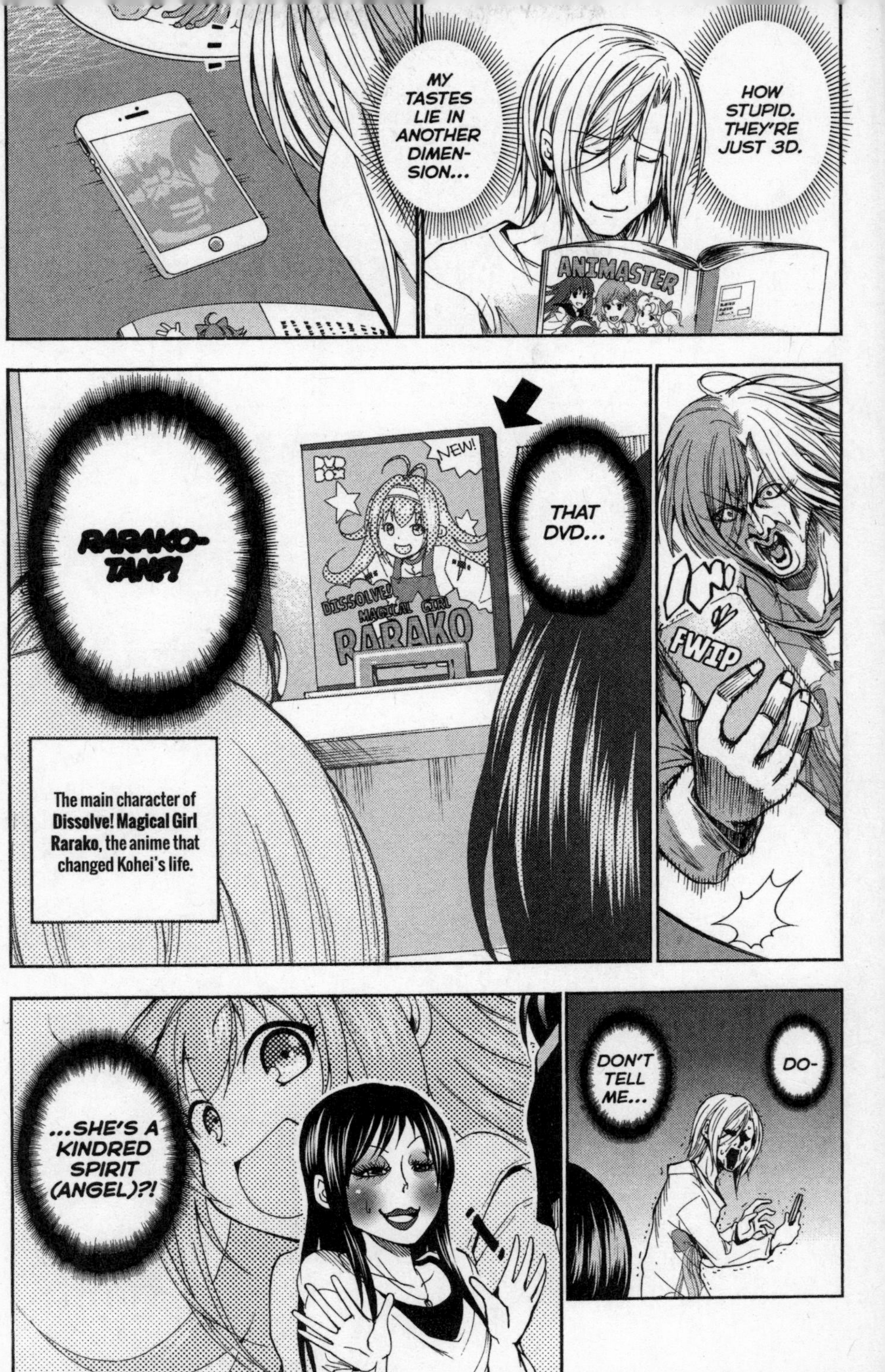
HOW STUPID. THEY'RE JUST 3D.
MY TASTES LIE IN ANOTHER DIMEN-SION...
ANIMASTER
FWIP
THAT DVD...
NEW!
DISSOLVE! MAGICAL GIRL RARAKO
RARAKO-TAN?!
The main character of **Dissolve! Magical Girl Rarako**, the anime that changed Kohei's life.
DO-
DON'T TELL ME...
...SHE'S A KINDRED SPIRIT (ANGEL)?!

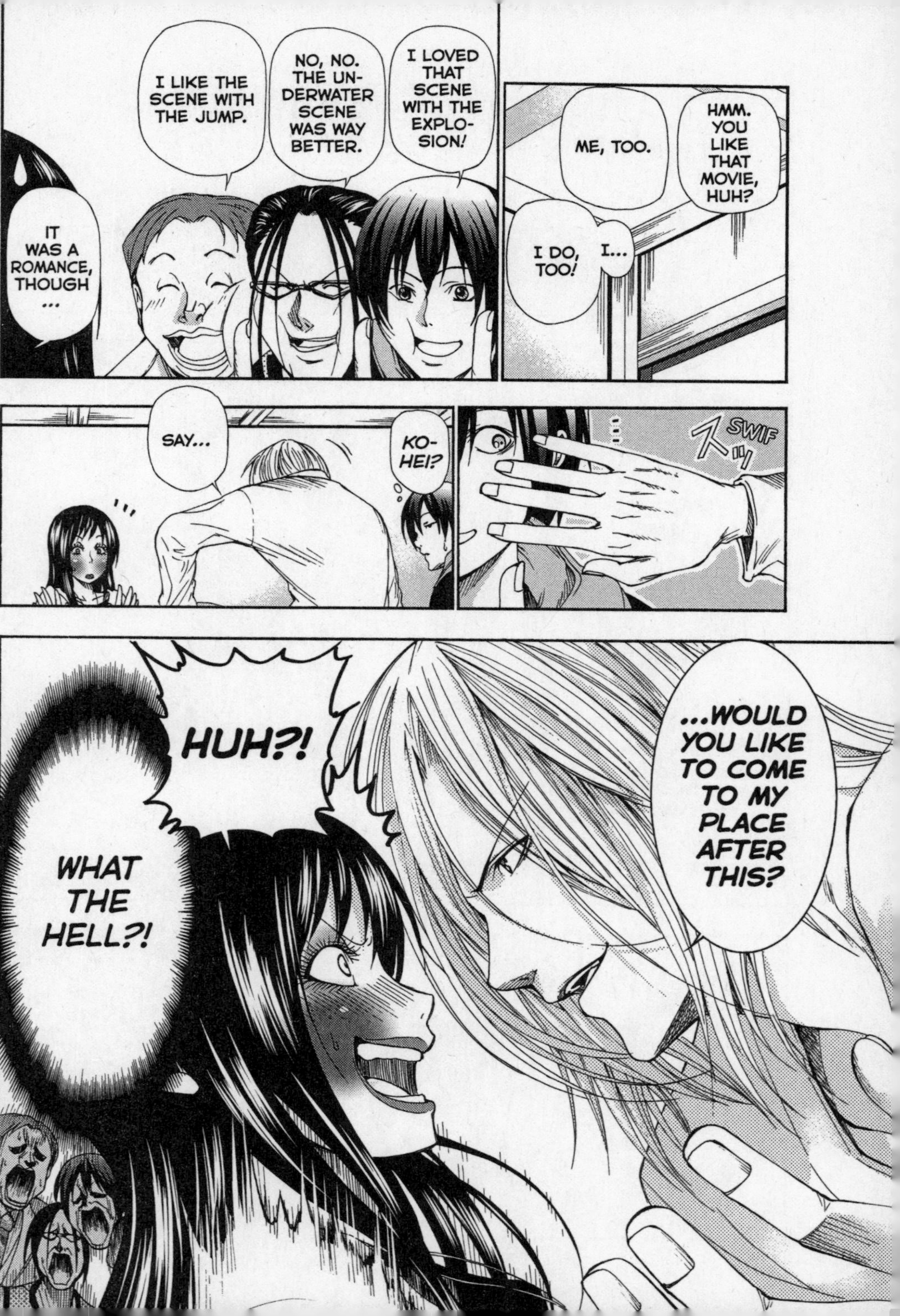
HMM. YOU LIKE THAT MOVIE, HUH?
ME, TOO.
I...
I DO, TOO!
I LOVED THAT SCENE WITH THE EXPLOSION!
NO, NO. THE UNDERWATER SCENE WAS WAY BETTER.
I LIKE THE SCENE WITH THE JUMP.
IT WAS A ROMANCE, THOUGH...
SWIF
...
KO-HEI?
SAY...
...WOULD YOU LIKE TO COME TO MY PLACE AFTER THIS?
HUH?!
WHAT THE HELL?!

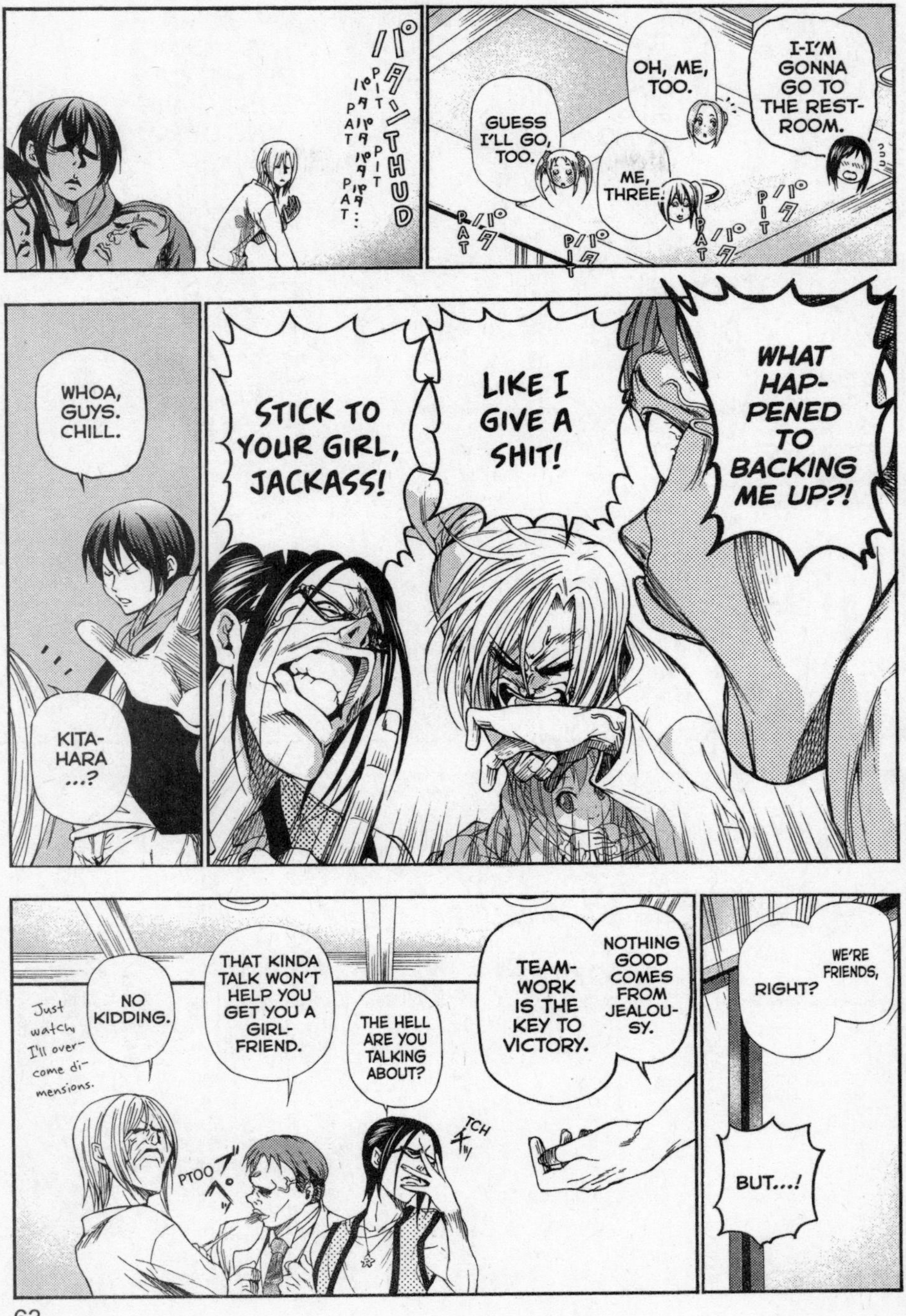
I-I'M GONNA GO TO THE REST-ROOM.
OH, ME, TOO.
ME, THREE.
GUESS I'LL GO, TOO.
PIT
PAT
PIT
PAT
THUD
PIT
PAT
PIT
PAT...
WHAT HAP-PENED TO BACKING ME UP?!
LIKE I GIVE A SHIT!
STICK TO YOUR GIRL, JACKASS!
WHOA, GUYS. CHILL.
KITA-HARA ...?
WE'RE FRIENDS, RIGHT?
BUT...!
NOTHING GOOD COMES FROM JEALOU-SY.
TEAM-WORK IS THE KEY TO VICTORY.
THE HELL ARE YOU TALKING ABOUT?
TCH
THAT KINDA TALK WON'T HELP YOU GET YOU A GIRL-FRIEND.
NO KIDDING.
Just watch. I'll over-come di-mensions.
PTOO

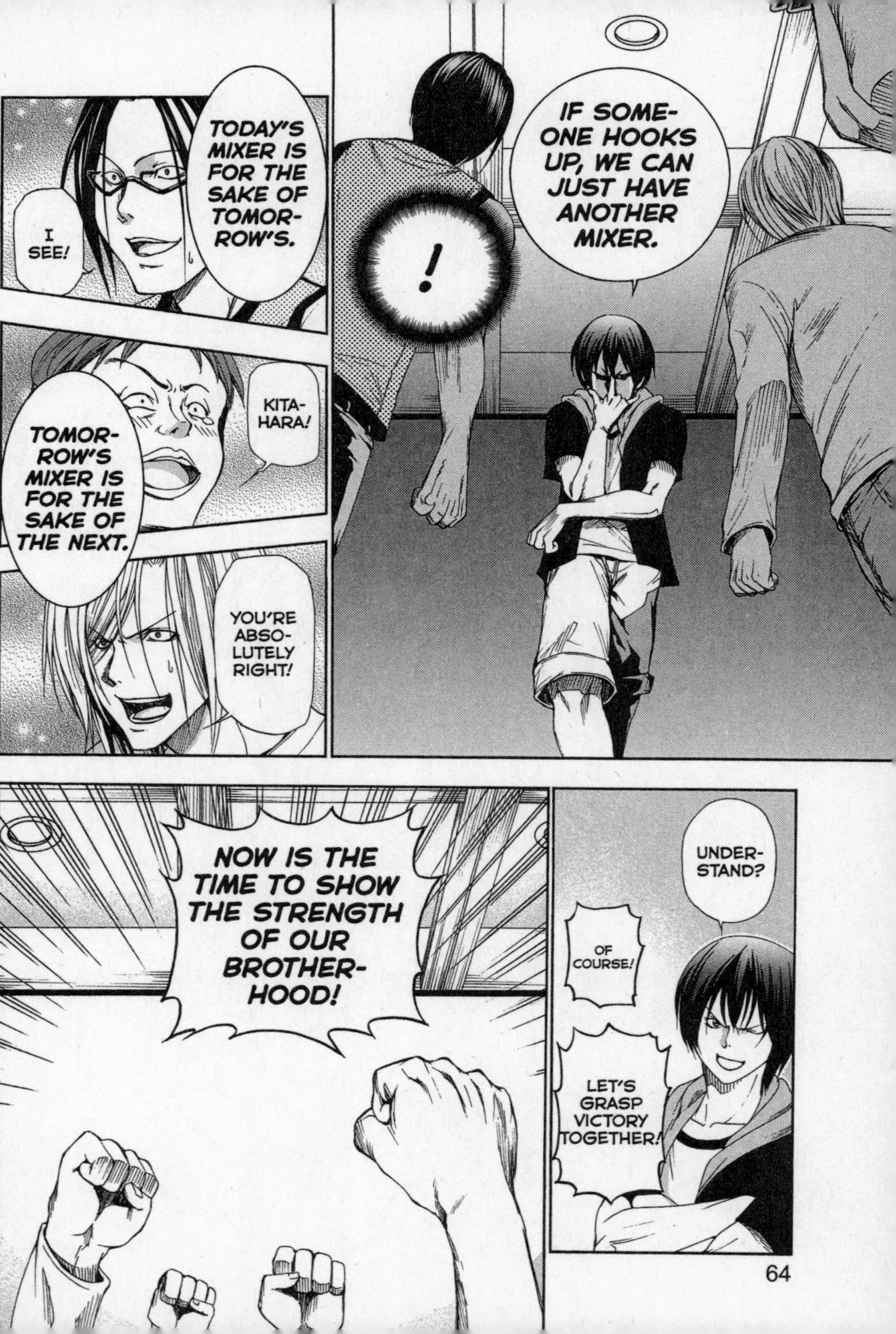
IF SOME-ONE HOOKS UP, WE CAN JUST HAVE ANOTHER MIXER.
!
TODAY'S MIXER IS FOR THE SAKE OF TOMOR-ROW'S.
I SEE!
KITA-HARA!
TOMOR-ROW'S MIXER IS FOR THE SAKE OF THE NEXT.
YOU'RE ABSO-LUTELY RIGHT!
UNDER-STAND?
OF COURSE!
LET'S GRASP VICTORY TOGETHER!
NOW IS THE TIME TO SHOW THE STRENGTH OF OUR BROTHER-HOOD!

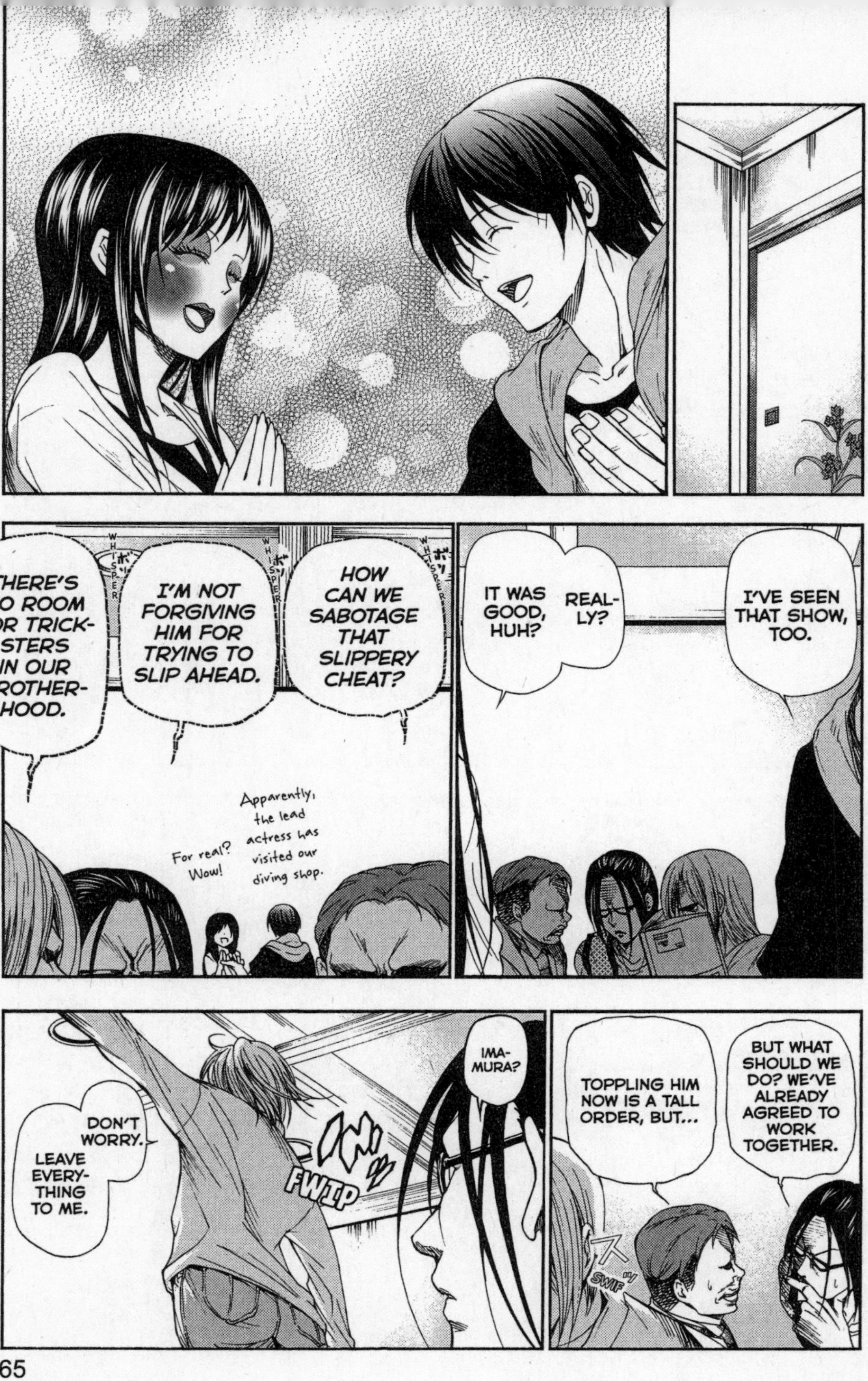
I'VE SEEN THAT SHOW, TOO.
REAL-LY?
IT WAS GOOD, HUH?
WHISPER
HOW CAN WE SABOTAGE THAT SLIPPERY CHEAT?
WHISPER
I'M NOT FORGIVING HIM FOR TRYING TO SLIP AHEAD.
WHISPER
WHISPER
THERE'S NO ROOM FOR TRICK-STERS IN OUR BROTHER-HOOD.
Apparently, the lead actress has visited our diving shop.
For real? Wow!
BUT WHAT SHOULD WE DO? WE'VE ALREADY AGREED TO WORK TOGETHER.
TOPPLING HIM NOW IS A TALL ORDER, BUT...
SWIF
IMA-MURA?
FWIP
DON'T WORRY. LEAVE EVERY-THING TO ME.

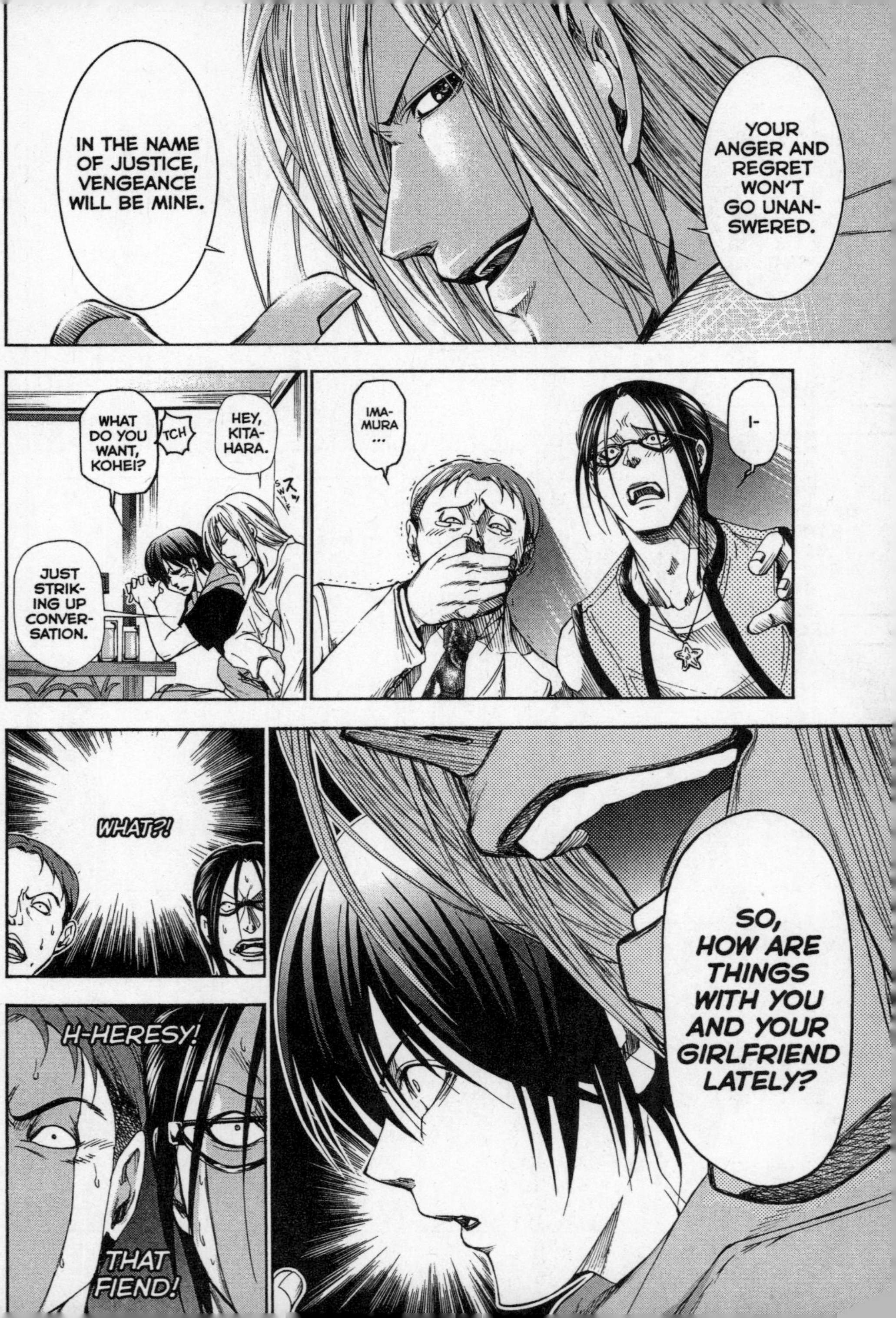
YOUR ANGER AND REGRET WON'T GO UNANSWERED.
IN THE NAME OF JUSTICE, VENGEANCE WILL BE MINE.
I-
IMAMURA...
HEY, KITAHARA.
スッ
SWIF
TCH
WHAT DO YOU WANT, KOHEI?
JUST STRIKING UP CONVERSATION.
SO, HOW ARE THINGS WITH YOU AND YOUR GIRLFRIEND LATELY?
WHAT?!
H-HERESY!
THAT FIEND!

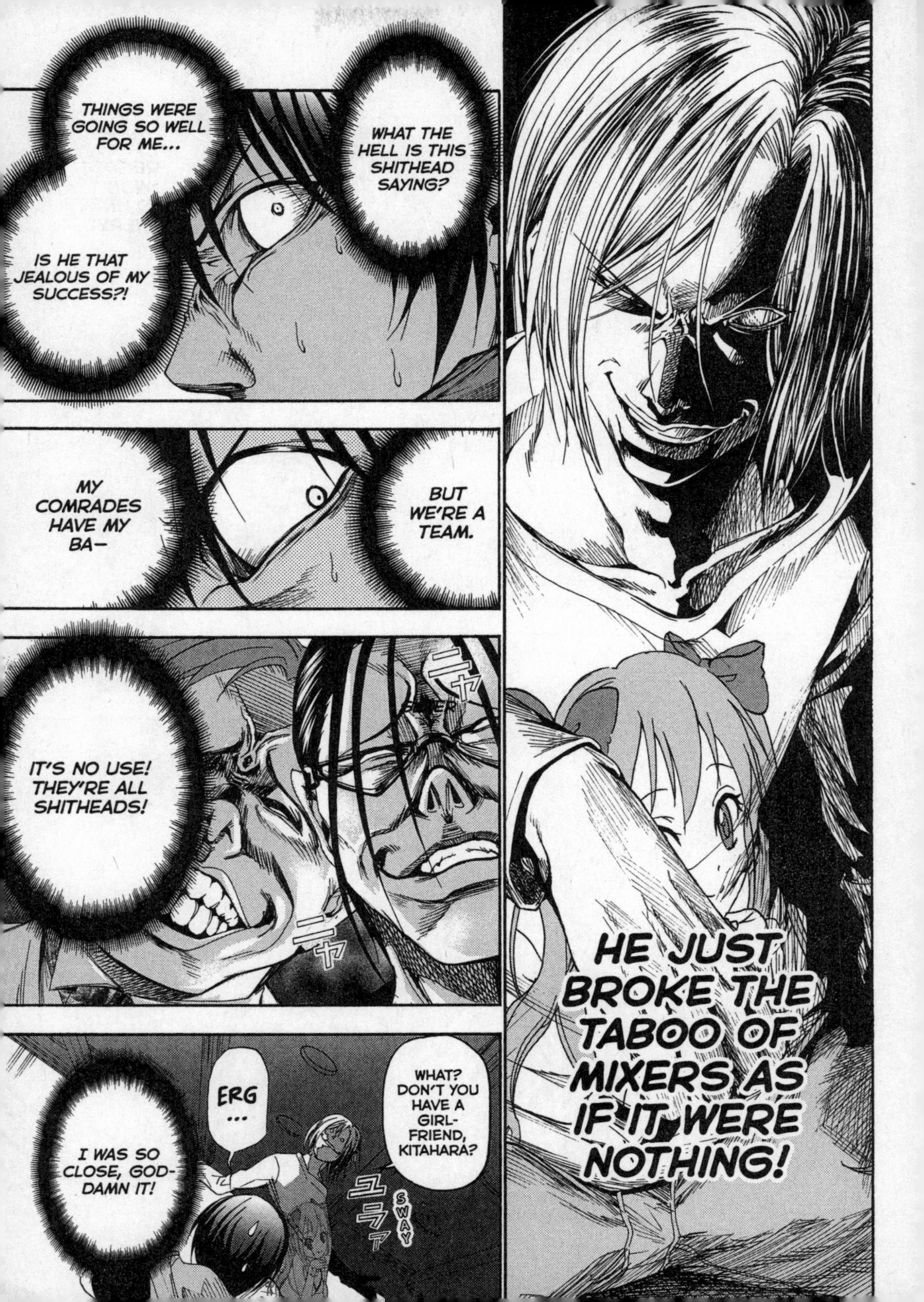
HE JUST BROKE THE TABOO OF MIXERS AS IF IT WERE NOTHING!
WHAT THE HELL IS THIS SHITHEAD SAYING?
THINGS WERE GOING SO WELL FOR ME...
IS HE THAT JEALOUS OF MY SUCCESS?!
BUT WE'RE A TEAM.
MY COMRADES HAVE MY BA—
ニヤ
IT'S NO USE! THEY'RE ALL SHITHEADS!
ニヤ
WHAT? DON'T YOU HAVE A GIRL-FRIEND, KITAHARA?
ERG ...
I WAS SO CLOSE, GOD-DAMN IT!
ユラァ
SWAY

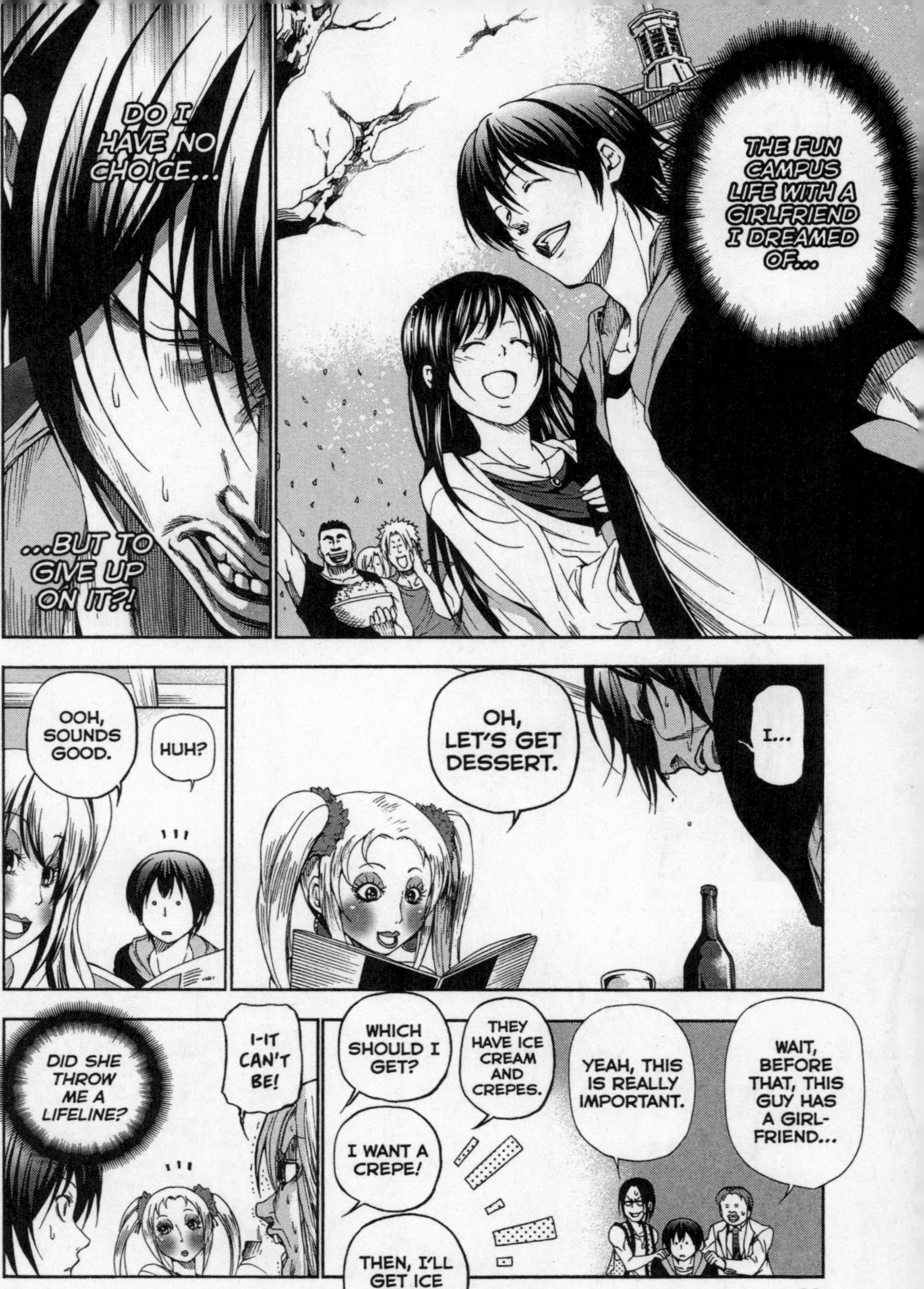
THE FUN CAMPUS LIFE WITH A GIRLFRIEND I DREAMED OF...
DO I HAVE NO CHOICE...
...BUT TO GIVE UP ON IT?!
I...
OH, LET'S GET DESSERT.
OOH, SOUNDS GOOD.
HUH?
WAIT, BEFORE THAT, THIS GUY HAS A GIRL-FRIEND...
YEAH, THIS IS REALLY IMPORTANT.
THEY HAVE ICE CREAM AND CREPES.
WHICH SHOULD I GET?
I WANT A CREPE!
THEN, I'LL GET ICE CREAM.
I-IT CAN'T BE!
DID SHE THROW ME A LIFELINE?

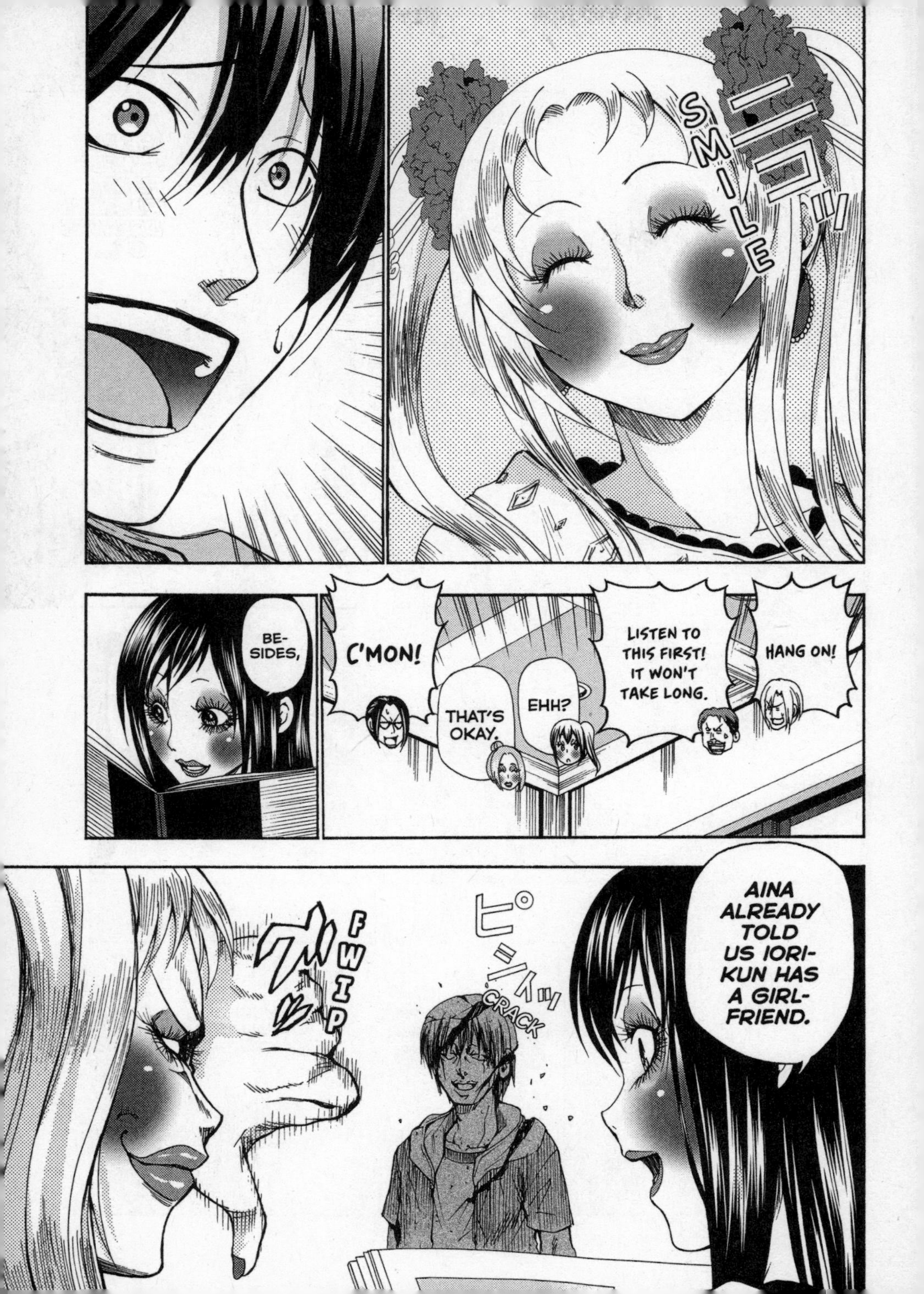

ニコッ
SMILE
HANG ON!
LISTEN TO THIS FIRST! IT WON'T TAKE LONG.
EHH?
THAT'S OKAY.
C'MON!
BE-SIDES,
AINA ALREADY TOLD US IORI-KUN HAS A GIRL-FRIEND.
CRACK
FWIP

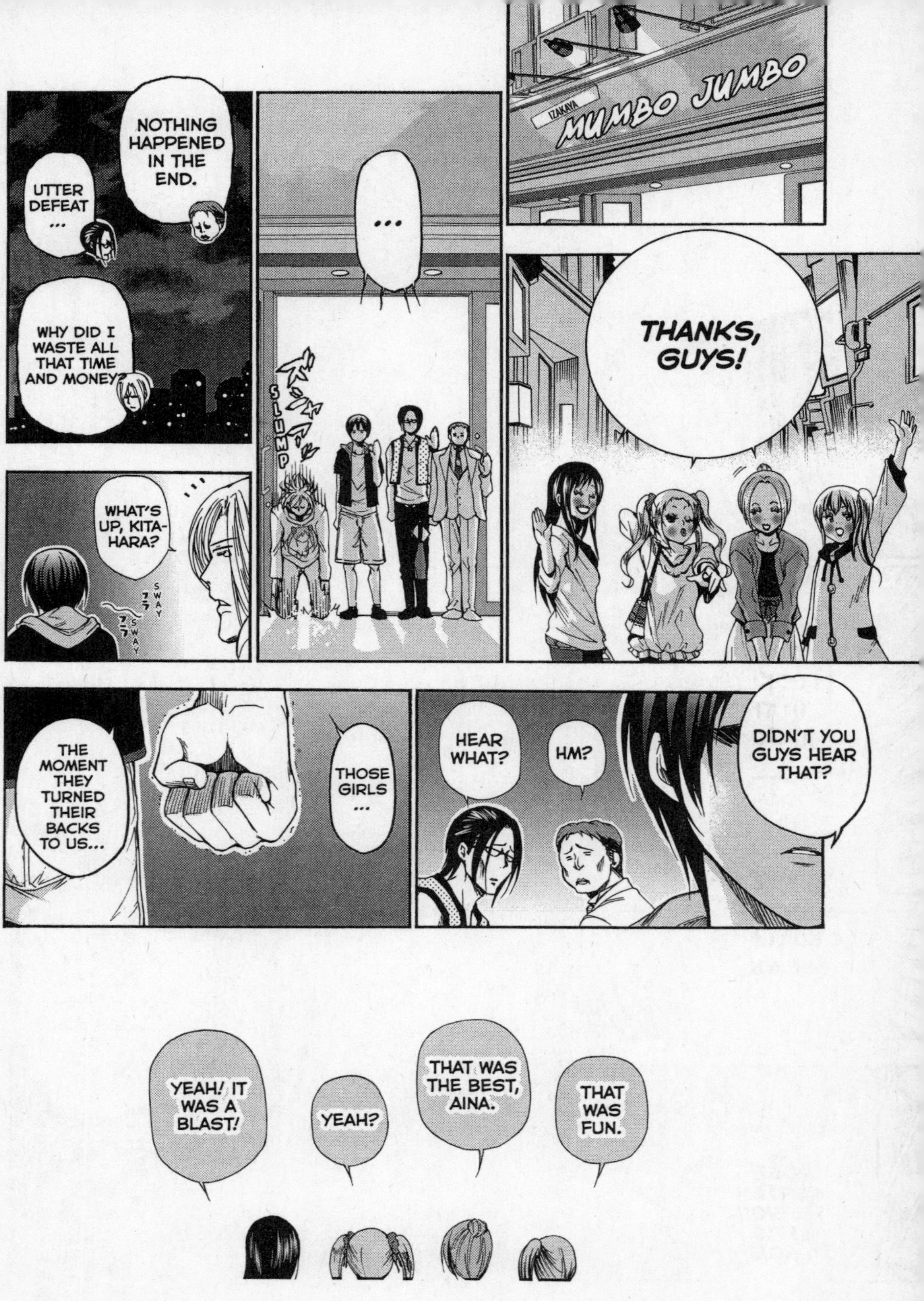
IZAKAYA
MUMBO JUMBO
THANKS, GUYS!
...
SLUMP
NOTHING HAPPENED IN THE END.
UTTER DEFEAT ...
WHY DID I WASTE ALL THAT TIME AND MONEY?
...
WHAT'S UP, KITA-HARA?
SWAY
SWAY
DIDN'T YOU GUYS HEAR THAT?
HM?
HEAR WHAT?
THOSE GIRLS ...
THE MOMENT THEY TURNED THEIR BACKS TO US...
THAT WAS FUN.
THAT WAS THE BEST, AINA.
YEAH?
YEAH! IT WAS A BLAST!

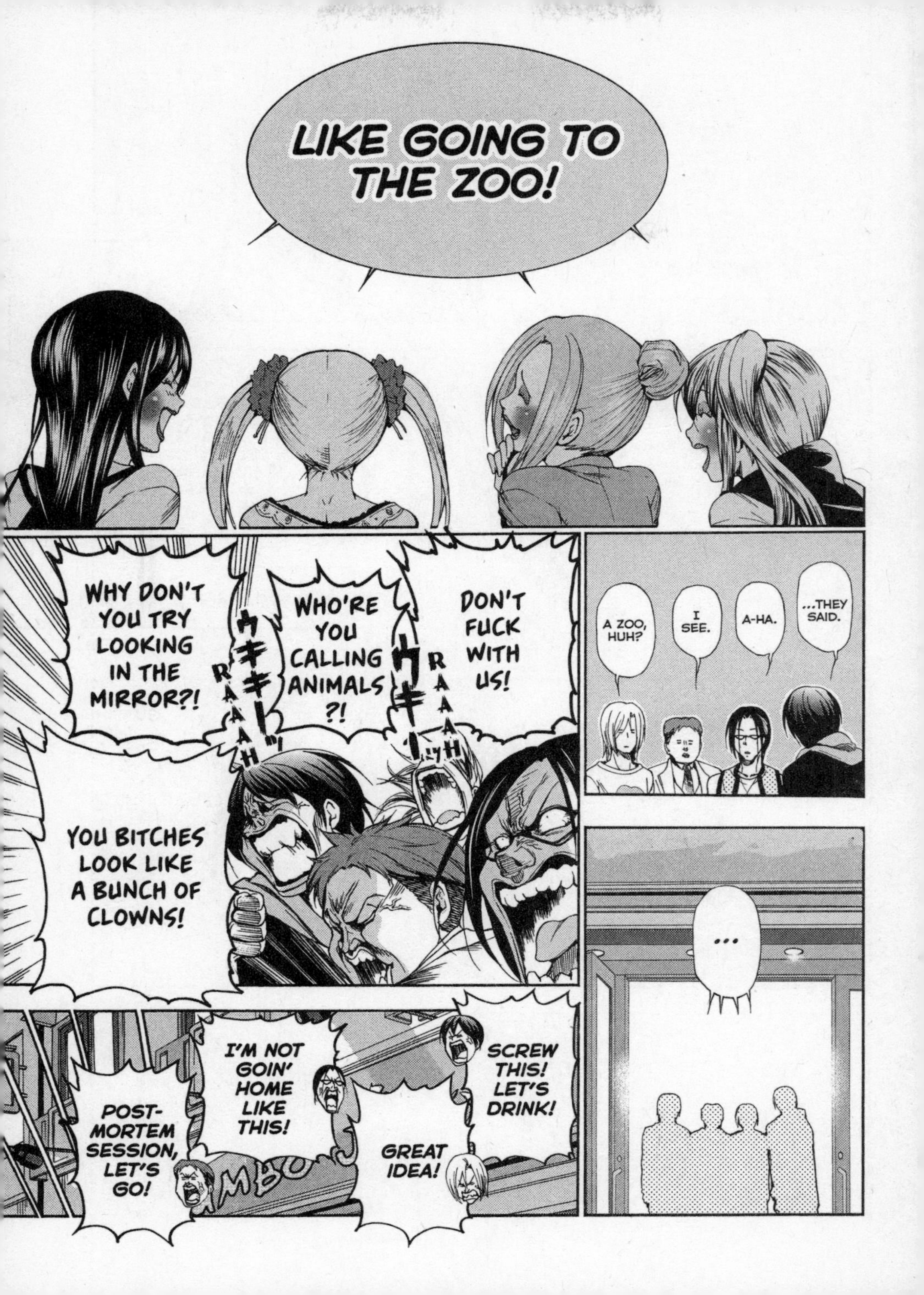
LIKE GOING TO THE ZOO!
...THEY SAID.
A-HA.
I SEE.
A ZOO, HUH?
...
DON'T FUCK WITH US!
RAAAAH
ウキーッ
WHO'RE YOU CALLING ANIMALS?!
RAAAAH
ウキキー!!
WHY DON'T YOU TRY LOOKING IN THE MIRROR?!
YOU BITCHES LOOK LIKE A BUNCH OF CLOWNS!
SCREW THIS! LET'S DRINK!
GREAT IDEA!
I'M NOT GOIN' HOME LIKE THIS!
POST-MORTEM SESSION, LET'S GO!

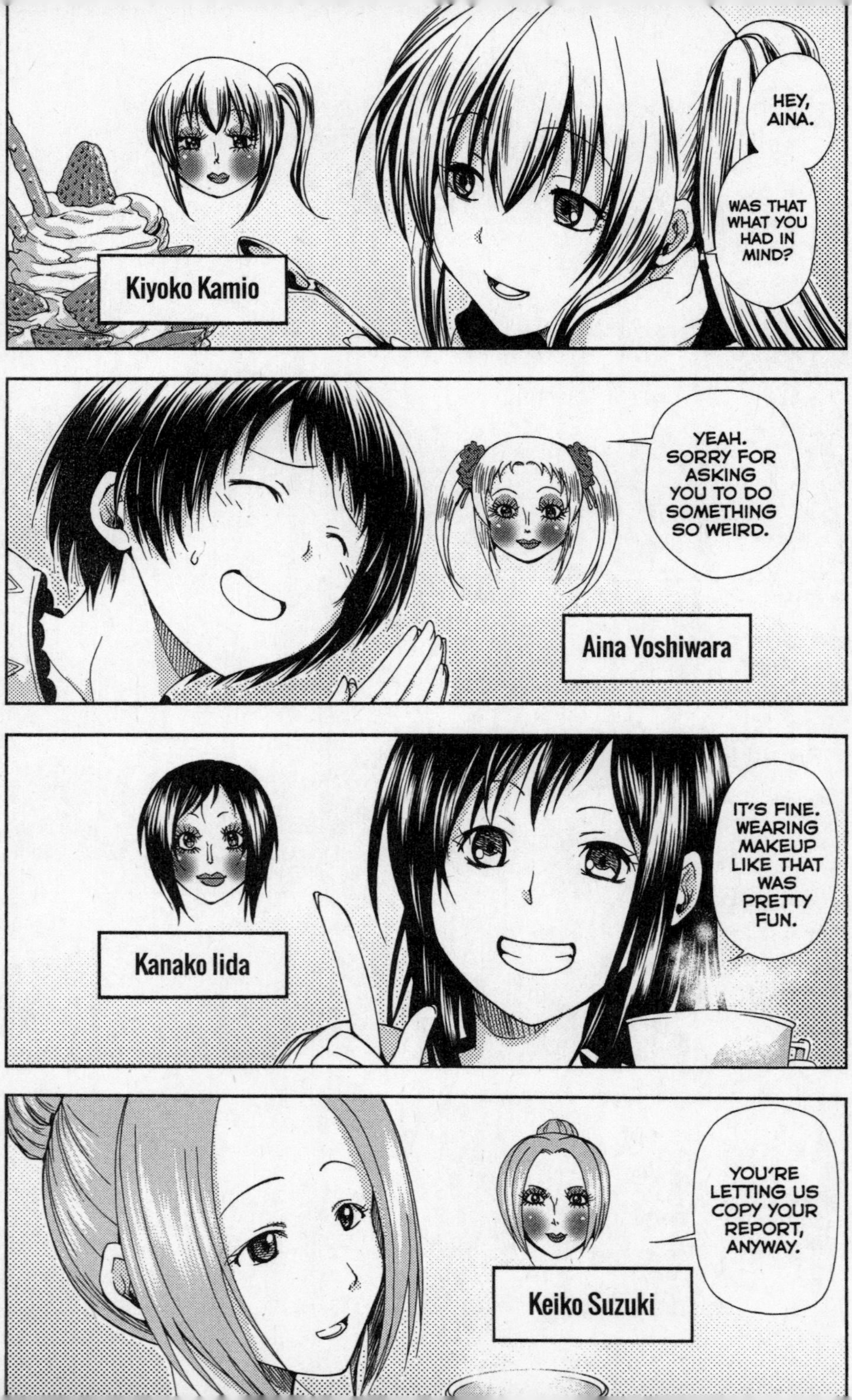
HEY, AINA.
WAS THAT WHAT YOU HAD IN MIND?
Kiyoko Kamio
YEAH. SORRY FOR ASKING YOU TO DO SOMETHING SO WEIRD.
Aina Yoshiwara
IT'S FINE. WEARING MAKEUP LIKE THAT WAS PRETTY FUN.
Kanako Iida
YOU'RE LETTING US COPY YOUR REPORT, ANYWAY.
Keiko Suzuki

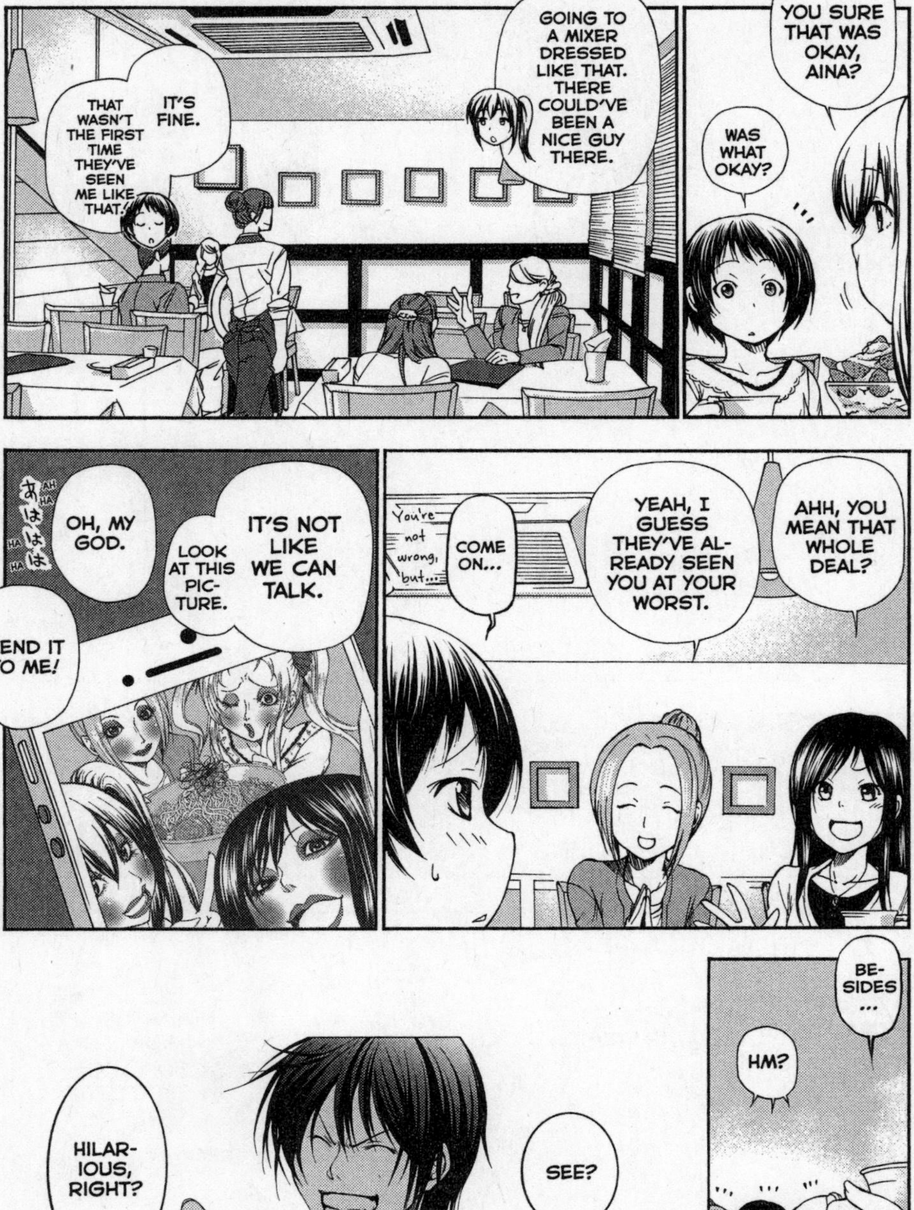
YOU SURE THAT WAS OKAY, AINA?
WAS WHAT OKAY?
GOING TO A MIXER DRESSED LIKE THAT. THERE COULD'VE BEEN A NICE GUY THERE.
IT'S FINE.
THAT WASN'T THE FIRST TIME THEY'VE SEEN ME LIKE THAT.
AHH, YOU MEAN THAT WHOLE DEAL?
YEAH, I GUESS THEY'VE AL-READY SEEN YOU AT YOUR WORST.
COME ON...
You're not wrong, but...
IT'S NOT LIKE WE CAN TALK.
LOOK AT THIS PIC-TURE.
OH, MY GOD.
あははは AH HA HA HA
SEND IT TO ME!
BE-SIDES...
HM?
SEE?
HILAR-IOUS, RIGHT?

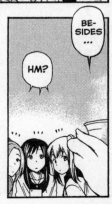

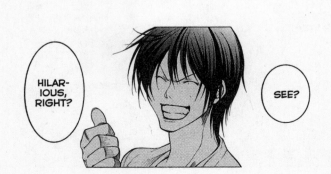

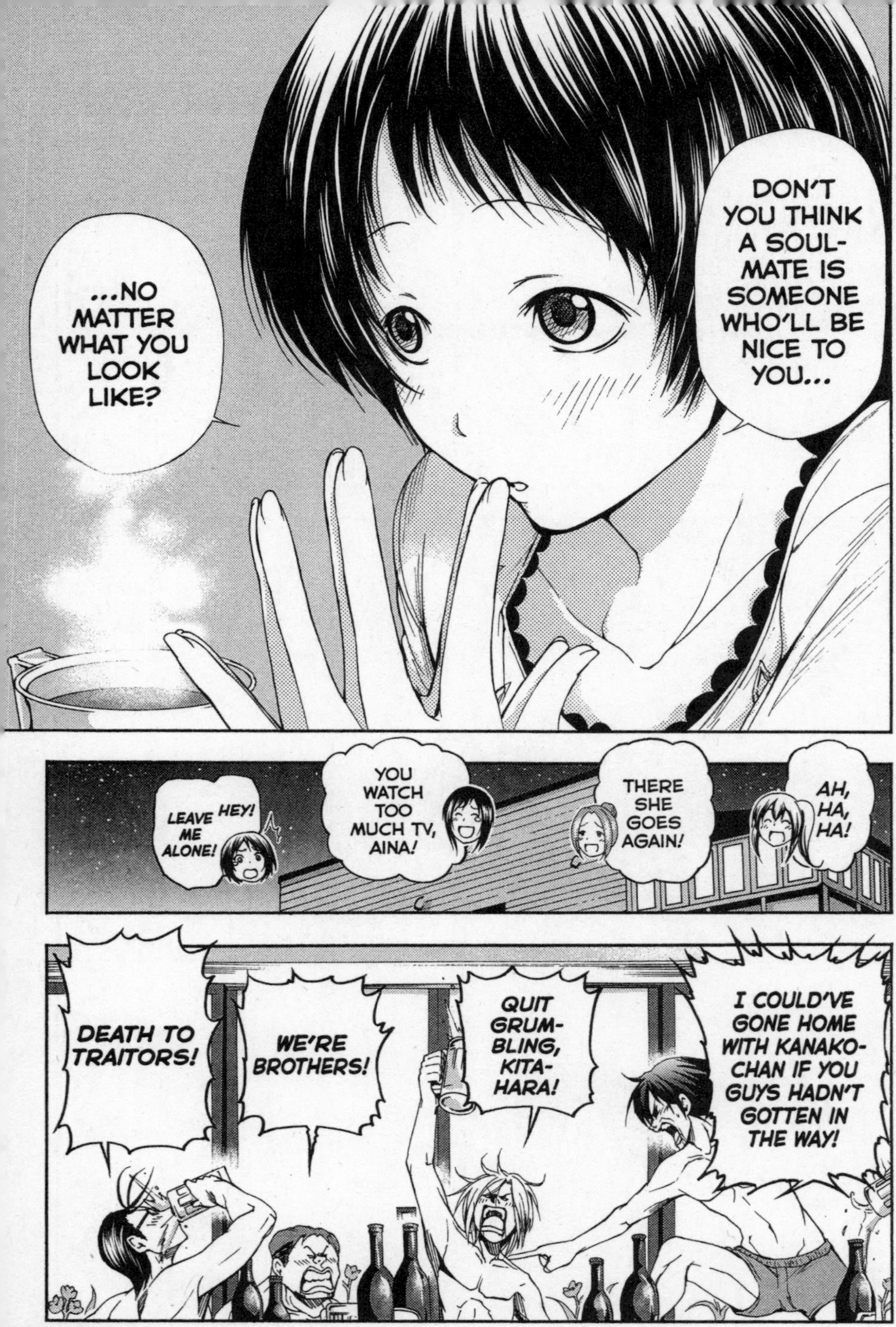
DON'T YOU THINK A SOUL-MATE IS SOMEONE WHO'LL BE NICE TO YOU...
...NO MATTER WHAT YOU LOOK LIKE?
AH, HA, HA!
THERE SHE GOES AGAIN!
YOU WATCH TOO MUCH TV, AINA!
HEY!
LEAVE ME ALONE!
I COULD'VE GONE HOME WITH KANAKO-CHAN IF YOU GUYS HADN'T GOTTEN IN THE WAY!
QUIT GRUM-BLING, KITA-HARA!
WE'RE BROTHERS!
DEATH TO TRAITORS!

CH.10 / End

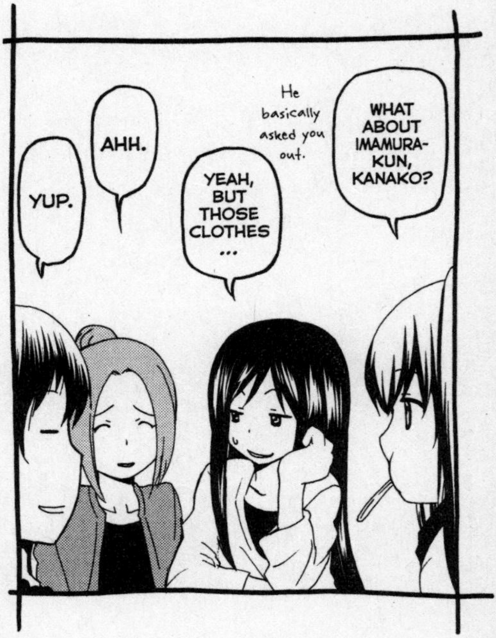
WHAT ABOUT IMAMURA-KUN, KANAKO?
He basically asked you out.
YEAH, BUT THOSE CLOTHES ...
AHH.
YUP.

Grand Blue
Dreaming

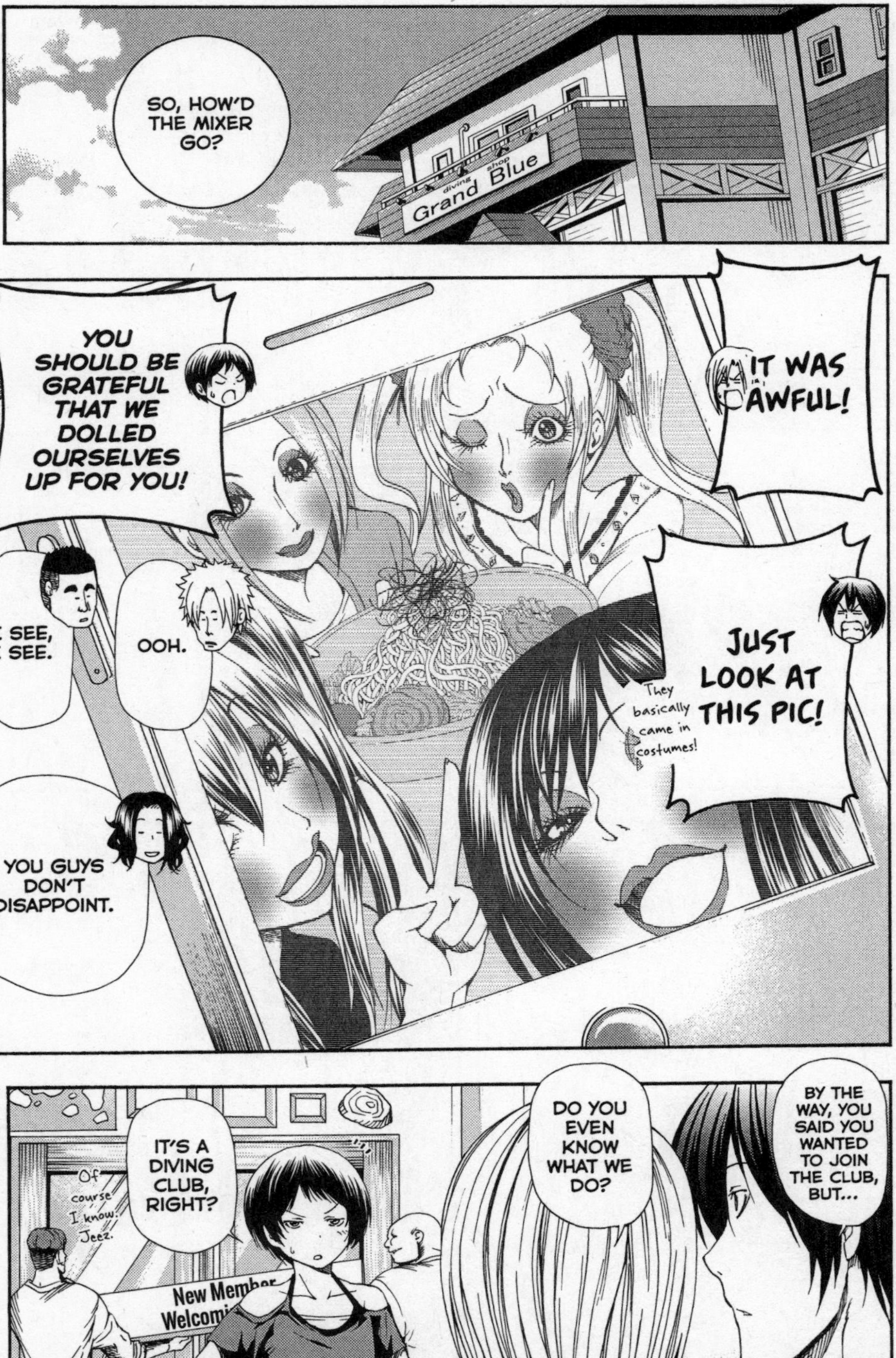
SO, HOW'D THE MIXER GO?
diving shop
Grand Blue
IT WAS AWFUL!
JUST LOOK AT THIS PIC!
They basically came in costumes!
YOU SHOULD BE GRATEFUL THAT WE DOLLED OURSELVES UP FOR YOU!
OOH.
I SEE, I SEE.
YOU GUYS DON'T DISAPPOINT.
BY THE WAY, YOU SAID YOU WANTED TO JOIN THE CLUB, BUT...
DO YOU EVEN KNOW WHAT WE DO?
IT'S A DIVING CLUB, RIGHT?
Of course I know. Jeez.
New Member

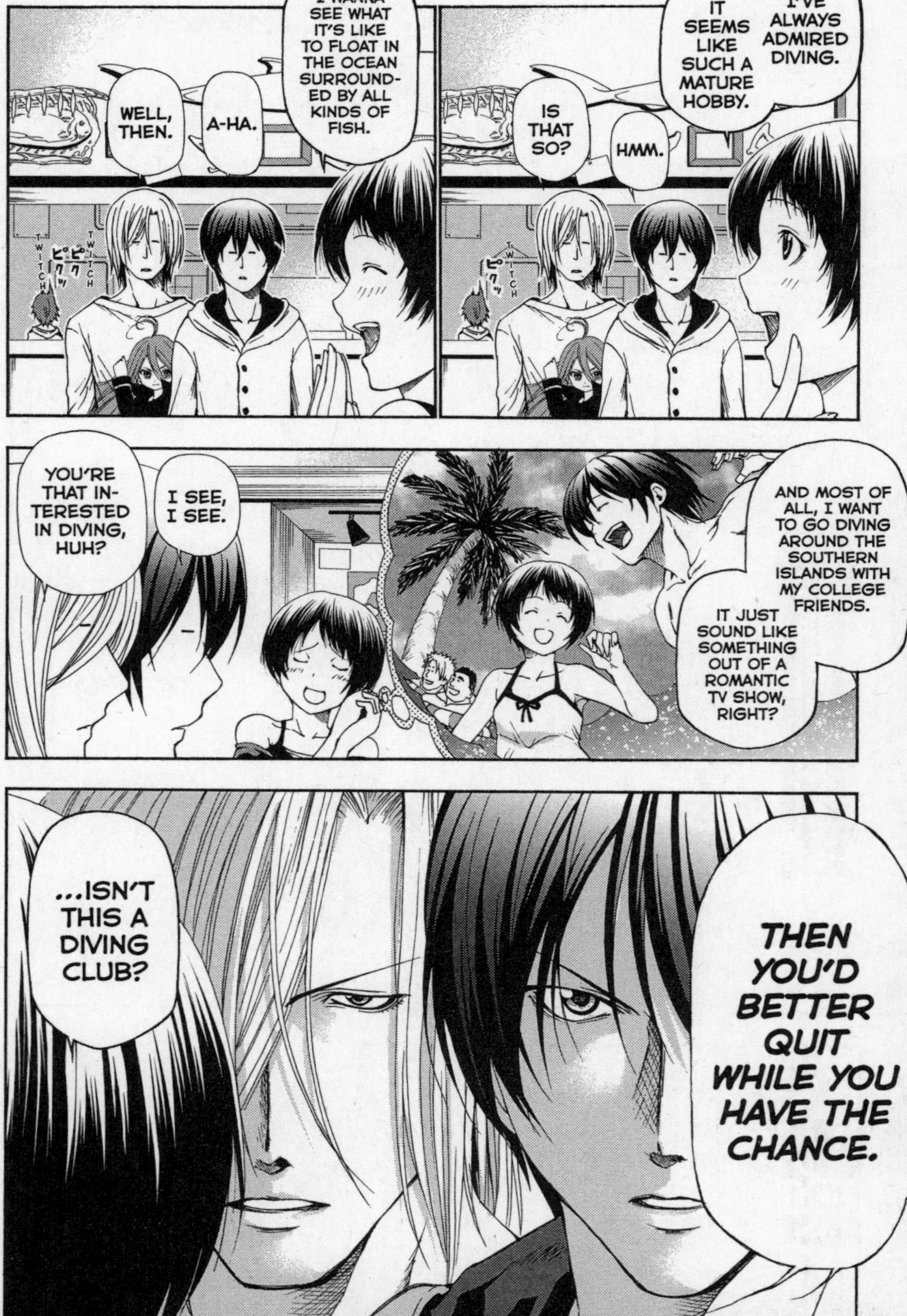
I'VE ALWAYS ADMIRED DIVING.
IT SEEMS LIKE SUCH A MATURE HOBBY.
HMM.
IS THAT SO?
TWITCH
I WANNA SEE WHAT IT'S LIKE TO FLOAT IN THE OCEAN SURROUND-ED BY ALL KINDS OF FISH.
A-HA.
WELL, THEN.
TWITCH TWITCH
AND MOST OF ALL, I WANT TO GO DIVING AROUND THE SOUTHERN ISLANDS WITH MY COLLEGE FRIENDS.
IT JUST SOUND LIKE SOMETHING OUT OF A ROMANTIC TV SHOW, RIGHT?
I SEE, I SEE.
YOU'RE THAT IN-TERESTED IN DIVING, HUH?
THEN YOU'D BETTER QUIT WHILE YOU HAVE THE CHANCE.
...ISN'T THIS A DIVING CLUB?

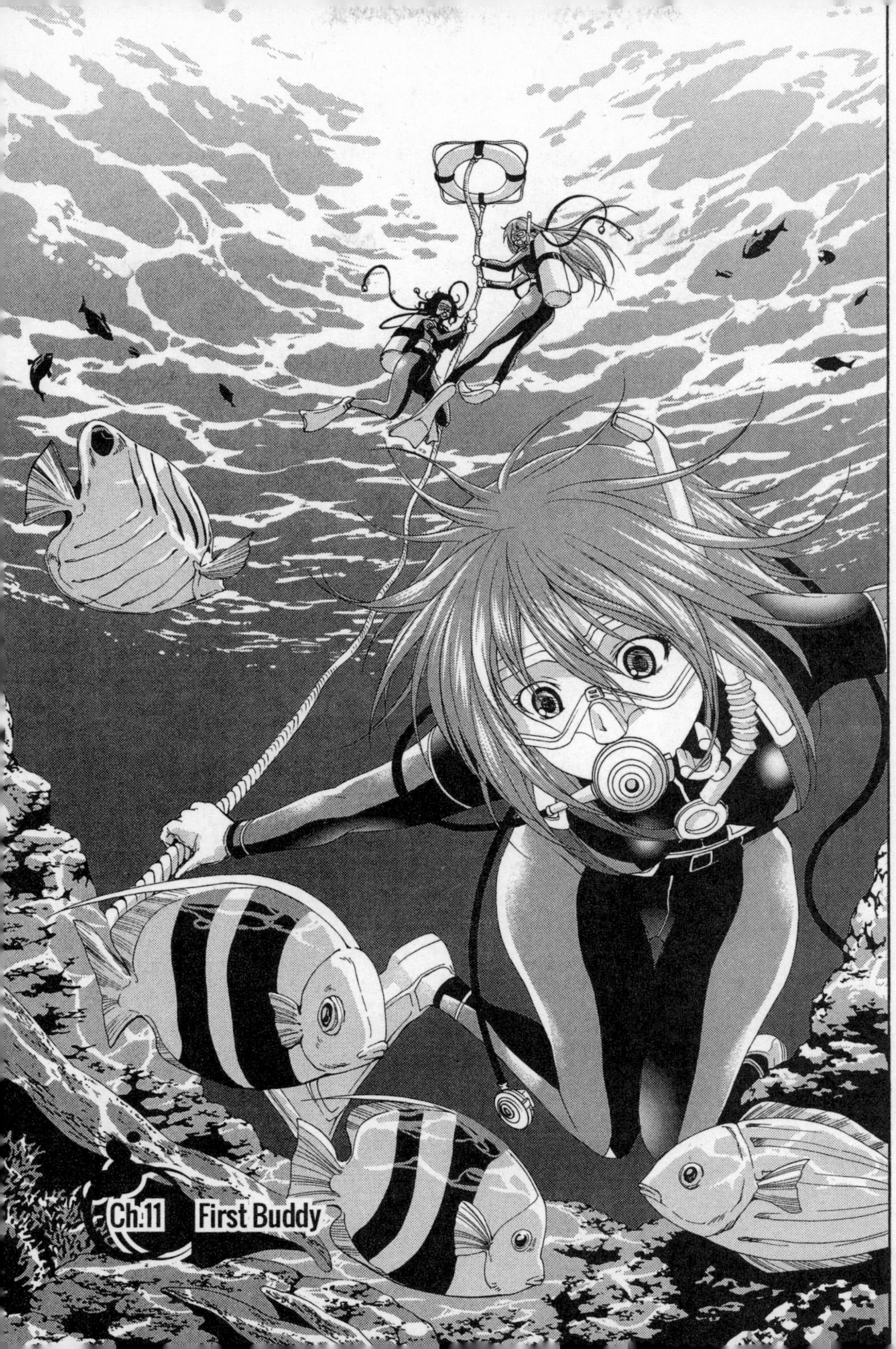
Ch.11 First Buddy

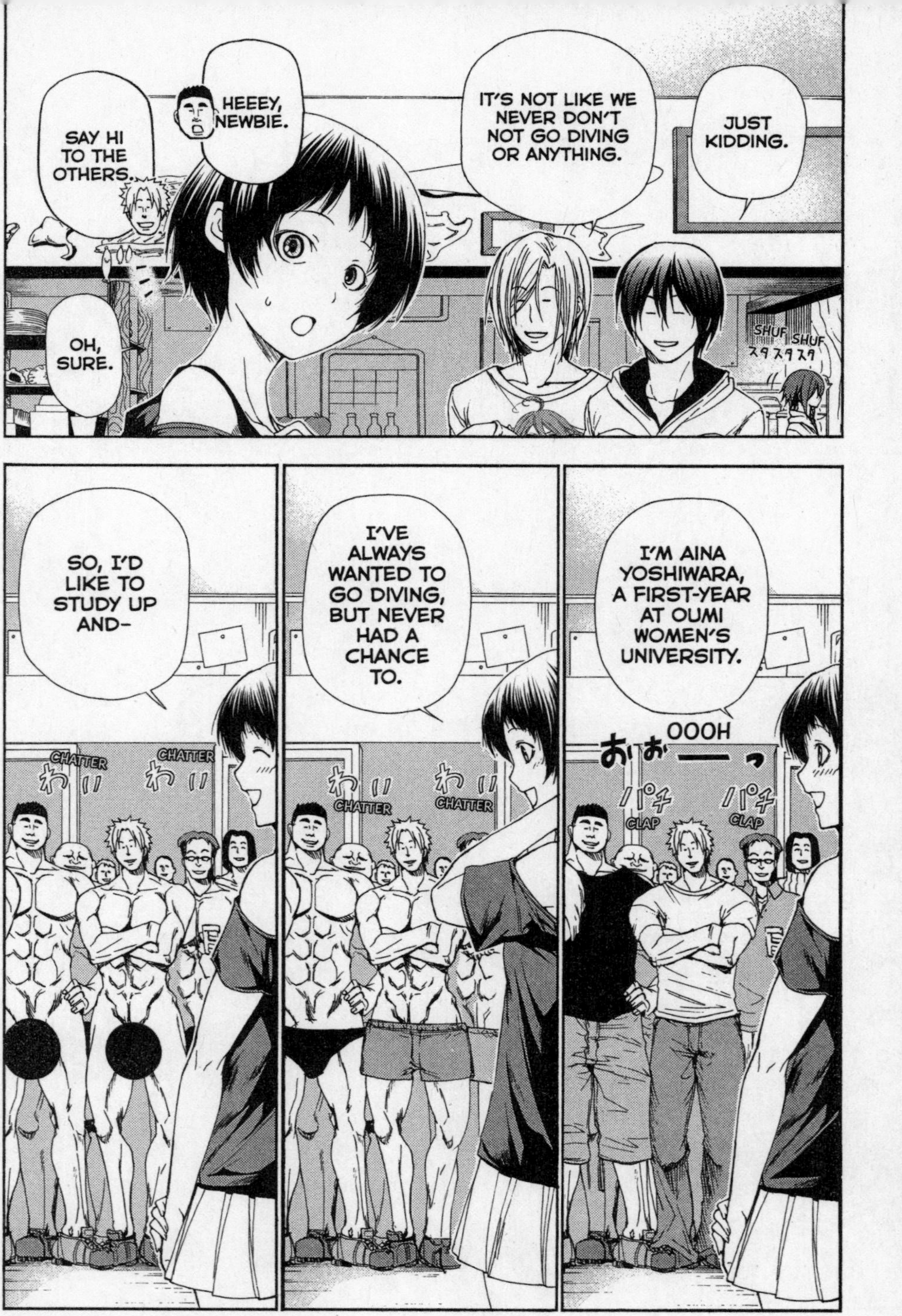
JUST KIDDING.
IT'S NOT LIKE WE NEVER DON'T NOT GO DIVING OR ANYTHING.
SHUF SHUF
スタスタスタ
HEEEY, NEWBIE.
SAY HI TO THE OTHERS.
OH, SURE.
I'M AINA YOSHIWARA, A FIRST-YEAR AT OUMI WOMEN'S UNIVERSITY.
おぉーーっ
OOOH
パチ
CLAP
パチ
CLAP
I'VE ALWAYS WANTED TO GO DIVING, BUT NEVER HAD A CHANCE TO.
CHATTER
CHATTER
SO, I'D LIKE TO STUDY UP AND–
CHATTER
CHATTER

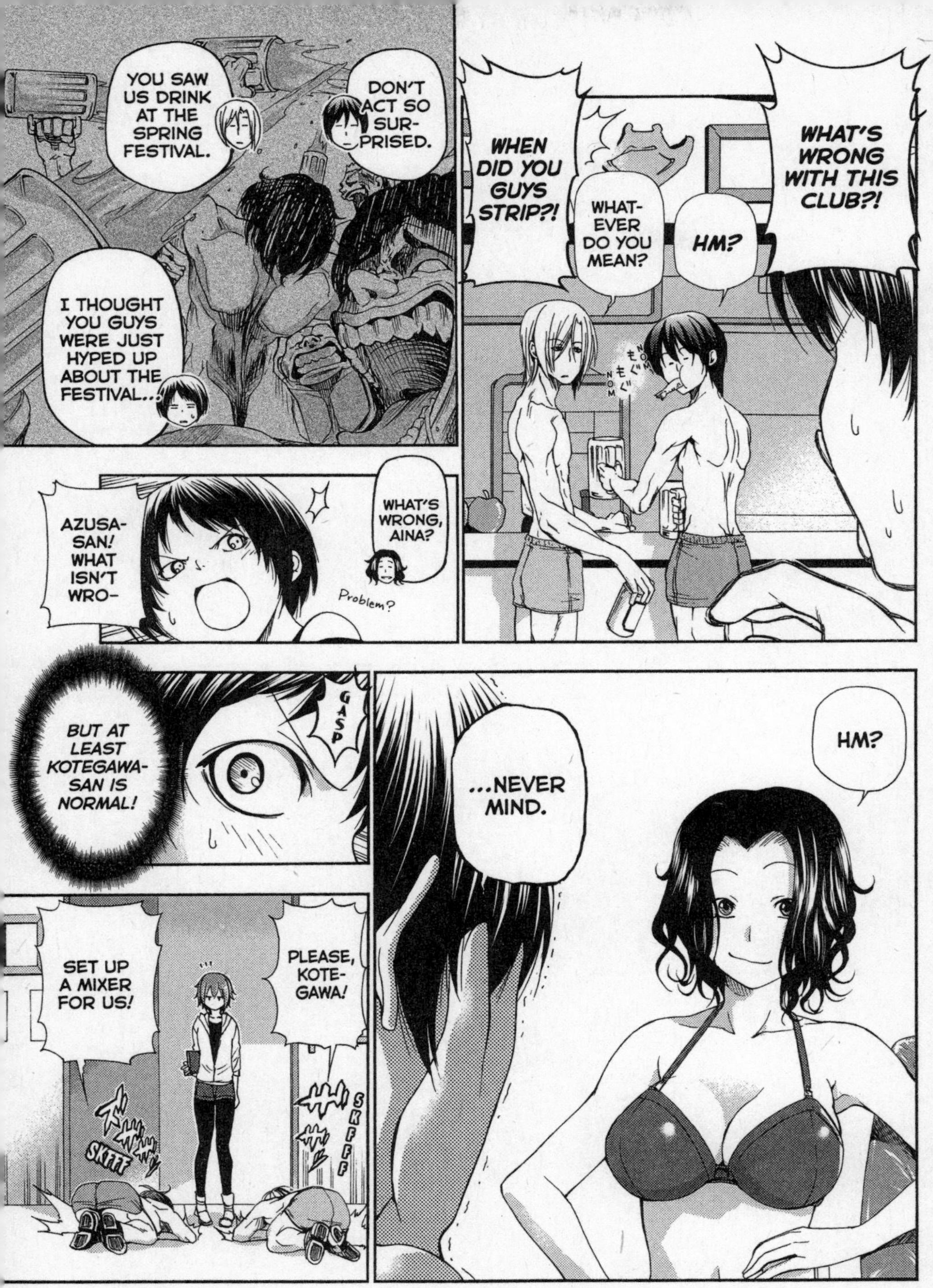
WHAT'S WRONG WITH THIS CLUB?!
HM?
WHAT-EVER DO YOU MEAN?
WHEN DID YOU GUYS STRIP?!
NOM NOM
DON'T ACT SO SUR-PRISED.
YOU SAW US DRINK AT THE SPRING FESTIVAL.
I THOUGHT YOU GUYS WERE JUST HYPED UP ABOUT THE FESTIVAL...
WHAT'S WRONG, AINA?
Problem?
AZUSA-SAN! WHAT ISN'T WRO-
HM?
...NEVER MIND.
GASP
BUT AT LEAST KOTEGAWA-SAN IS NORMAL!
PLEASE, KOTE-GAWA!
SET UP A MIXER FOR US!
SKFFF
SKFFF

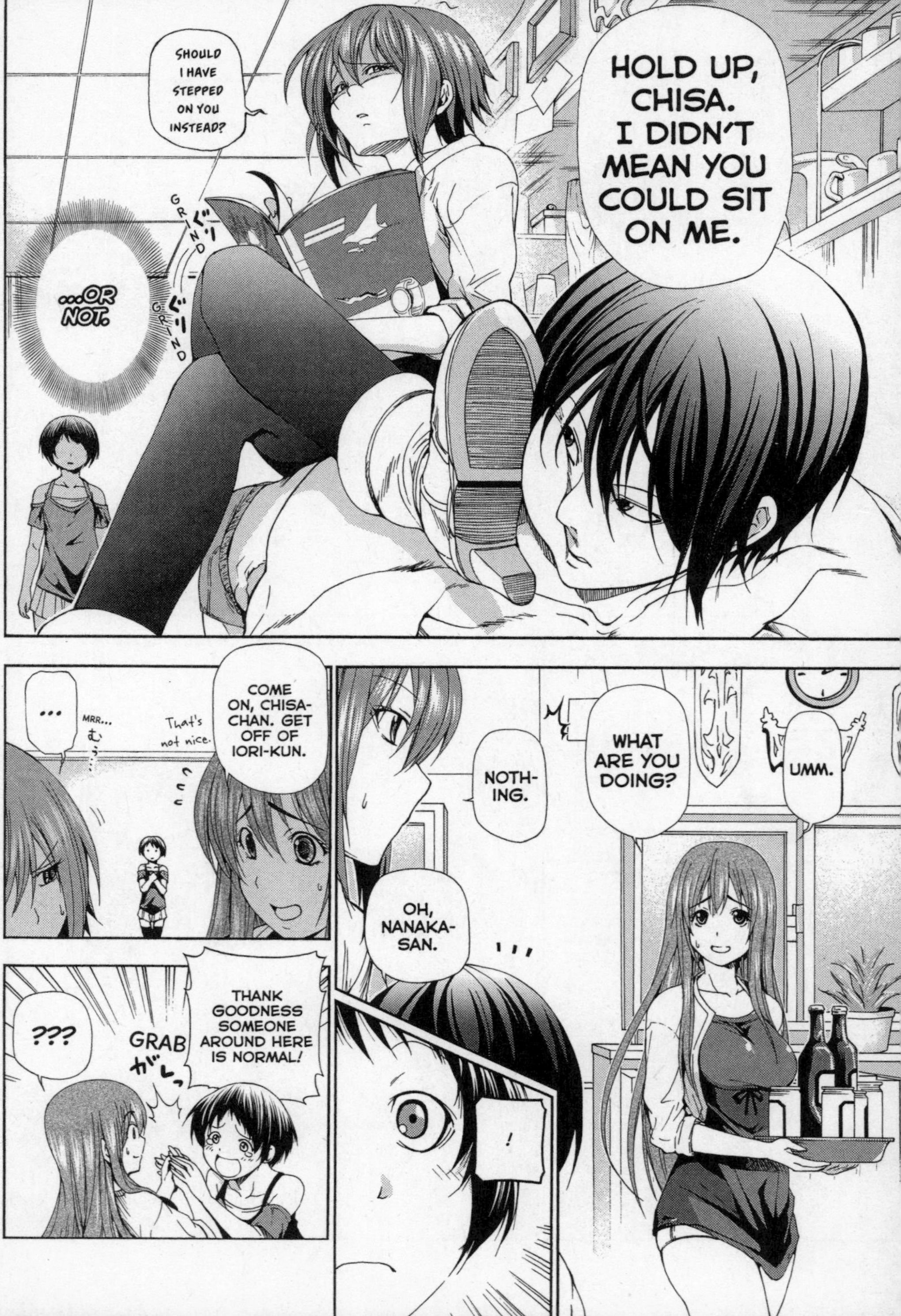
HOLD UP, CHISA. I DIDN'T MEAN YOU COULD SIT ON ME.
SHOULD I HAVE STEPPED ON YOU INSTEAD?
GRIND
GRIND
...OR NOT.
UMM.
WHAT ARE YOU DOING?
NOTHING.
OH, NANAKA-SAN.
COME ON, CHISA-CHAN. GET OFF OF IORI-KUN.
That's not nice.
MRR...
...
!
THANK GOODNESS SOMEONE AROUND HERE IS NORMAL!
GRAB
???

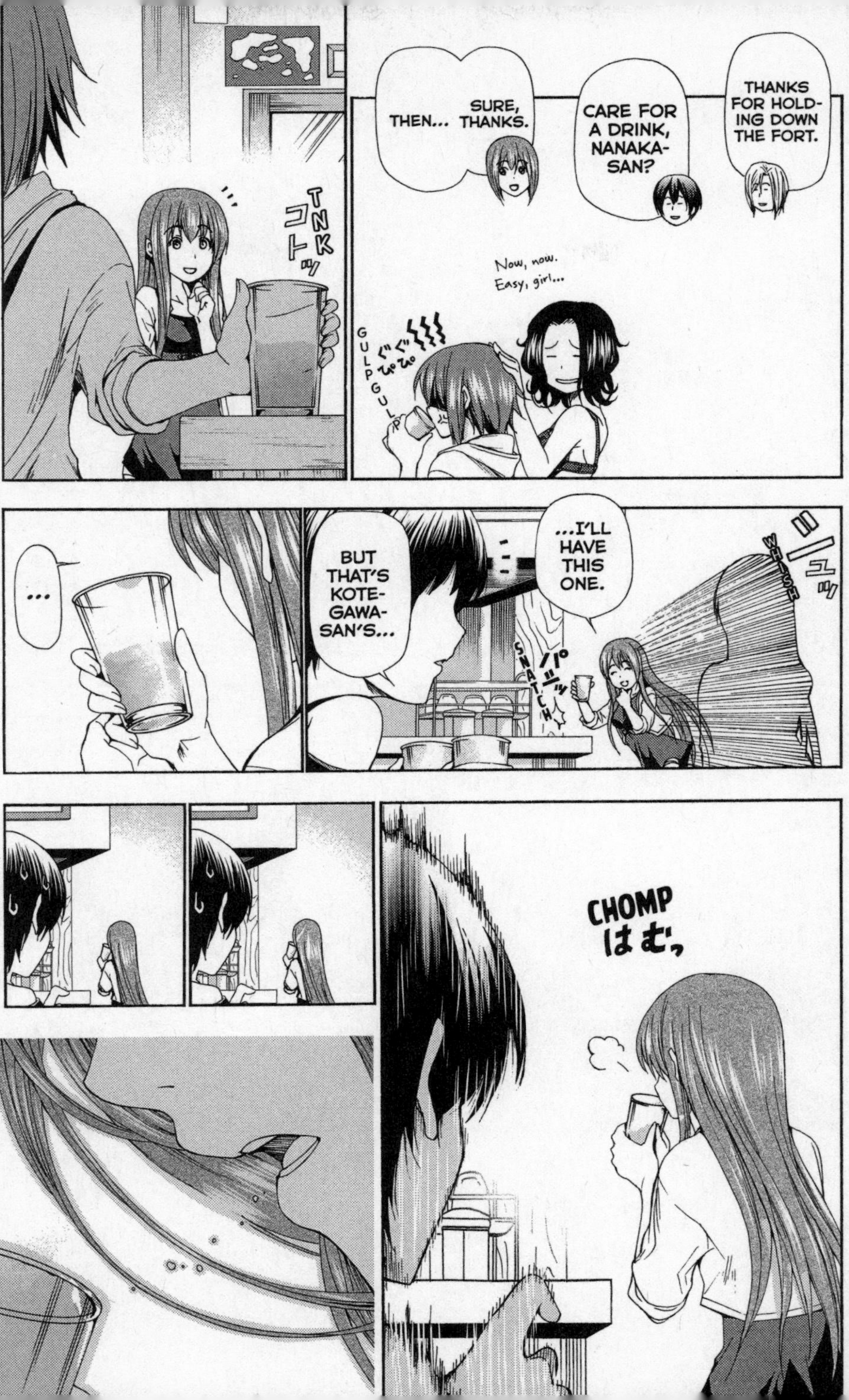
THANKS FOR HOLDING DOWN THE FORT.
CARE FOR A DRINK, NANAKA-SAN?
SURE, THANKS.
THEN...
Now, now. Easy, girl...
GULP GULP
ぐびぐび
TNK
コトッ
WHISH
ニュッ
...I'LL HAVE THIS ONE.
SNATCH
パッ
BUT THAT'S KOTEGAWA-SAN'S...
...
CHOMP
はむっ

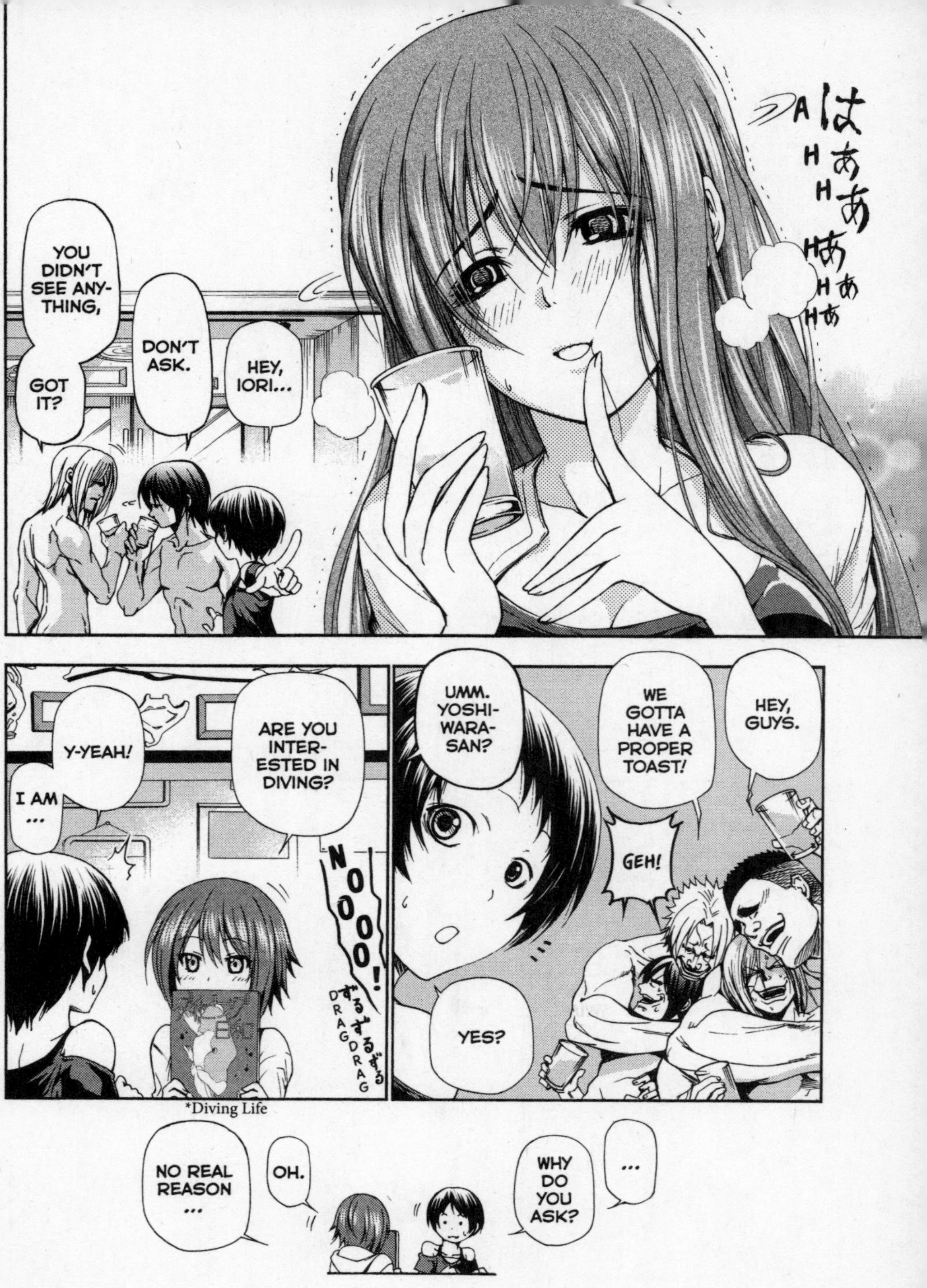
はあああああ
AHHHHH
HEY, IORI...
DON'T ASK.
YOU DIDN'T SEE ANYTHING,
GOT IT?
HEY, GUYS.
WE GOTTA HAVE A PROPER TOAST!
UMM. YOSHIWARA-SAN?
GEH!
YES?
NOOOOO!
ずるずるずる
DRAGDRAG
ARE YOU INTERESTED IN DIVING?
Y-YEAH!
I AM ...
...
WHY DO YOU ASK?
OH.
NO REAL REASON ...

*Diving Life

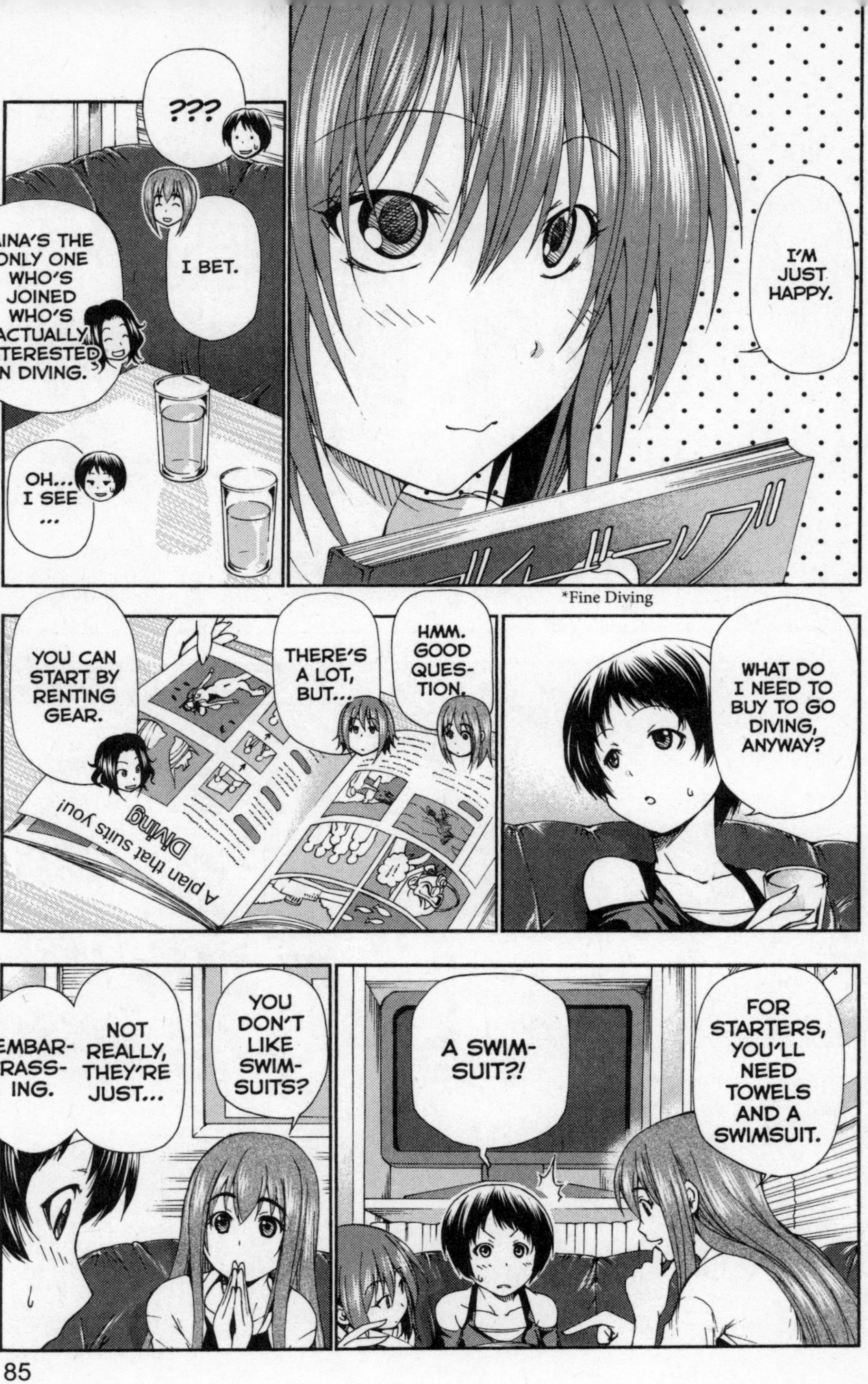
I'M JUST HAPPY.
???
I BET.
AINA'S THE ONLY ONE WHO'S JOINED WHO'S ACTUALLY INTERESTED IN DIVING.
OH... I SEE ...
WHAT DO I NEED TO BUY TO GO DIVING, ANYWAY?
HMM. GOOD QUES-TION.
THERE'S A LOT, BUT...
YOU CAN START BY RENTING GEAR.
A plan that suits you!
Diving
FOR STARTERS, YOU'LL NEED TOWELS AND A SWIMSUIT.
A SWIM-SUIT?!
YOU DON'T LIKE SWIM-SUITS?
NOT REALLY, THEY'RE JUST...
EMBAR-RASS-ING.

*Fine Diving

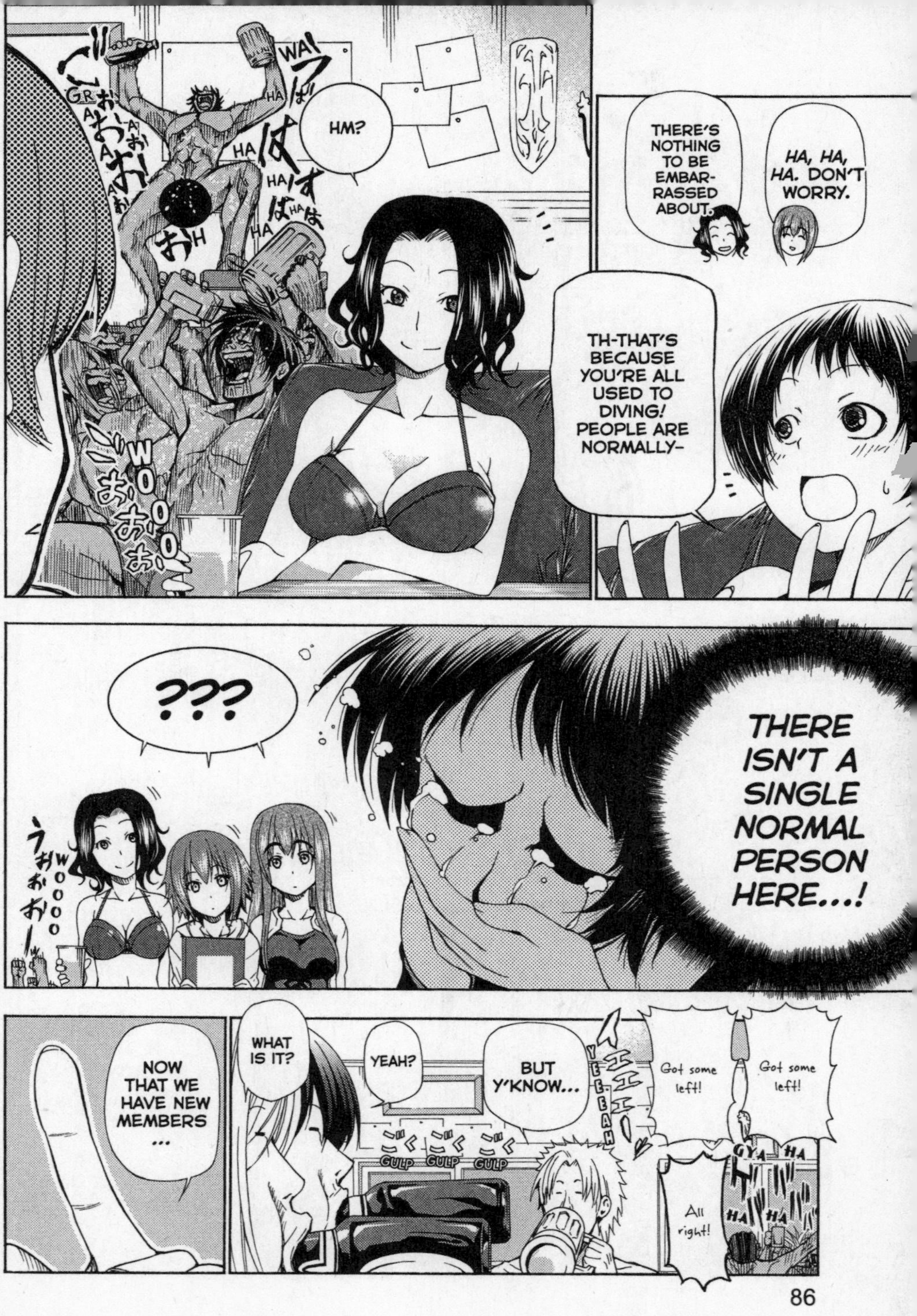

HA, HA, HA. DON'T WORRY.
THERE'S NOTHING TO BE EMBARRASSED ABOUT.
TH-THAT'S BECAUSE YOU'RE ALL USED TO DIVING! PEOPLE ARE NORMALLY-
HM?
WAHAHAHAHAHAHA
GRAAAAH
WOOOO
THERE ISN'T A SINGLE NORMAL PERSON HERE...!
???
WOOOO
Got some left!
Got some left!
GYAHA HAHAHA
All right!
YEEEAH
BUT Y'KNOW...
YEAH?
WHAT IS IT?
GULP GULP GULP
NOW THAT WE HAVE NEW MEMBERS ...

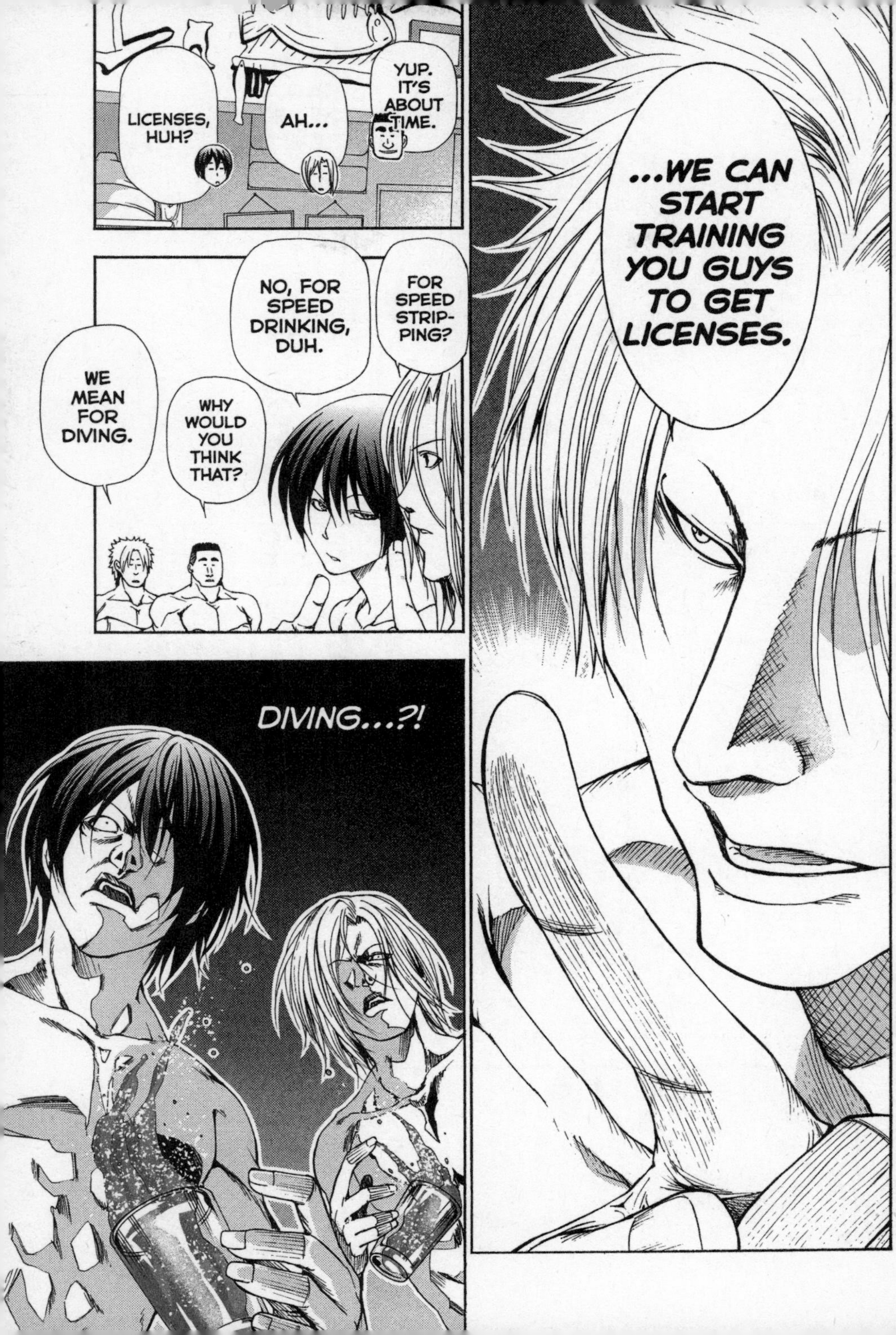
...WE CAN START TRAINING YOU GUYS TO GET LICENSES.
YUP. IT'S ABOUT TIME.
AH...
LICENSES, HUH?
FOR SPEED STRIP-PING?
NO, FOR SPEED DRINKING, DUH.
WHY WOULD YOU THINK THAT?
WE MEAN FOR DIVING.
DIVING...?!

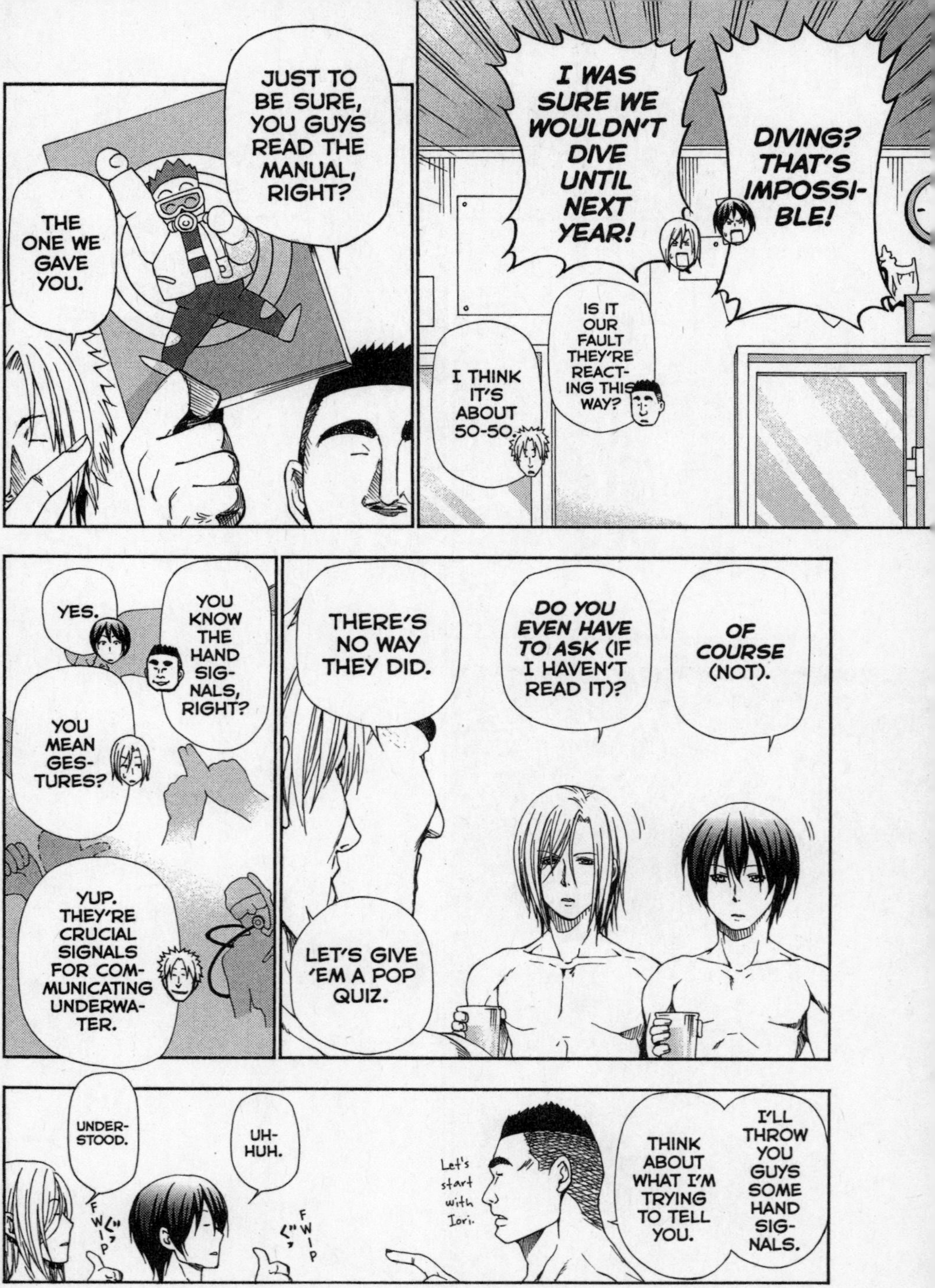
DIVING? THAT'S IMPOSSIBLE!
I WAS SURE WE WOULDN'T DIVE UNTIL NEXT YEAR!
IS IT OUR FAULT THEY'RE REACTING THIS WAY?
I THINK IT'S ABOUT 50-50.
JUST TO BE SURE, YOU GUYS READ THE MANUAL, RIGHT?
THE ONE WE GAVE YOU.
OF COURSE (NOT).
DO YOU EVEN HAVE TO ASK (IF I HAVEN'T READ IT)?
THERE'S NO WAY THEY DID.
LET'S GIVE 'EM A POP QUIZ.
YOU KNOW THE HAND SIGNALS, RIGHT?
YES.
YOU MEAN GESTURES?
YUP. THEY'RE CRUCIAL SIGNALS FOR COMMUNICATING UNDERWATER.
I'LL THROW YOU GUYS SOME HAND SIGNALS.
THINK ABOUT WHAT I'M TRYING TO TELL YOU.
Let's start with Iori.
FWIP
UH-HUH.
FWIP
UNDERSTOOD.

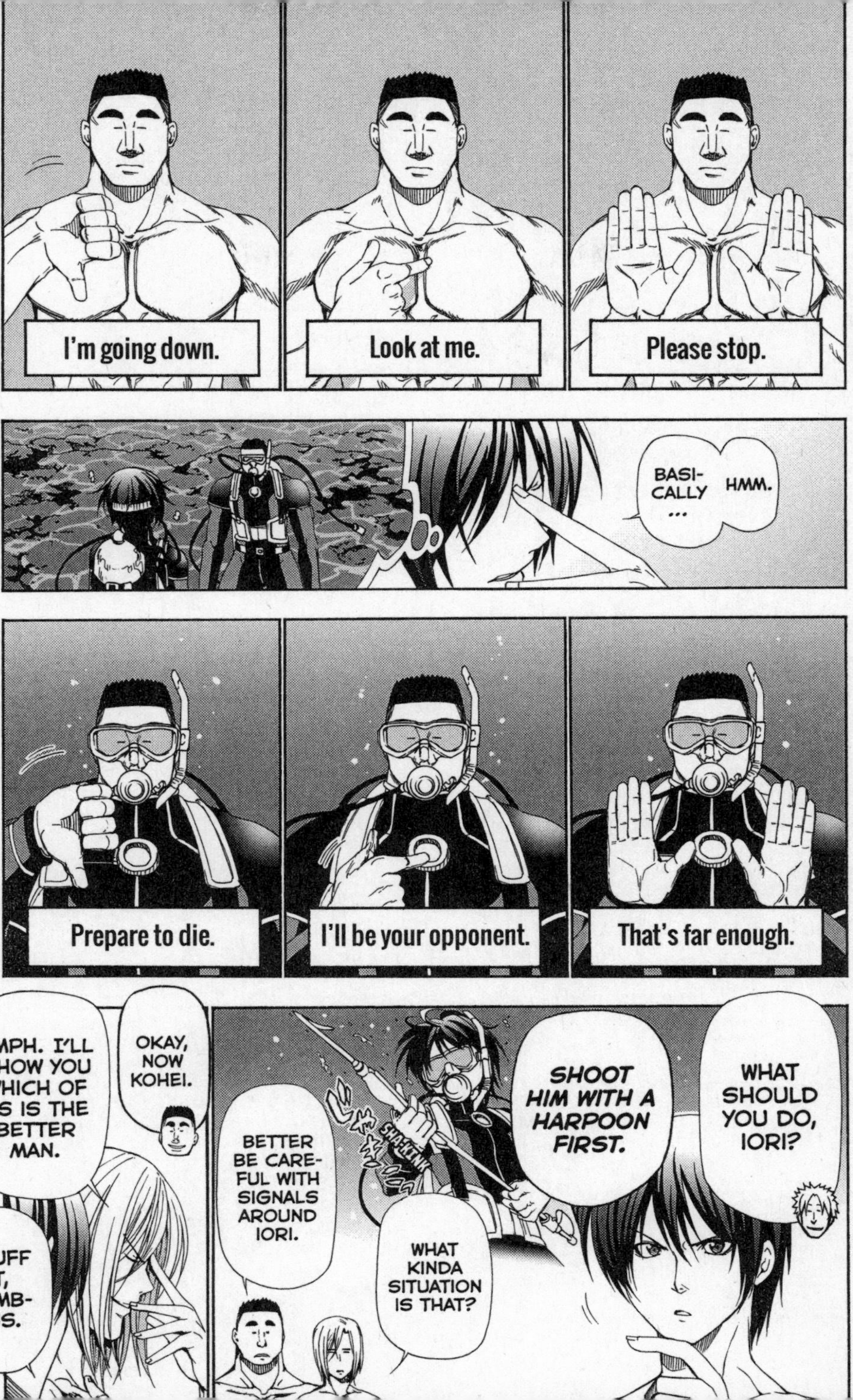
Please stop.
Look at me.
I'm going down.
HMM.
BASI-CALLY ...
That's far enough.
I'll be your opponent.
Prepare to die.
WHAT SHOULD YOU DO, IORI?
SHOOT HIM WITH A HARPOON FIRST.
SHA-KINK
BETTER BE CARE-FUL WITH SIGNALS AROUND IORI.
WHAT KINDA SITUATION IS THAT?
OKAY, NOW KOHEI.
HMPH. I'LL SHOW YOU WHICH OF US IS THE BETTER MAN.
STUFF IT, DUMB-ASS.

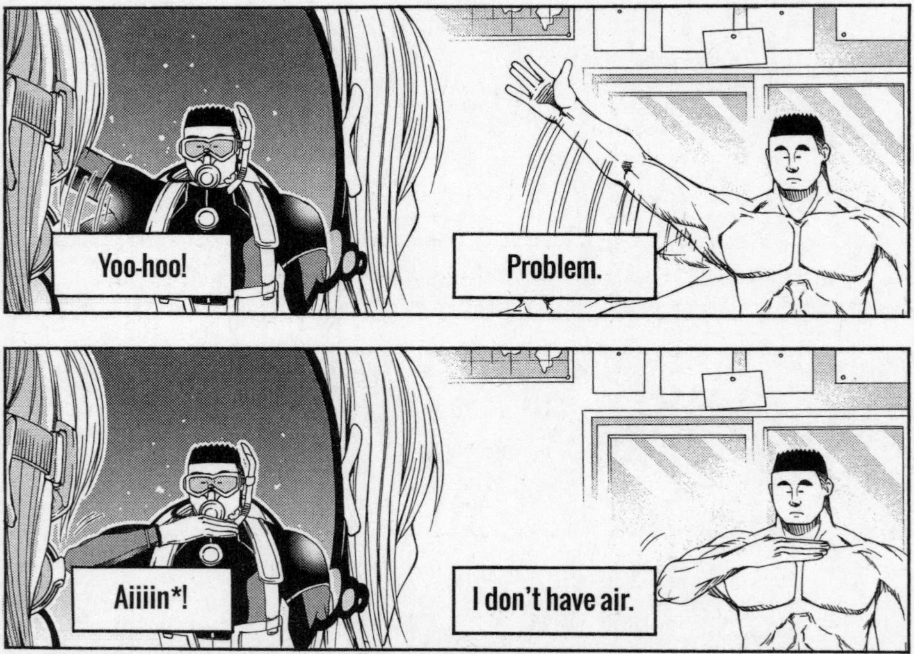
Problem.
Yoo-hoo!
I don't have air.
Aiiiin*!

*A reference to Bakatono-sama, a character played by the comedian Ken Shimura.

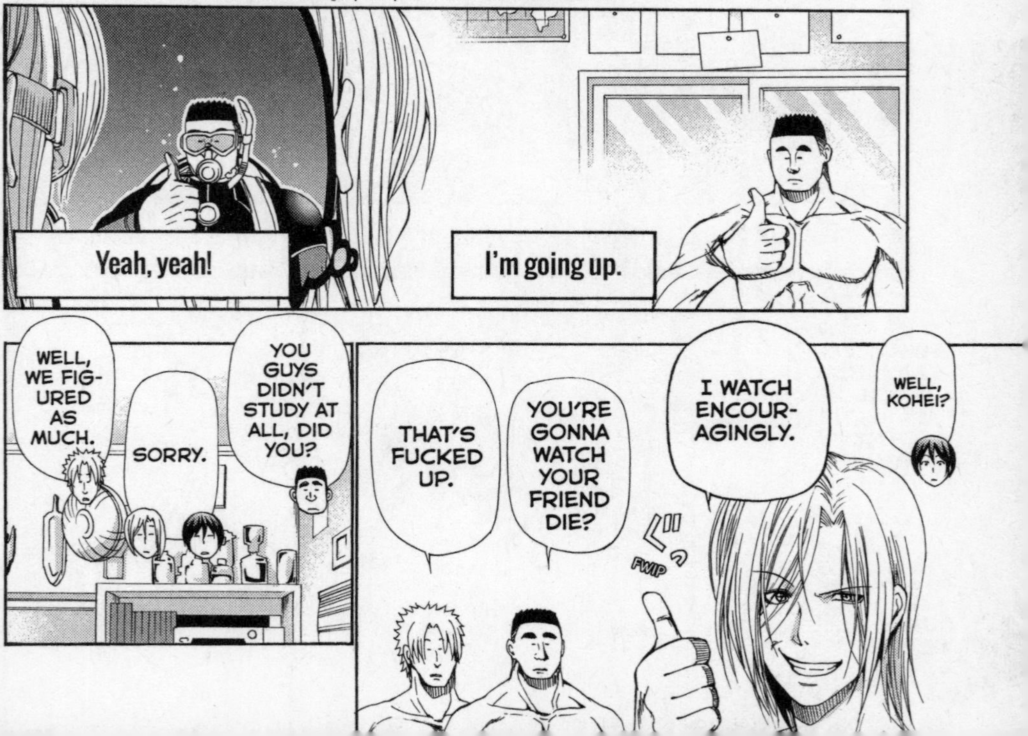
I'm going up.
Yeah, yeah!
WELL, KOHEI?
I WATCH ENCOUR-AGINGLY.
YOU'RE GONNA WATCH YOUR FRIEND DIE?
THAT'S FUCKED UP.
FWIP
YOU GUYS DIDN'T STUDY AT ALL, DID YOU?
SORRY.
WELL, WE FIG-URED AS MUCH.

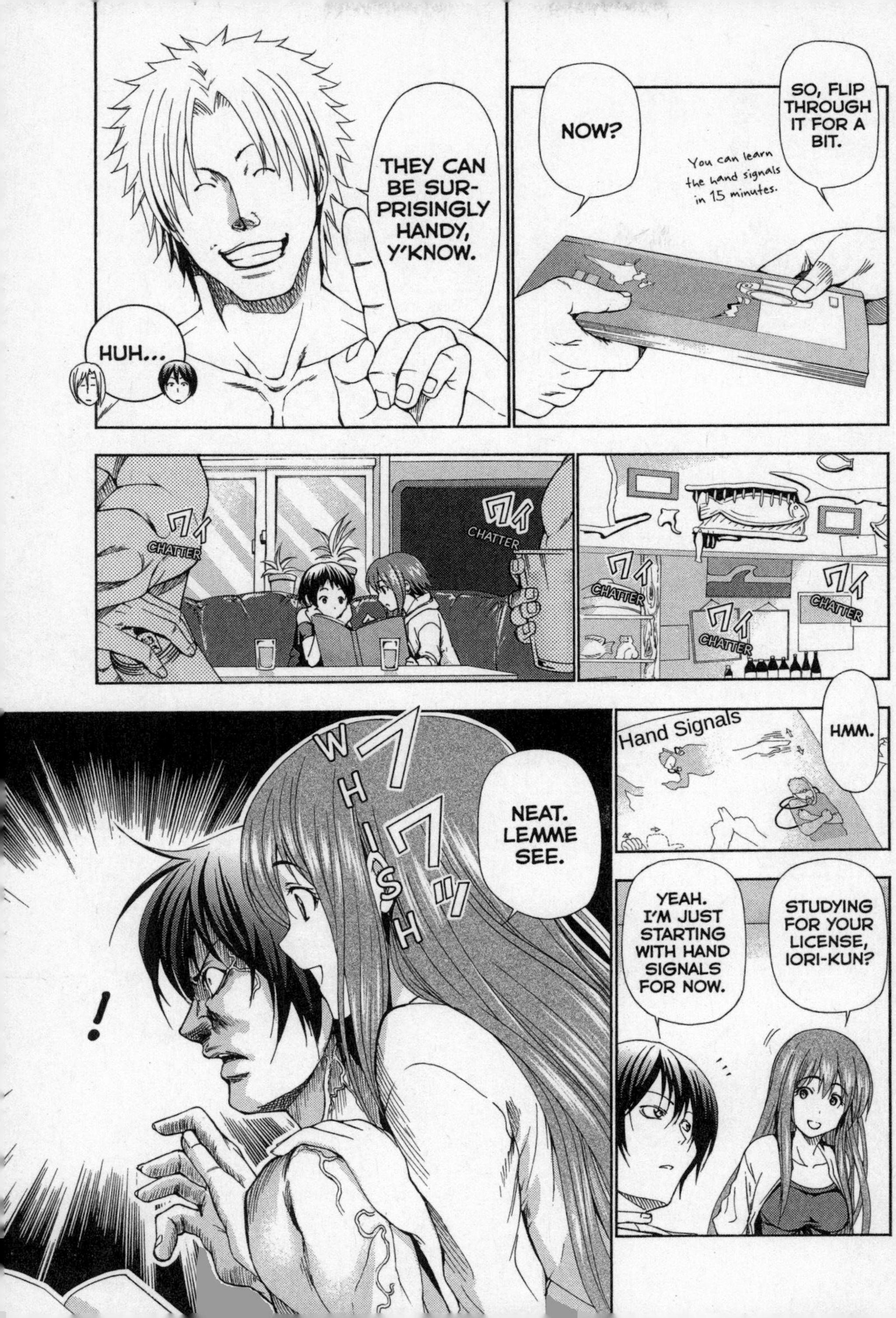
SO, FLIP THROUGH IT FOR A BIT.
NOW?
You can learn the hand signals in 15 minutes.
THEY CAN BE SUR-PRISINGLY HANDY, Y'KNOW.
HUH...
ワイ
CHATTER
ワイ
CHATTER
ワイ
CHATTER
ワイ
CHATTER
ワイ
CHATTER
Hand Signals
HMM.
STUDYING FOR YOUR LICENSE, IORI-KUN?
YEAH. I'M JUST STARTING WITH HAND SIGNALS FOR NOW.
フワッ
WHISH
NEAT. LEMME SEE.
!

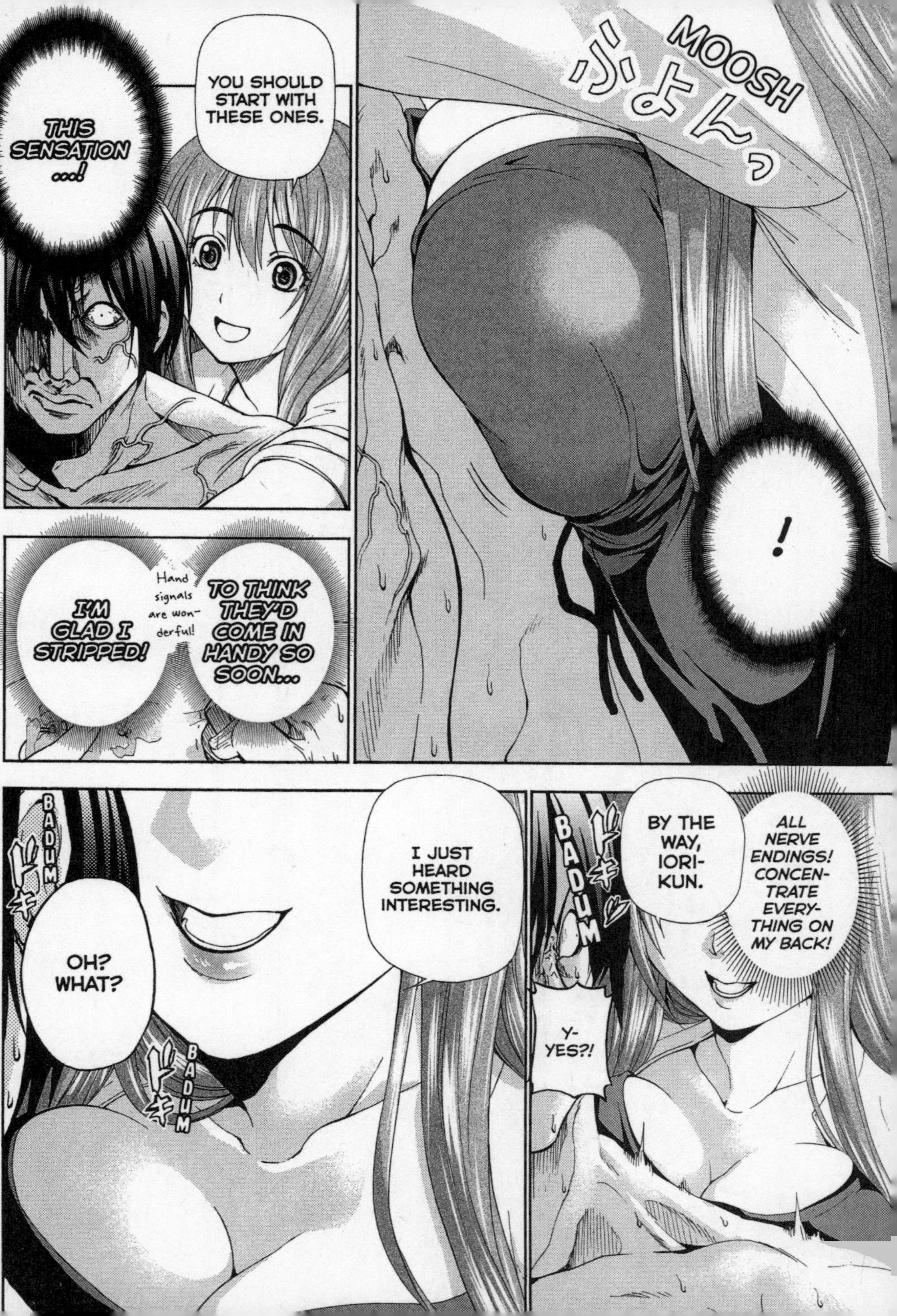
MOOSH
ぷよんっ
!
YOU SHOULD START WITH THESE ONES.
THIS SENSATION ...!
TO THINK THEY'D COME IN HANDY SO SOON...
Hand signals are won-derful!
I'M GLAD I STRIPPED!
ALL NERVE ENDINGS! CONCEN-TRATE EVERY-THING ON MY BACK!
BY THE WAY, IORI-KUN.
BADUM
ドキ
Y-YES?!
I JUST HEARD SOMETHING INTERESTING.
BADUM
ドキ
OH? WHAT?
BADUM
ドキ

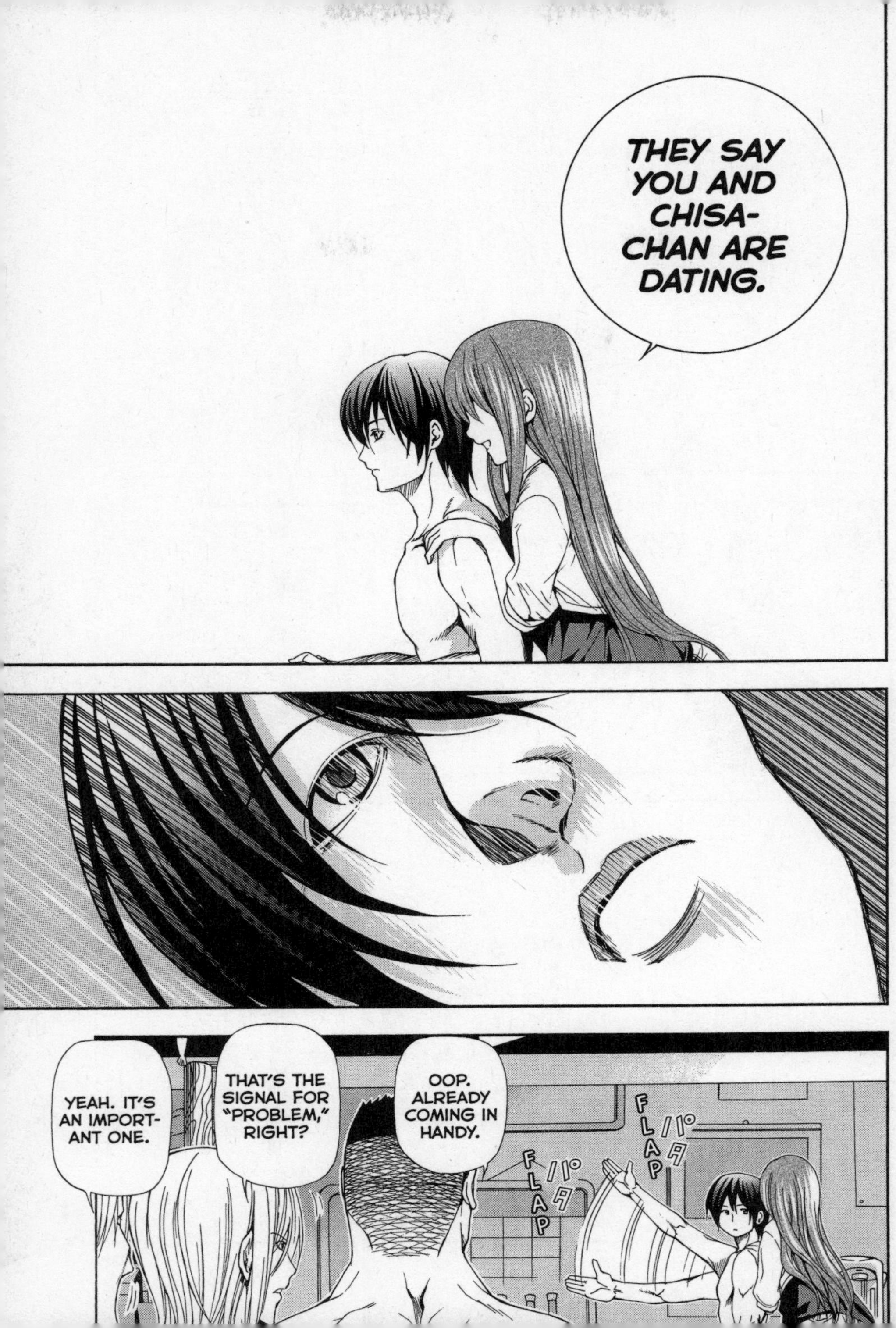
THEY SAY YOU AND CHISA-CHAN ARE DATING.
FLAP
FLAP
OOP. ALREADY COMING IN HANDY.
THAT'S THE SIGNAL FOR "PROBLEM," RIGHT?
YEAH. IT'S AN IMPORT-ANT ONE.

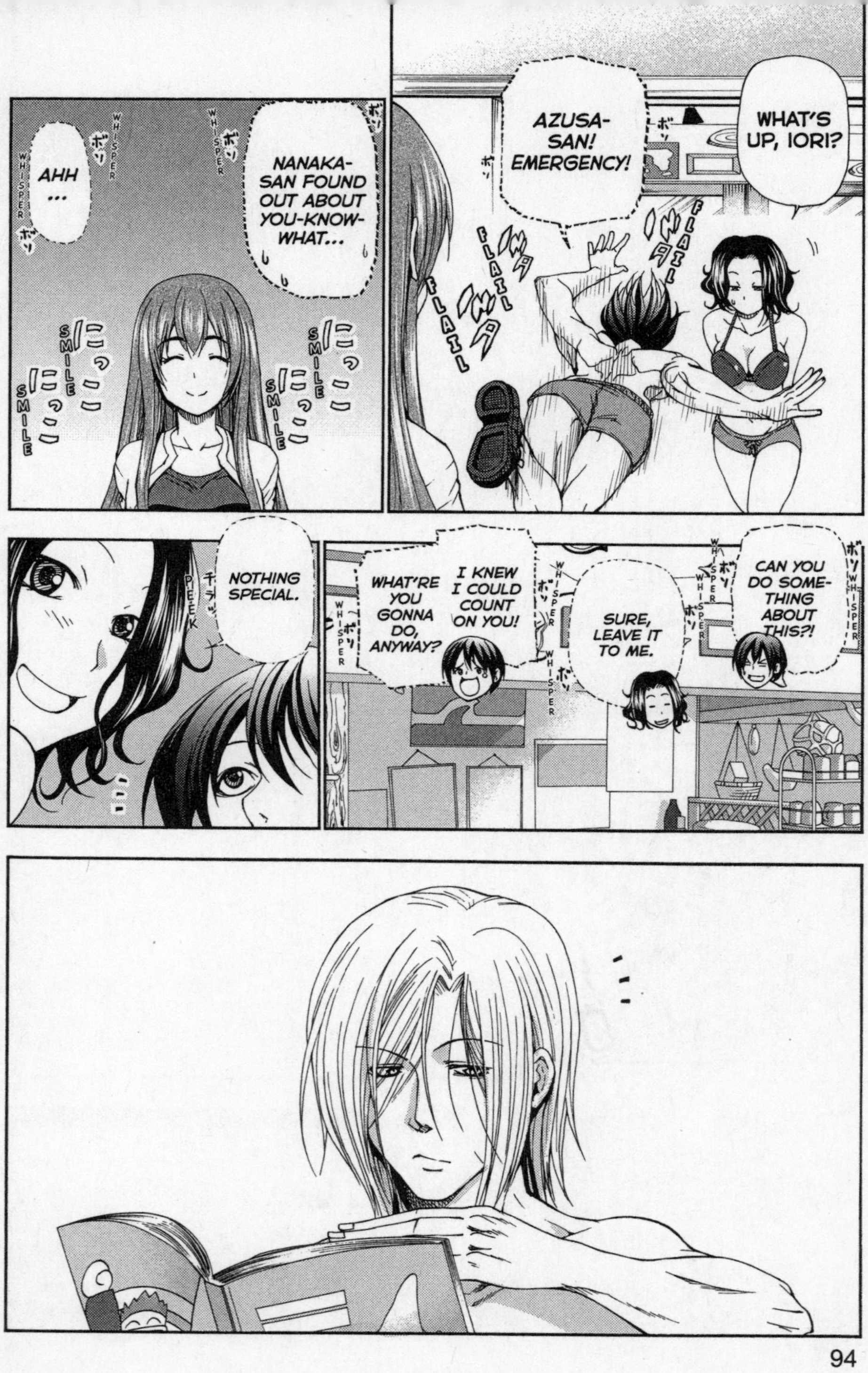
WHAT'S UP, IORI?
AZUSA-SAN! EMERGENCY!
FLAIL FLAIL FLAIL
NANAKA-SAN FOUND OUT ABOUT YOU-KNOW-WHAT...
WHISPER WHISPER WHISPER
AHH ...
SMILE SMILE SMILE SMILE
CAN YOU DO SOMETHING ABOUT THIS?!
WHISPER WHISPER
SURE, LEAVE IT TO ME.
WHISPER WHISPER
I KNEW I COULD COUNT ON YOU!
WHAT'RE YOU GONNA DO, ANYWAY?
WHISPER
NOTHING SPECIAL.
PEEK

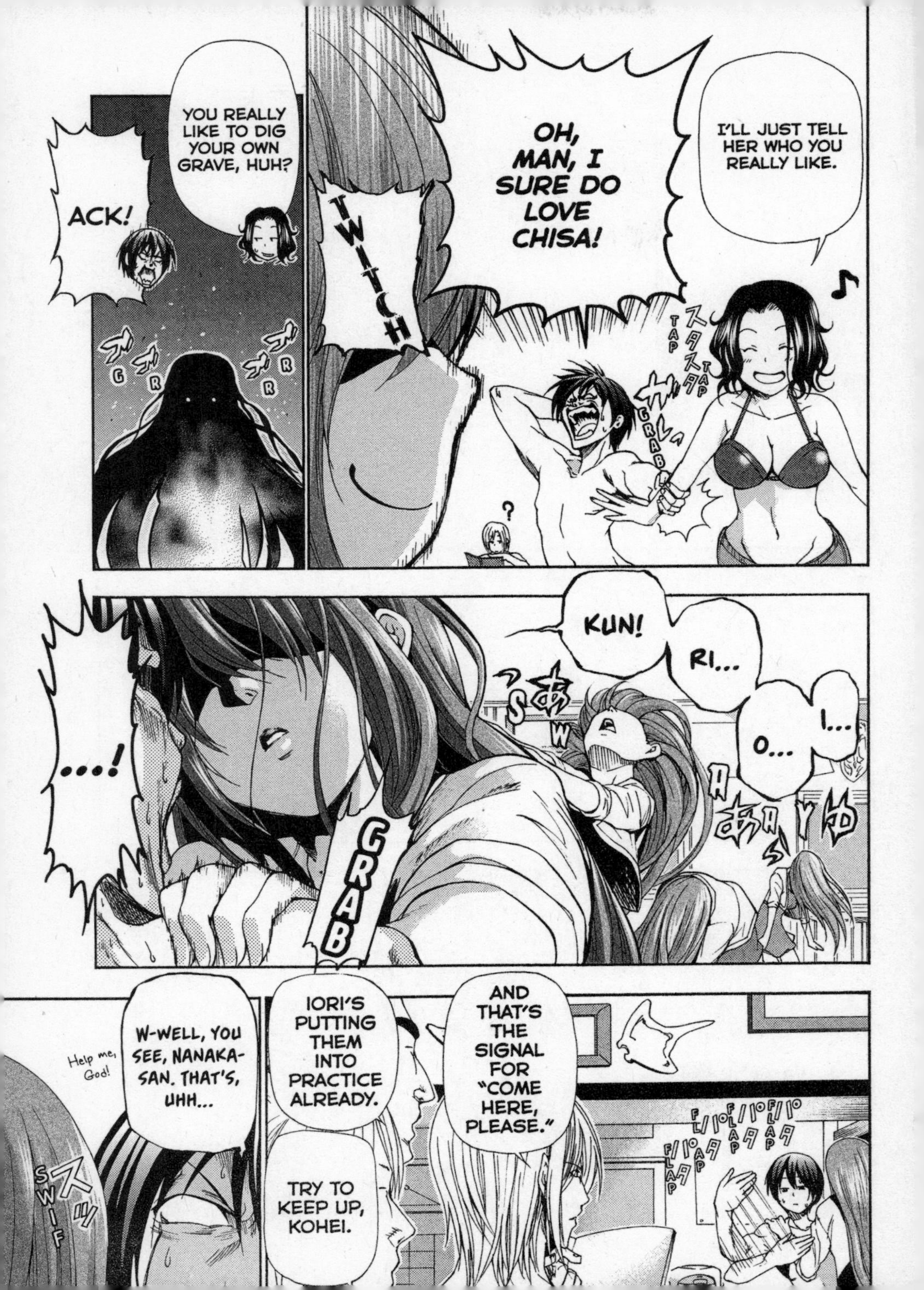
I'LL JUST TELL HER WHO YOU REALLY LIKE.
OH, MAN, I SURE DO LOVE CHISA!
TWITCH
TAP TAP
GRAB
?
YOU REALLY LIKE TO DIG YOUR OWN GRAVE, HUH?
ACK!
GRRR
I...
O...
RI...
KUN!
SW
GRAB
...!
FLAP FLAP
AND THAT'S THE SIGNAL FOR "COME HERE, PLEASE."
IORI'S PUTTING THEM INTO PRACTICE ALREADY.
TRY TO KEEP UP, KOHEI.
W-WELL, YOU SEE, NANAKA-SAN. THAT'S, UHH...
Help me, God!
SWIF

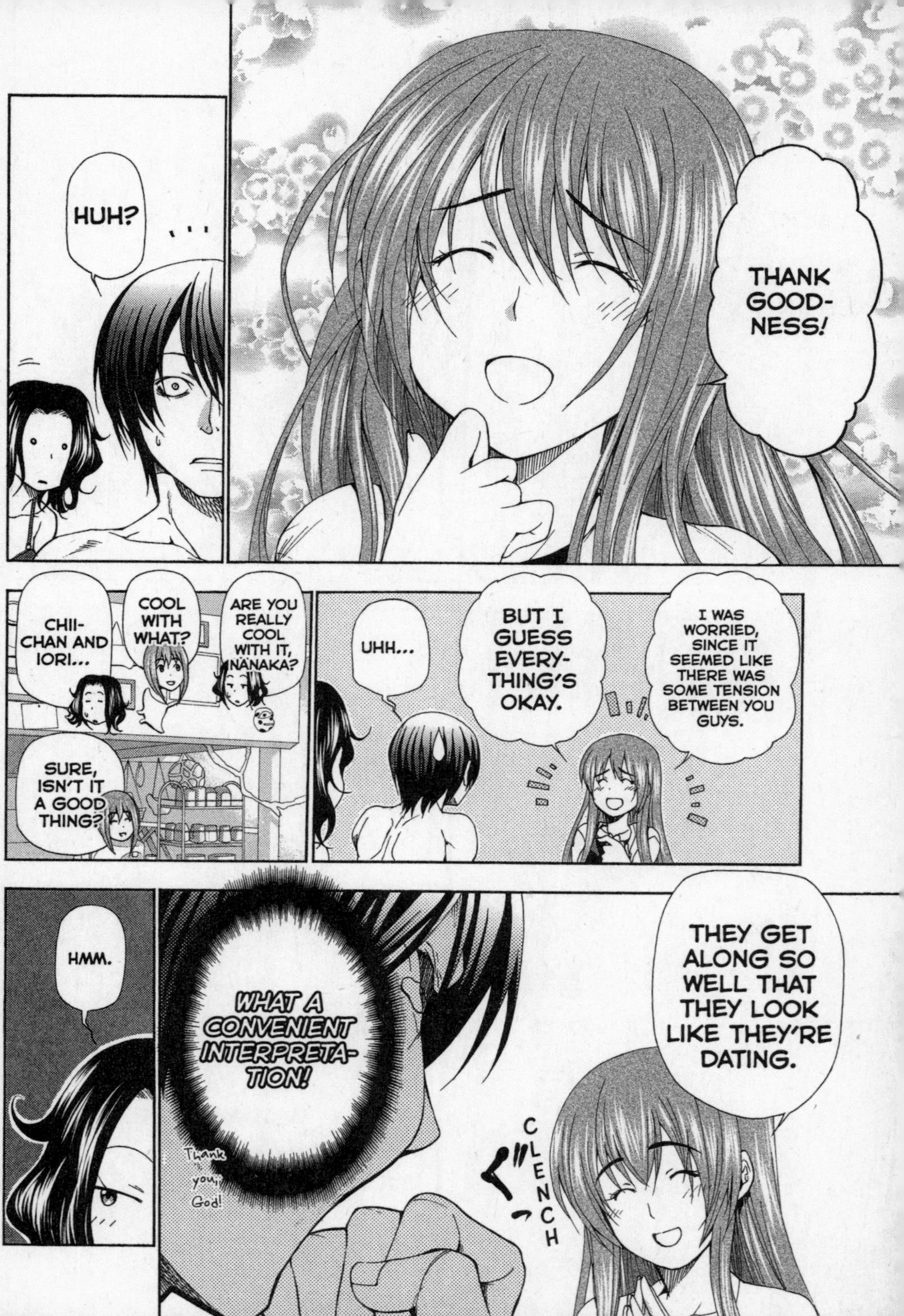
THANK GOOD-NESS!
HUH?
...
I WAS WORRIED, SINCE IT SEEMED LIKE THERE WAS SOME TENSION BETWEEN YOU GUYS.
BUT I GUESS EVERY-THING'S OKAY.
UHH...
ARE YOU REALLY COOL WITH IT, NANAKA?
COOL WITH WHAT?
CHII-CHAN AND IORI...
SURE, ISN'T IT A GOOD THING?
THEY GET ALONG SO WELL THAT THEY LOOK LIKE THEY'RE DATING.
CLENCH
WHAT A CONVENIENT INTERPRETA-TION!
Thank you, God!
HMM.

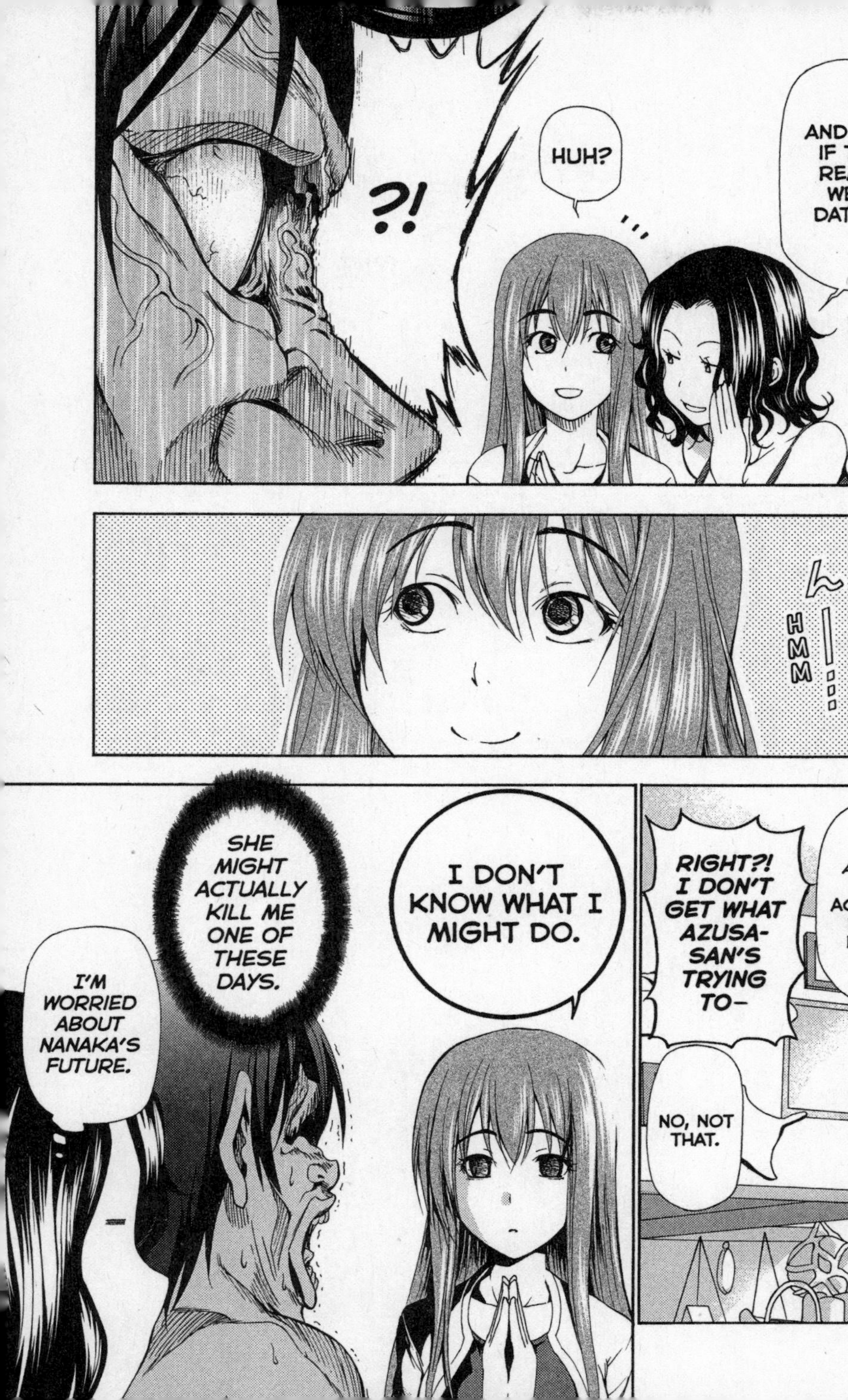
AND WHAT IF THEY REALLY WERE DATING?
HUH?
?!
ん
HMM
AH, HA, HA. I ACTUALLY DON'T KNOW.
RIGHT?! I DON'T GET WHAT AZUSA-SAN'S TRYING TO—
NO, NOT THAT.
I DON'T KNOW WHAT I MIGHT DO.
SHE MIGHT ACTUALLY KILL ME ONE OF THESE DAYS.
I'M WORRIED ABOUT NANAKA'S FUTURE.

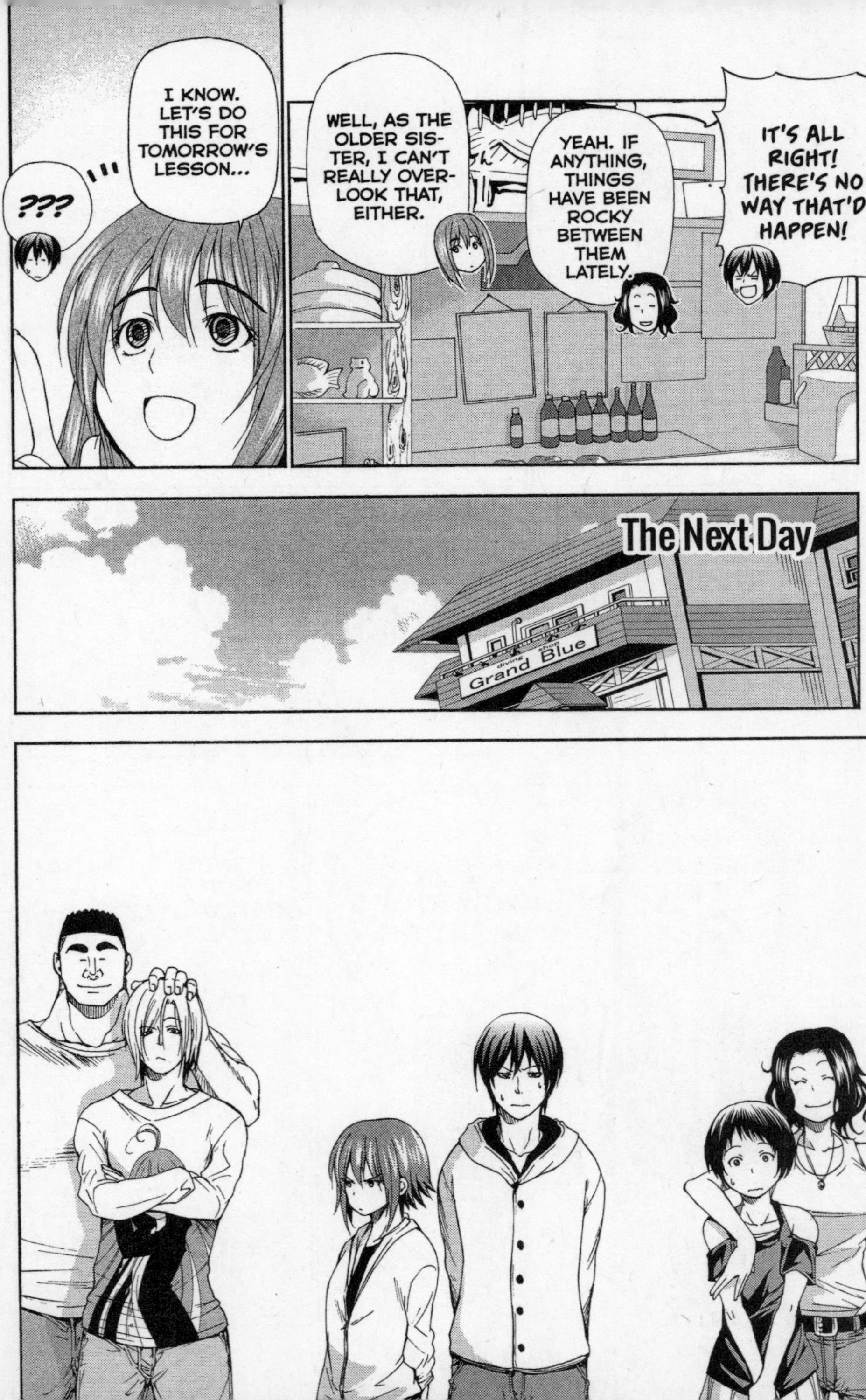
IT'S ALL RIGHT! THERE'S NO WAY THAT'D HAPPEN!
YEAH. IF ANYTHING, THINGS HAVE BEEN ROCKY BETWEEN THEM LATELY.
WELL, AS THE OLDER SISTER, I CAN'T REALLY OVERLOOK THAT, EITHER.
I KNOW. LET'S DO THIS FOR TOMORROW'S LESSON...
!!
???
The Next Day
diving shop
Grand Blue

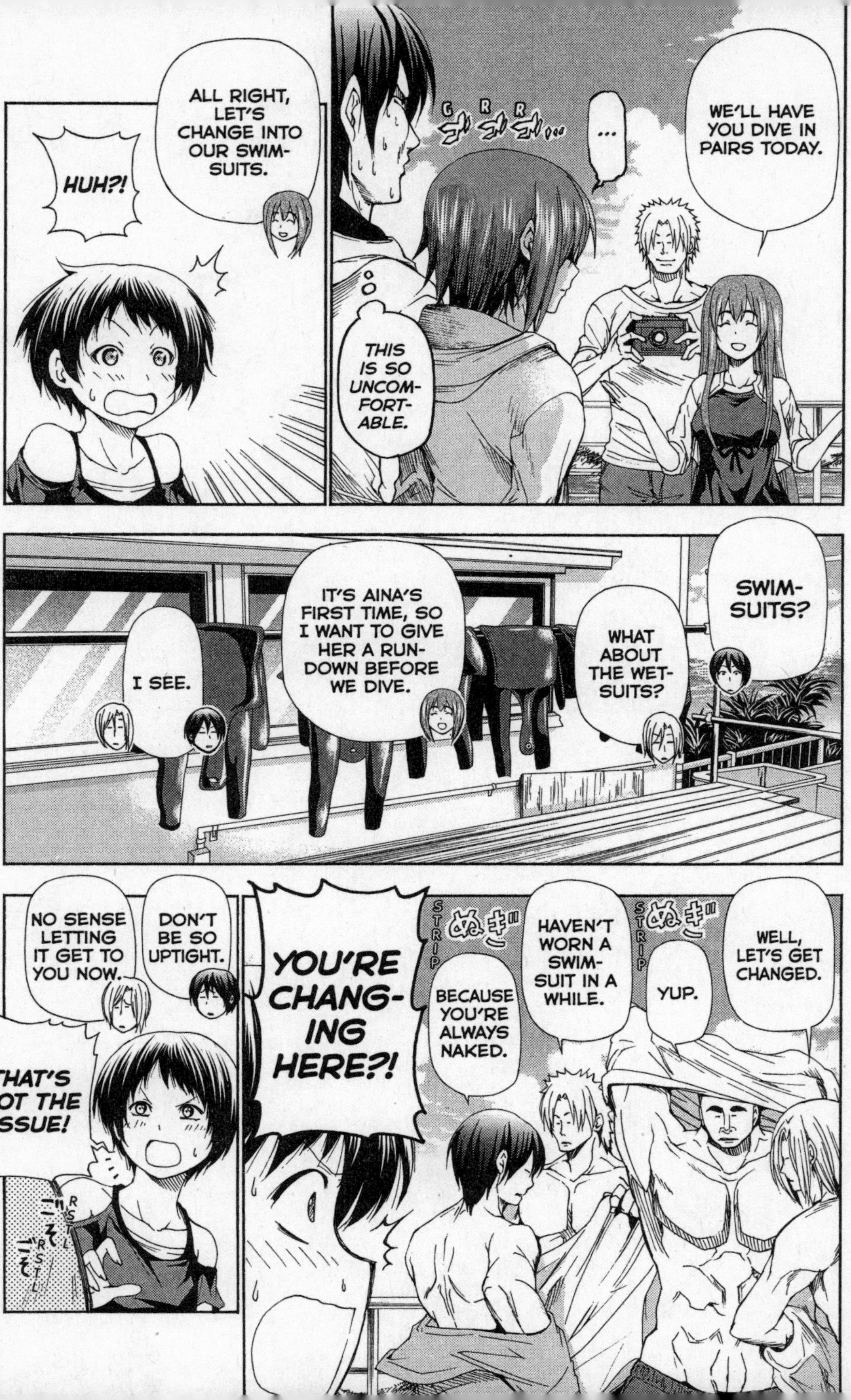
WE'LL HAVE YOU DIVE IN PAIRS TODAY.
GRRR
ゴゴゴ...
...
THIS IS SO UNCOM-FORT-ABLE.
ALL RIGHT, LET'S CHANGE INTO OUR SWIM-SUITS.
HUH?!
SWIM-SUITS?
WHAT ABOUT THE WET-SUITS?
IT'S AINA'S FIRST TIME, SO I WANT TO GIVE HER A RUN-DOWN BEFORE WE DIVE.
I SEE.
WELL, LET'S GET CHANGED.
YUP.
STRIP ぬぎ
HAVEN'T WORN A SWIM-SUIT IN A WHILE.
BECAUSE YOU'RE ALWAYS NAKED.
STRIP ぬぎ
YOU'RE CHANG-ING HERE?!
DON'T BE SO UPTIGHT.
NO SENSE LETTING IT GET TO YOU NOW.
THAT'S NOT THE ISSUE!
RSTL ごそ
RSTL ごそ

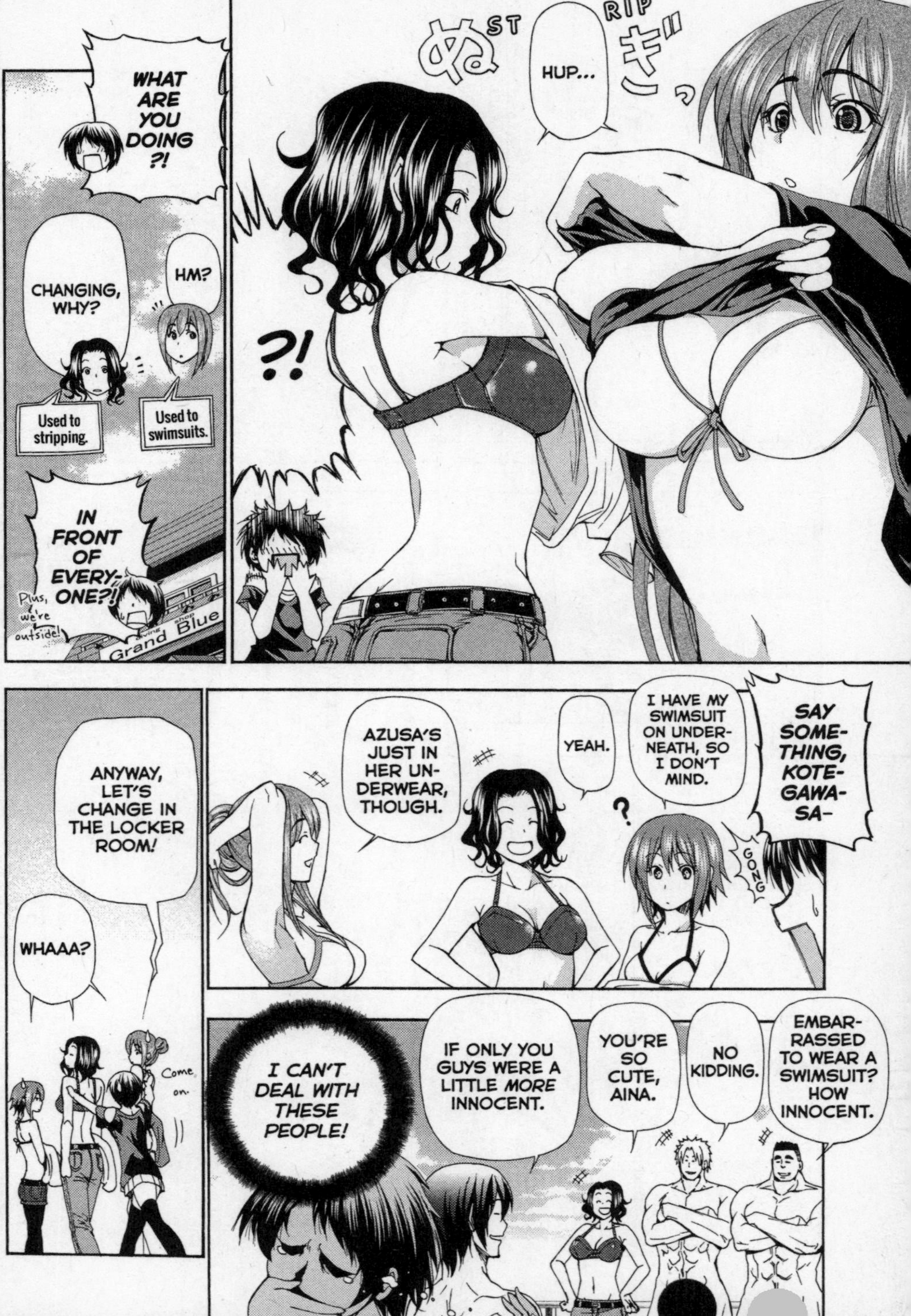
ぬ ST
HUP...
ぎっ RIP
?!
WHAT ARE YOU DOING?!
HM?
CHANGING, WHY?
Used to swimsuits.
Used to stripping.
IN FRONT OF EVERY-ONE?!
Plus, we're outside!
diving shop Grand Blue
SAY SOME-THING, KOTE-GAWA-SA-
GONG
?
I HAVE MY SWIMSUIT ON UNDER-NEATH, SO I DON'T MIND.
YEAH.
AZUSA'S JUST IN HER UN-DERWEAR, THOUGH.
EMBAR-RASSED TO WEAR A SWIMSUIT? HOW INNOCENT.
NO KIDDING.
YOU'RE SO CUTE, AINA.
IF ONLY YOU GUYS WERE A LITTLE MORE INNOCENT.
I CAN'T DEAL WITH THESE PEOPLE!
ANYWAY, LET'S CHANGE IN THE LOCKER ROOM!
WHAAA?
Come on.

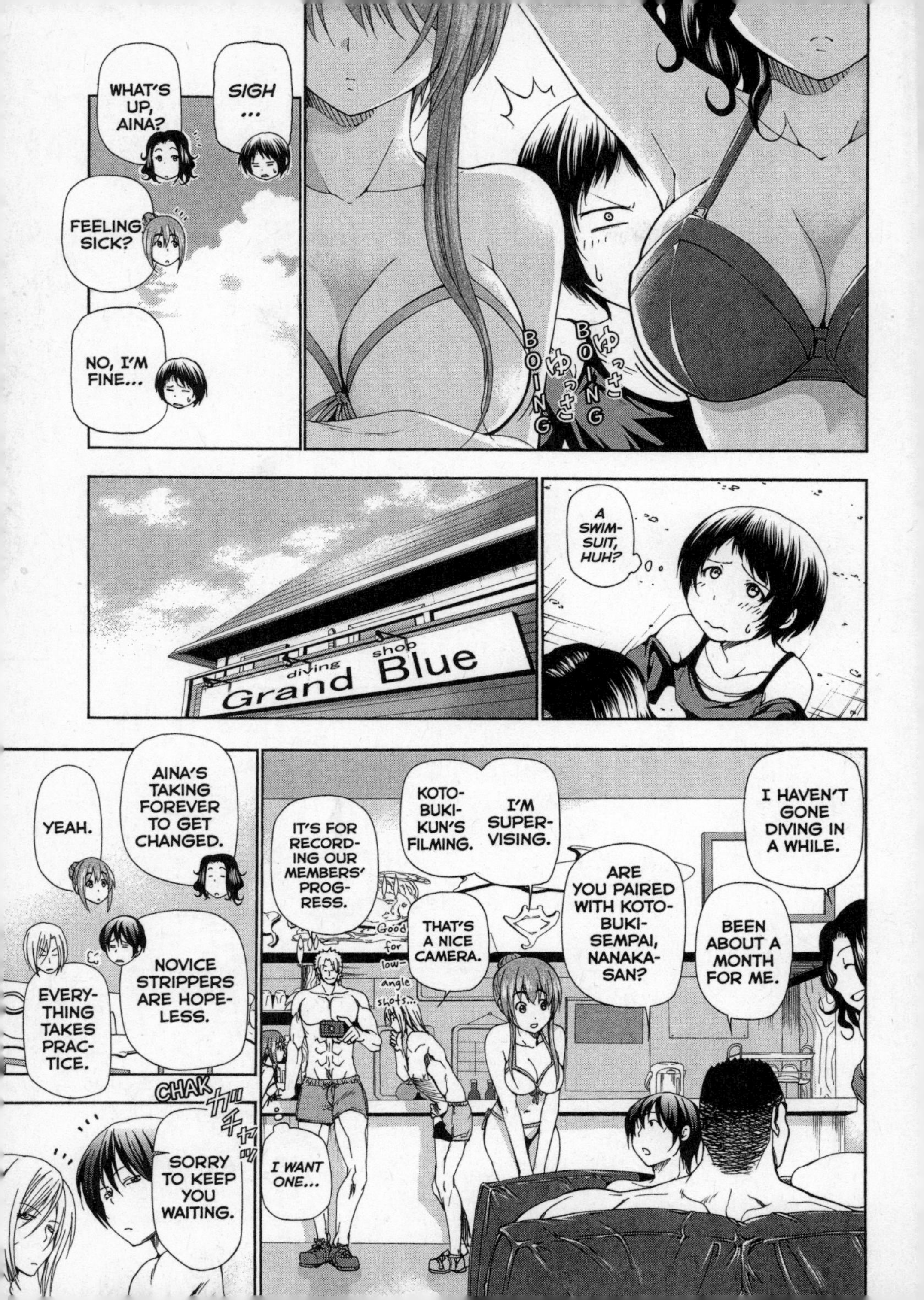
BOING
ゆっさ
BOING
ゆっさ
SIGH...
WHAT'S UP, AINA?
FEELING SICK?
NO, I'M FINE...
A SWIMSUIT, HUH?
diving shop Grand Blue
I HAVEN'T GONE DIVING IN A WHILE.
BEEN ABOUT A MONTH FOR ME.
ARE YOU PAIRED WITH KOTOBUKI-SEMPAI, NANAKA-SAN?
I'M SUPERVISING.
KOTOBUKI-KUN'S FILMING.
IT'S FOR RECORDING OUR MEMBERS' PROGRESS.
THAT'S A NICE CAMERA.
Good for low-angle shots...
I WANT ONE...
AINA'S TAKING FOREVER TO GET CHANGED.
YEAH.
NOVICE STRIPPERS ARE HOPELESS.
EVERYTHING TAKES PRACTICE.
CHAK
ガチャッ
SORRY TO KEEP YOU WAITING.

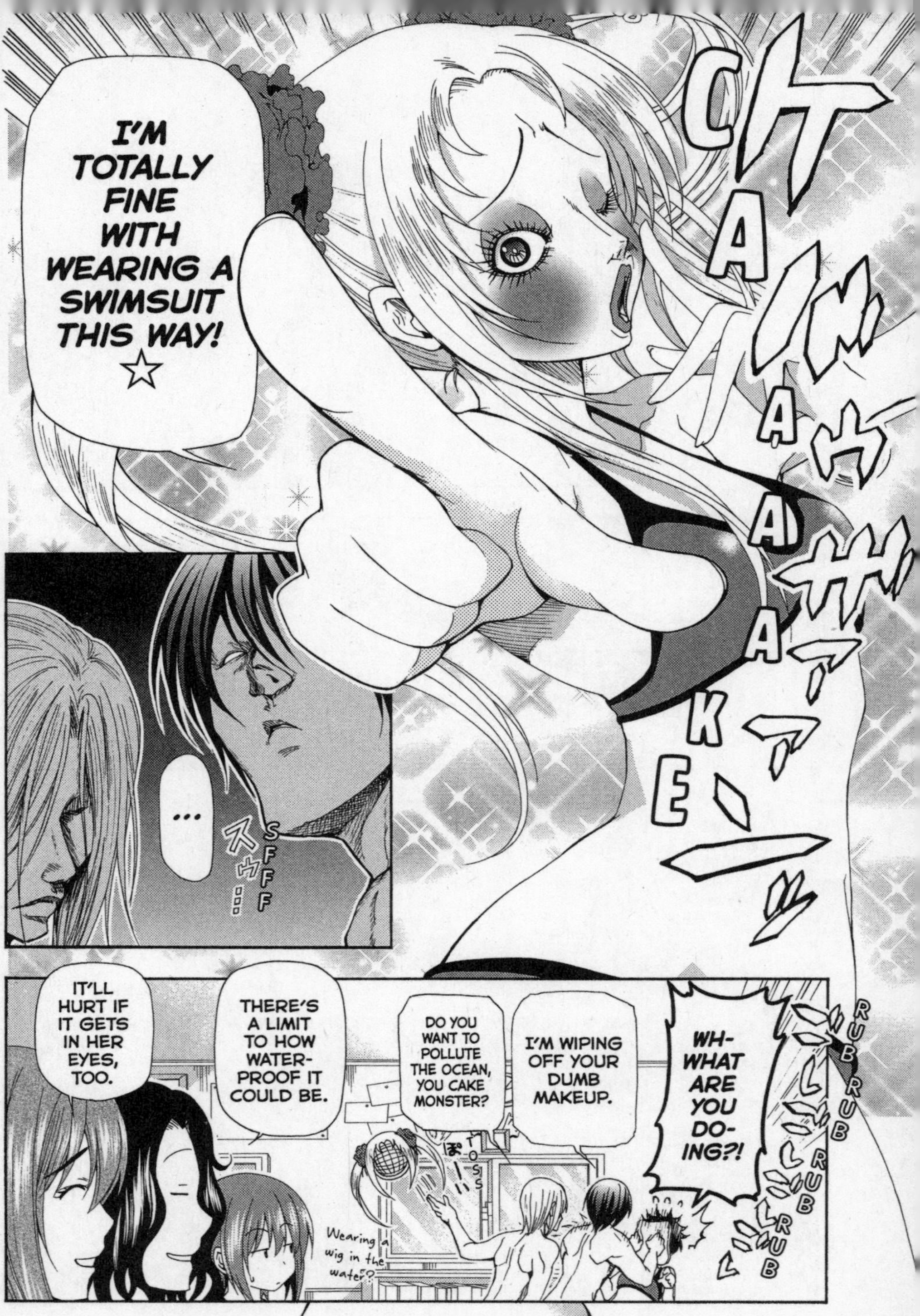
CAAAAKE
I'M TOTALLY FINE WITH WEARING A SWIMSUIT THIS WAY! ☆
...
SFFF
WH-WHAT ARE YOU DO-ING?!
RUB RUB RUB RUB
I'M WIPING OFF YOUR DUMB MAKEUP.
DO YOU WANT TO POLLUTE THE OCEAN, YOU CAKE MONSTER?
TOSS
THERE'S A LIMIT TO HOW WATER-PROOF IT COULD BE.
IT'LL HURT IF IT GETS IN HER EYES, TOO.
Wearing a wig in the water?

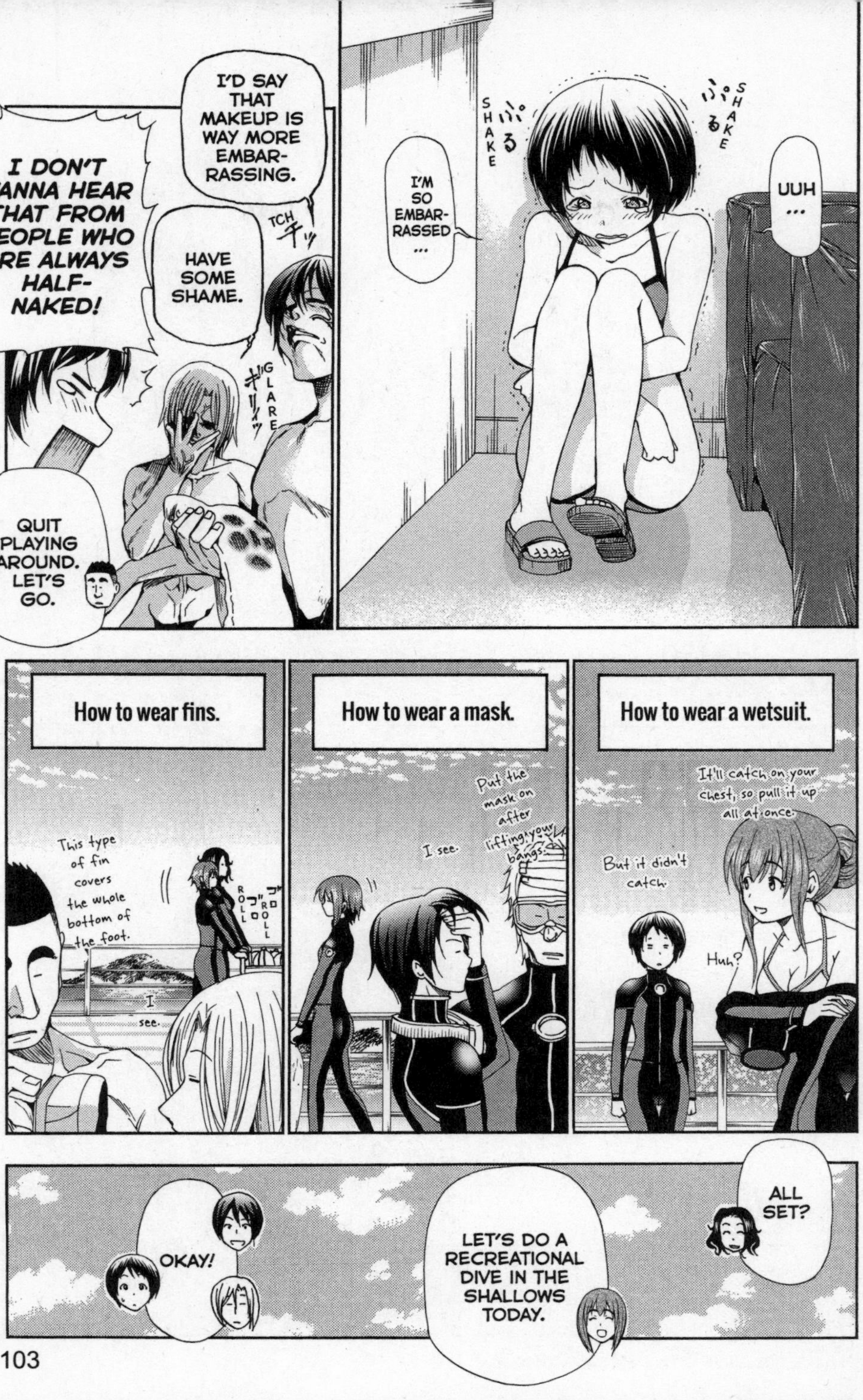
SHAKE ぷる
SHAKE ぷる
UUH...
I'M SO EMBARRASSED...
I'D SAY THAT MAKEUP IS WAY MORE EMBARRASSING.
TCH チッ
HAVE SOME SHAME.
I DON'T WANNA HEAR THAT FROM PEOPLE WHO ARE ALWAYS HALF-NAKED!
GLARE ギリッ
QUIT PLAYING AROUND. LET'S GO.
How to wear a wetsuit.
It'll catch on your chest, so pull it up all at once.
Huh?
But it didn't catch.
How to wear a mask.
Put the mask on after lifting your bangs.
I see.
How to wear fins.
This type of fin covers the whole bottom of the foot.
ROLL ゴロ ROLL ゴロ
I see.
ALL SET?
LET'S DO A RECREATIONAL DIVE IN THE SHALLOWS TODAY.
OKAY!

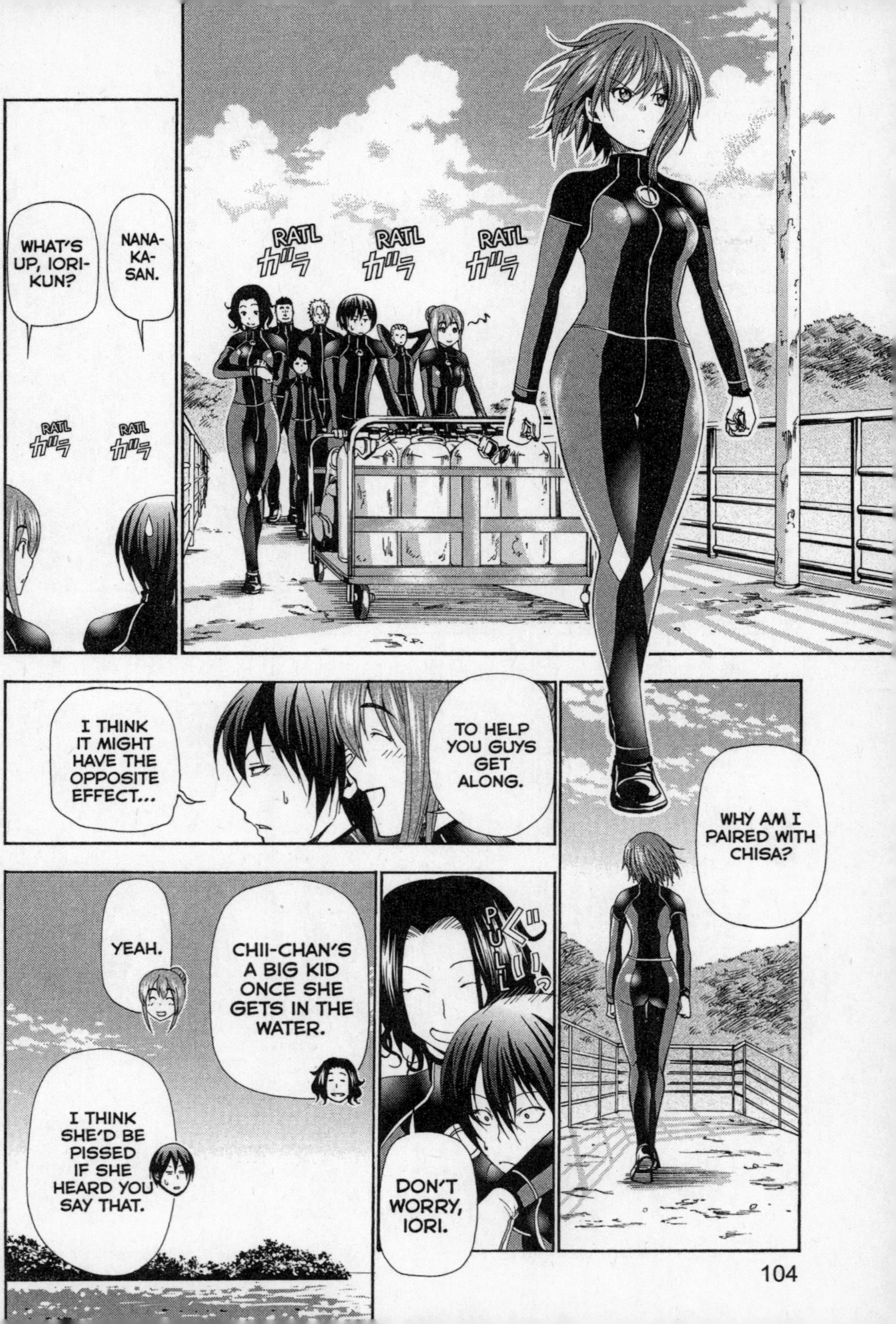
RATL ガラ
RATL ガラ
RATL ガラ
NANA-KA-SAN.
WHAT'S UP, IORI-KUN?
RATL ガラ
RATL ガラ
WHY AM I PAIRED WITH CHISA?
TO HELP YOU GUYS GET ALONG.
I THINK IT MIGHT HAVE THE OPPOSITE EFFECT...
PULL ぐいっ
DON'T WORRY, IORI.
CHII-CHAN'S A BIG KID ONCE SHE GETS IN THE WATER.
YEAH.
I THINK SHE'D BE PISSED IF SHE HEARD YOU SAY THAT.

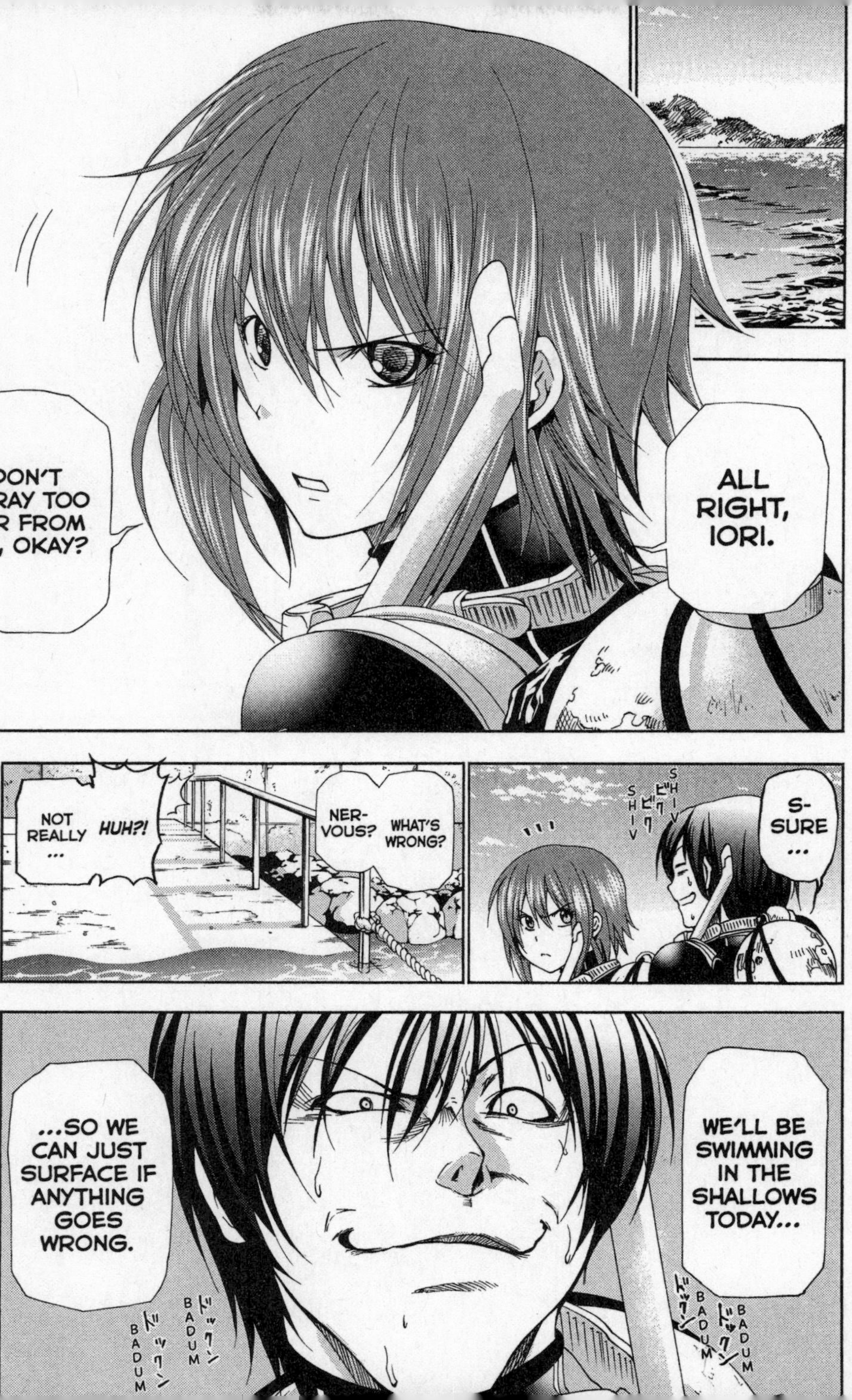
ALL RIGHT, IORI.
DON'T STRAY TOO FAR FROM ME, OKAY?
SHIV SHIV
S- SURE ...
WHAT'S WRONG?
NERVOUS?
HUH?!
NOT REALLY ...
WE'LL BE SWIMMING IN THE SHALLOWS TODAY...
BADUM BADUM
...SO WE CAN JUST SURFACE IF ANYTHING GOES WRONG.
BADUM BADUM

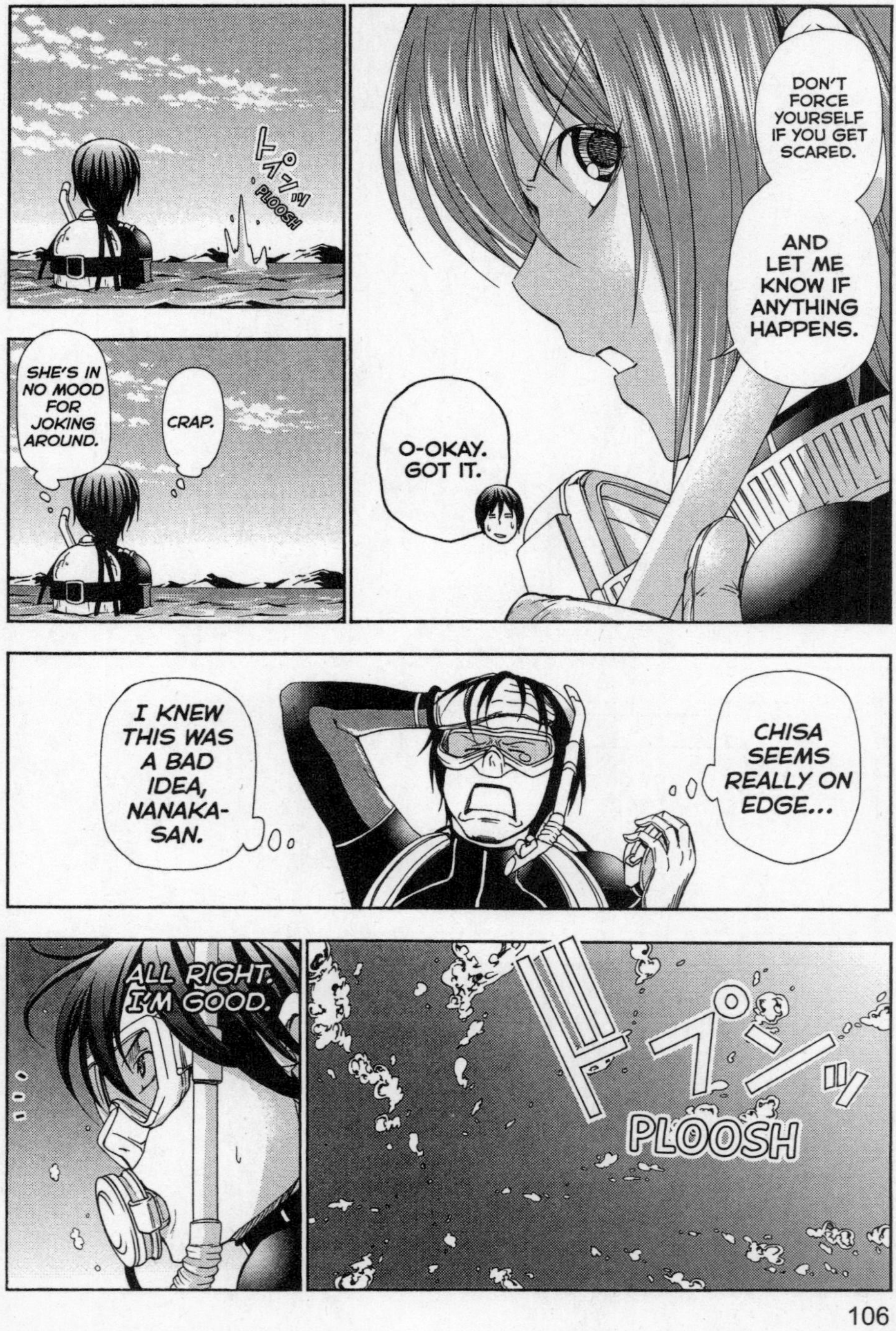

DON'T FORCE YOURSELF IF YOU GET SCARED.
AND LET ME KNOW IF ANYTHING HAPPENS.
O-OKAY. GOT IT.
トプンッ
PLOOSH
CRAP.
SHE'S IN NO MOOD FOR JOKING AROUND.
CHISA SEEMS REALLY ON EDGE...
I KNEW THIS WAS A BAD IDEA, NANAKA-SAN.
ドプンッ
PLOOSH
ALL RIGHT. I'M GOOD.

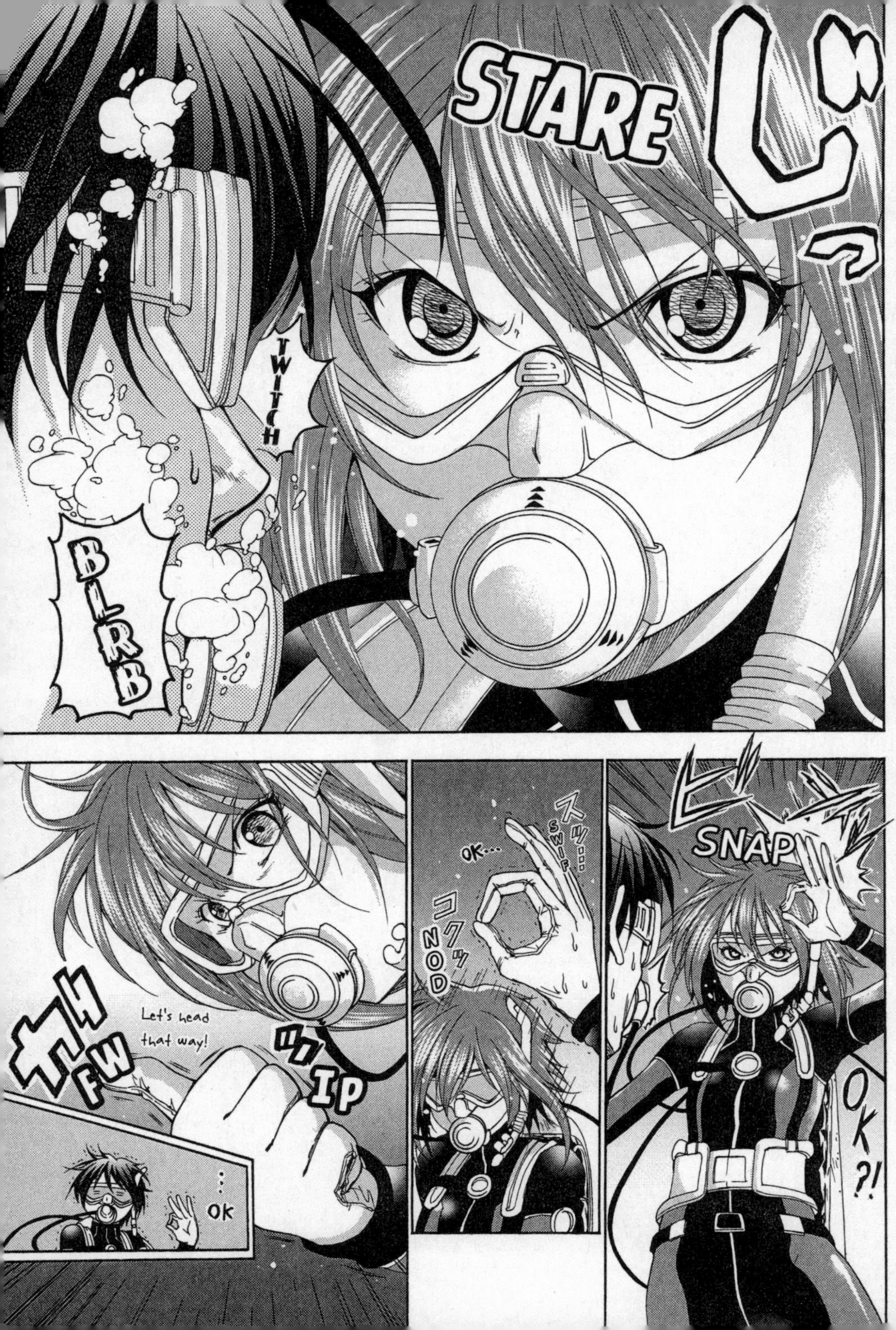

STARE
じっ
TWITCH
BLRB
SNAP
OK?!
SWIF
OK...
NOD
Let's head that way!
FW
IP
...OK

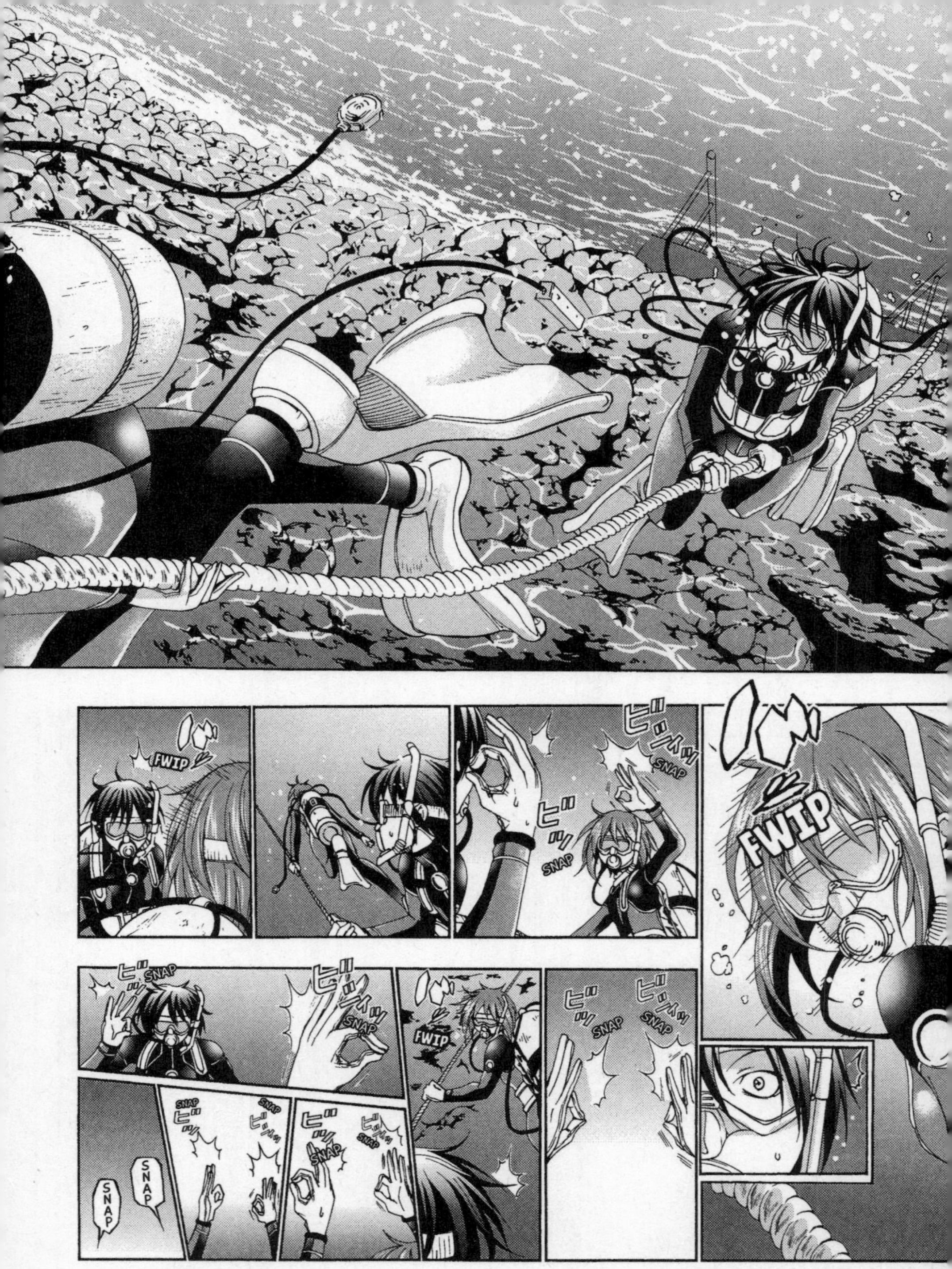
FWIP
SNAP
SNAP
FWIP
SNAP
SNAP
FWIP
SNAP
SNAP
SNAP
SNAP
SNAP
SNAP
SNAP

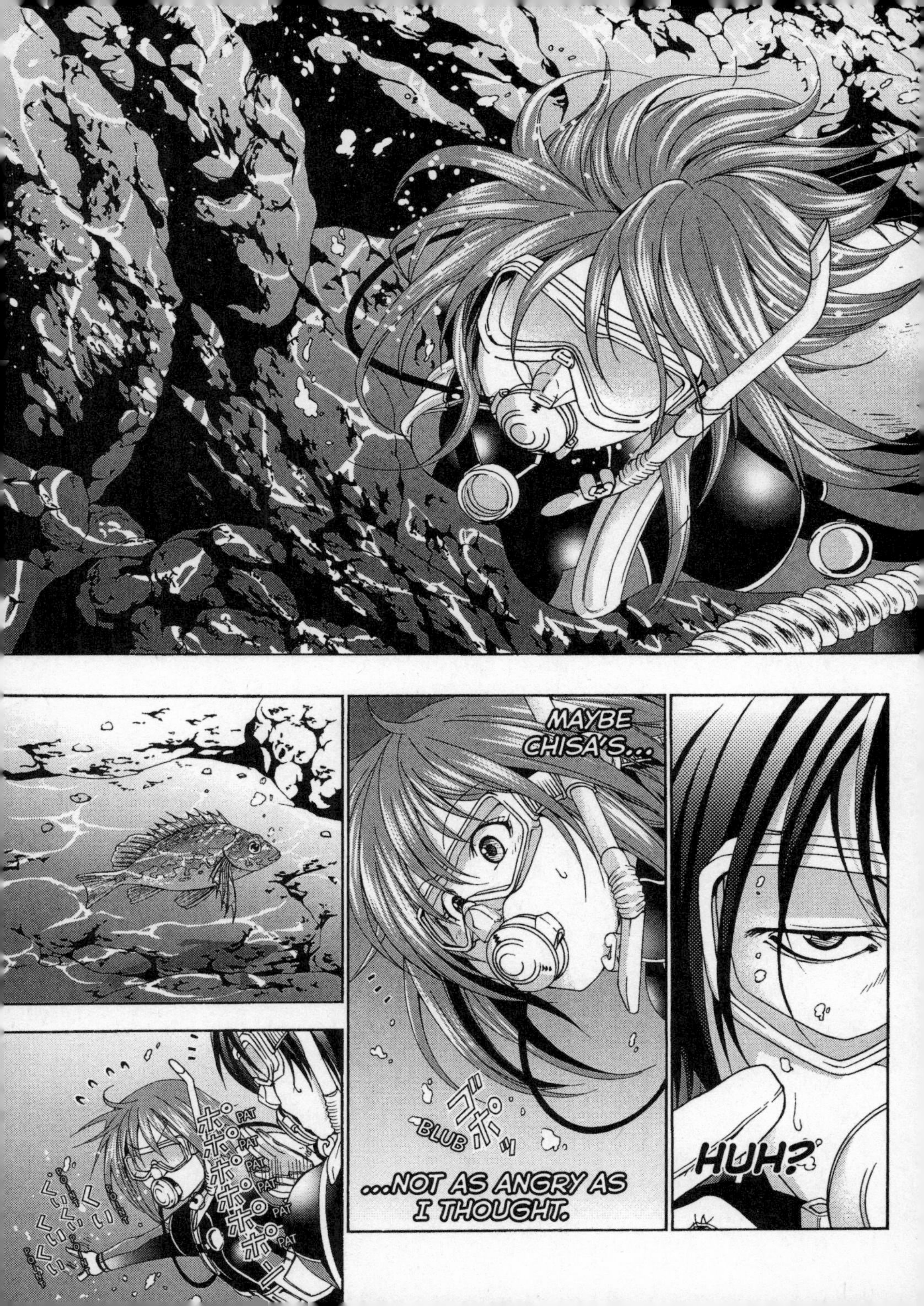
HUH?
MAYBE CHISA'S...
BLUB
...NOT AS ANGRY AS I THOUGHT.
PAT
PAT
PAT
PAT
PAT

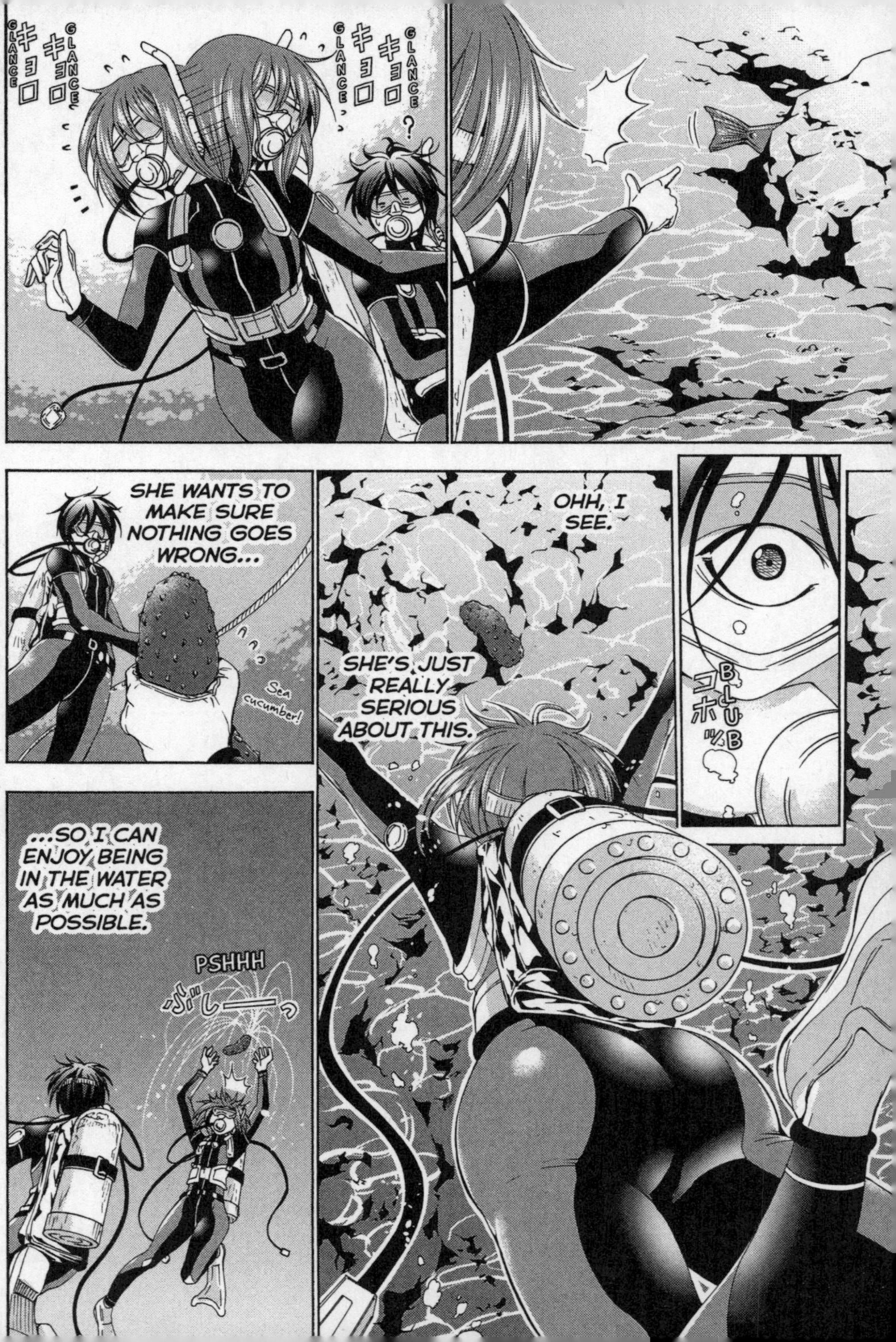
GLANCE
キョロ
GLANCE
キョロ
?
GLANCE
キョロ
GLANCE
キョロ
BLUB
コポ
BLUB
ッ
OHH, I SEE.
SHE'S JUST REALLY SERIOUS ABOUT THIS.
SHE WANTS TO MAKE SURE NOTHING GOES WRONG...
Sea cucumber!
...SO I CAN ENJOY BEING IN THE WATER AS MUCH AS POSSIBLE.
PSHHH
ぶしーっ

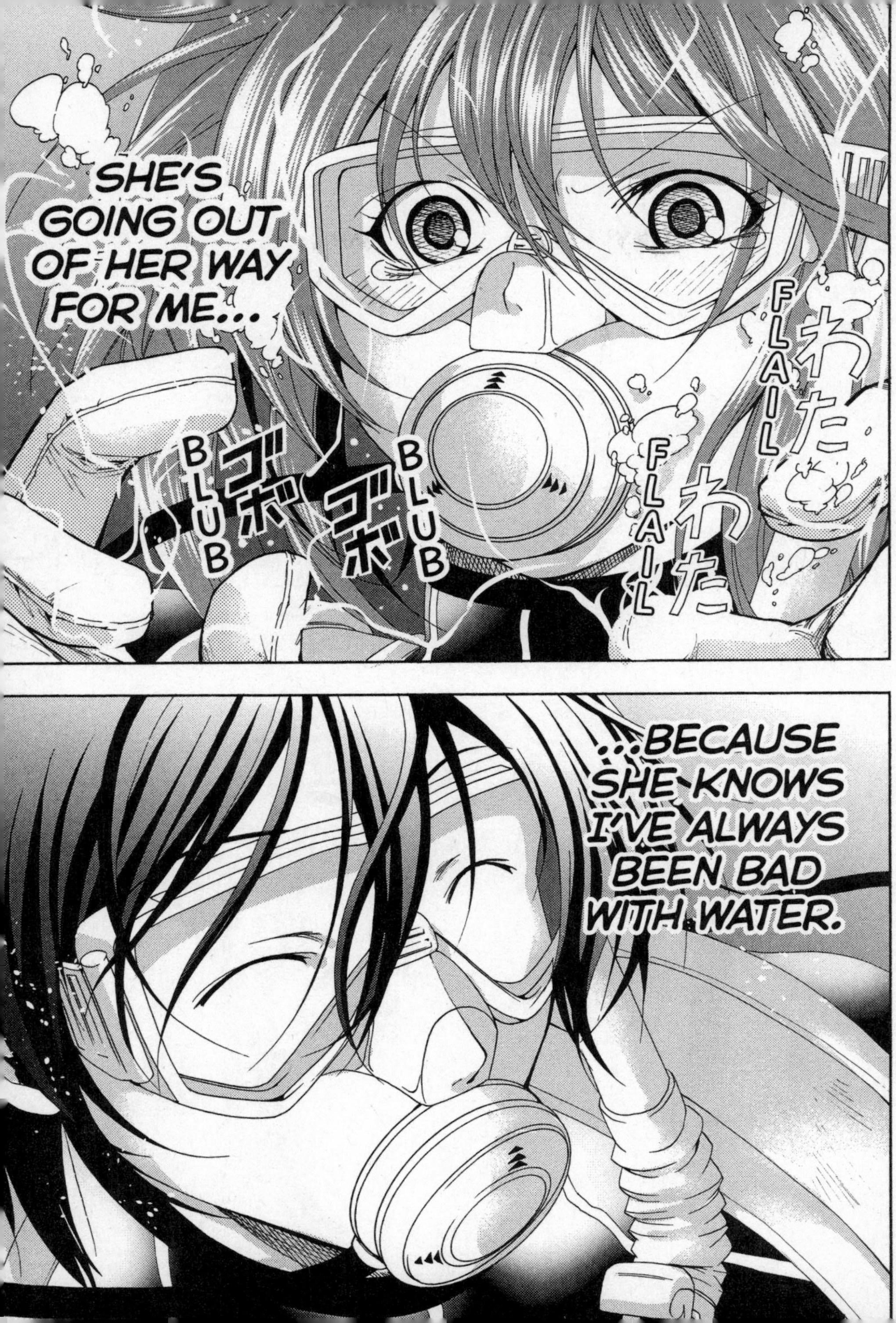
わたわた FLAIL FLAIL
SHE'S GOING OUT OF HER WAY FOR ME...
ゴボゴボ BLUB BLUB
...BECAUSE SHE KNOWS I'VE ALWAYS BEEN BAD WITH WATER.

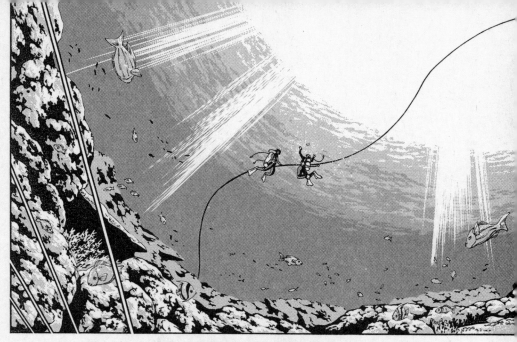

...SO FUN!

THAT WAS...

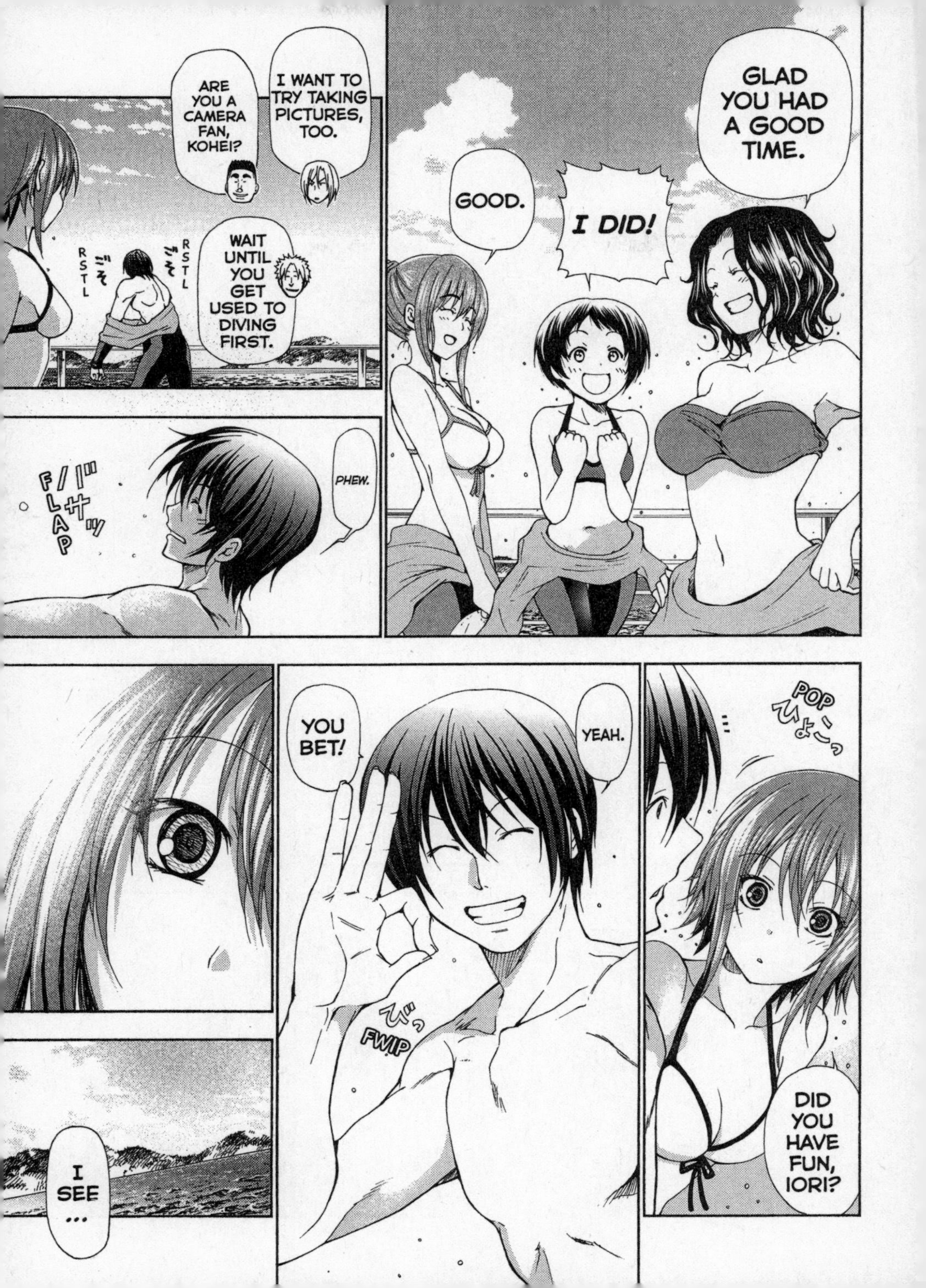
GLAD YOU HAD A GOOD TIME.
I DID!
GOOD.
I WANT TO TRY TAKING PICTURES, TOO.
ARE YOU A CAMERA FAN, KOHEI?
WAIT UNTIL YOU GET USED TO DIVING FIRST.
ごそ RSTL
ごそ RSTL
PHEW.
バサッ FLAP
ひょこっ POP
DID YOU HAVE FUN, IORI?
YEAH.
YOU BET!
びっ FWIP
I SEE...

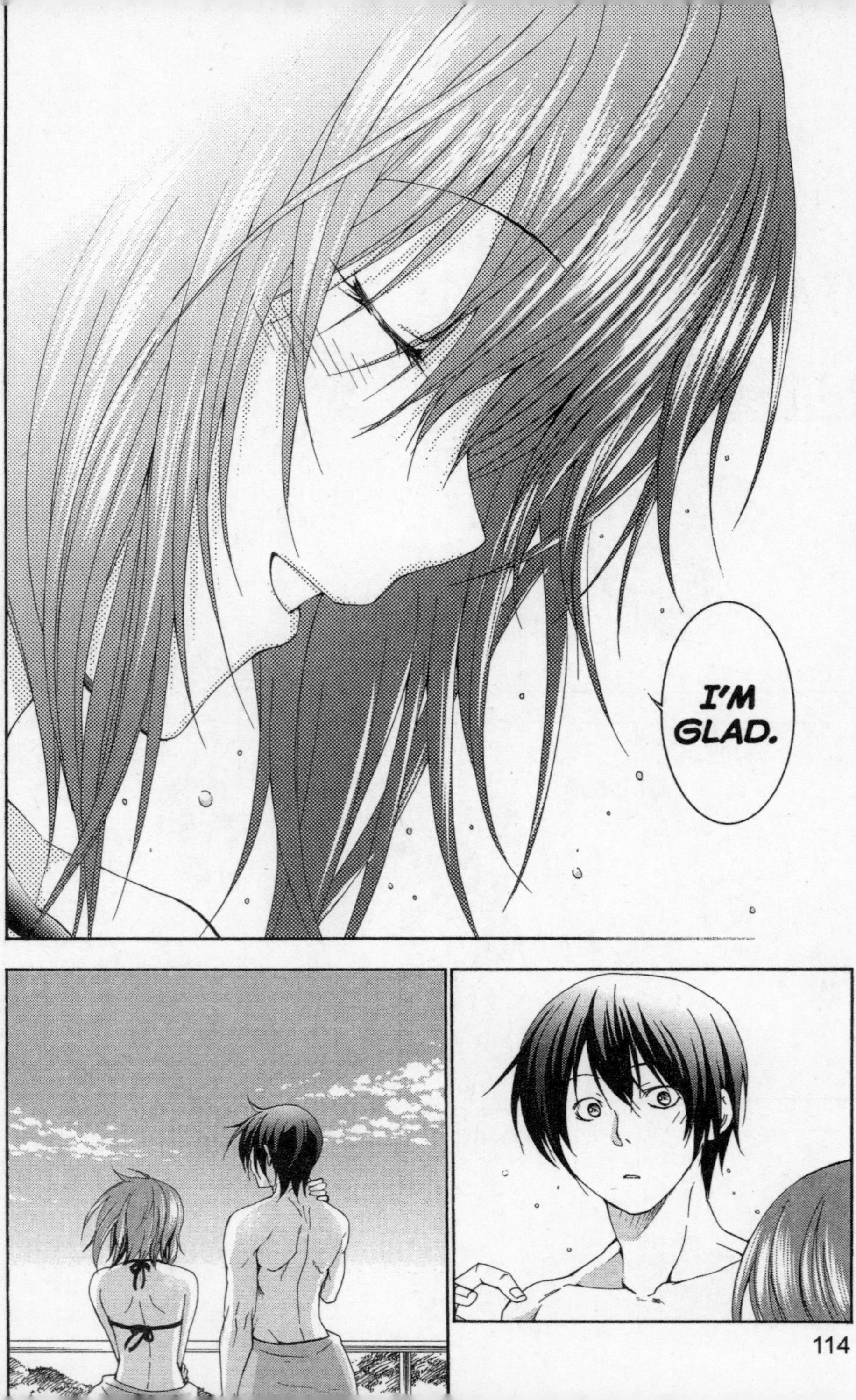
I'M GLAD.

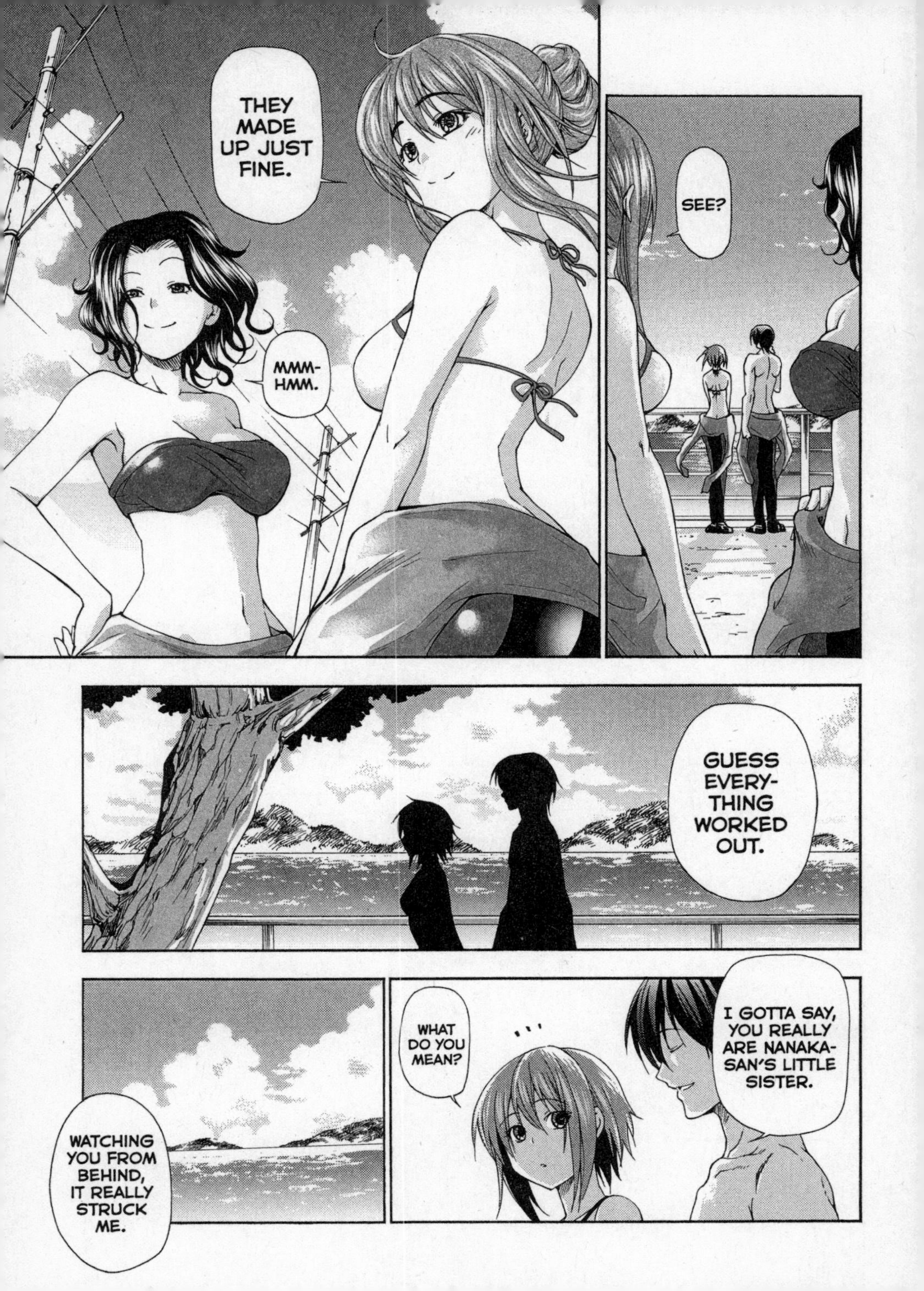
SEE?
THEY MADE UP JUST FINE.
MMM-HMM.
GUESS EVERY-THING WORKED OUT.
I GOTTA SAY, YOU REALLY ARE NANAKA-SAN'S LITTLE SISTER.
...
WHAT DO YOU MEAN?
WATCHING YOU FROM BEHIND, IT REALLY STRUCK ME.

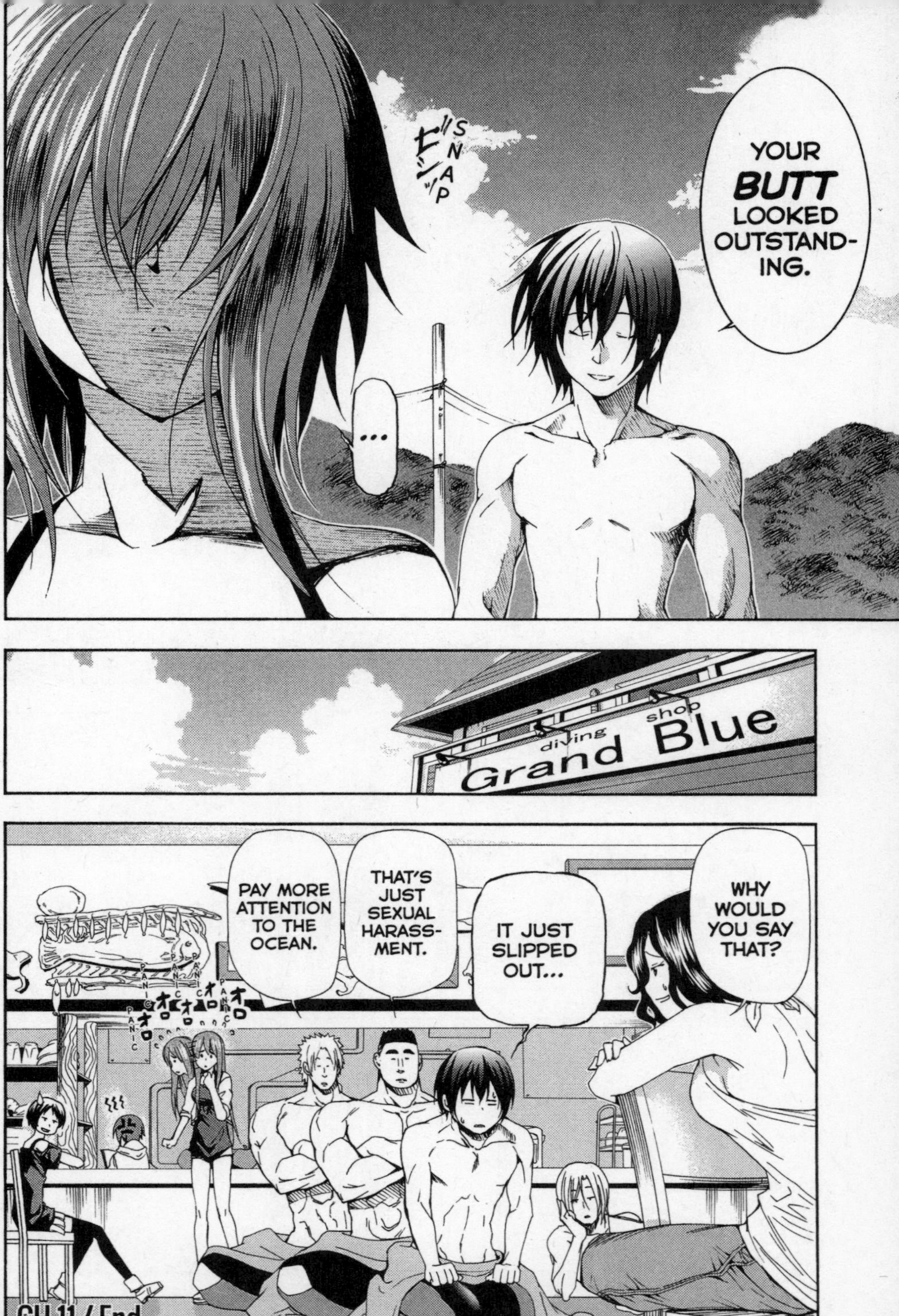

YOUR BUTT LOOKED OUTSTANDING.
...
SNAP
diving shop Grand Blue
WHY WOULD YOU SAY THAT?
IT JUST SLIPPED OUT...
THAT'S JUST SEXUAL HARASS-MENT.
PAY MORE ATTENTION TO THE OCEAN.
PANIC PANIC PANIC PANIC
CH.11 / End

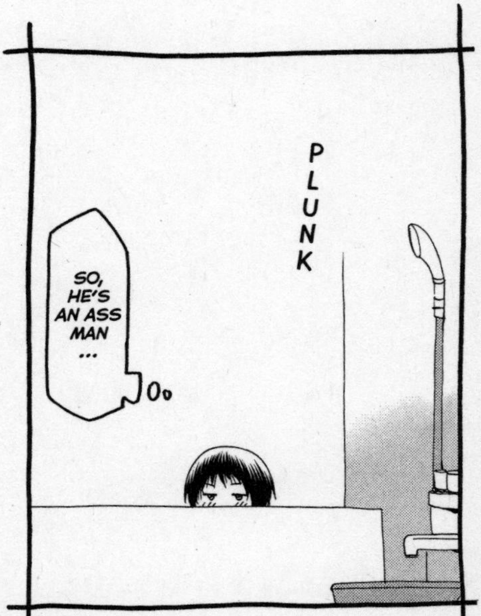
PLUNK
SO, HE'S AN ASS MAN ...

Grand Blue Dreaming

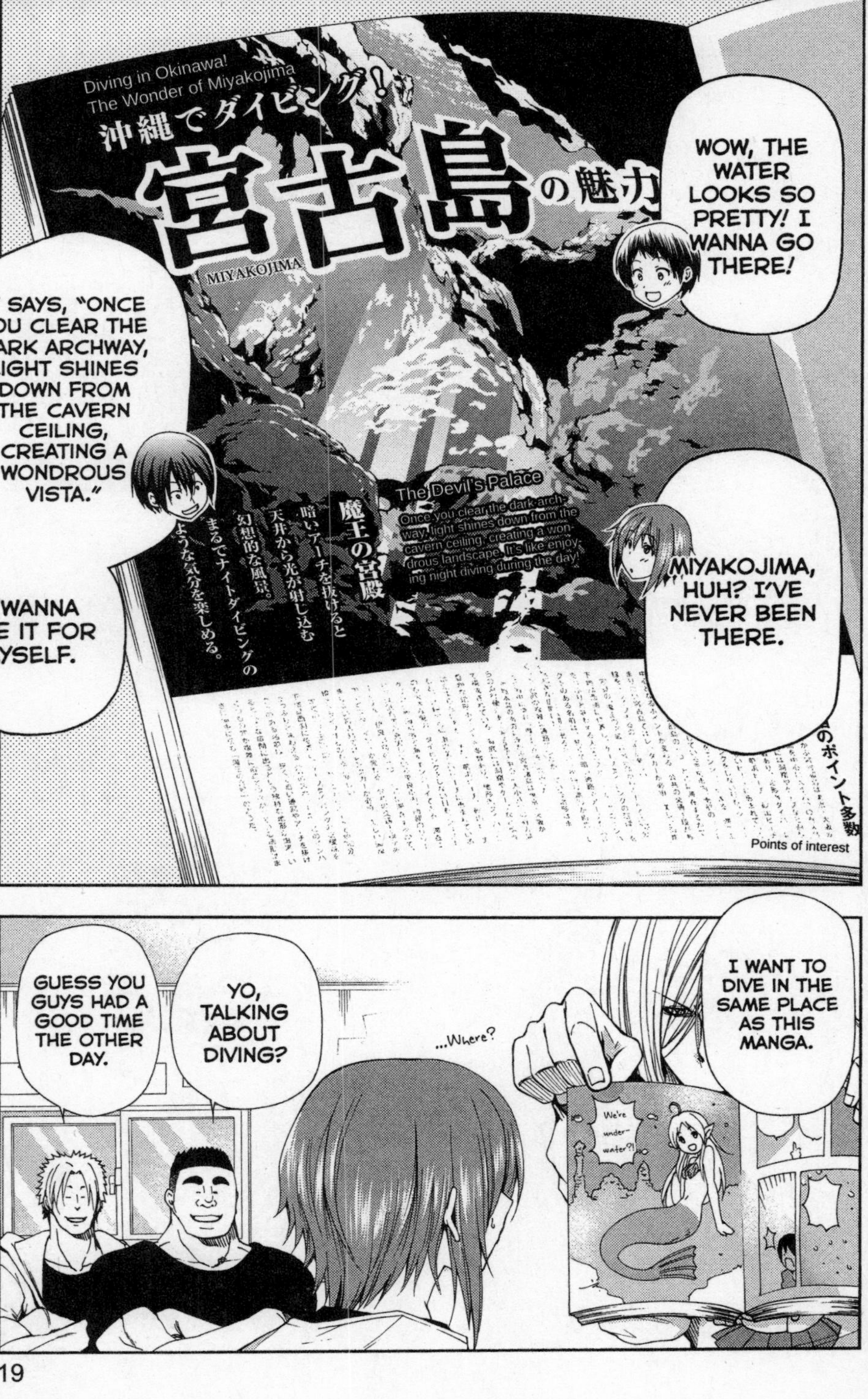
Diving in Okinawa!
The Wonder of Miyakojima
沖縄でダイビング！
宮古島の魅力
MIYAKOJIMA
WOW, THE WATER LOOKS SO PRETTY! I WANNA GO THERE!
IT SAYS, "ONCE YOU CLEAR THE DARK ARCHWAY, LIGHT SHINES DOWN FROM THE CAVERN CEILING, CREATING A WONDROUS VISTA."
魔王の宮殿
暗いアーチを抜けると天井から光が射し込む幻想的な風景。まるでナイトダイビングのような気分を楽しめる。
The Devil's Palace
Once you clear the dark archway, light shines down from the cavern ceiling, creating a wondrous landscape. It's like enjoying night diving during the day!
MIYAKOJIMA, HUH? I'VE NEVER BEEN THERE.
I WANNA SEE IT FOR MYSELF.
のポイント多数
Points of interest
I WANT TO DIVE IN THE SAME PLACE AS THIS MANGA.
...Where?
We're underwater?!
YO, TALKING ABOUT DIVING?
GUESS YOU GUYS HAD A GOOD TIME THE OTHER DAY.

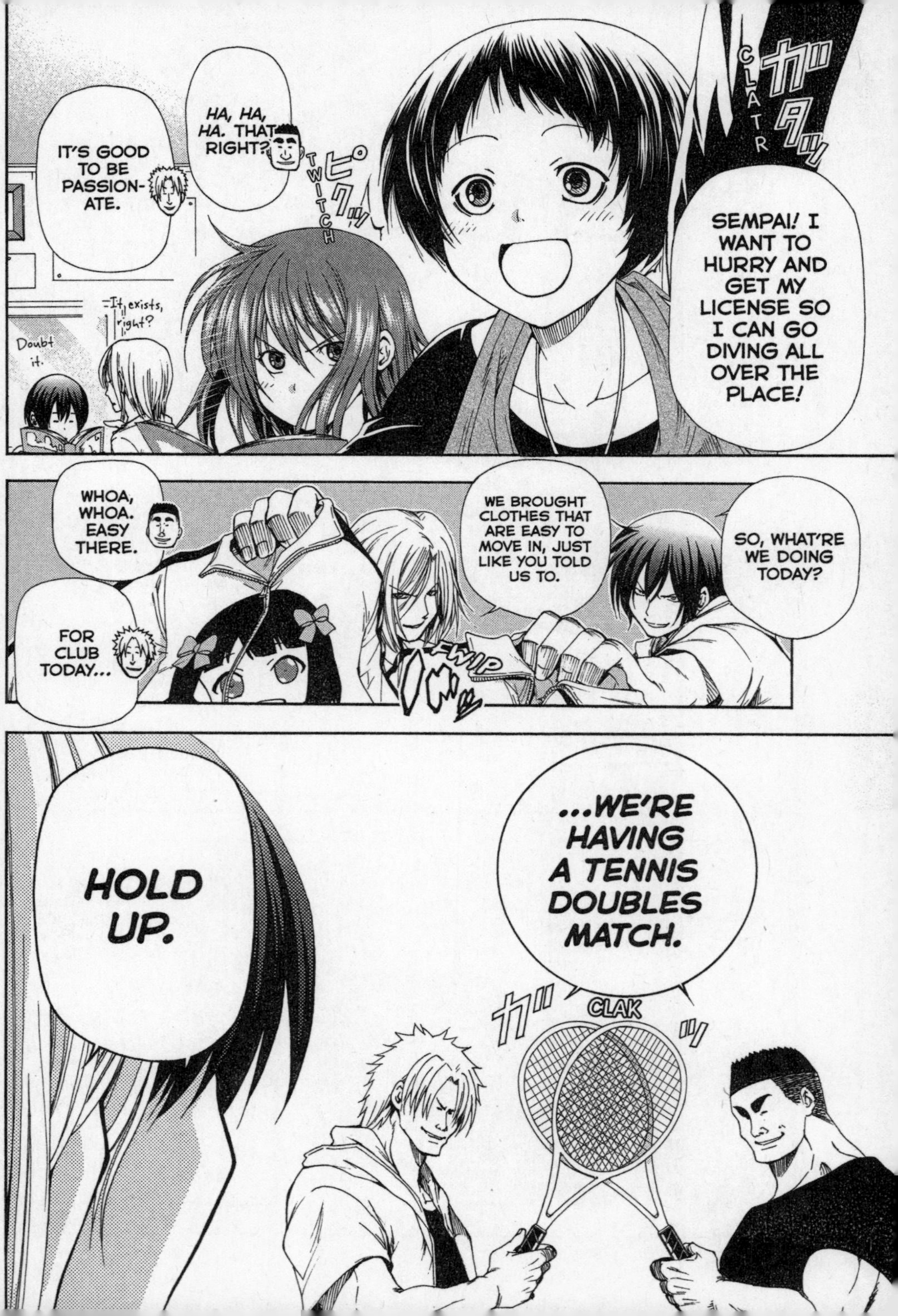
CLATR
ガタッ
SEMPAI! I WANT TO HURRY AND GET MY LICENSE SO I CAN GO DIVING ALL OVER THE PLACE!
TWITCH
ピクッ
HA, HA, HA. THAT RIGHT?
IT'S GOOD TO BE PASSION-ATE.
It exists, right?
Doubt it.
SO, WHAT'RE WE DOING TODAY?
WE BROUGHT CLOTHES THAT ARE EASY TO MOVE IN, JUST LIKE YOU TOLD US TO.
FWIP
WHOA, WHOA. EASY THERE.
FOR CLUB TODAY...
...WE'RE HAVING A TENNIS DOUBLES MATCH.
CLAK
ガッ
HOLD UP.

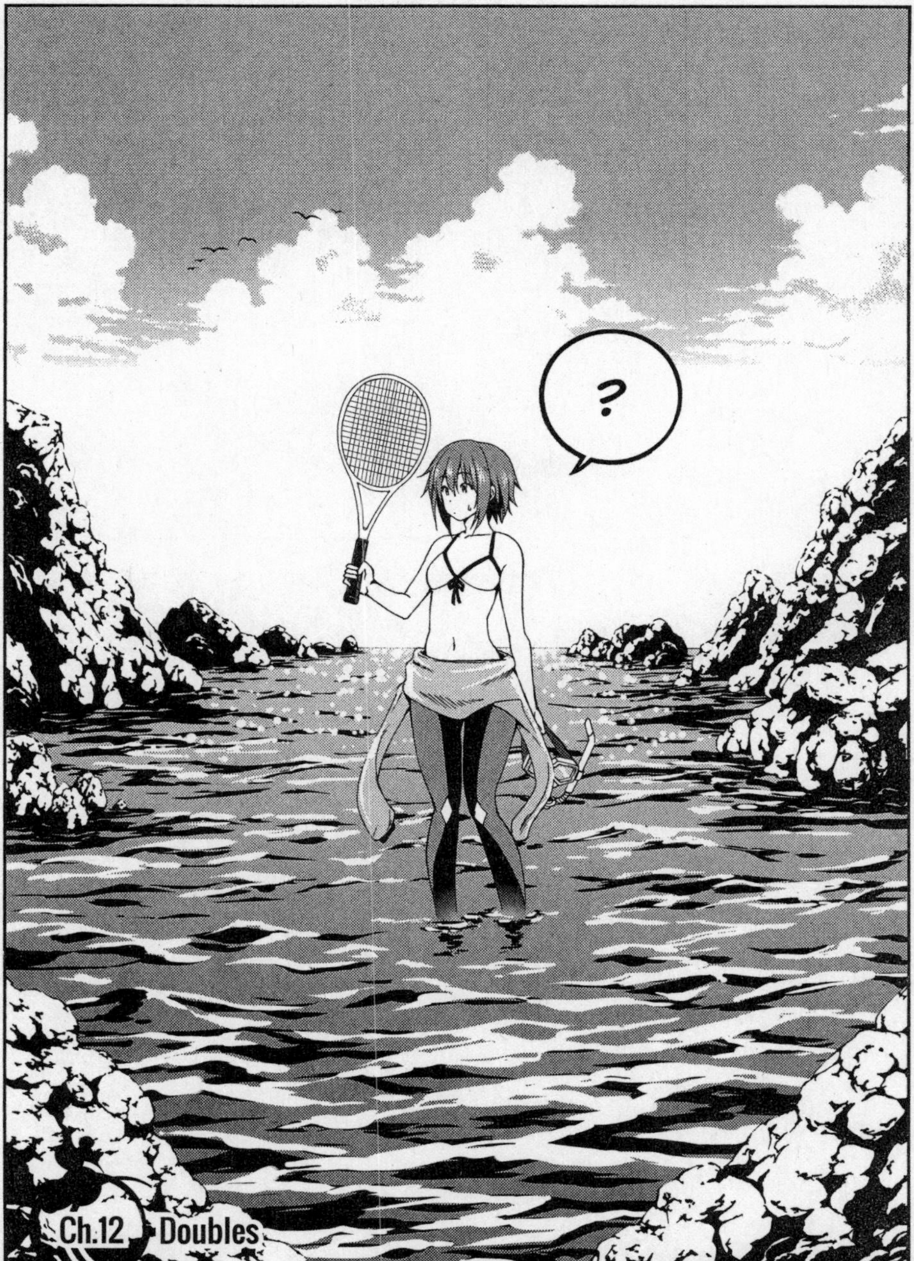
?
Ch.12 Doubles

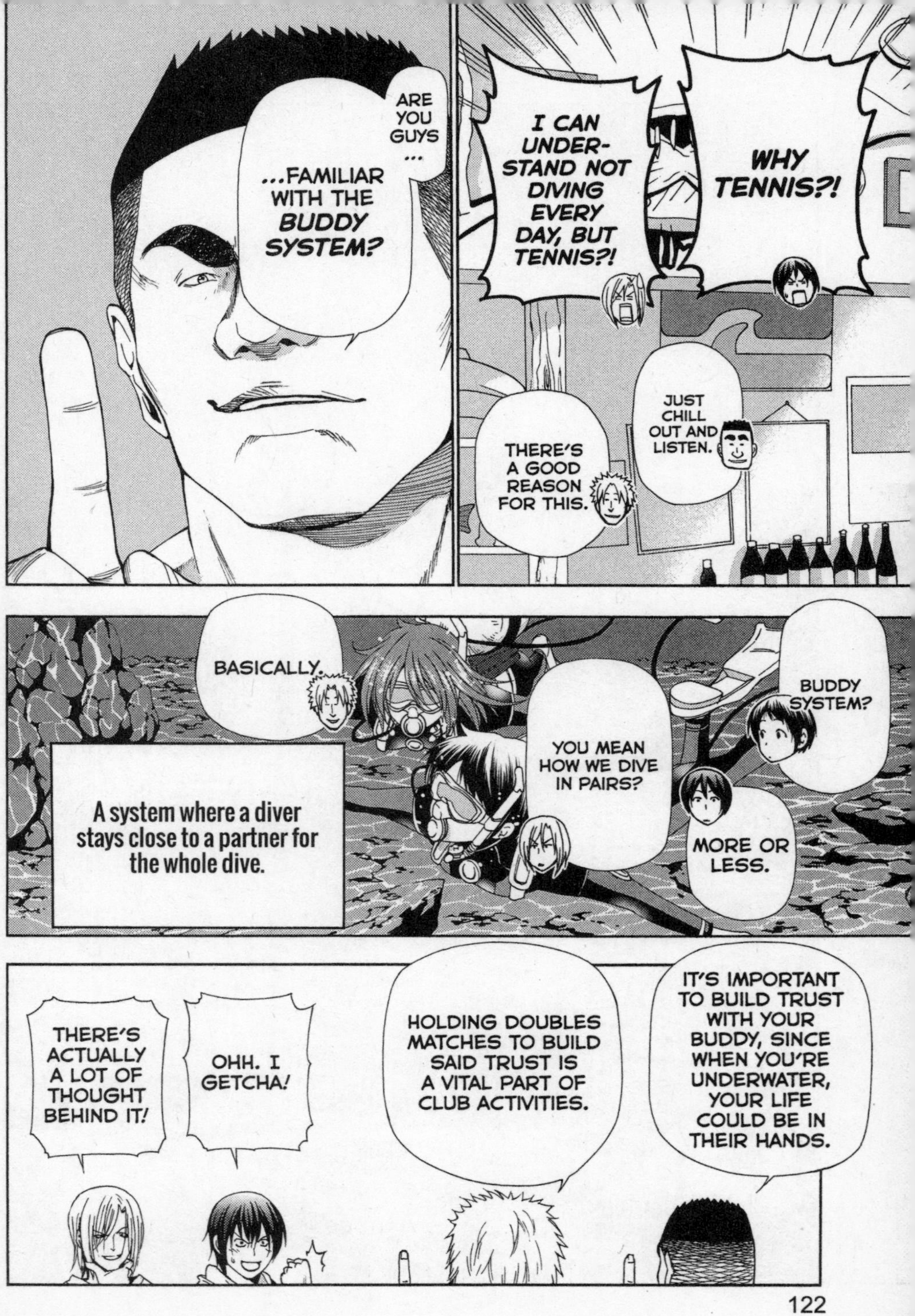
WHY TENNIS?!
I CAN UNDER-STAND NOT DIVING EVERY DAY, BUT TENNIS?!
JUST CHILL OUT AND LISTEN.
THERE'S A GOOD REASON FOR THIS.
ARE YOU GUYS...
...FAMILIAR WITH THE BUDDY SYSTEM?
BUDDY SYSTEM?
YOU MEAN HOW WE DIVE IN PAIRS?
MORE OR LESS.
BASICALLY.
A system where a diver stays close to a partner for the whole dive.
IT'S IMPORTANT TO BUILD TRUST WITH YOUR BUDDY, SINCE WHEN YOU'RE UNDERWATER, YOUR LIFE COULD BE IN THEIR HANDS.
HOLDING DOUBLES MATCHES TO BUILD SAID TRUST IS A VITAL PART OF CLUB ACTIVITIES.
OHH. I GETCHA!
THERE'S ACTUALLY A LOT OF THOUGHT BEHIND IT!

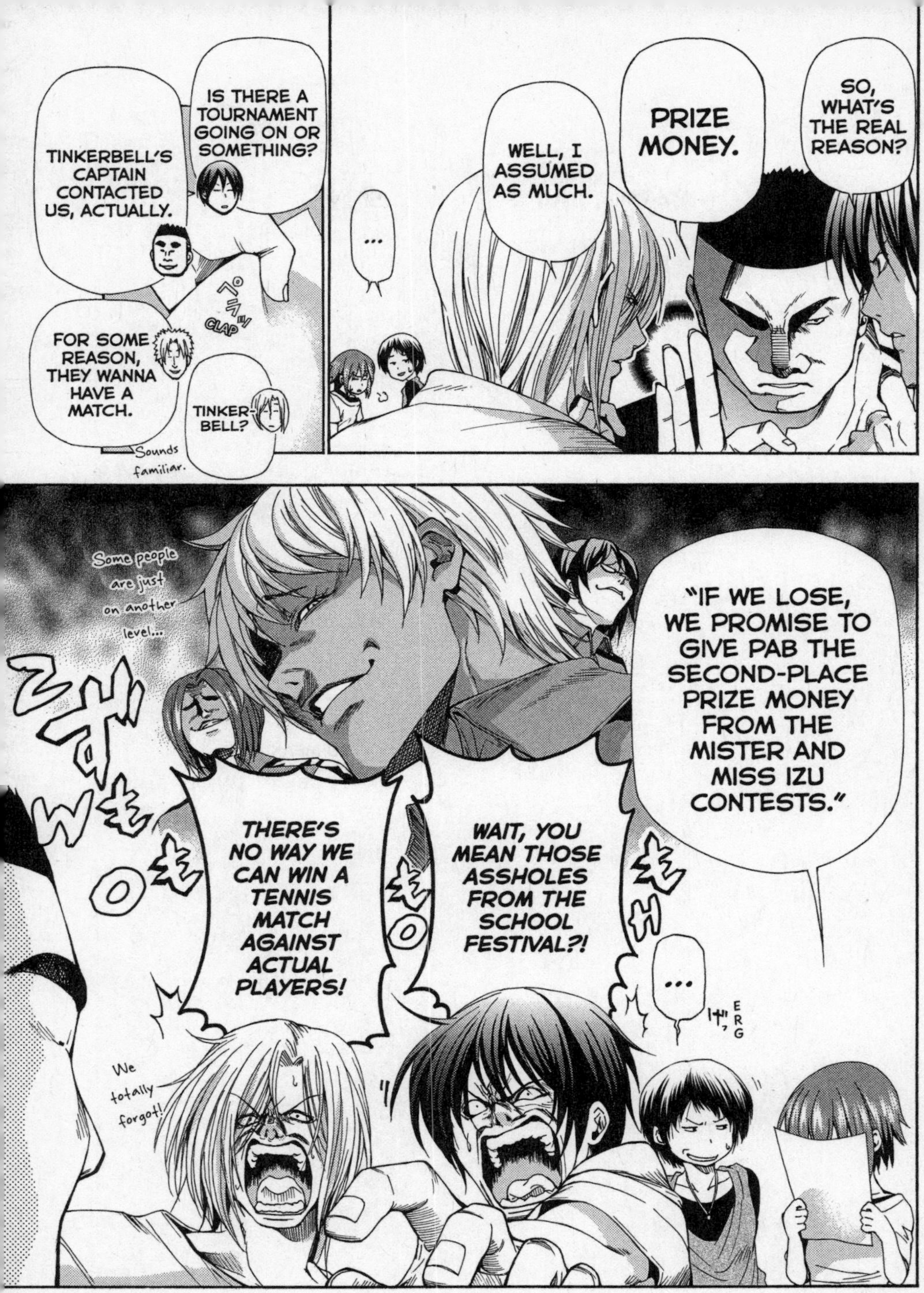
SO, WHAT'S THE REAL REASON?
PRIZE MONEY.
WELL, I ASSUMED AS MUCH.
...
IS THERE A TOURNAMENT GOING ON OR SOMETHING?
TINKERBELL'S CAPTAIN CONTACTED US, ACTUALLY.
CLAP
FOR SOME REASON, THEY WANNA HAVE A MATCH.
TINKER-BELL?
Sounds familiar.
"IF WE LOSE, WE PROMISE TO GIVE PAB THE SECOND-PLACE PRIZE MONEY FROM THE MISTER AND MISS IZU CONTESTS."
...
ERG
WAIT, YOU MEAN THOSE ASSHOLES FROM THE SCHOOL FESTIVAL?!
THERE'S NO WAY WE CAN WIN A TENNIS MATCH AGAINST ACTUAL PLAYERS!
Some people are just on another level...
We totally forgot!

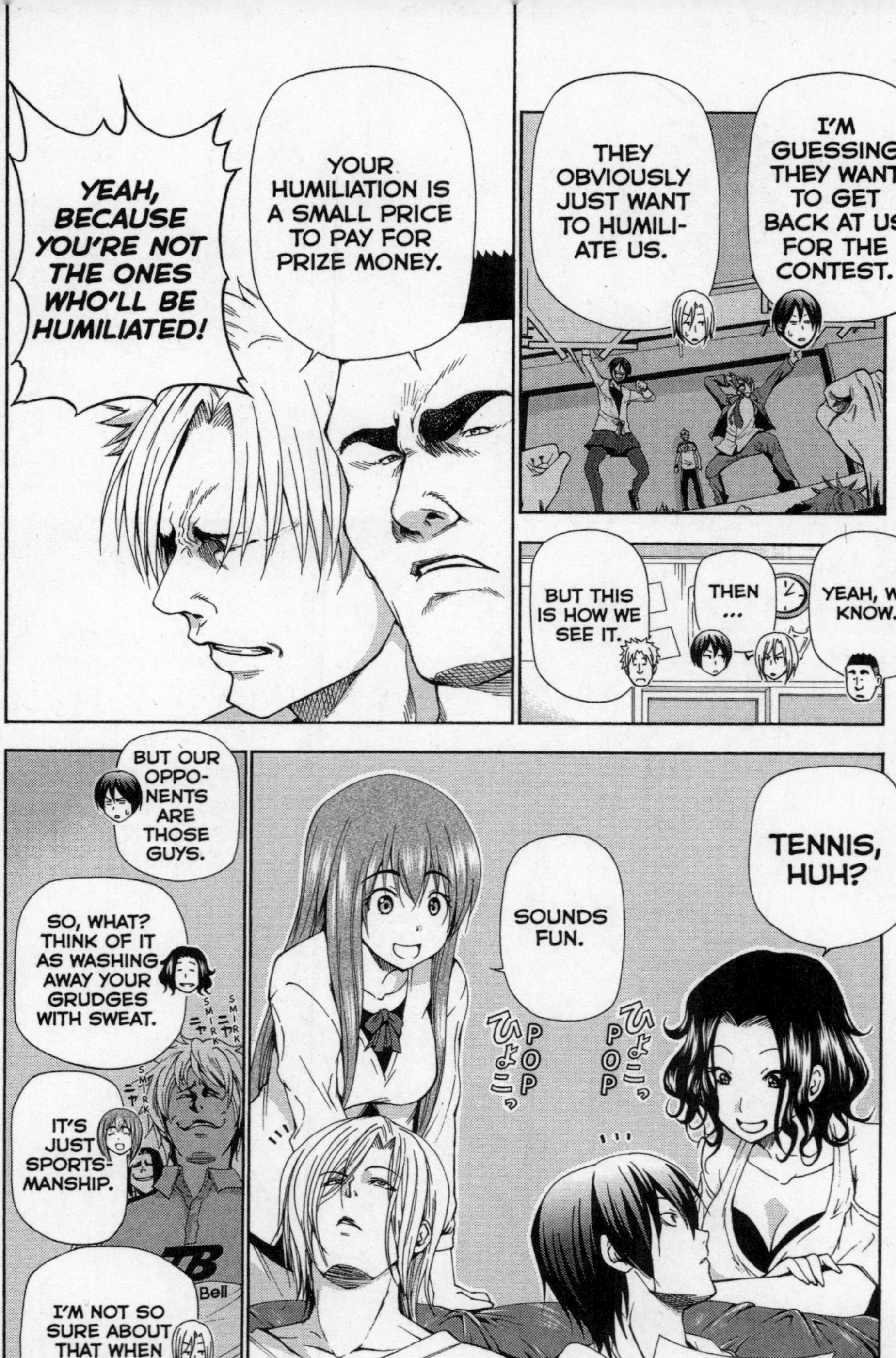
I'M GUESSING THEY WANT TO GET BACK AT US FOR THE CONTEST.
THEY OBVIOUSLY JUST WANT TO HUMILI-ATE US.
YEAH, WE KNOW.
THEN ...
BUT THIS IS HOW WE SEE IT.
YOUR HUMILIATION IS A SMALL PRICE TO PAY FOR PRIZE MONEY.
YEAH, BECAUSE YOU'RE NOT THE ONES WHO'LL BE HUMILIATED!
TENNIS, HUH?
SOUNDS FUN.
ひょこっ POP
ひょこっ POP
BUT OUR OPPO-NENTS ARE THOSE GUYS.
SO, WHAT? THINK OF IT AS WASHING AWAY YOUR GRUDGES WITH SWEAT.
SMIRK SMIRK
SMIRK
IT'S JUST SPORTS-MANSHIP.
Bell
I'M NOT SO SURE ABOUT THAT WHEN MONEY'S ON THE LINE.

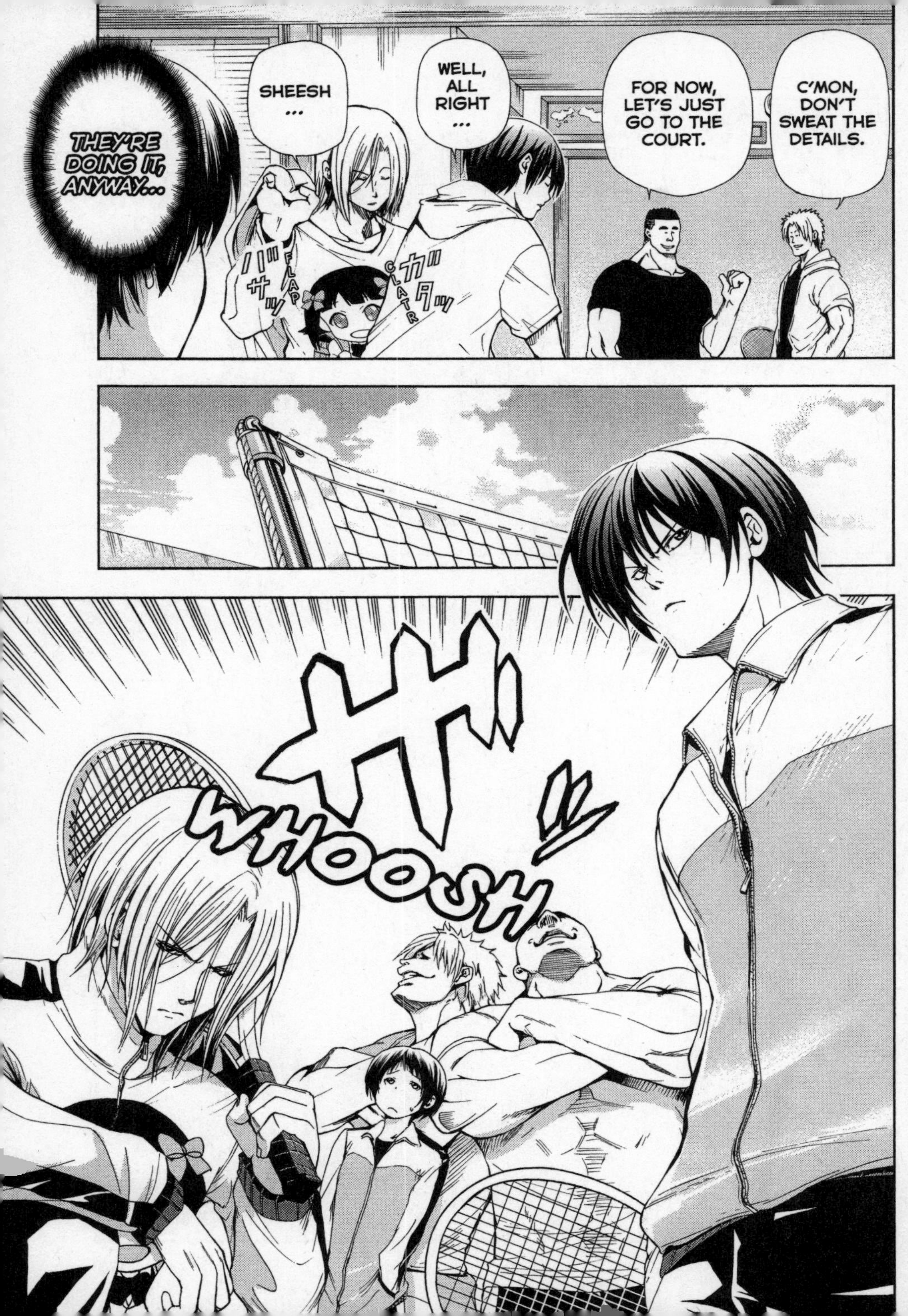
C'MON, DON'T SWEAT THE DETAILS.
FOR NOW, LET'S JUST GO TO THE COURT.
WELL, ALL RIGHT ...
SHEESH ...
THEY'RE DOING IT, ANYWAY...
ガタッ CLATR
バサッ FLAP
ザッ!! WHOOSH

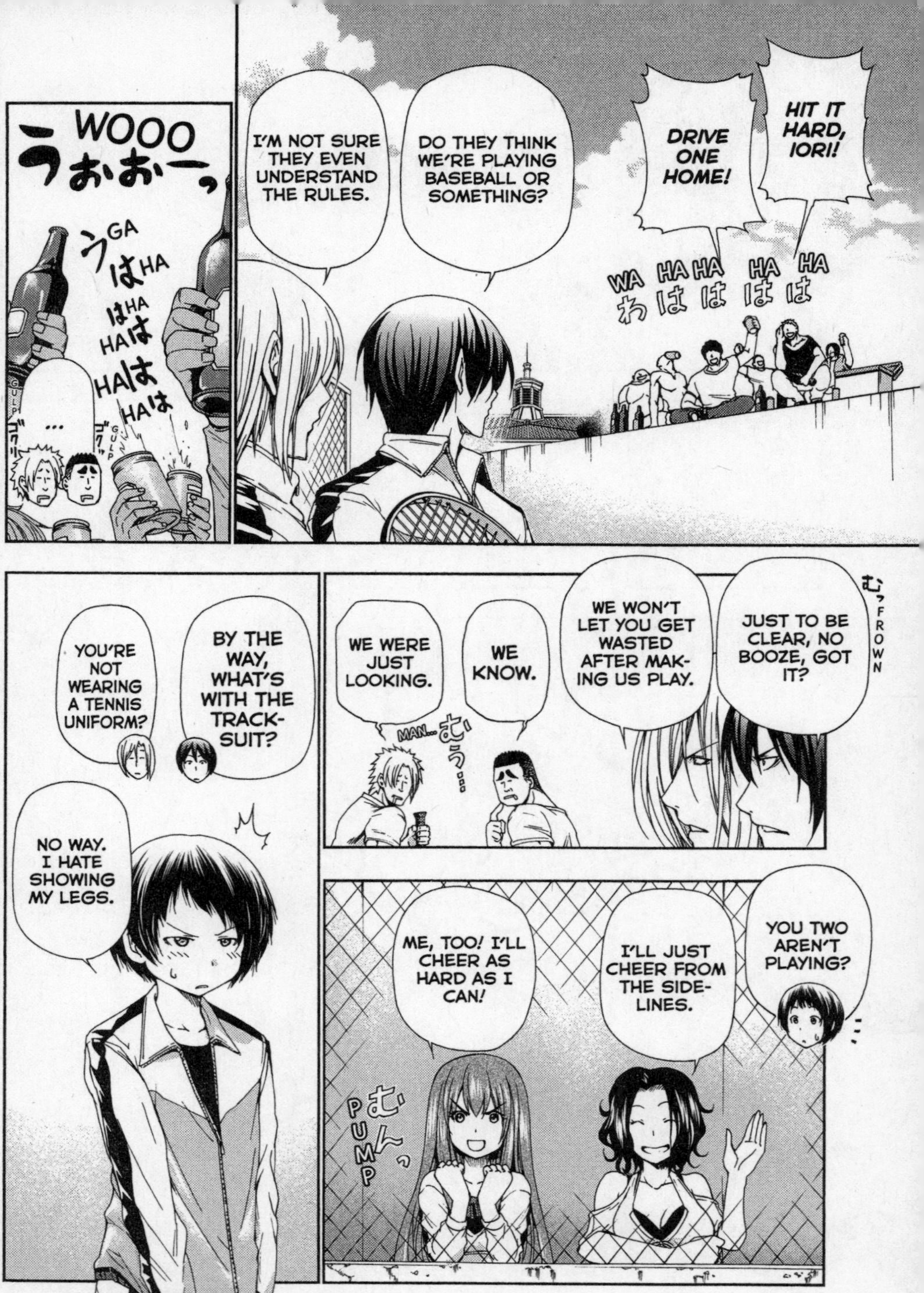

HIT IT HARD, IORI!
DRIVE ONE HOME!
WA HA HA HA HA
わははははは
DO THEY THINK WE'RE PLAYING BASEBALL OR SOMETHING?
I'M NOT SURE THEY EVEN UNDERSTAND THE RULES.
WOOO
うおおーっ
GA HA HA HA HA HA HA
うははははは
GULP GULP
ゴクッ ゴクッ
...
JUST TO BE CLEAR, NO BOOZE, GOT IT?
むっ FROWN
WE WON'T LET YOU GET WASTED AFTER MAKING US PLAY.
WE KNOW.
WE WERE JUST LOOKING.
MAN... むう...
YOU TWO AREN'T PLAYING?
I'LL JUST CHEER FROM THE SIDELINES.
ME, TOO! I'LL CHEER AS HARD AS I CAN!
PUMP PUMP むんっ
BY THE WAY, WHAT'S WITH THE TRACKSUIT?
YOU'RE NOT WEARING A TENNIS UNIFORM?
NO WAY. I HATE SHOWING MY LEGS.

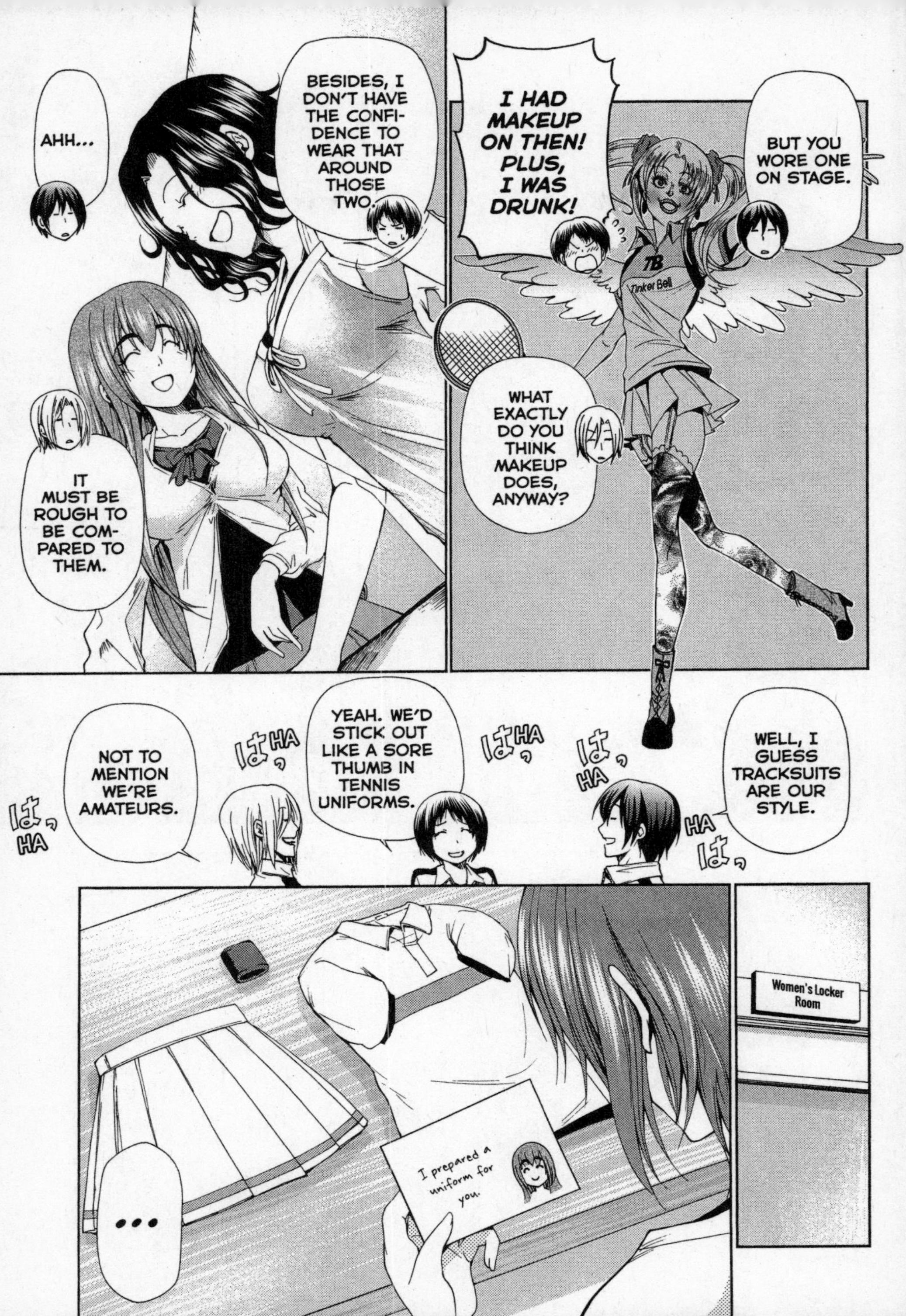
BUT YOU WORE ONE ON STAGE.
I HAD MAKEUP ON THEN! PLUS, I WAS DRUNK!
WHAT EXACTLY DO YOU THINK MAKEUP DOES, ANYWAY?
Tinker Bell
BESIDES, I DON'T HAVE THE CONFIDENCE TO WEAR THAT AROUND THOSE TWO.
AHH...
IT MUST BE ROUGH TO BE COMPARED TO THEM.
WELL, I GUESS TRACKSUITS ARE OUR STYLE.
はっ HA
はっ HA
はっ HA
YEAH. WE'D STICK OUT LIKE A SORE THUMB IN TENNIS UNIFORMS.
はっ HA
NOT TO MENTION WE'RE AMATEURS.
はっ HA
Women's Locker Room
I prepared a uniform for you.
...

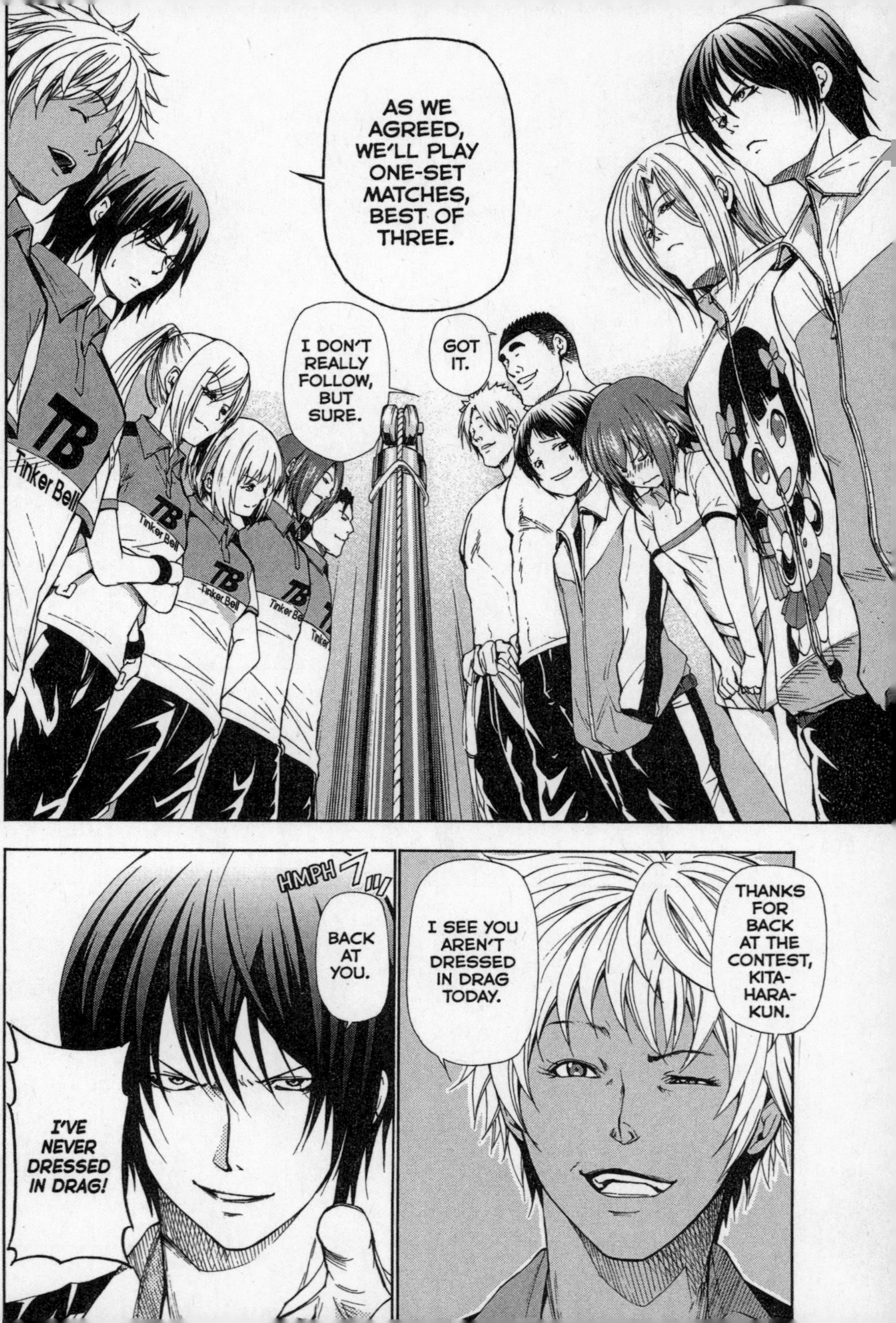
AS WE AGREED, WE'LL PLAY ONE-SET MATCHES, BEST OF THREE.
GOT IT.
I DON'T REALLY FOLLOW, BUT SURE.
Tinker Bell
THANKS FOR BACK AT THE CONTEST, KITA-HARA-KUN.
I SEE YOU AREN'T DRESSED IN DRAG TODAY.
HMPH
BACK AT YOU.
I'VE NEVER DRESSED IN DRAG!

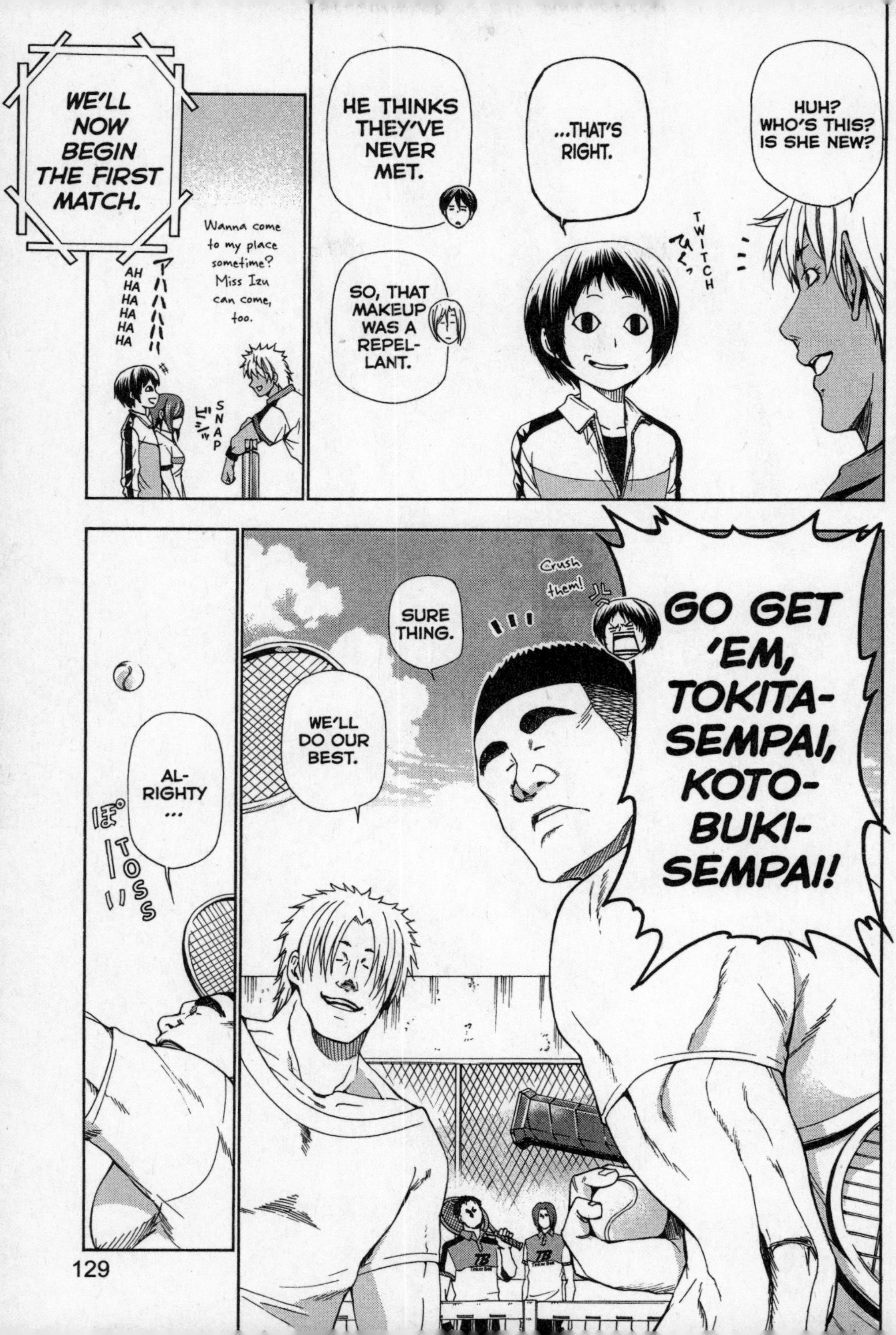
HUH? WHO'S THIS? IS SHE NEW?
TWITCH
...THAT'S RIGHT.
HE THINKS THEY'VE NEVER MET.
SO, THAT MAKEUP WAS A REPELLANT.
WE'LL NOW BEGIN THE FIRST MATCH.
Wanna come to my place sometime? Miss Izu can come, too.
AH HA HA HA HA HA
SNAP
GO GET 'EM, TOKITA-SEMPAI, KOTOBUKI-SEMPAI!
Crush them!
SURE THING.
WE'LL DO OUR BEST.
ALRIGHTY...
TOSS

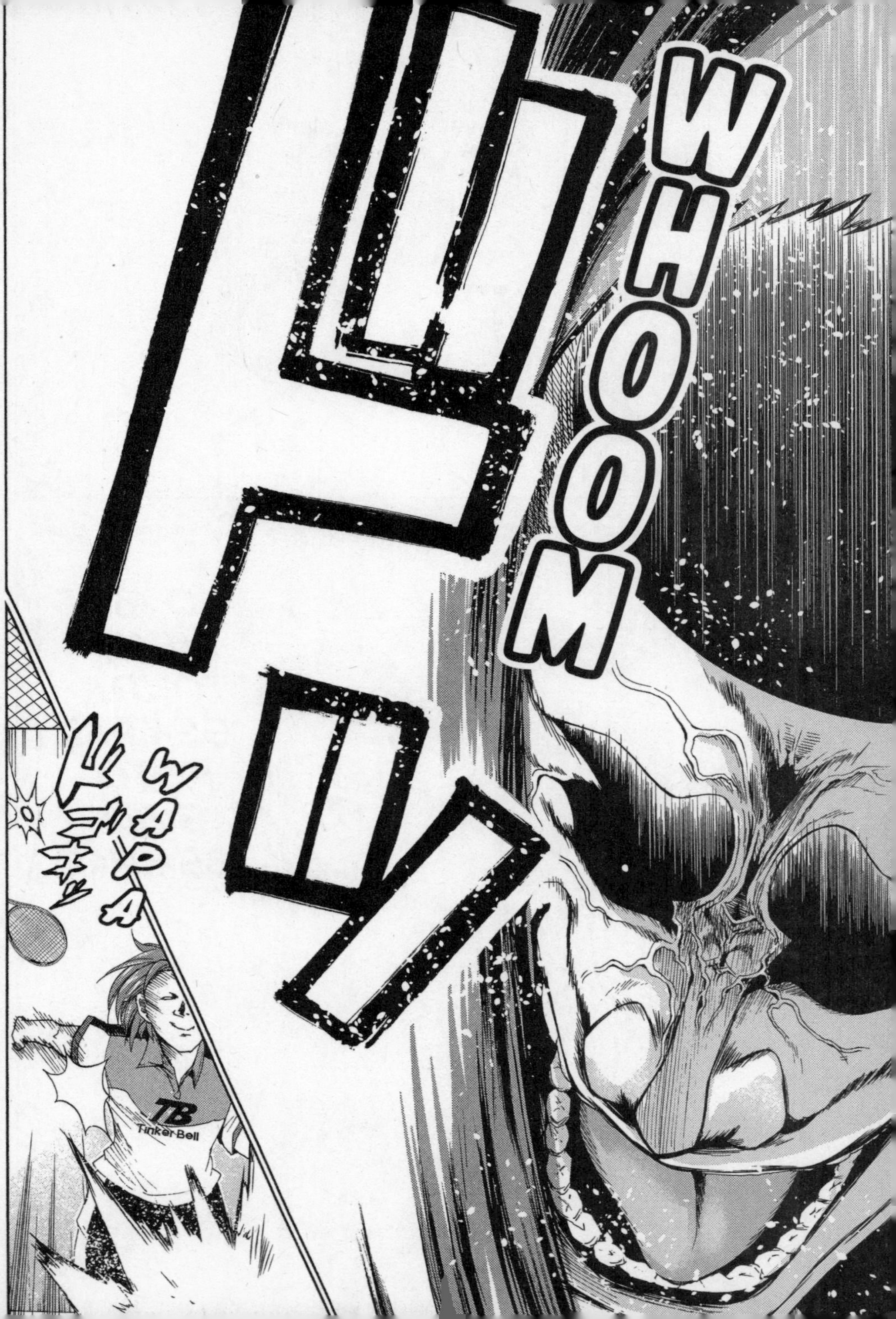
WHOOM
ドゴッ
WAPA
パキャ
TB
Tinker Bell

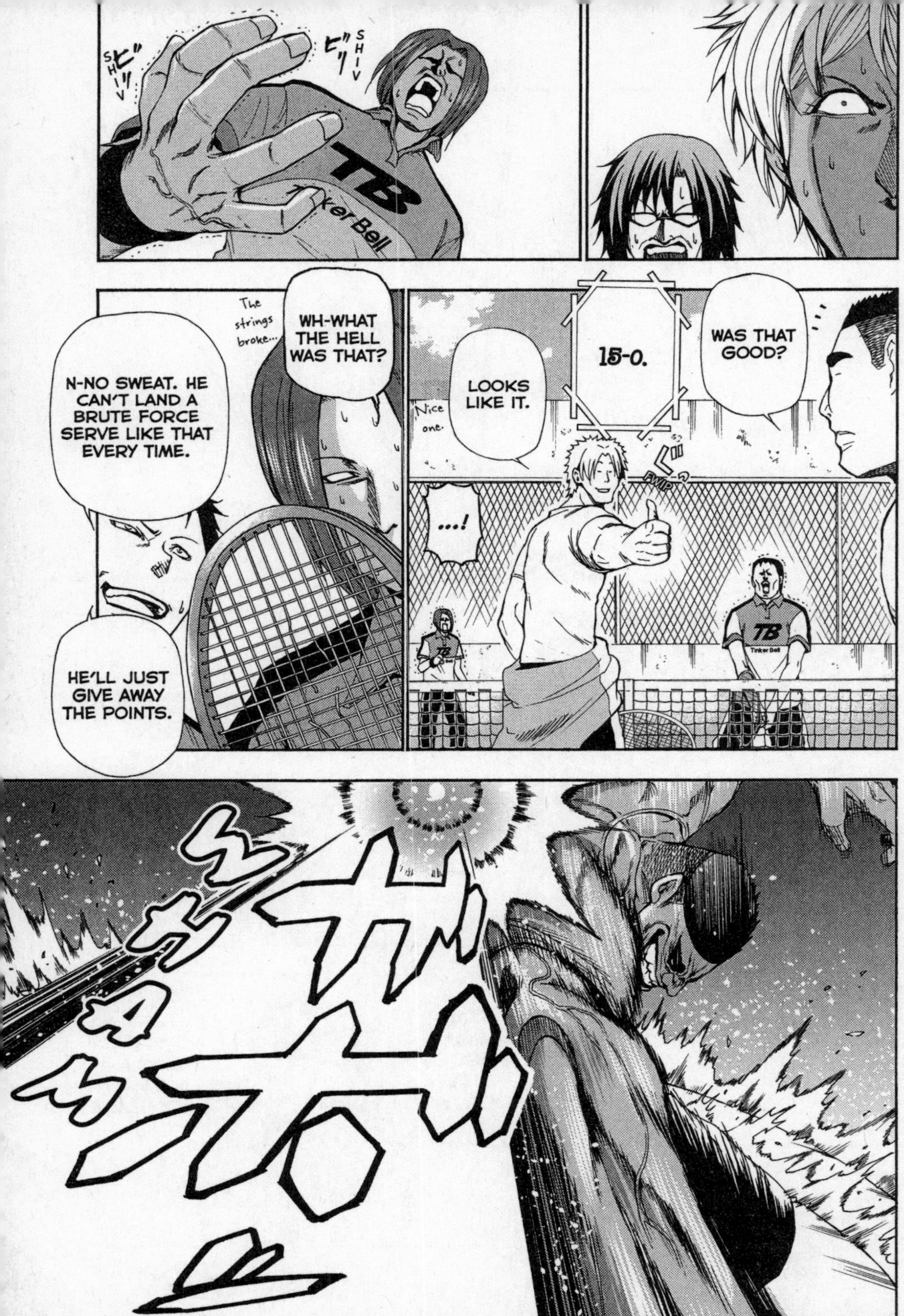
SHIV
SHIV
WAS THAT GOOD?
15-0.
LOOKS LIKE IT.
Nice one.
FWIP
...!
WH-WHAT THE HELL WAS THAT?
The strings broke...
N-NO SWEAT. HE CAN'T LAND A BRUTE FORCE SERVE LIKE THAT EVERY TIME.
HE'LL JUST GIVE AWAY THE POINTS.

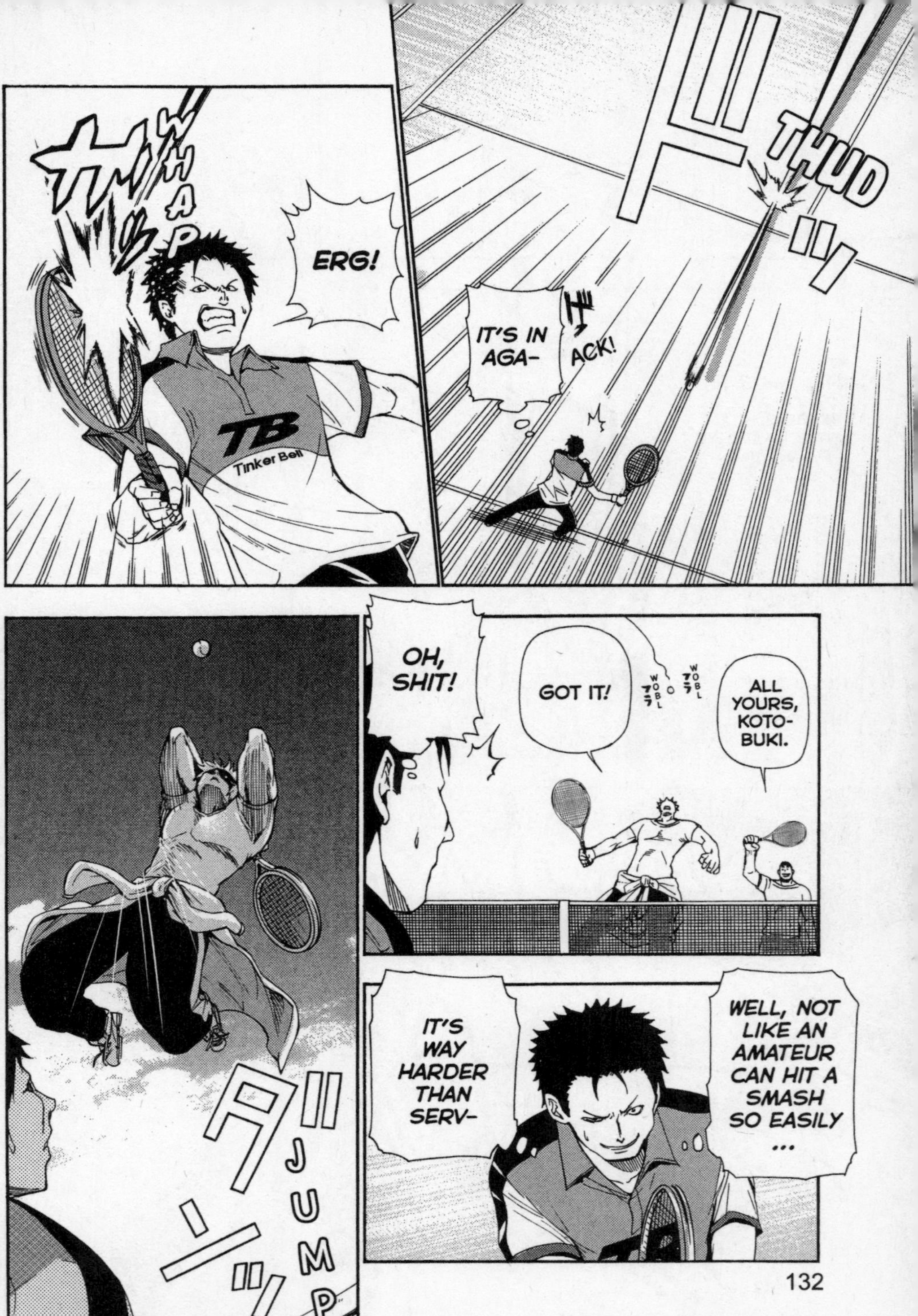
THUD
IT'S IN AGA-
ACK!
WHAP
ERG!
ALL YOURS, KOTOBUKI.
WOBL
WOBL
GOT IT!
OH, SHIT!
WELL, NOT LIKE AN AMATEUR CAN HIT A SMASH SO EASILY ...
IT'S WAY HARDER THAN SERV-
JUMP

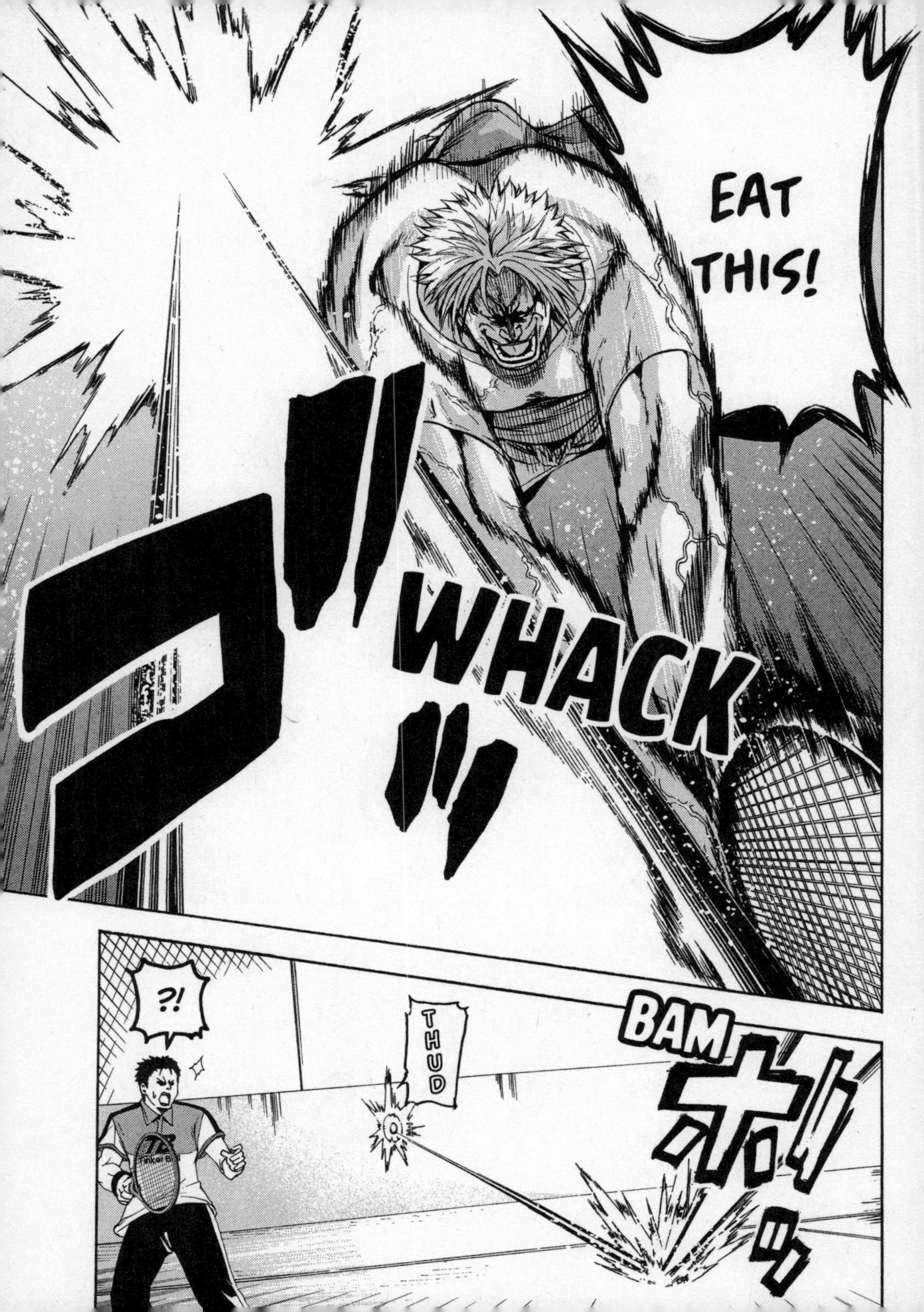
EAT THIS!
WHACK
BAM
THUD
?!

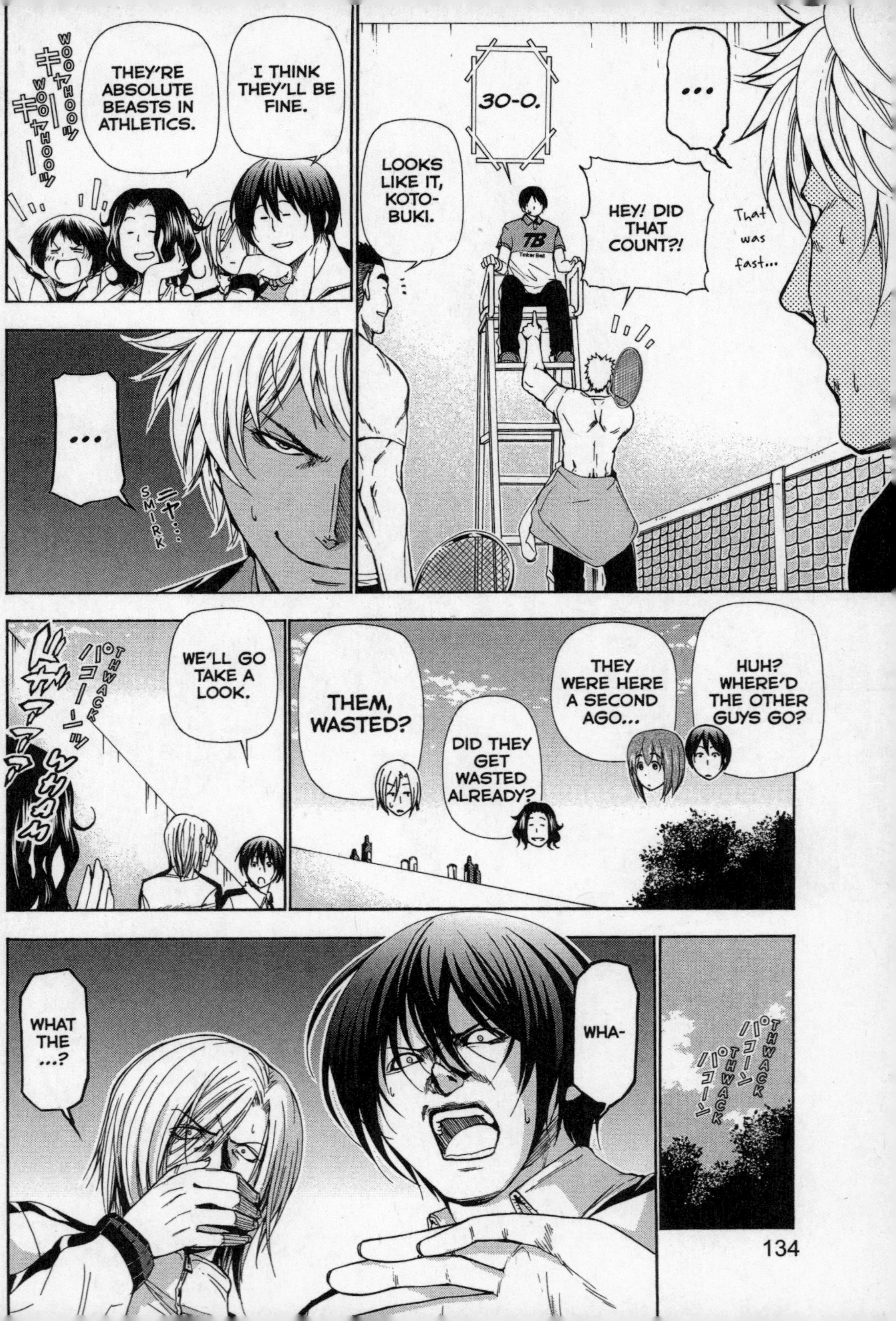
...
That was fast...
30-0.
HEY! DID THAT COUNT?!
LOOKS LIKE IT, KOTO-BUKI.
I THINK THEY'LL BE FINE.
THEY'RE ABSOLUTE BEASTS IN ATHLETICS.
キャーーッ WOOHOO
キャーーッ WOOHOO
...
ニヤ... SMIRK
HUH? WHERE'D THE OTHER GUYS GO?
THEY WERE HERE A SECOND AGO...
DID THEY GET WASTED ALREADY?
THEM, WASTED?
WE'LL GO TAKE A LOOK.
パコーーンッ THWACK
ドガァァァ WHAM
パコーン THWACK
パコーン THWACK
WHA-
WHAT THE ...?

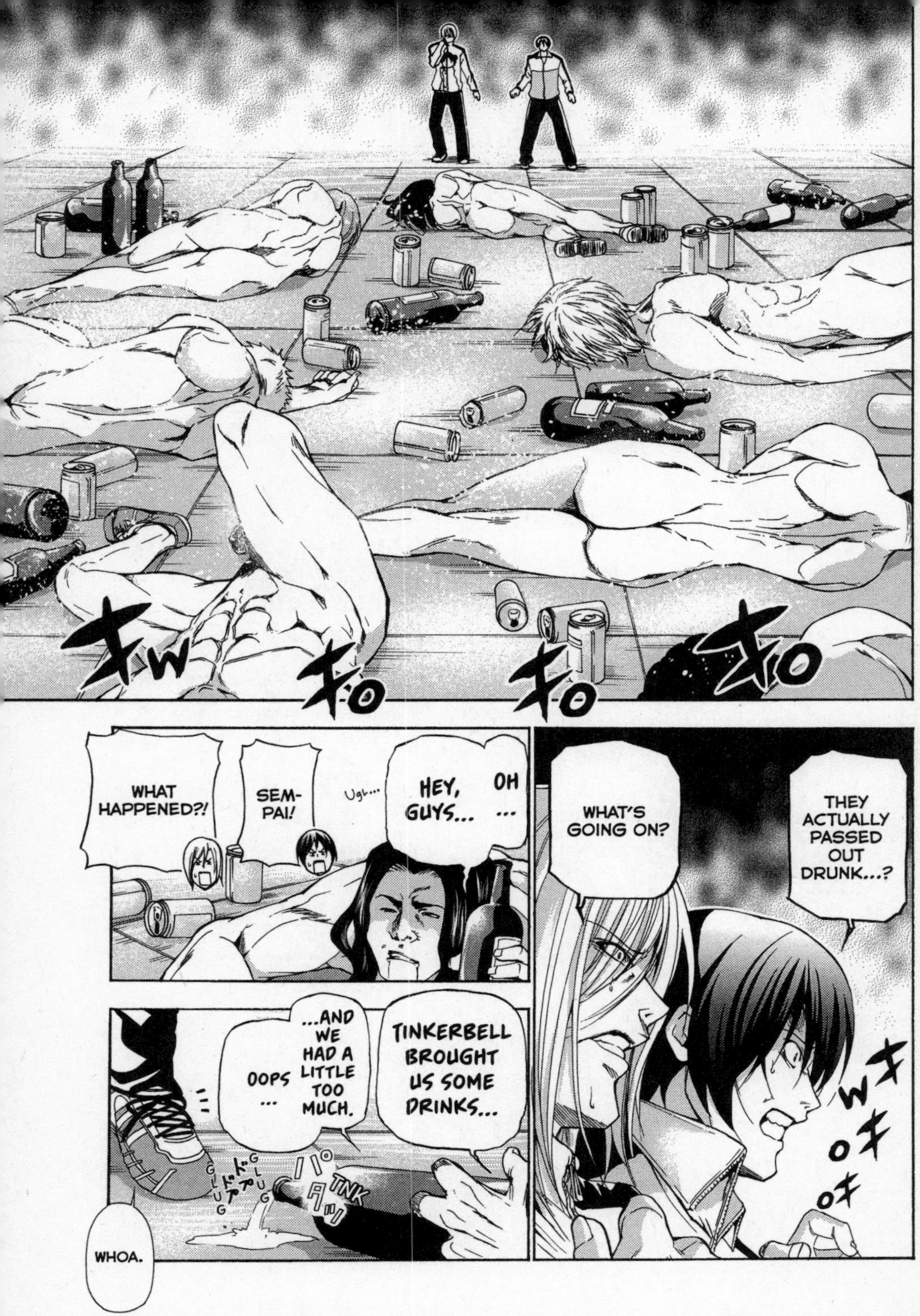
THEY ACTUALLY PASSED OUT DRUNK...?
WHAT'S GOING ON?
OH ...
HEY, GUYS...
Ugh...
SEM-PAI!
WHAT HAPPENED?!
TINKERBELL BROUGHT US SOME DRINKS...
...AND WE HAD A LITTLE TOO MUCH.
OOPS ...
TNK
GLUG
GLUG
WHOA.

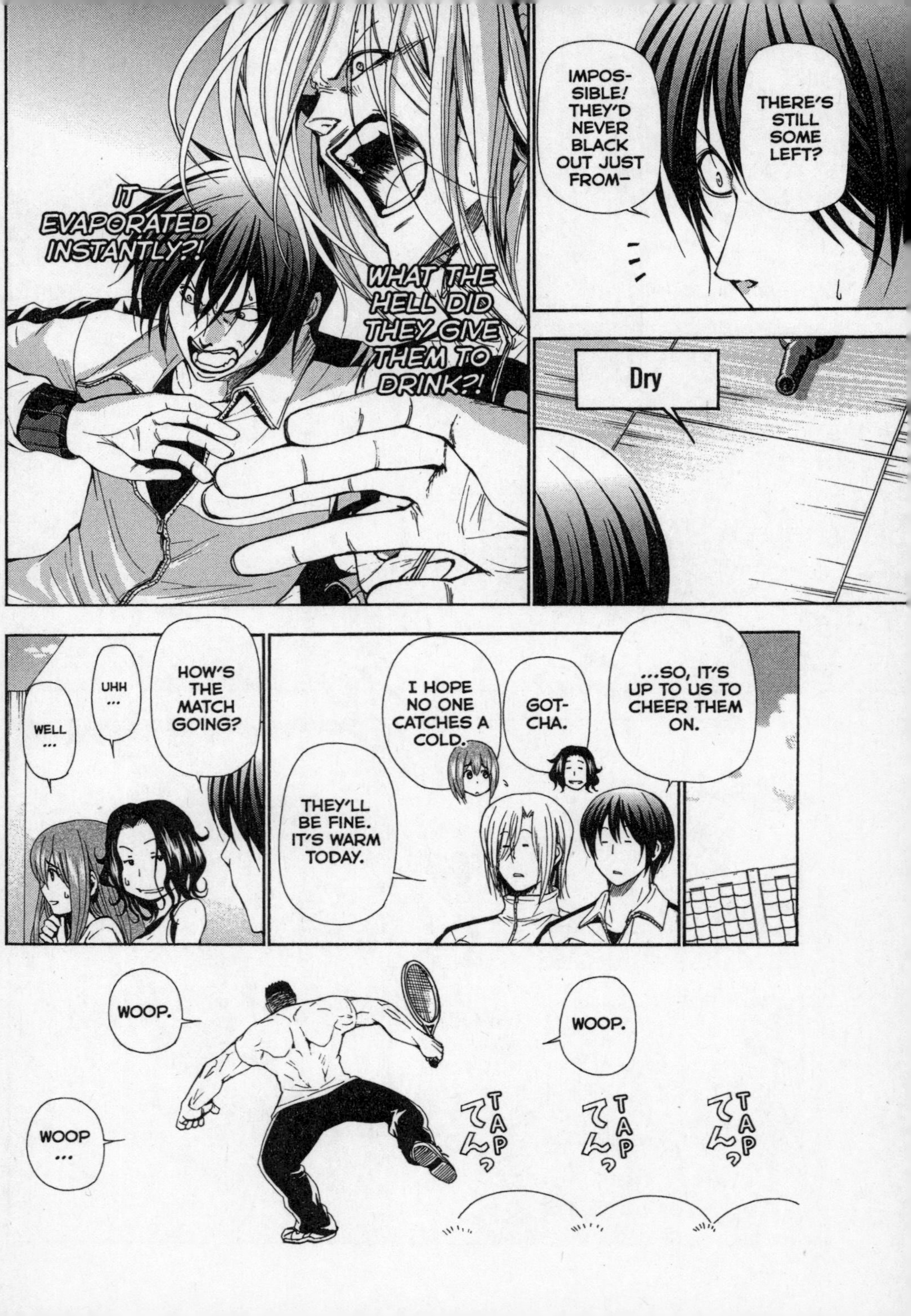
THERE'S STILL SOME LEFT?
IMPOS-SIBLE! THEY'D NEVER BLACK OUT JUST FROM-
Dry
IT EVAPORATED INSTANTLY?!
WHAT THE HELL DID THEY GIVE THEM TO DRINK?!
...SO, IT'S UP TO US TO CHEER THEM ON.
GOT-CHA.
I HOPE NO ONE CATCHES A COLD.
THEY'LL BE FINE. IT'S WARM TODAY.
HOW'S THE MATCH GOING?
UHH ...
WELL ...
WOOP.
WOOP.
TAP てんっ
TAP てんっ
TAP てんっ
WOOP ...

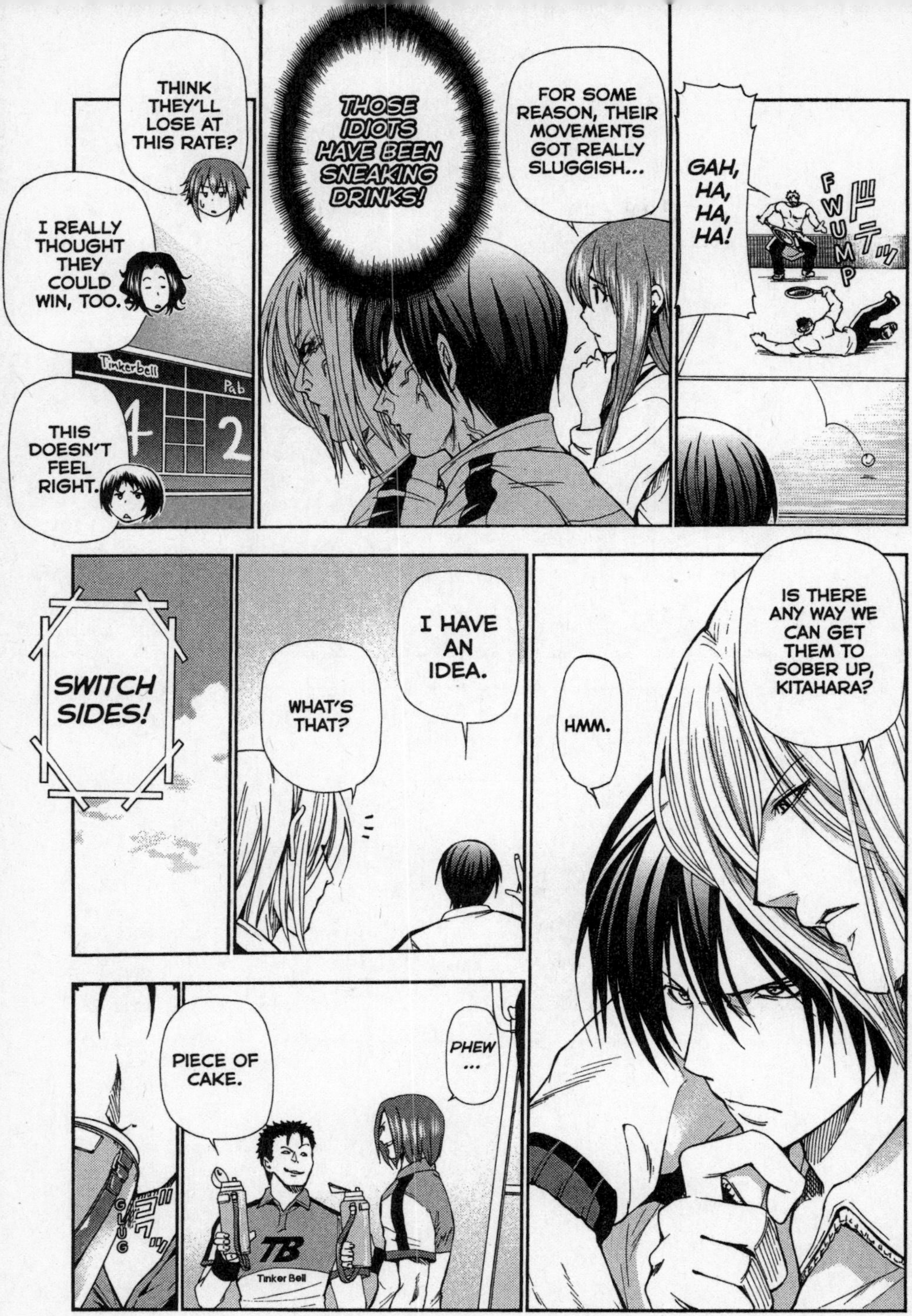
GAH, HA, HA, HA!
FWUMP
ドテッ
FOR SOME REASON, THEIR MOVEMENTS GOT REALLY SLUGGISH...
THOSE IDIOTS HAVE BEEN SNEAKING DRINKS!
THINK THEY'LL LOSE AT THIS RATE?
I REALLY THOUGHT THEY COULD WIN, TOO.
Tinkerbell
Pab
4 2
THIS DOESN'T FEEL RIGHT.
IS THERE ANY WAY WE CAN GET THEM TO SOBER UP, KITAHARA?
HMM.
I HAVE AN IDEA.
WHAT'S THAT?
SWITCH SIDES!
PHEW ...
PIECE OF CAKE.
TB
Tinker Bell
GLUG
ゴクッ

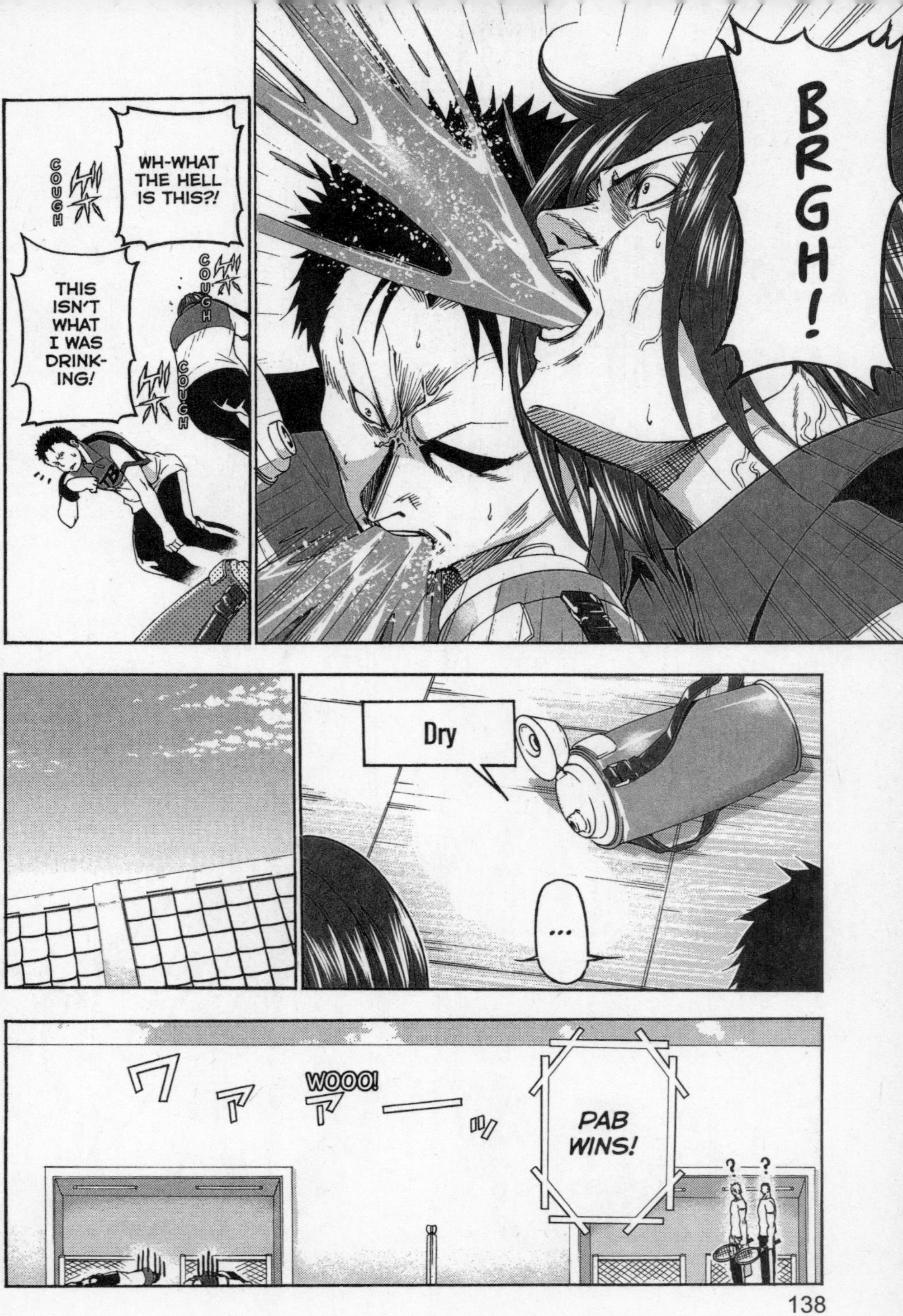
BRGH!
COUGH
WH-WHAT THE HELL IS THIS?!
COUGH
THIS ISN'T WHAT I WAS DRINK-ING!
COUGH
Dry
...
WOOO!
PAB WINS!
?
?

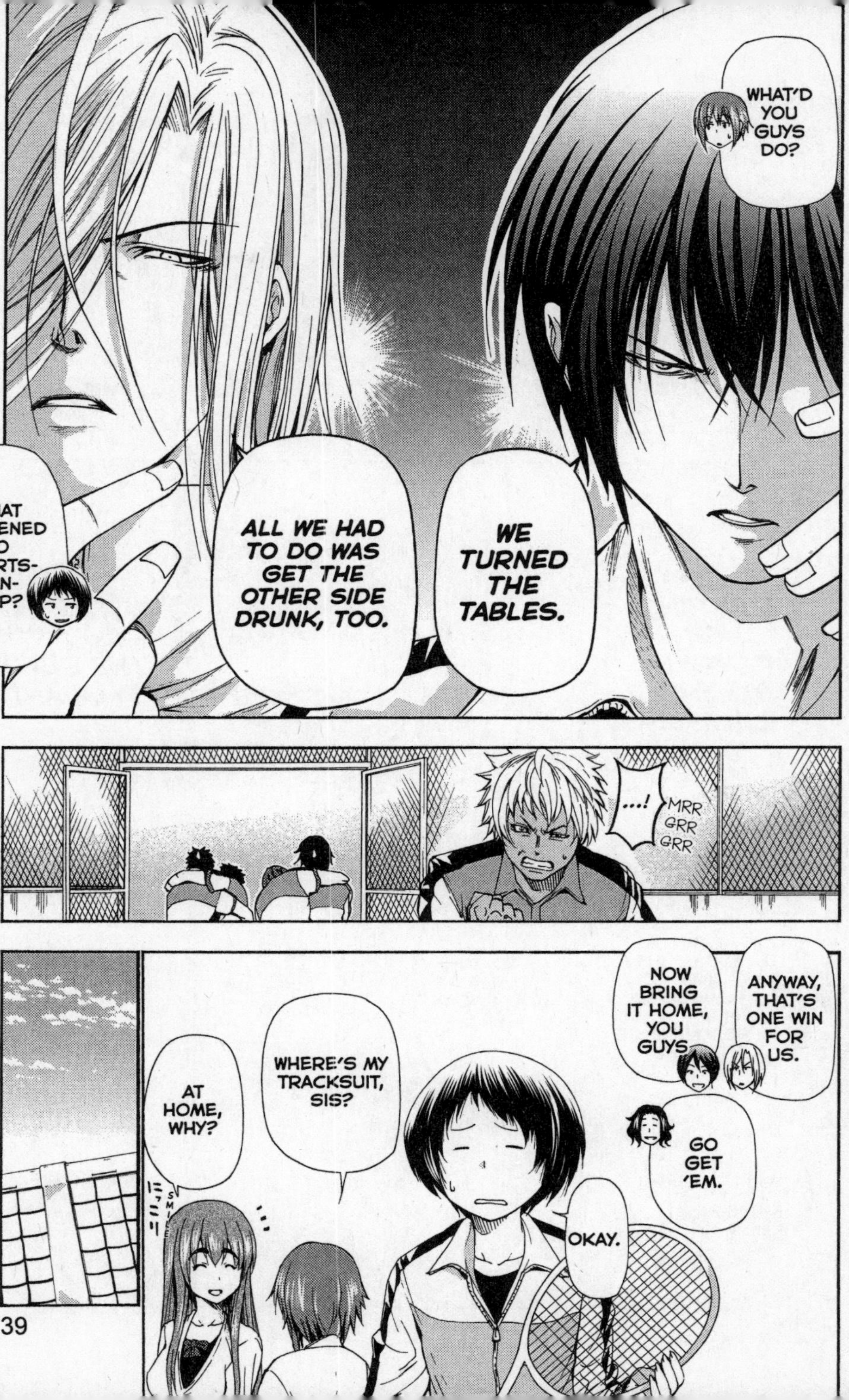
WHAT'D YOU GUYS DO?
WE TURNED THE TABLES.
ALL WE HAD TO DO WAS GET THE OTHER SIDE DRUNK, TOO.
WHAT HAPPENED TO SPORTS-MAN-SHIP?
MRR GRR GRR
...!
ANYWAY, THAT'S ONE WIN FOR US.
NOW BRING IT HOME, YOU GUYS.
GO GET 'EM.
OKAY.
WHERE'S MY TRACKSUIT, SIS?
AT HOME, WHY?
SMILE

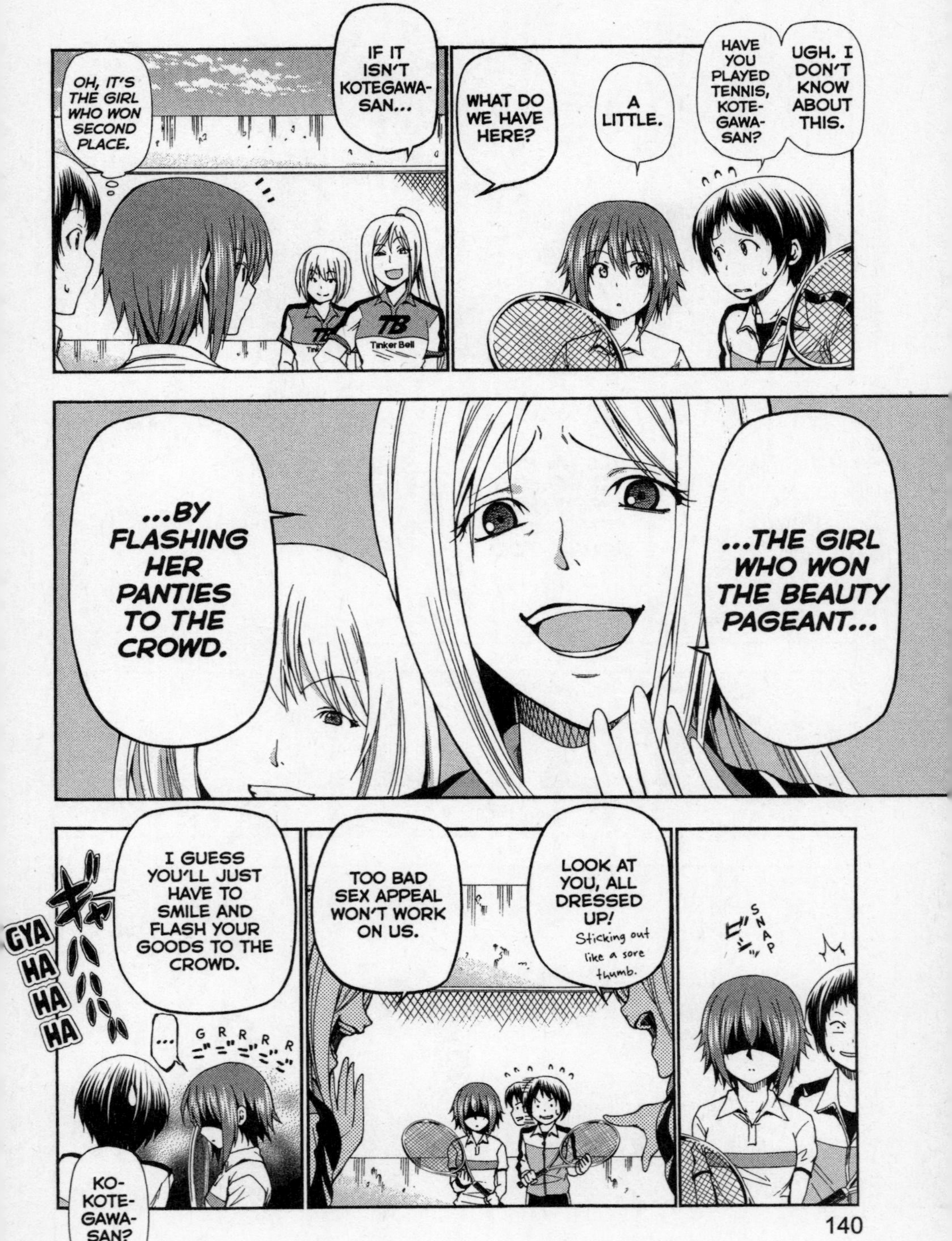
UGH. I DON'T KNOW ABOUT THIS.
HAVE YOU PLAYED TENNIS, KOTE-GAWA-SAN?
A LITTLE.
WHAT DO WE HAVE HERE?
IF IT ISN'T KOTEGAWA-SAN...
OH, IT'S THE GIRL WHO WON SECOND PLACE.
...THE GIRL WHO WON THE BEAUTY PAGEANT...
...BY FLASHING HER PANTIES TO THE CROWD.
SNAP
LOOK AT YOU, ALL DRESSED UP!
Sticking out like a sore thumb.
TOO BAD SEX APPEAL WON'T WORK ON US.
I GUESS YOU'LL JUST HAVE TO SMILE AND FLASH YOUR GOODS TO THE CROWD.
GYA HA HA HA HA
...
GRRRR
KO-KOTE-GAWA-SAN?

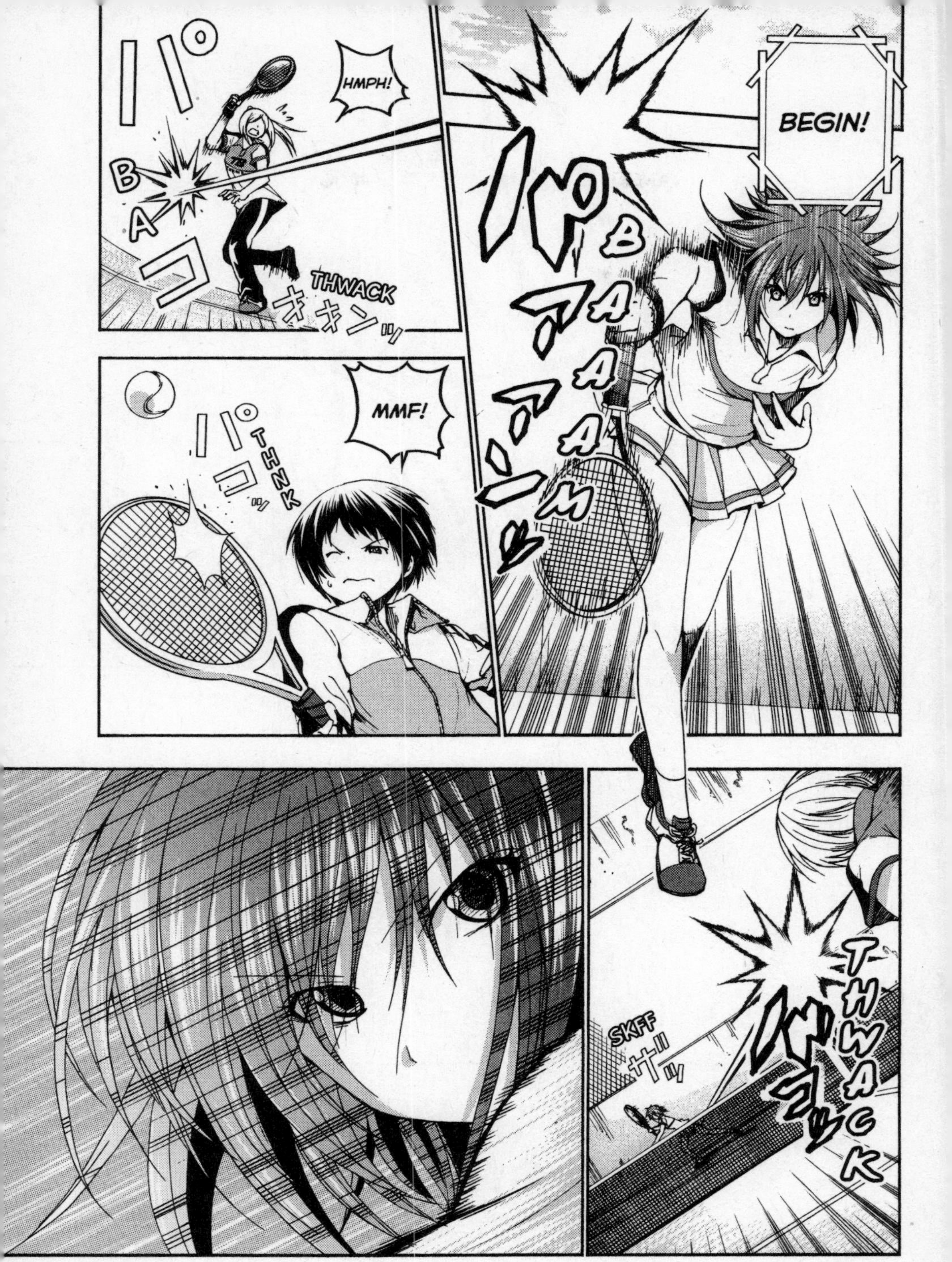
BEGIN!
BAAAAAM
HMPH!
BA
THWACK
MMF!
THNK
THWACK
SKFF

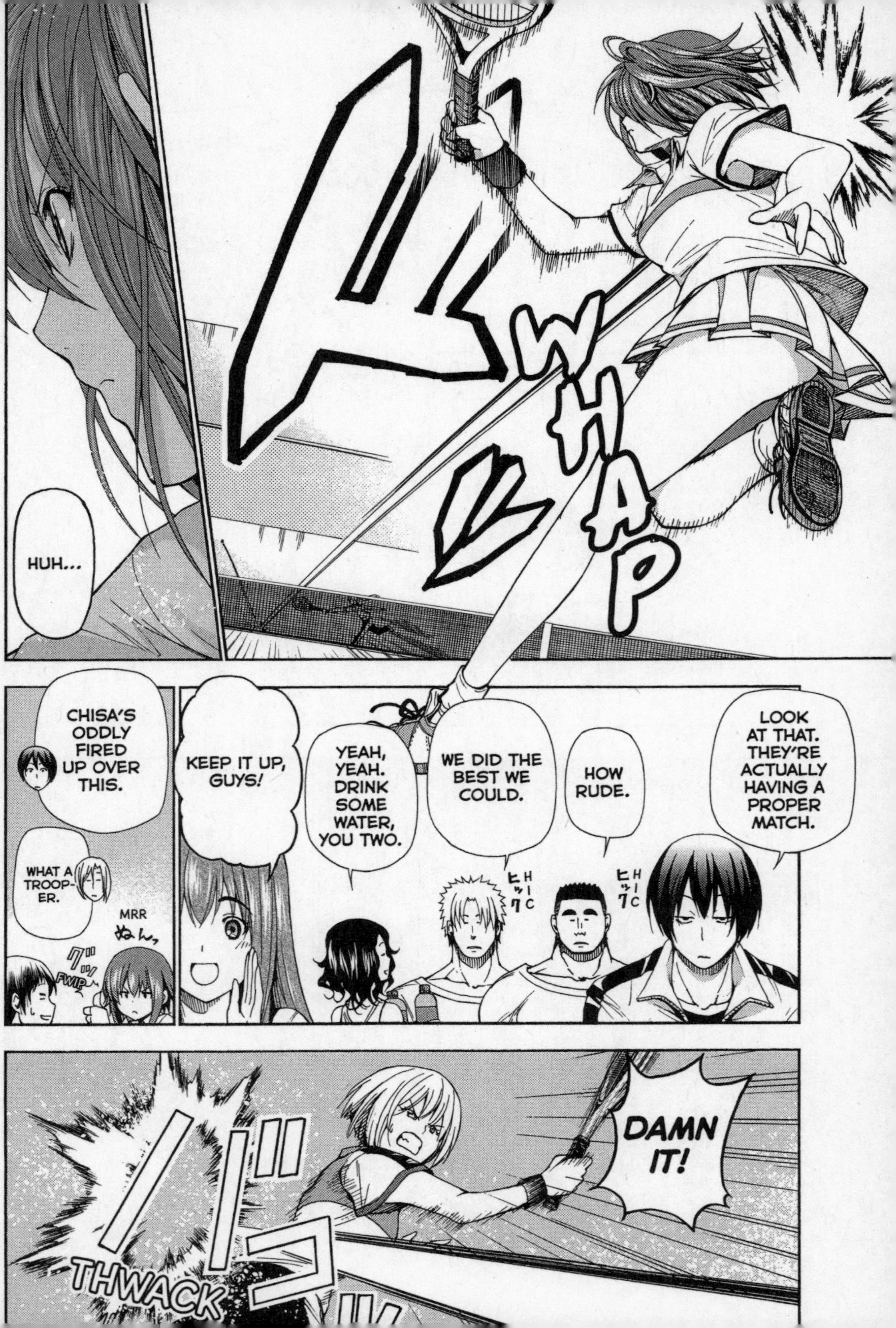
WHAP
HUH...
LOOK AT THAT. THEY'RE ACTUALLY HAVING A PROPER MATCH.
HOW RUDE.
HIC
WE DID THE BEST WE COULD.
HIC
YEAH, YEAH. DRINK SOME WATER, YOU TWO.
KEEP IT UP, GUYS!
CHISA'S ODDLY FIRED UP OVER THIS.
WHAT A TROOPER.
MRR
FWIP
DAMN IT!
THWACK

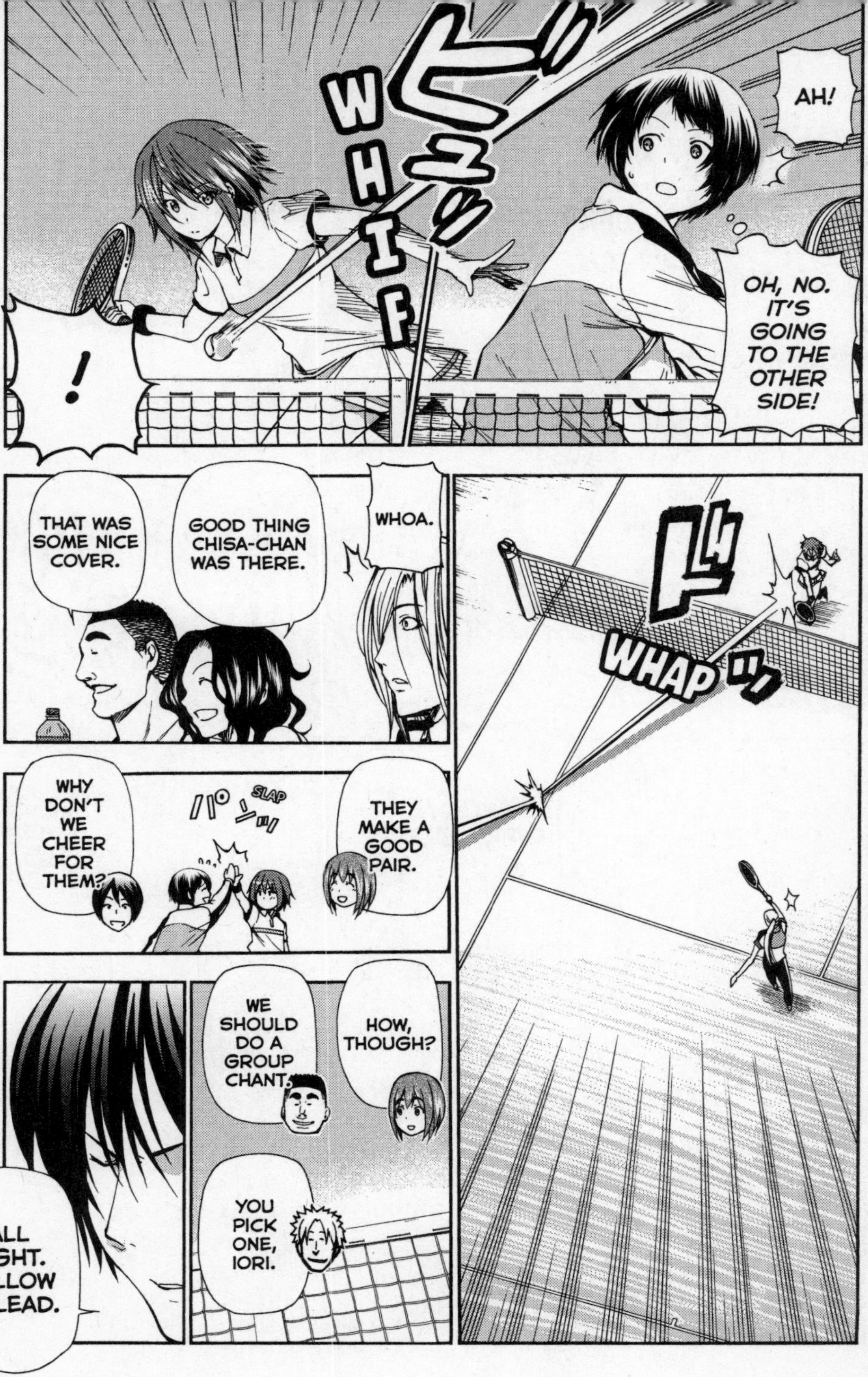
AH!
OH, NO. IT'S GOING TO THE OTHER SIDE!
WHIFF
!
WHAP
WHOA.
GOOD THING CHISA-CHAN WAS THERE.
THAT WAS SOME NICE COVER.
THEY MAKE A GOOD PAIR.
SLAP
WHY DON'T WE CHEER FOR THEM?
HOW, THOUGH?
WE SHOULD DO A GROUP CHANT.
YOU PICK ONE, IORI.
ALL RIGHT. FOLLOW MY LEAD.

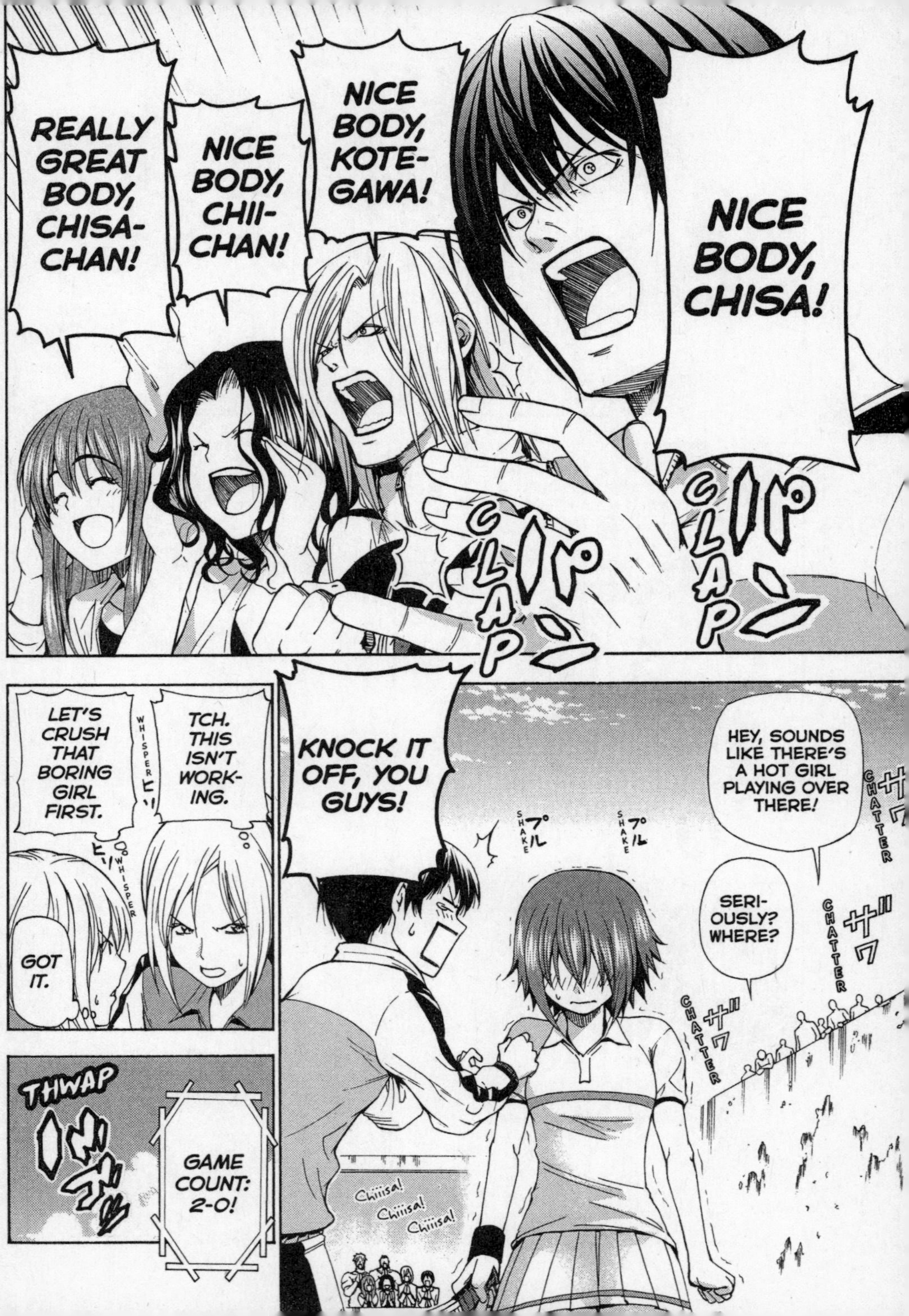
NICE BODY, CHISA!
NICE BODY, KOTEGAWA!
NICE BODY, CHII-CHAN!
REALLY GREAT BODY, CHISA-CHAN!
CLAP
CLAP
CHATTER ザワ
HEY, SOUNDS LIKE THERE'S A HOT GIRL PLAYING OVER THERE!
CHATTER ザワ
SERIOUSLY? WHERE?
CHATTER ザワ
SHAKE プル
SHAKE プル
KNOCK IT OFF, YOU GUYS!
Chiiisa! Chiiisa! Chiiisa!
TCH. THIS ISN'T WORKING.
WHISPER
LET'S CRUSH THAT BORING GIRL FIRST.
WHISPER
GOT IT.
THWAP
GAME COUNT: 2-0!

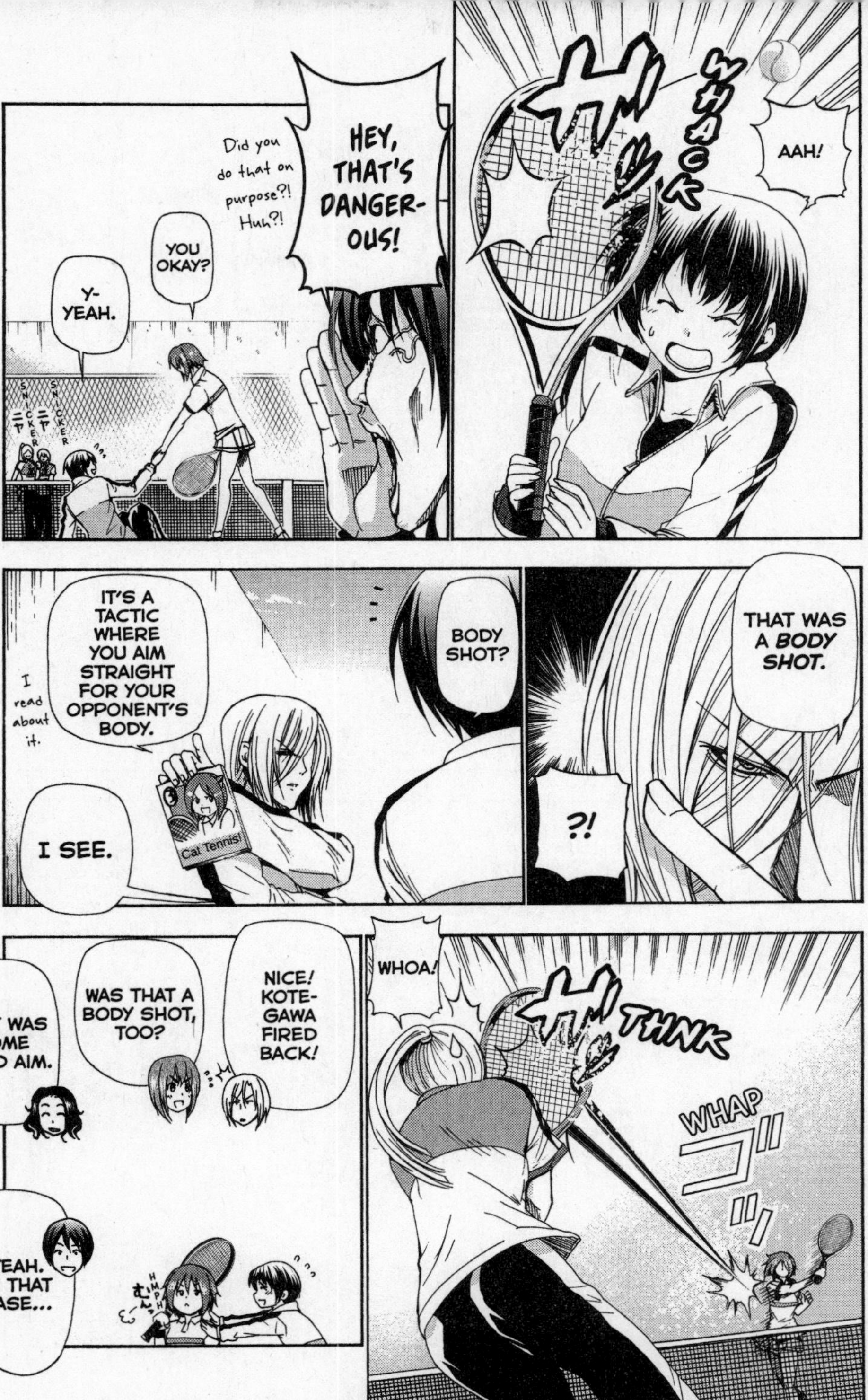
WHACK
AAH!
HEY, THAT'S DANGER-OUS!
Did you do that on purpose?! Huh?!
YOU OKAY?
Y-YEAH.
SNICKER
SNICKER
THAT WAS A BODY SHOT.
?!
BODY SHOT?
IT'S A TACTIC WHERE YOU AIM STRAIGHT FOR YOUR OPPONENT'S BODY.
I read about it.
Cat Tennis!
I SEE.
WHOA!
THNK
WHAP
NICE! KOTE-GAWA FIRED BACK!
WAS THAT A BODY SHOT, TOO?
THAT WAS SOME GOOD AIM.
YEAH. IN THAT CASE...
HMPH

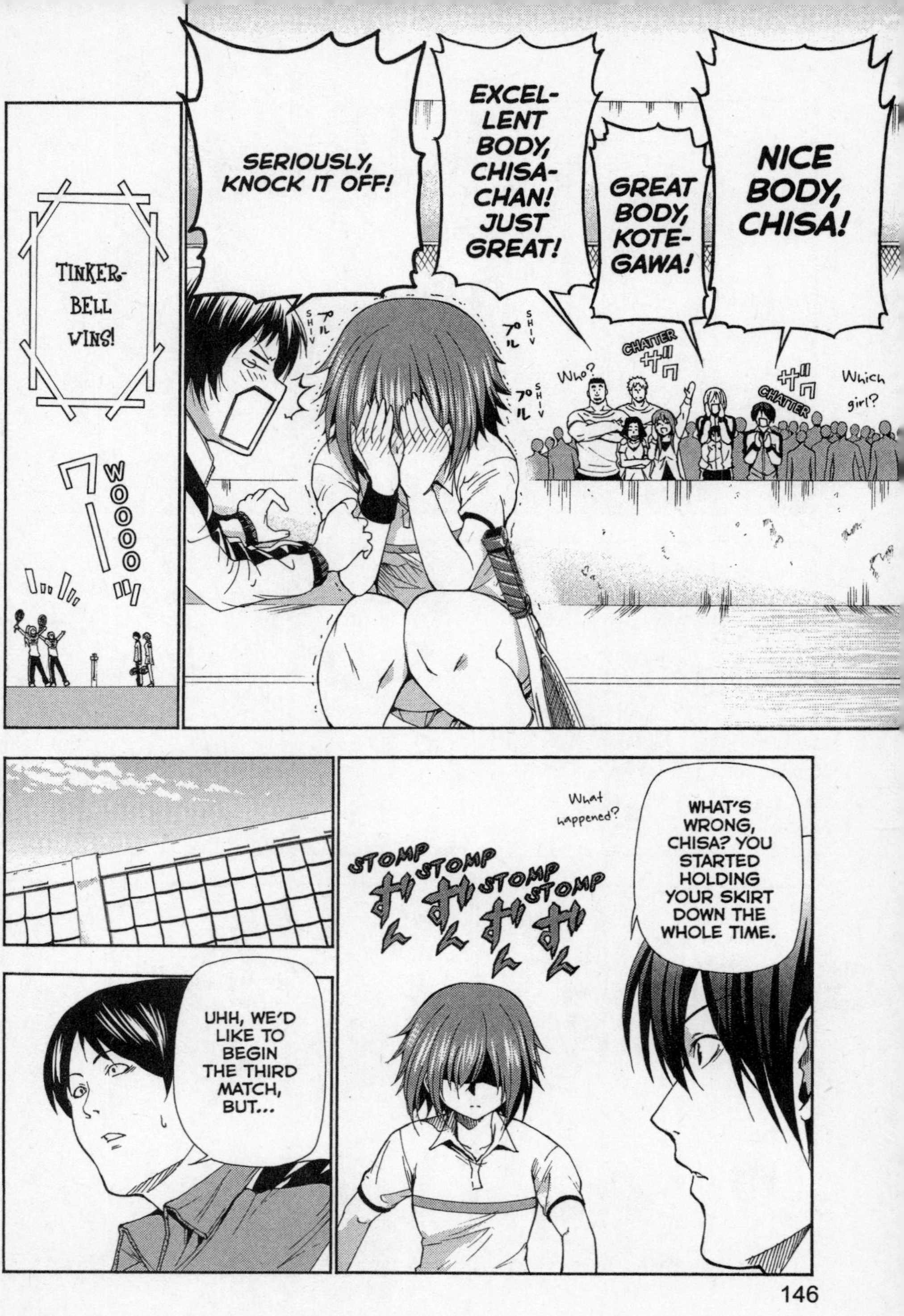
NICE BODY, CHISA!
GREAT BODY, KOTE-GAWA!
EXCEL-LENT BODY, CHISA-CHAN! JUST GREAT!
SERIOUSLY, KNOCK IT OFF!
SHIV
SHIV
SHIV
Which girl?
CHATTER
CHATTER
Who?
TINKER-BELL WINS!
WOOOOO
What happened?
WHAT'S WRONG, CHISA? YOU STARTED HOLDING YOUR SKIRT DOWN THE WHOLE TIME.
STOMP STOMP STOMP STOMP
UHH, WE'D LIKE TO BEGIN THE THIRD MATCH, BUT...

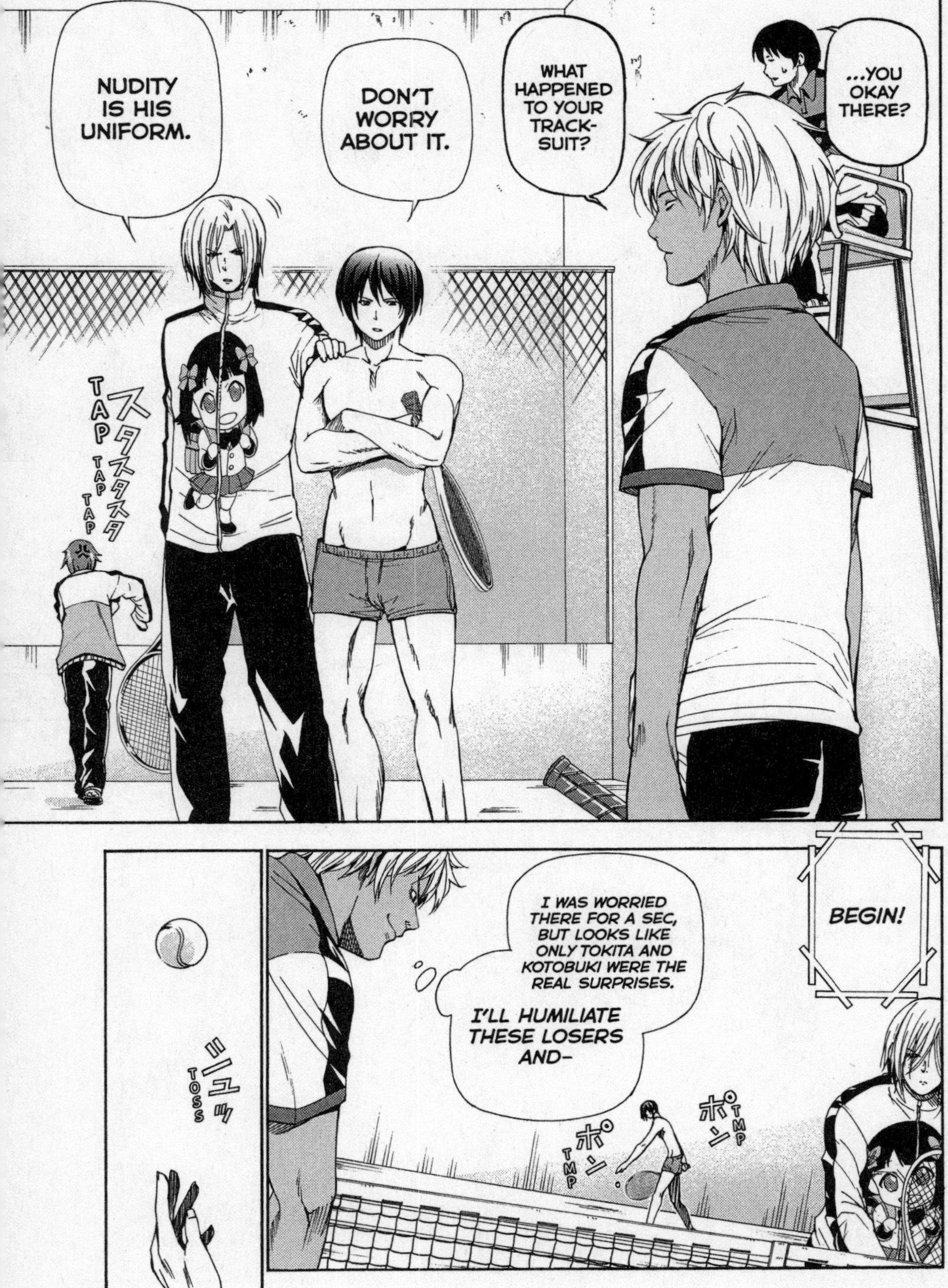
...YOU OKAY THERE?
WHAT HAPPENED TO YOUR TRACK-SUIT?
DON'T WORRY ABOUT IT.
NUDITY IS HIS UNIFORM.
スタスタスタ
TAP TAP TAP
BEGIN!
I WAS WORRIED THERE FOR A SEC, BUT LOOKS LIKE ONLY TOKITA AND KOTOBUKI WERE THE REAL SURPRISES.
I'LL HUMILIATE THESE LOSERS AND-
ポン
TMP
ポン
TMP
シュッ
TOSS

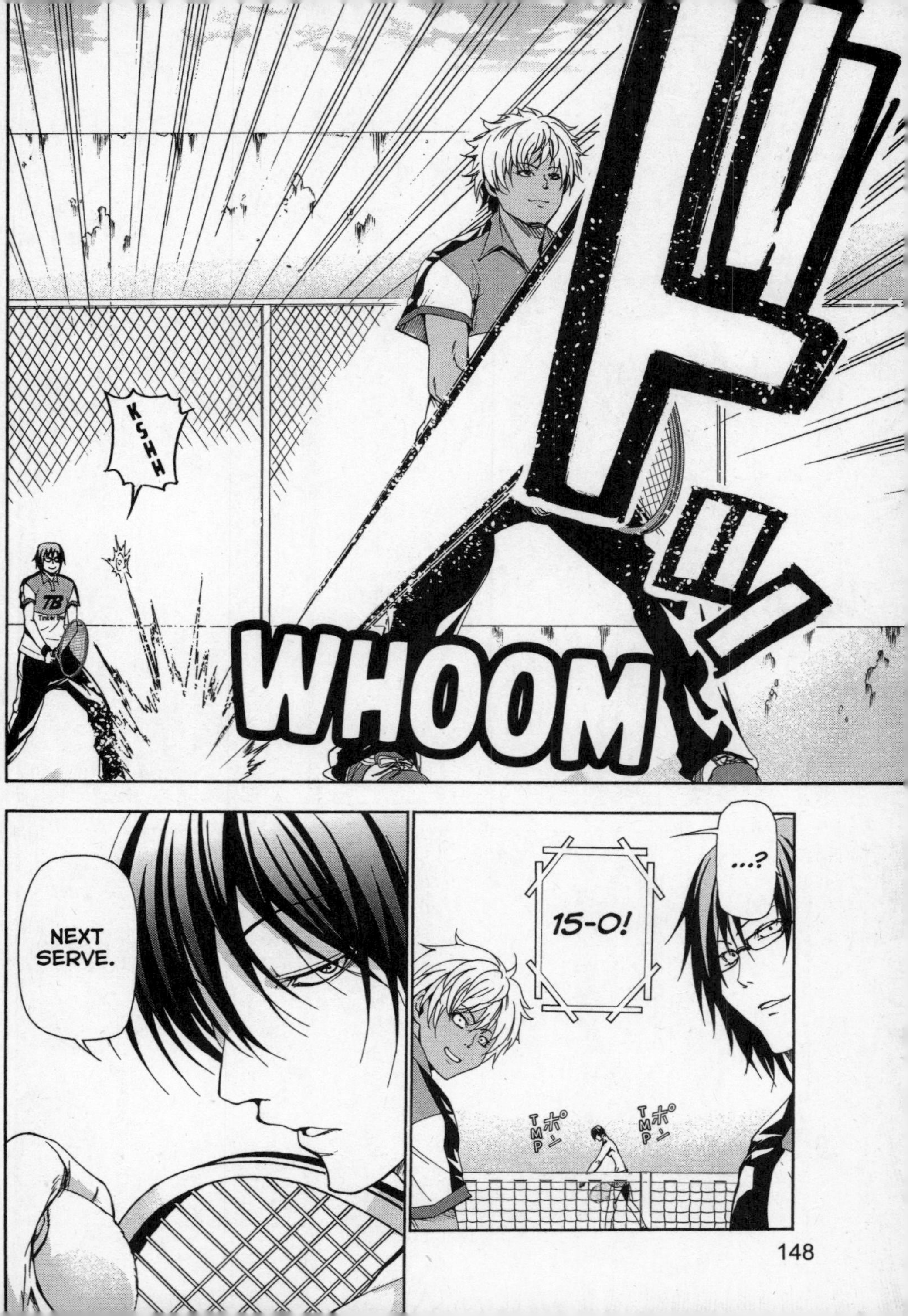
KSHH
WHOOM
...?
15-0!
TMP
TMP
NEXT SERVE.

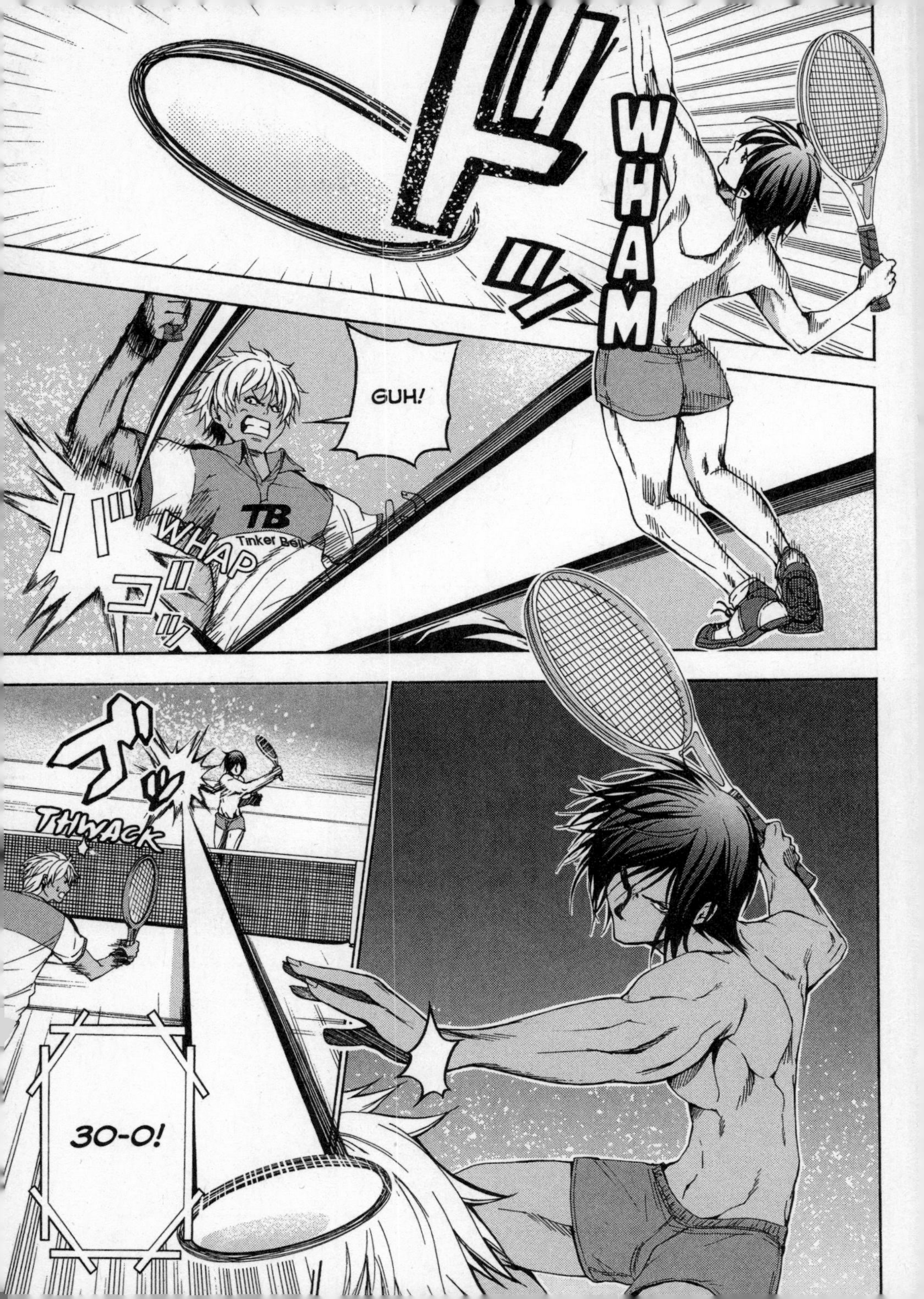
WHAM
GUH!
WHAP
THWACK
30-0!

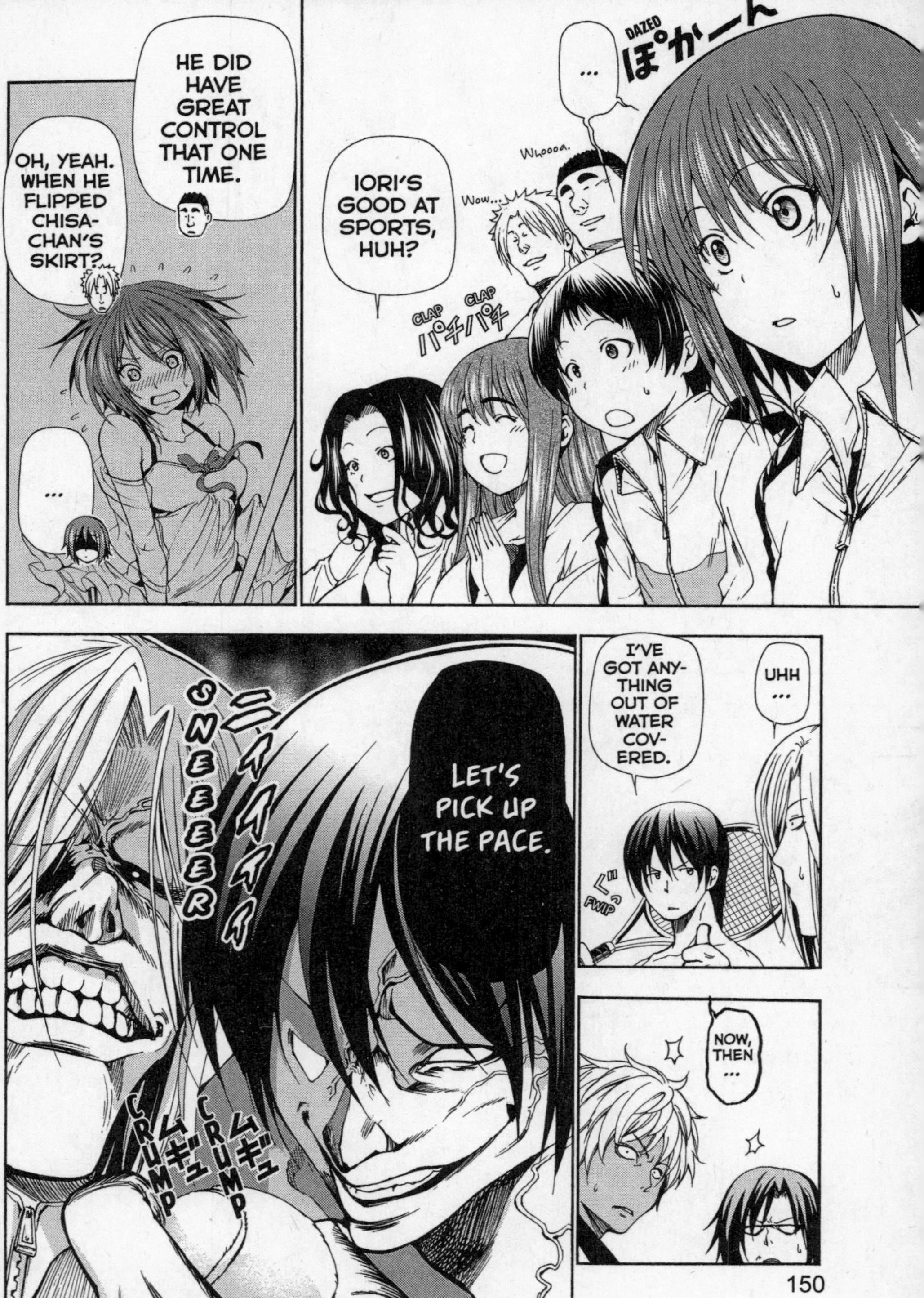
DAZED
ぽかーん
...
Whoooa.
Wow...
IORI'S GOOD AT SPORTS, HUH?
CLAP CLAP
パチパチ
HE DID HAVE GREAT CONTROL THAT ONE TIME.
OH, YEAH. WHEN HE FLIPPED CHISA-CHAN'S SKIRT?
...
UHH ...
I'VE GOT ANYTHING OUT OF WATER COVERED.
FWIP
ぐっ
NOW, THEN ...
LET'S PICK UP THE PACE.
SNEEEER
ニィィィィ
CRUMP CRUMP
ムギュ ムギュ

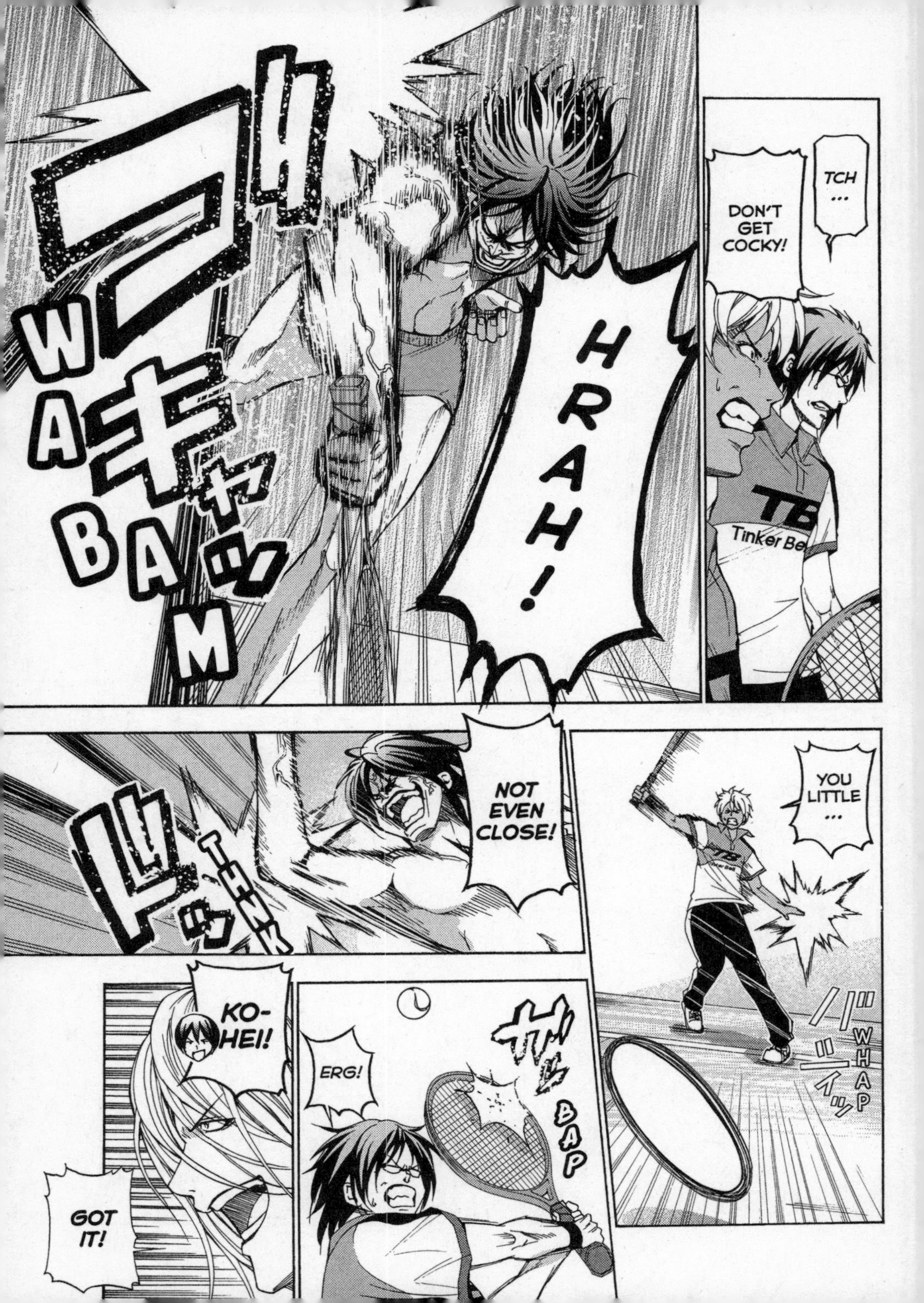

TCH ...
DON'T GET COCKY!
HRAH!
WABAM
YOU LITTLE ...
NOT EVEN CLOSE!
THUNK
WHAP
ERG!
BAP
KO-HEI!
GOT IT!

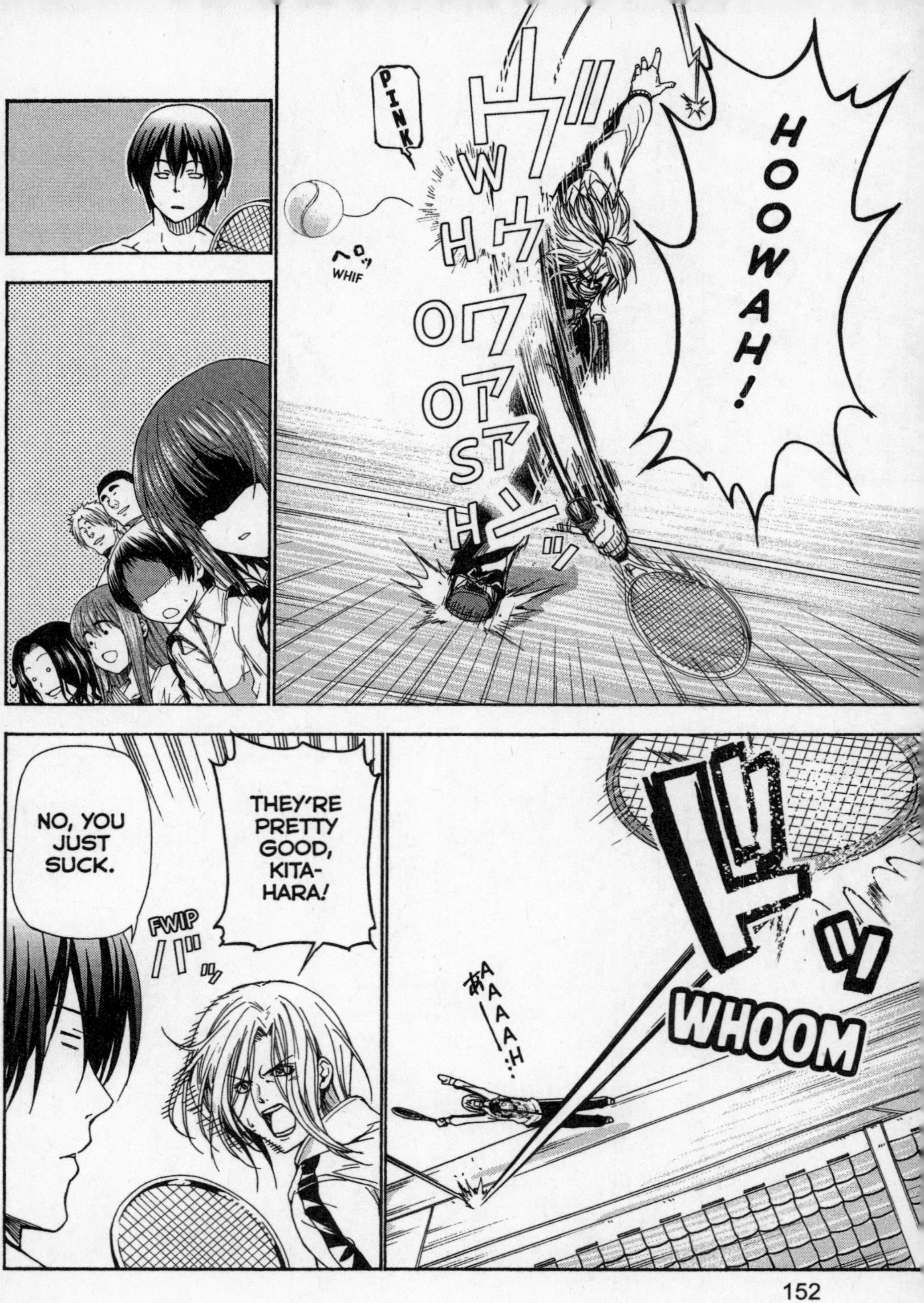
HOOWAH!
PINK
WHOOSH
WHIF
WHOOM
AAAAAH
THEY'RE PRETTY GOOD, KITA-HARA!
FWIP
NO, YOU JUST SUCK.

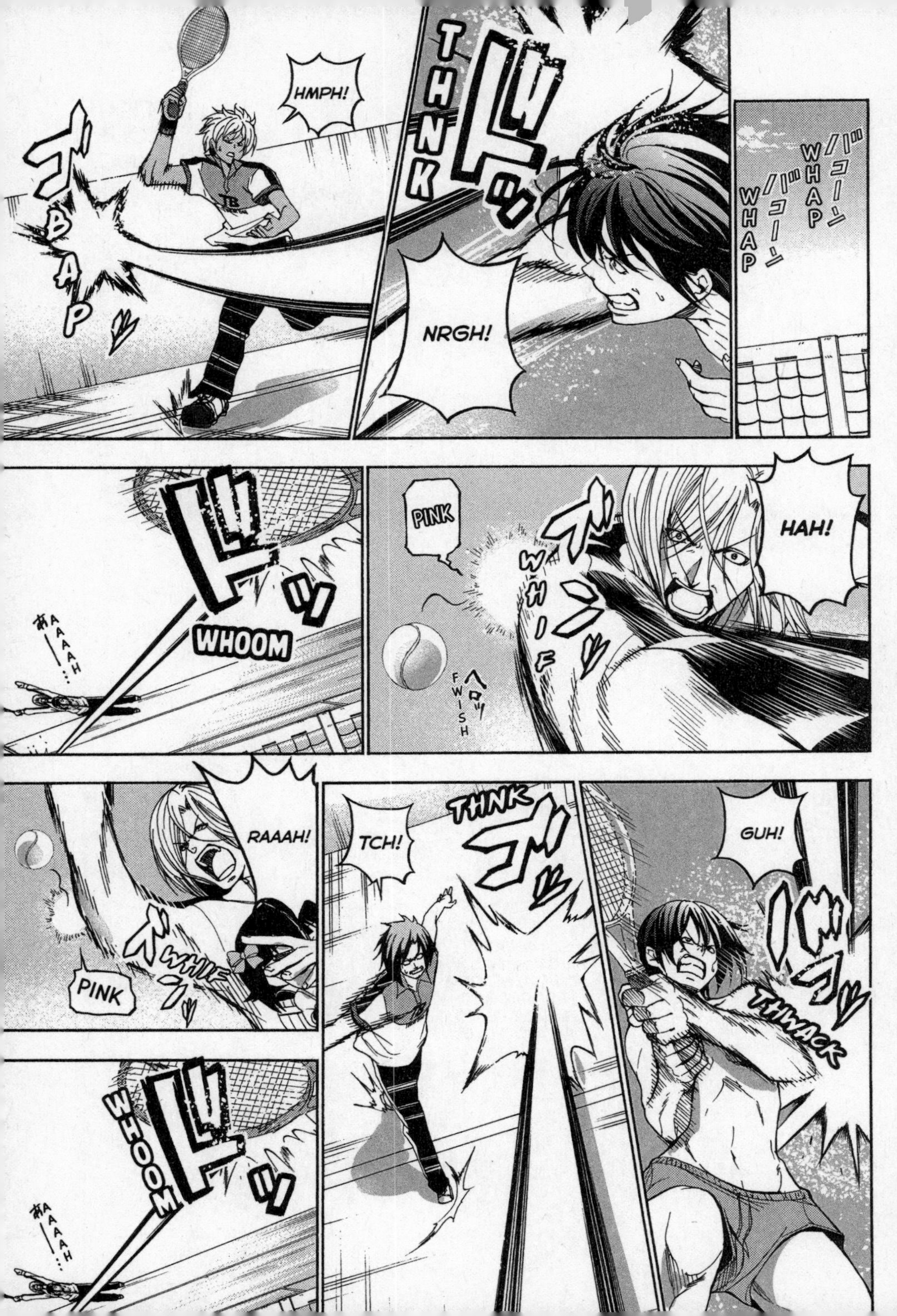
WHAP
WHAP
THNK
NRGH!
HMPH!
BAP
HAH!
PINK
WHIF
FWISH
WHOOM
AAAAH...
GUH!
THWACK
TCH!
THNK
RAAAH!
WHIF
PINK
WHOOM
AAAAH...

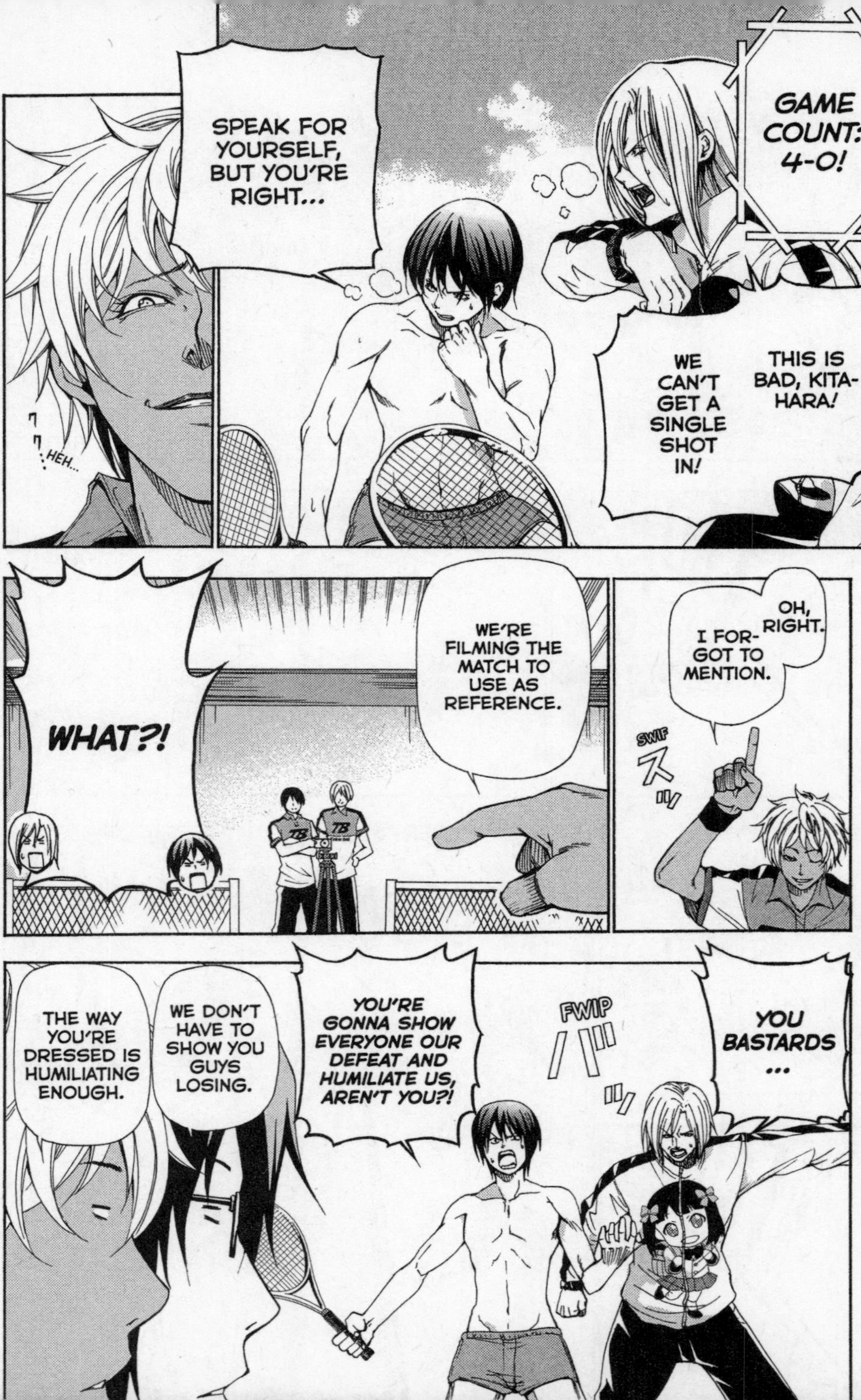
GAME COUNT: 4-0!
THIS IS BAD, KITA-HARA!
WE CAN'T GET A SINGLE SHOT IN!
SPEAK FOR YOURSELF, BUT YOU'RE RIGHT...
HEH...
OH, RIGHT.
I FOR-GOT TO MENTION.
SWIF
WE'RE FILMING THE MATCH TO USE AS REFERENCE.
WHAT?!
YOU BASTARDS...
FWIP
YOU'RE GONNA SHOW EVERYONE OUR DEFEAT AND HUMILIATE US, AREN'T YOU?!
WE DON'T HAVE TO SHOW YOU GUYS LOSING.
THE WAY YOU'RE DRESSED IS HUMILIATING ENOUGH.

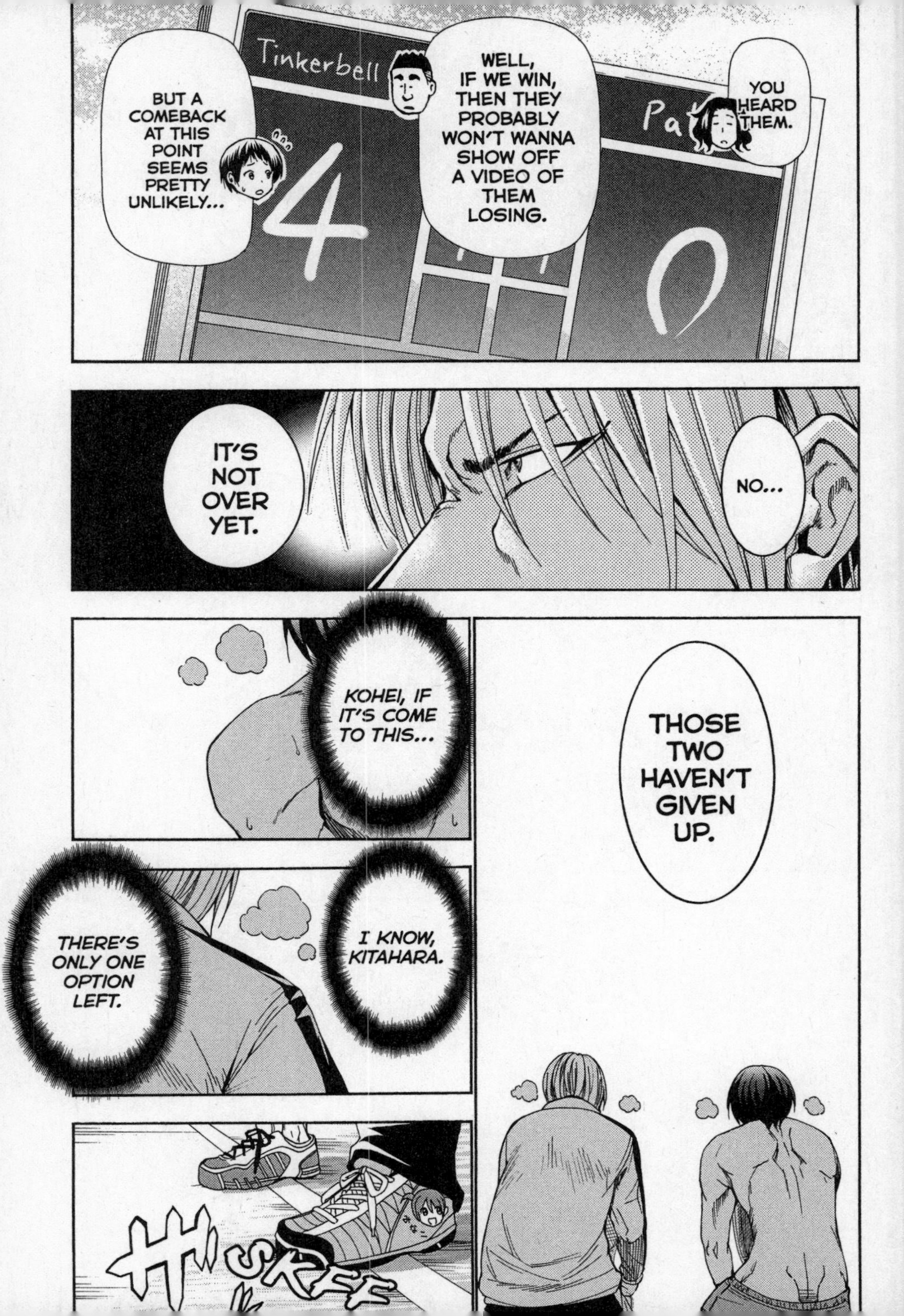
Tinkerbell
Pat
YOU HEARD THEM.
WELL, IF WE WIN, THEN THEY PROBABLY WON'T WANNA SHOW OFF A VIDEO OF THEM LOSING.
BUT A COMEBACK AT THIS POINT SEEMS PRETTY UNLIKELY...
4
0
NO...
IT'S NOT OVER YET.
THOSE TWO HAVEN'T GIVEN UP.
KOHEI, IF IT'S COME TO THIS...
I KNOW, KITAHARA.
THERE'S ONLY ONE OPTION LEFT.
SKEE

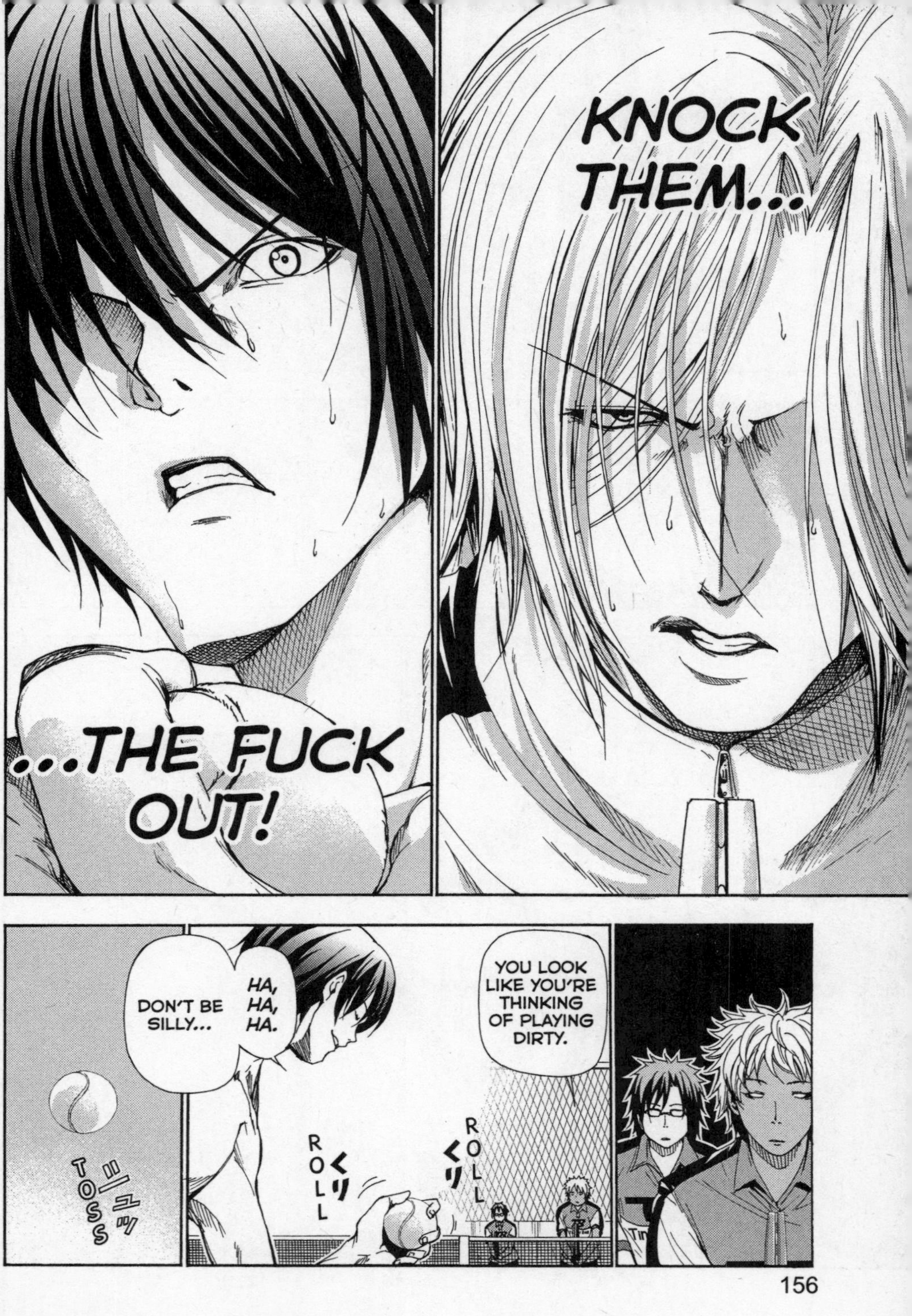
KNOCK THEM...
...THE FUCK OUT!
YOU LOOK LIKE YOU'RE THINKING OF PLAYING DIRTY.
HA, HA, HA.
DON'T BE SILLY...
くり ROLL
くり ROLL
TOSS

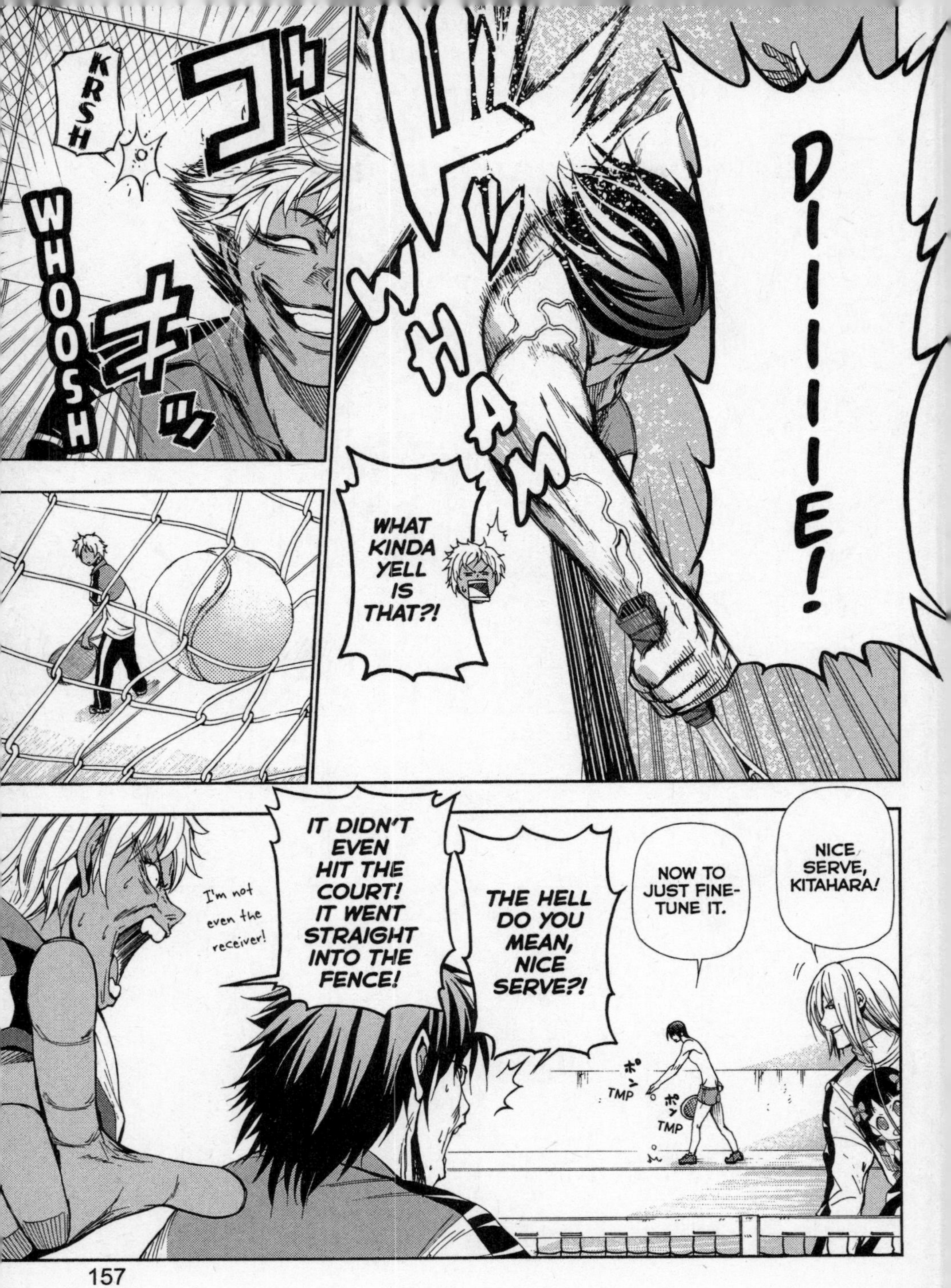
DIIIE!
WHAM
WHAT KINDA YELL IS THAT?!
KRSH
WHOOSH
NICE SERVE, KITAHARA!
NOW TO JUST FINE-TUNE IT.
TMP
TMP
THE HELL DO YOU MEAN, NICE SERVE?!
IT DIDN'T EVEN HIT THE COURT! IT WENT STRAIGHT INTO THE FENCE!
I'm not even the receiver!

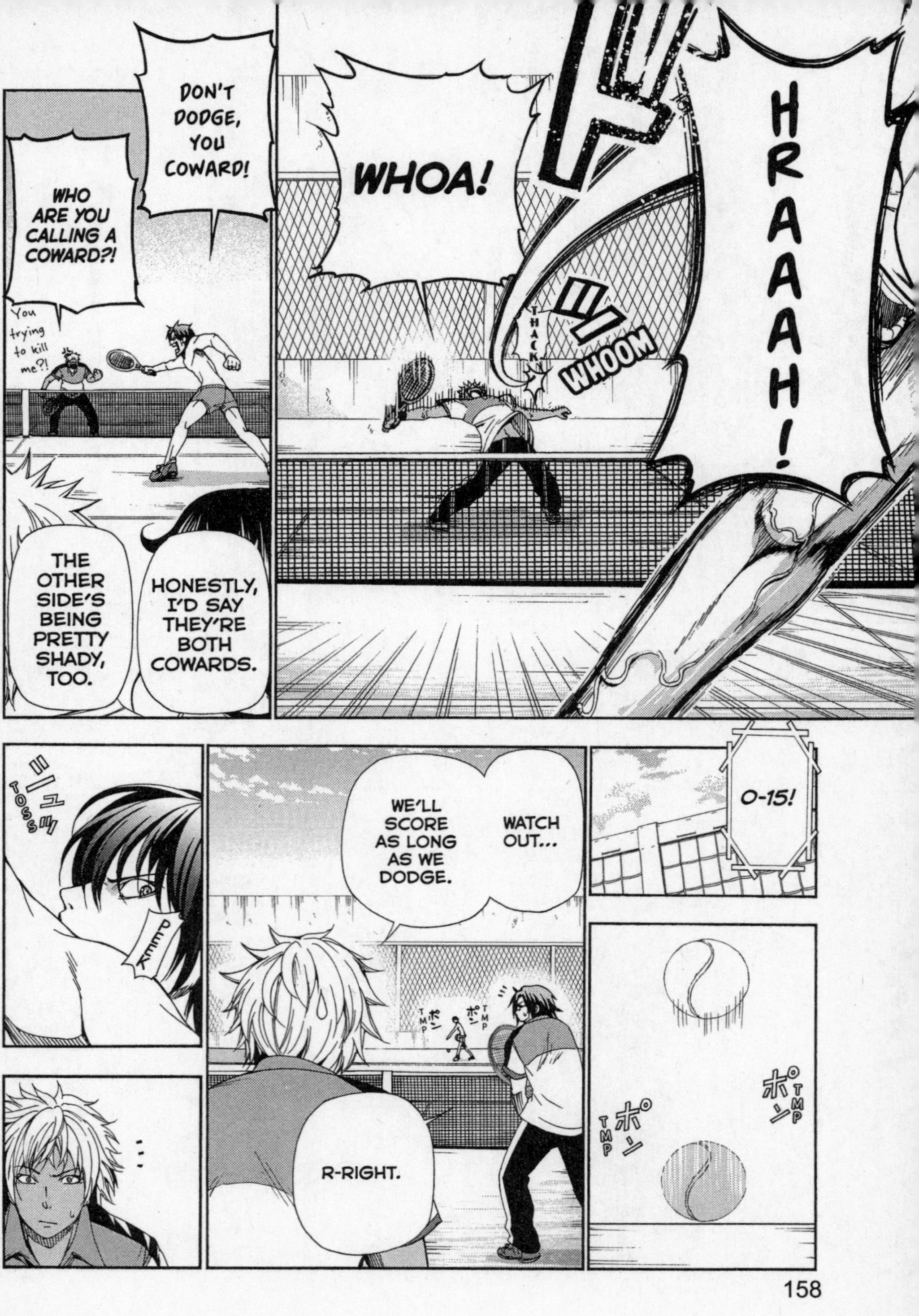
HRAAAH!
WHOA!
THACK
WHOOM
DON'T DODGE, YOU COWARD!
WHO ARE YOU CALLING A COWARD?!
You trying to kill me?!
HONESTLY, I'D SAY THEY'RE BOTH COWARDS.
THE OTHER SIDE'S BEING PRETTY SHADY, TOO.
O-15!
TMP
TMP
WATCH OUT...
WE'LL SCORE AS LONG AS WE DODGE.
TMP
TMP
R-RIGHT.
TOSS
PEEK
...

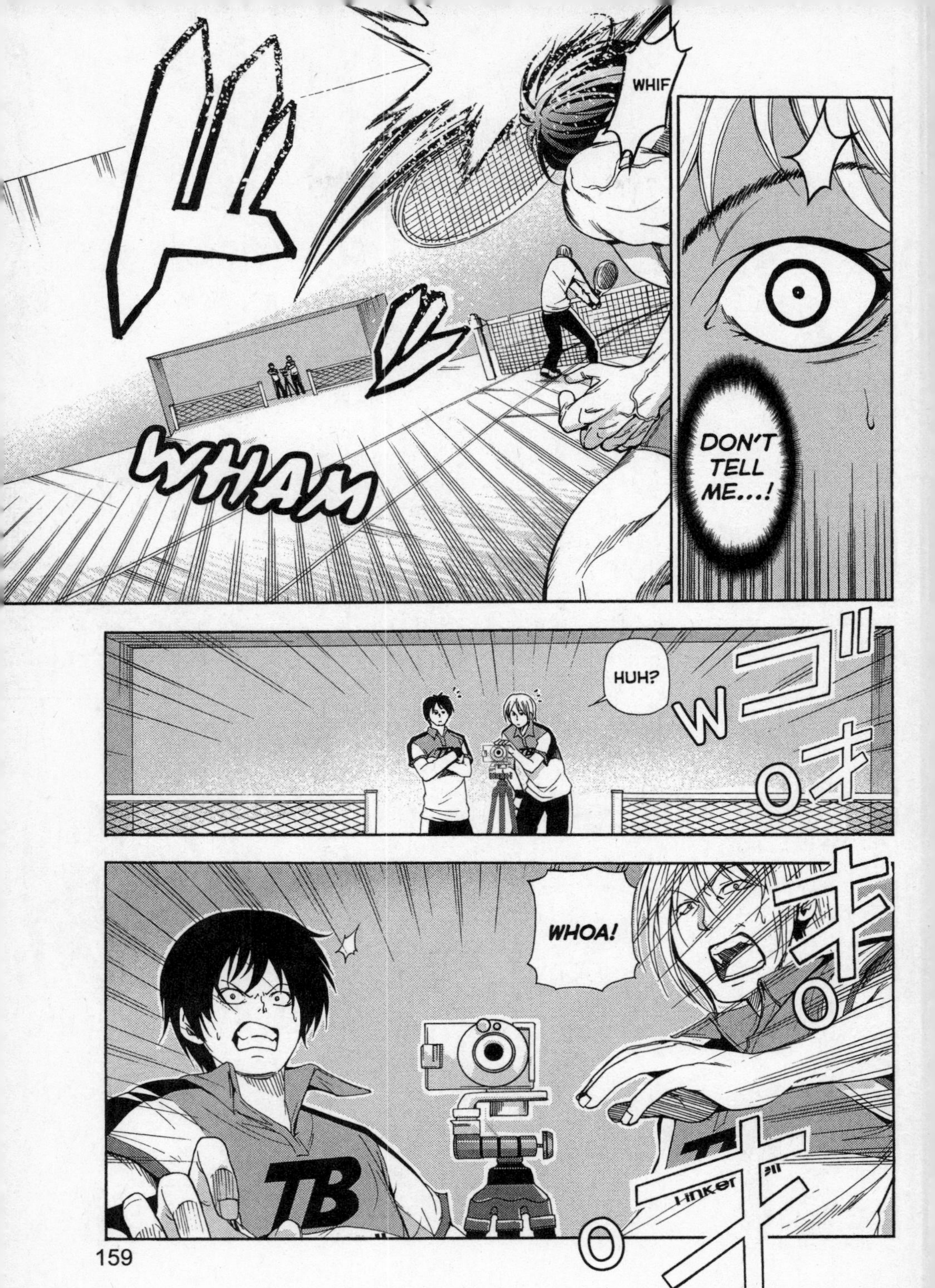
DON'T TELL ME...!
WHIF
WHAM
HUH?
W
O
WHOA!
O
O

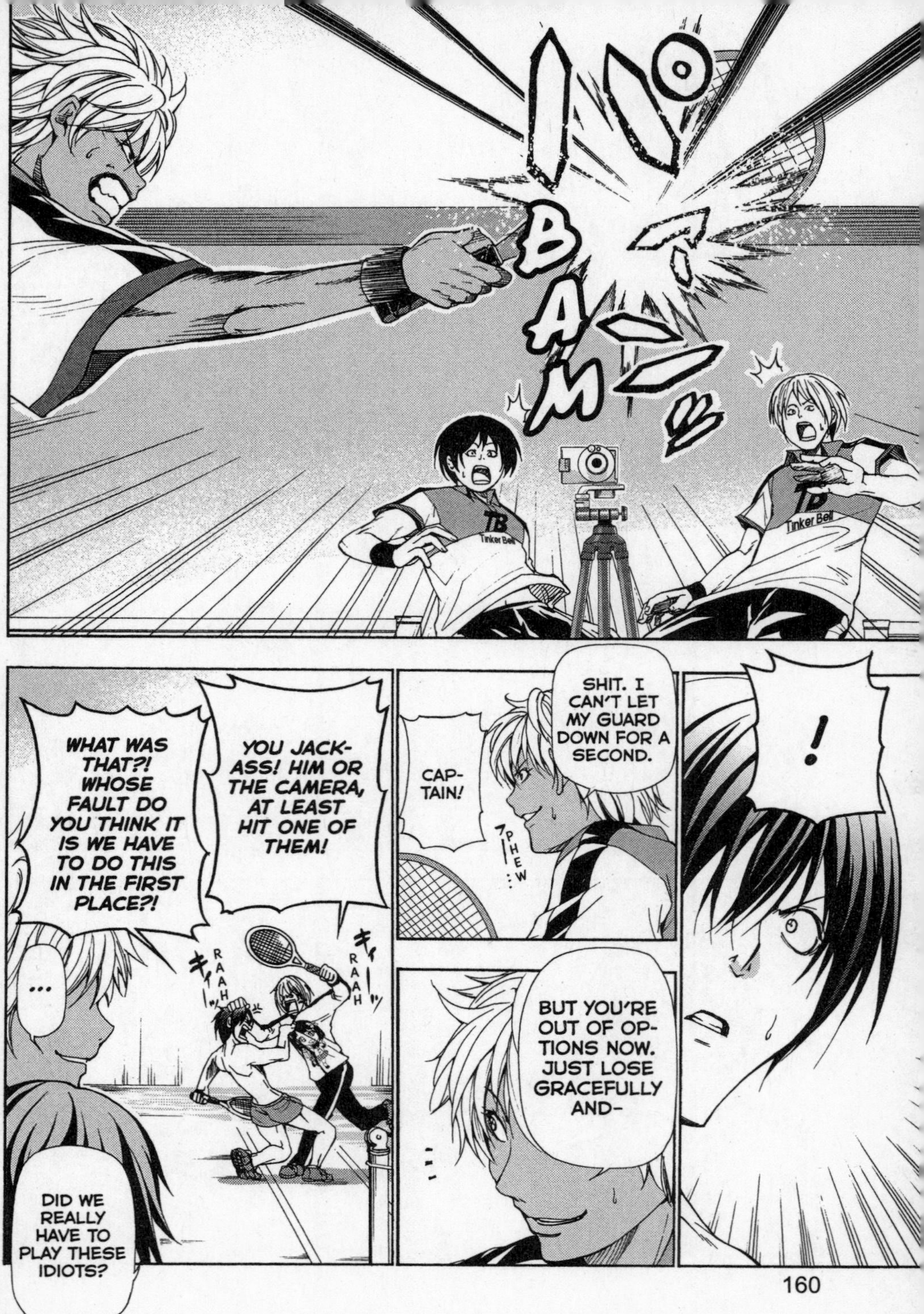
BAM
!
SHIT. I CAN'T LET MY GUARD DOWN FOR A SECOND.
CAP-TAIN!
PHEW...
BUT YOU'RE OUT OF OPTIONS NOW. JUST LOSE GRACEFULLY AND-
YOU JACK-ASS! HIM OR THE CAMERA, AT LEAST HIT ONE OF THEM!
WHAT WAS THAT?! WHOSE FAULT DO YOU THINK IT IS WE HAVE TO DO THIS IN THE FIRST PLACE?!
RAAH
RAAH
...
DID WE REALLY HAVE TO PLAY THESE IDIOTS?

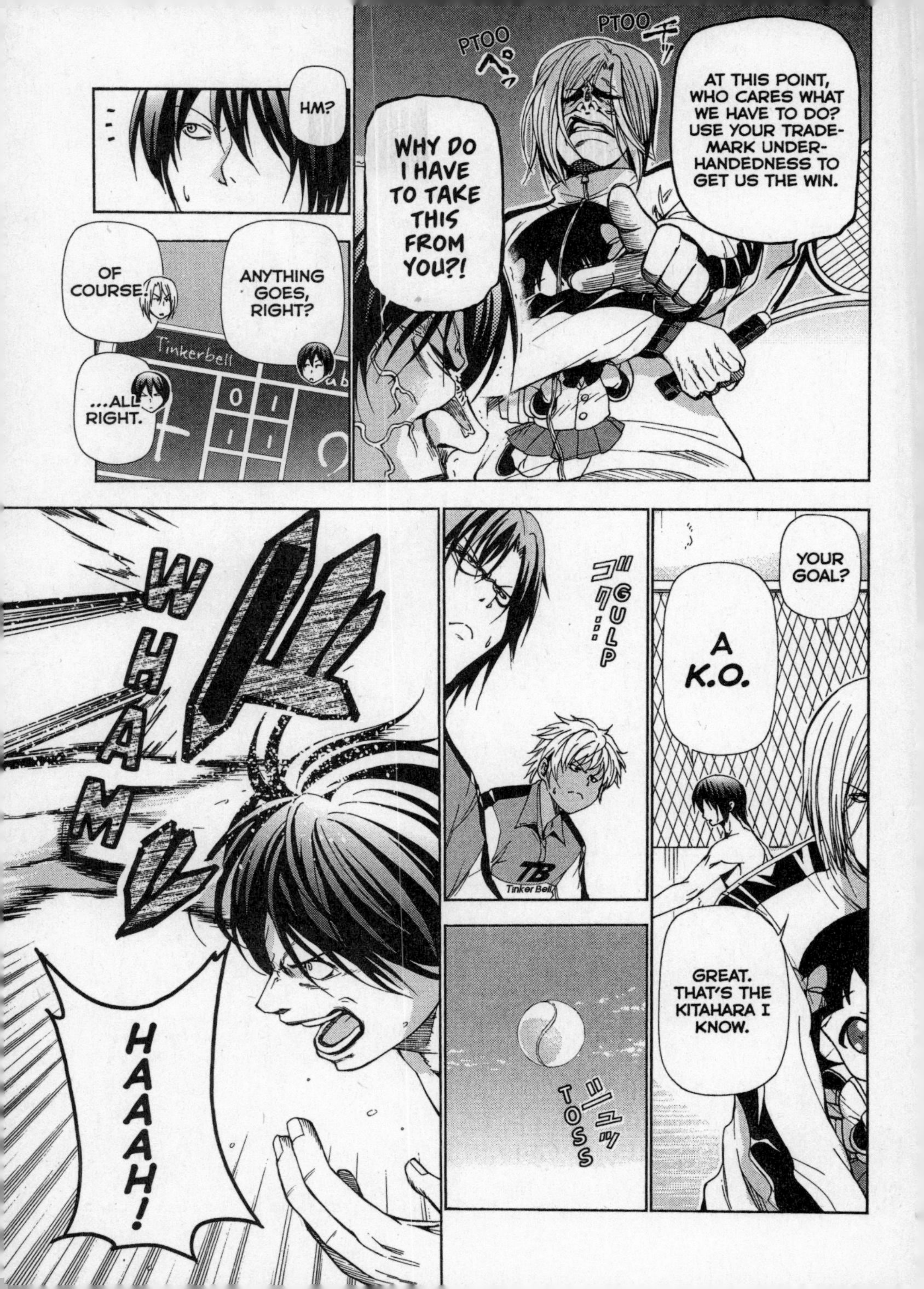

PTOO
PTOO
AT THIS POINT, WHO CARES WHAT WE HAVE TO DO? USE YOUR TRADE-MARK UNDER-HANDEDNESS TO GET US THE WIN.
WHY DO I HAVE TO TAKE THIS FROM YOU?!
HM?
ANYTHING GOES, RIGHT?
OF COURSE.
...ALL RIGHT.
Tinkerbell
YOUR GOAL?
A K.O.
GREAT. THAT'S THE KITAHARA I KNOW.
GULP
Tinker Bell
TOSS
WHAM
HAAAH!

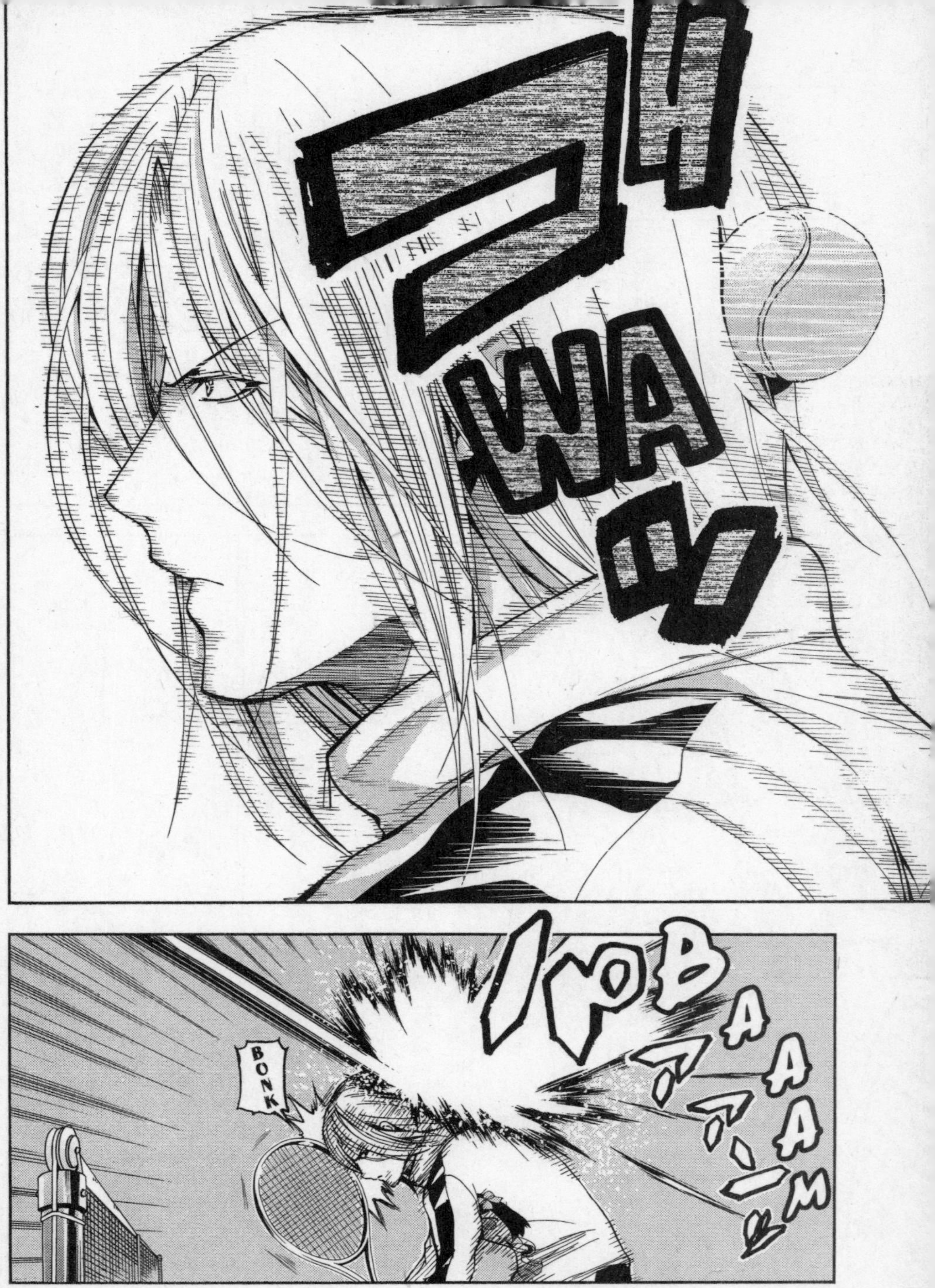
WA
BONK
BAAAM

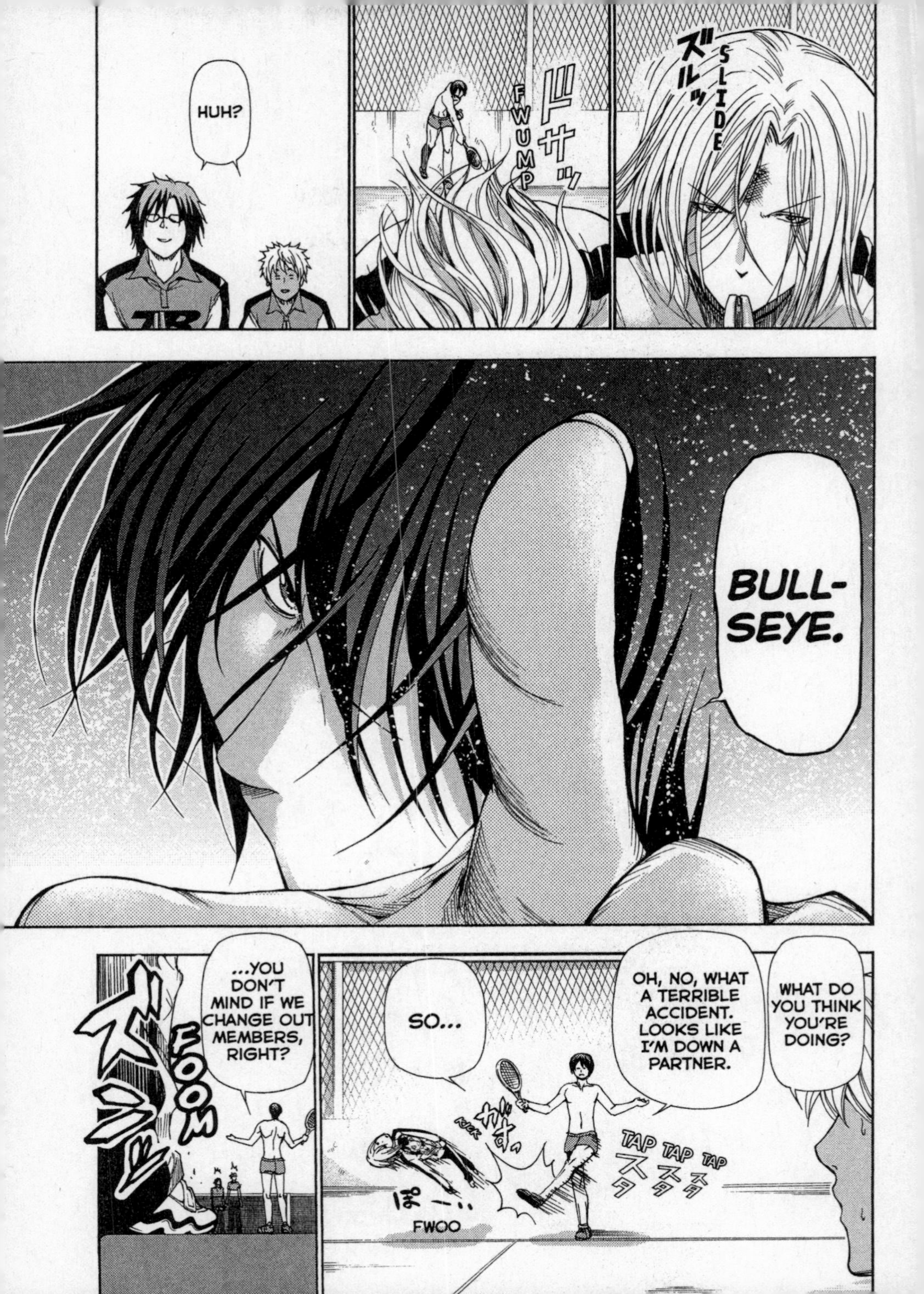
SLIDE
FWUMP
HUH?
BULL-SEYE.
WHAT DO YOU THINK YOU'RE DOING?
OH, NO, WHAT A TERRIBLE ACCIDENT. LOOKS LIKE I'M DOWN A PARTNER.
SO...
KICK
TAP TAP TAP
FWOO
...YOU DON'T MIND IF WE CHANGE OUT MEMBERS, RIGHT?
FOOOM

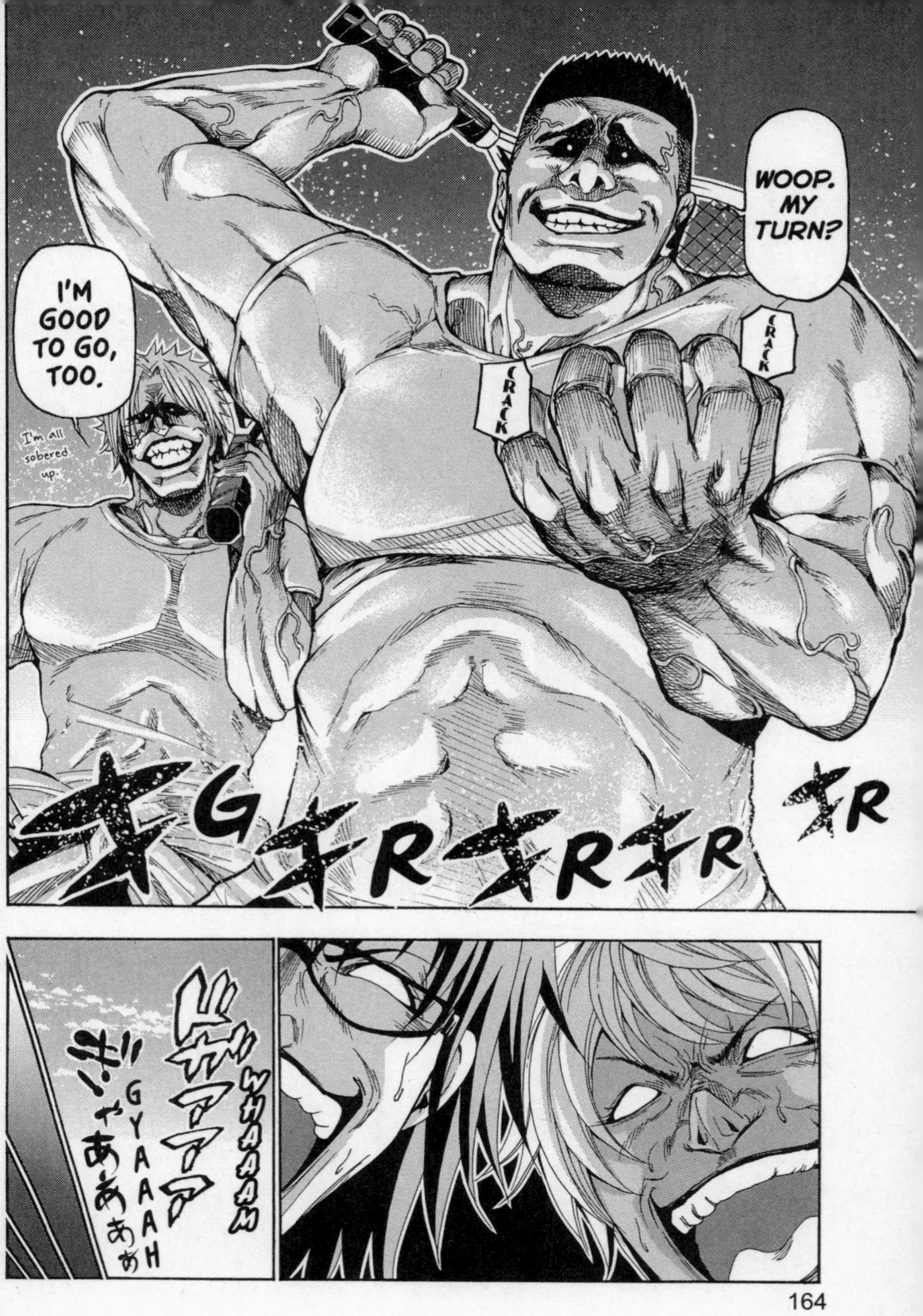
WOOP. MY TURN?
CRACK
CRACK
I'M GOOD TO GO, TOO.
I'm all sobered up.
GRRRR
WHAAAAM
GYAAAH

Tinkerbell

Pab

4

0	1
1	1
2	

6

Victory!

IT WAS A GREAT CHACHACHA MATCH. WOW, THAT WAS FUN.

WELL, WE WON, SO WHO CARES?

SO MUCH FOR SPORTS-MANSHIP.

YOU SAID DO WHAT-EVER IT TAKES!

WHAT WAS THAT FOR, ASS-HOLE?!

I MEANT AGAINST THEM!

GOOD THING KOHEI-KUN WASN'T HURT.

RAAAH!ッ

RAAAH!ッ

キ||||ッ

キ||||ッ

キ||||ッ

YOU WEREN'T IN A CLUB?!

NO, BUT I GOT INTO IT AFTER I TOOK ENTRANCE EXAMS.

NAH.

DID YOU PLAY TENNIS IN HIGH SCHOOL?

YOU WERE PRETTY GOOD OUT THERE, IORI.

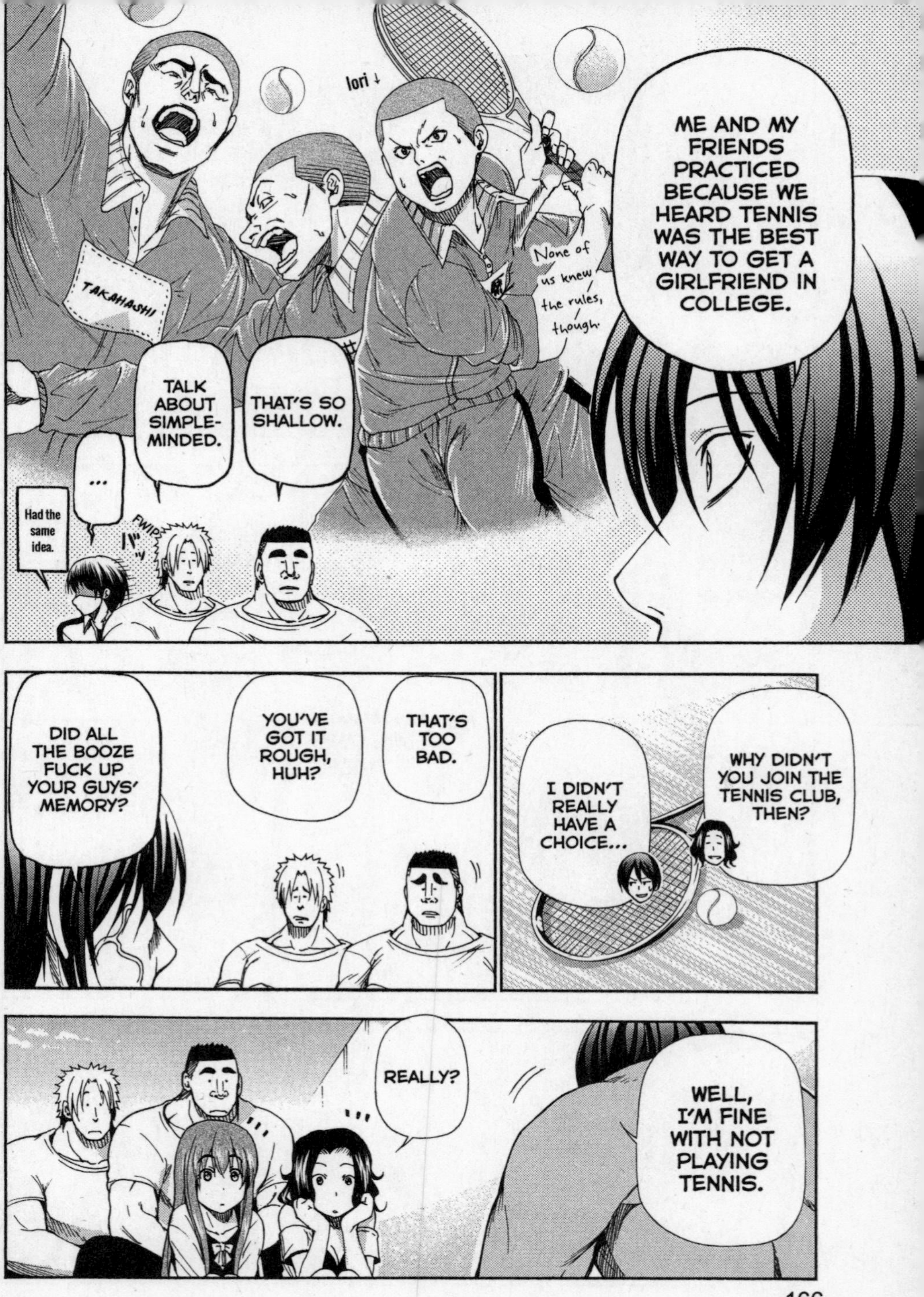
ME AND MY FRIENDS PRACTICED BECAUSE WE HEARD TENNIS WAS THE BEST WAY TO GET A GIRLFRIEND IN COLLEGE.
None of us knew the rules, though.
Iori ↓
TAKAHASHI
THAT'S SO SHALLOW.
TALK ABOUT SIMPLE-MINDED.
...
FWIP
Had the same idea.
WHY DIDN'T YOU JOIN THE TENNIS CLUB, THEN?
I DIDN'T REALLY HAVE A CHOICE...
THAT'S TOO BAD.
YOU'VE GOT IT ROUGH, HUH?
DID ALL THE BOOZE FUCK UP YOUR GUYS' MEMORY?
WELL, I'M FINE WITH NOT PLAYING TENNIS.
REALLY?

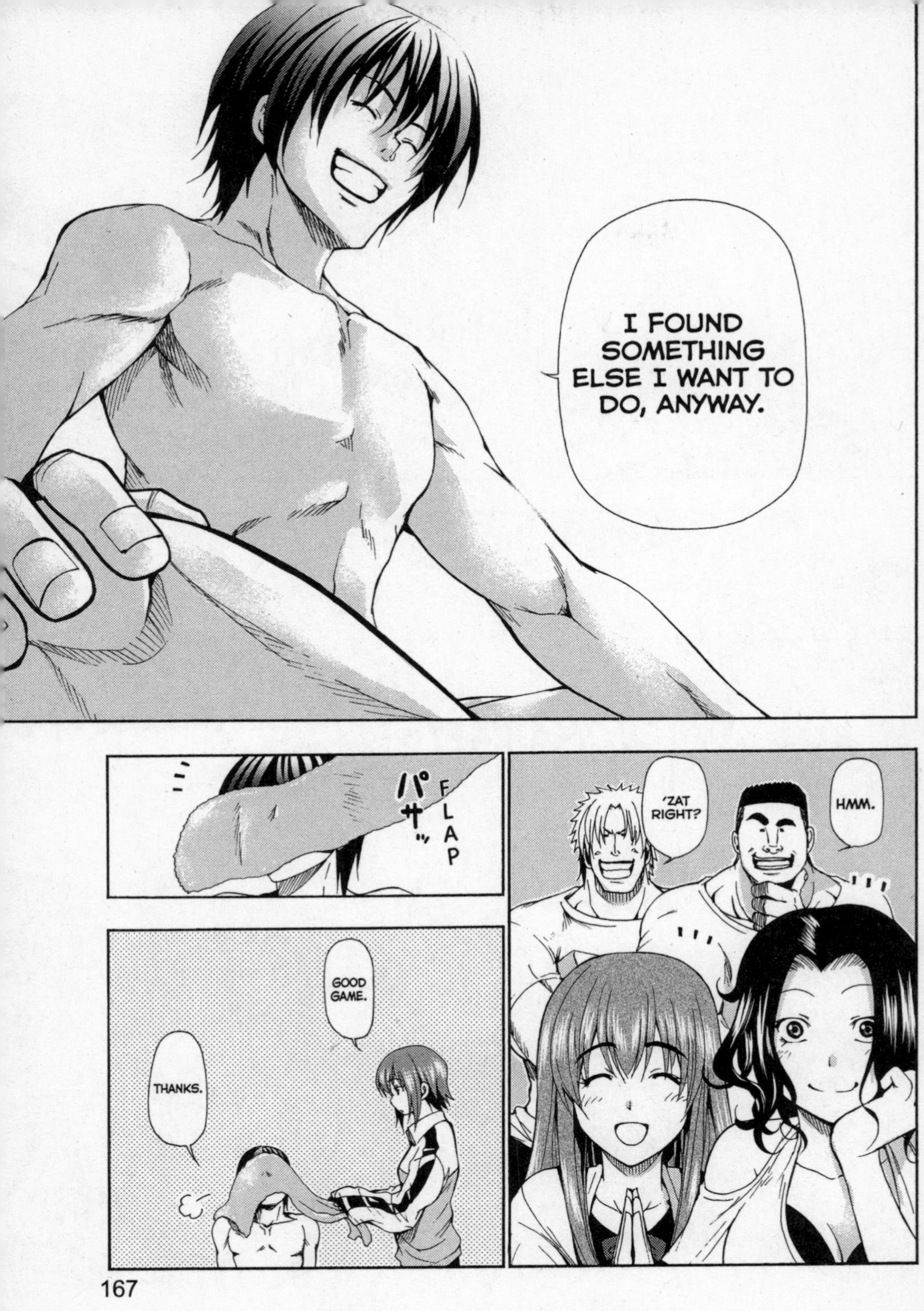
I FOUND SOMETHING ELSE I WANT TO DO, ANYWAY.
HMM.
'ZAT RIGHT?
パサッ
FLAP
GOOD GAME.
THANKS.

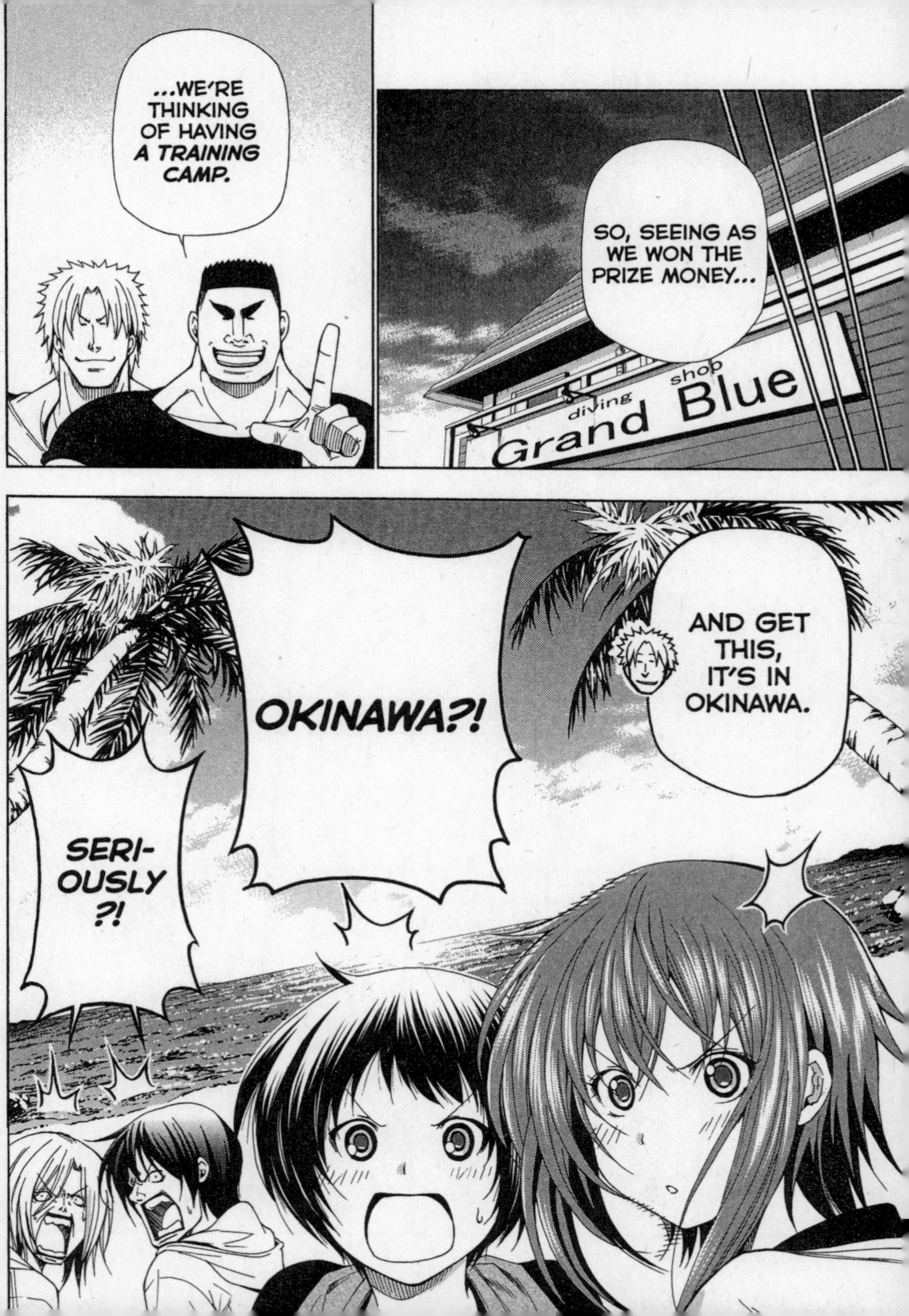
SO, SEEING AS WE WON THE PRIZE MONEY...
diving shop Grand Blue
...WE'RE THINKING OF HAVING A TRAINING CAMP.
AND GET THIS, IT'S IN OKINAWA.
OKINAWA?!
SERI-OUSLY ?!

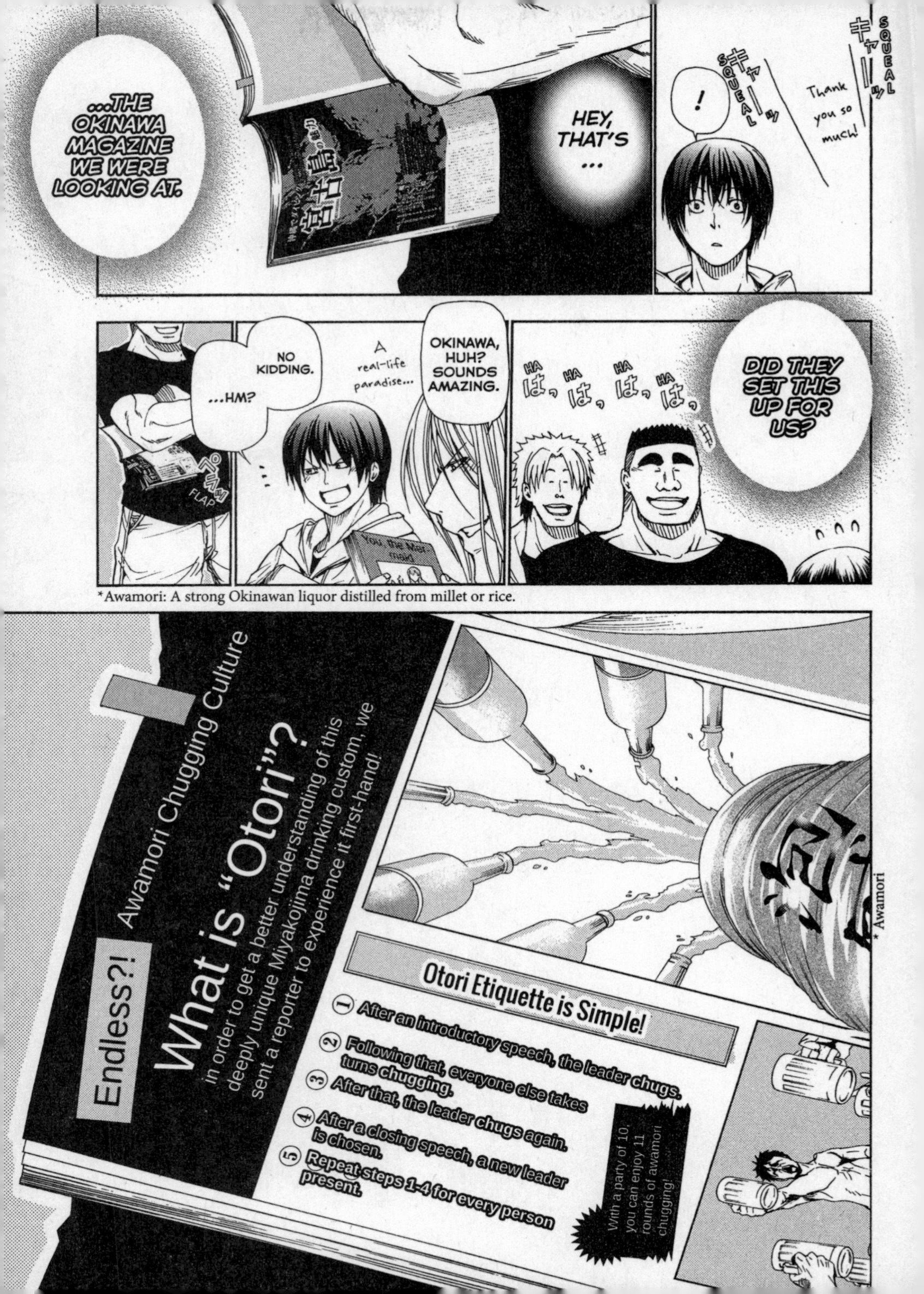

!
SQUEAL
SQUEAL
Thank you so much!
HEY, THAT'S ...
...THE OKINAWA MAGAZINE WE WERE LOOKING AT.
DID THEY SET THIS UP FOR US?
HA HA HA HA
OKINAWA, HUH? SOUNDS AMAZING.
A real-life paradise...
NO KIDDING.
...HM?
FLAP
You, the Mer-maid
Endless?! Awamori Chugging Culture
What is "Otori"?
in order to get a better understanding of this deeply unique Miyakojima drinking custom, we sent a reporter to experience it first-hand!
Otori Etiquette is Simple!
1 After an introductory speech, the leader chugs.
2 Following that, everyone else takes turns chugging.
3 After that, the leader chugs again.
4 After a closing speech, a new leader is chosen.
5 Repeat steps 1-4 for every person present.
With a party of 10, you can enjoy 11 rounds of awamori chugging!
* Awamori

*Awamori: A strong Okinawan liquor distilled from millet or rice.

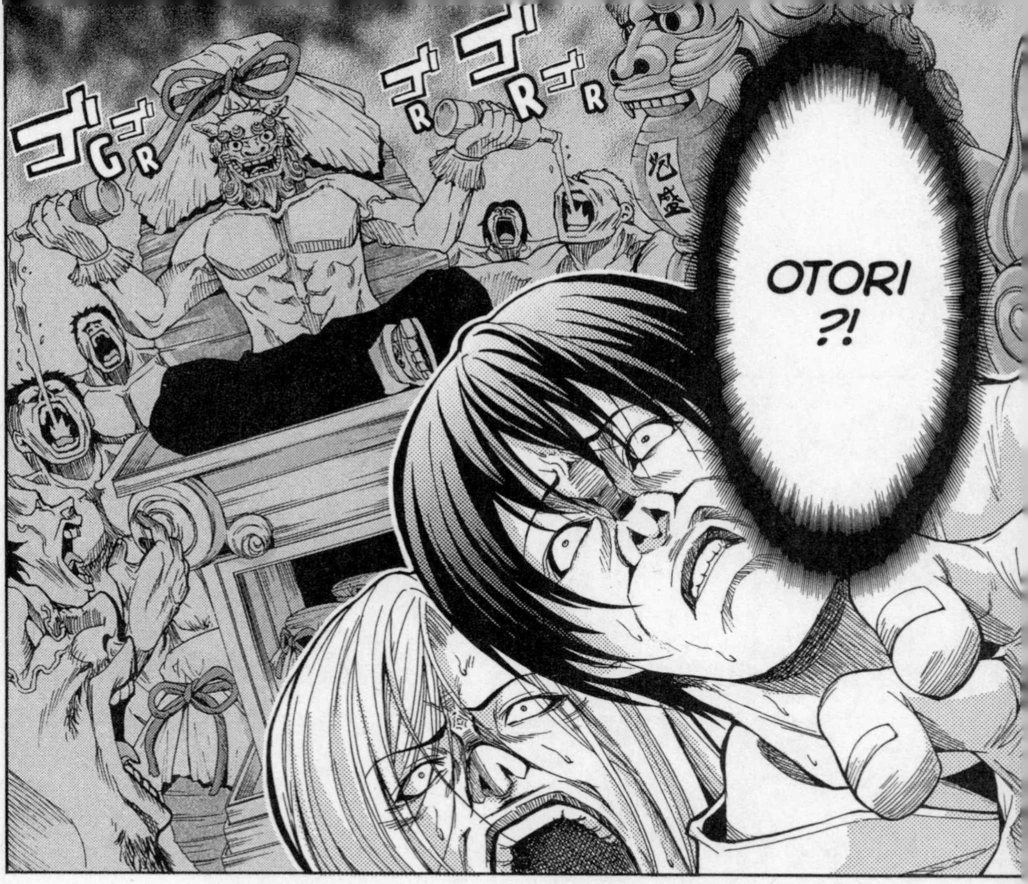
OTORI ?!
ゴRゴRゴR
ゴGゴR

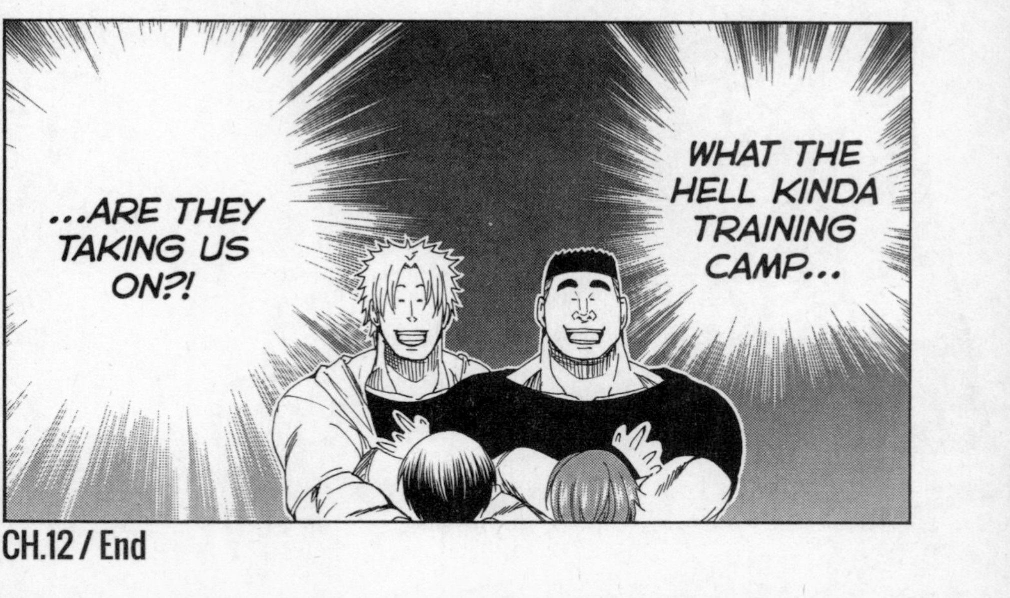
WHAT THE HELL KINDA TRAINING CAMP...
...ARE THEY TAKING US ON?!

CH.12 / End

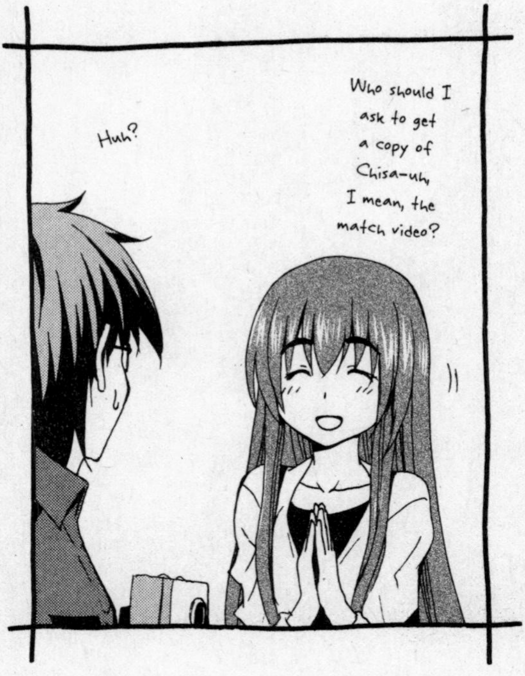
Who should I ask to get a copy of Chisa-uh, I mean, the match video?
Huh?

A SIDE STORY FROM LEFT FIELD

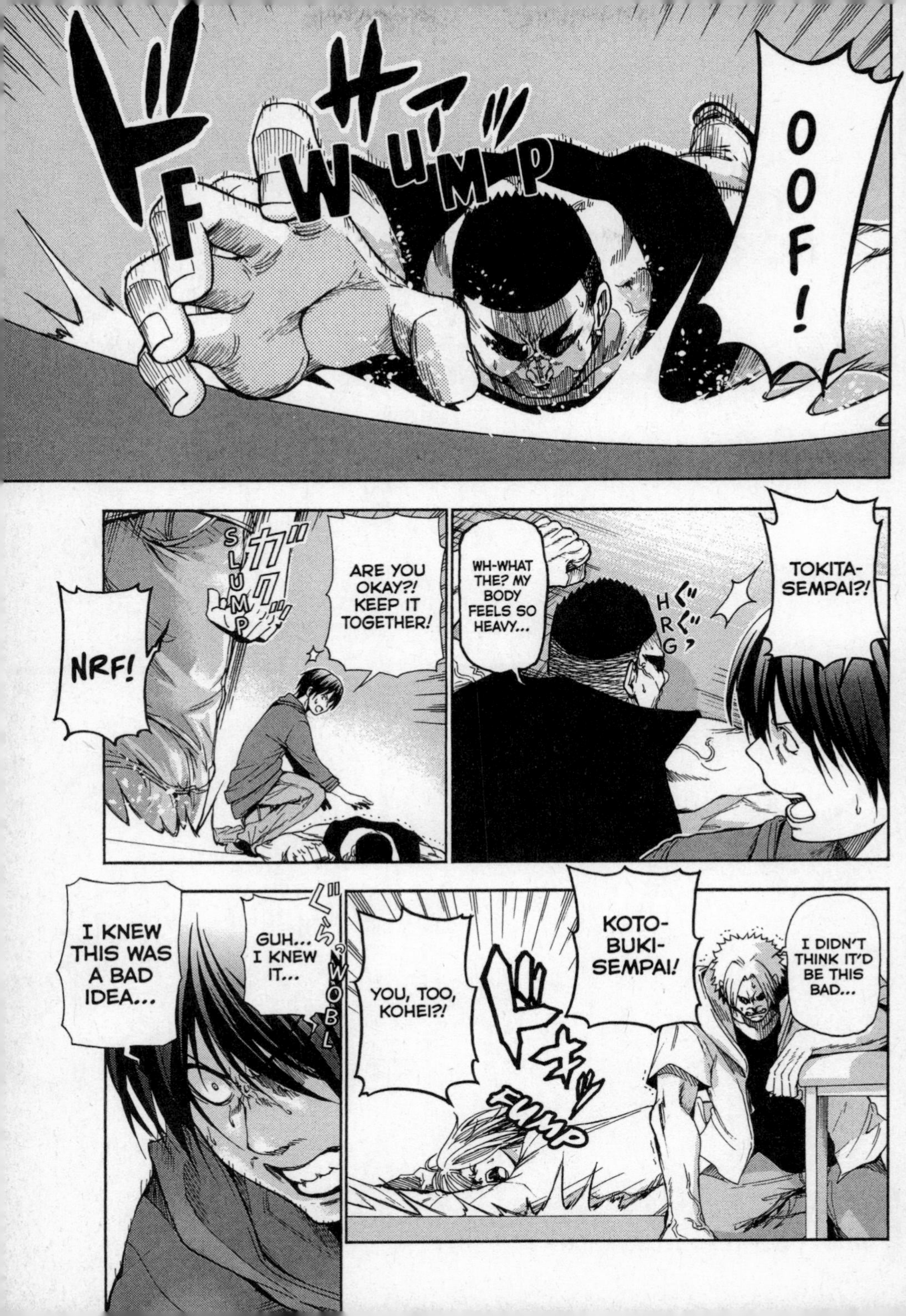
OOF!
FWUMP
TOKITA-SEMPAI?!
HRG
WH-WHAT THE? MY BODY FEELS SO HEAVY...
ARE YOU OKAY?! KEEP IT TOGETHER!
SLUMP
NRF!
I DIDN'T THINK IT'D BE THIS BAD...
KOTO-BUKI-SEMPAI!
YOU, TOO, KOHEI?!
FUMP
GUH... I KNEW IT...
WOBL
I KNEW THIS WAS A BAD IDEA...

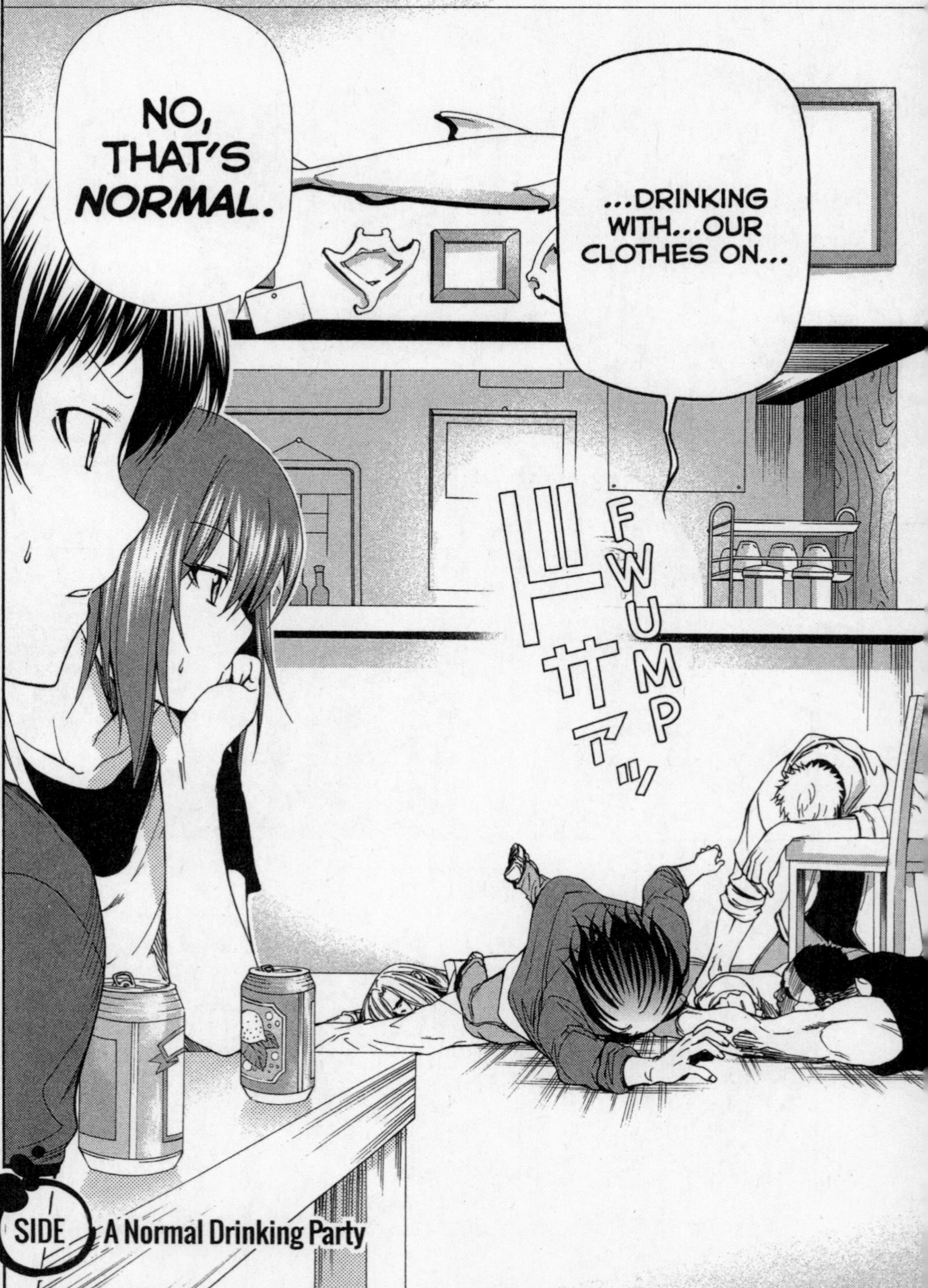
...DRINKING WITH...OUR CLOTHES ON...
NO, THAT'S *NORMAL*.
ドサァッ
FWUMP
SIDE A Normal Drinking Party

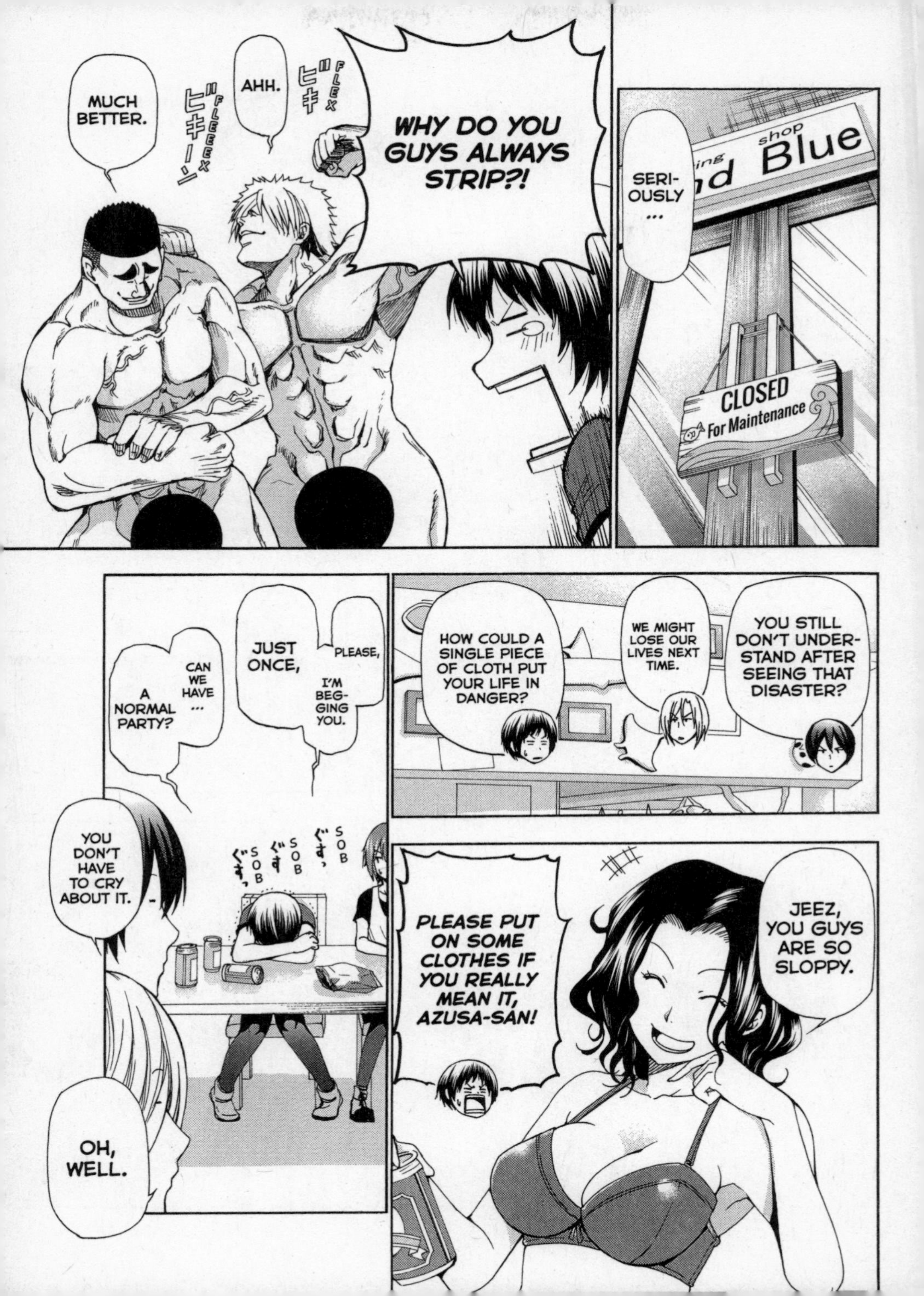
SERI-OUSLY...
ing shop
d Blue
CLOSED
For Maintenance
WHY DO YOU GUYS ALWAYS STRIP?!
FLEX ビキ
AHH.
FLEEEX ビキーン
MUCH BETTER.
YOU STILL DON'T UNDER-STAND AFTER SEEING THAT DISASTER?
WE MIGHT LOSE OUR LIVES NEXT TIME.
HOW COULD A SINGLE PIECE OF CLOTH PUT YOUR LIFE IN DANGER?
JEEZ, YOU GUYS ARE SO SLOPPY.
PLEASE PUT ON SOME CLOTHES IF YOU REALLY MEAN IT, AZUSA-SAN!
PLEASE, I'M BEG-GING YOU.
JUST ONCE,
CAN WE HAVE...
A NORMAL PARTY?
SOB ぐすっ
SOB ぐす
SOB ぐすっ
YOU DON'T HAVE TO CRY ABOUT IT.
OH, WELL.

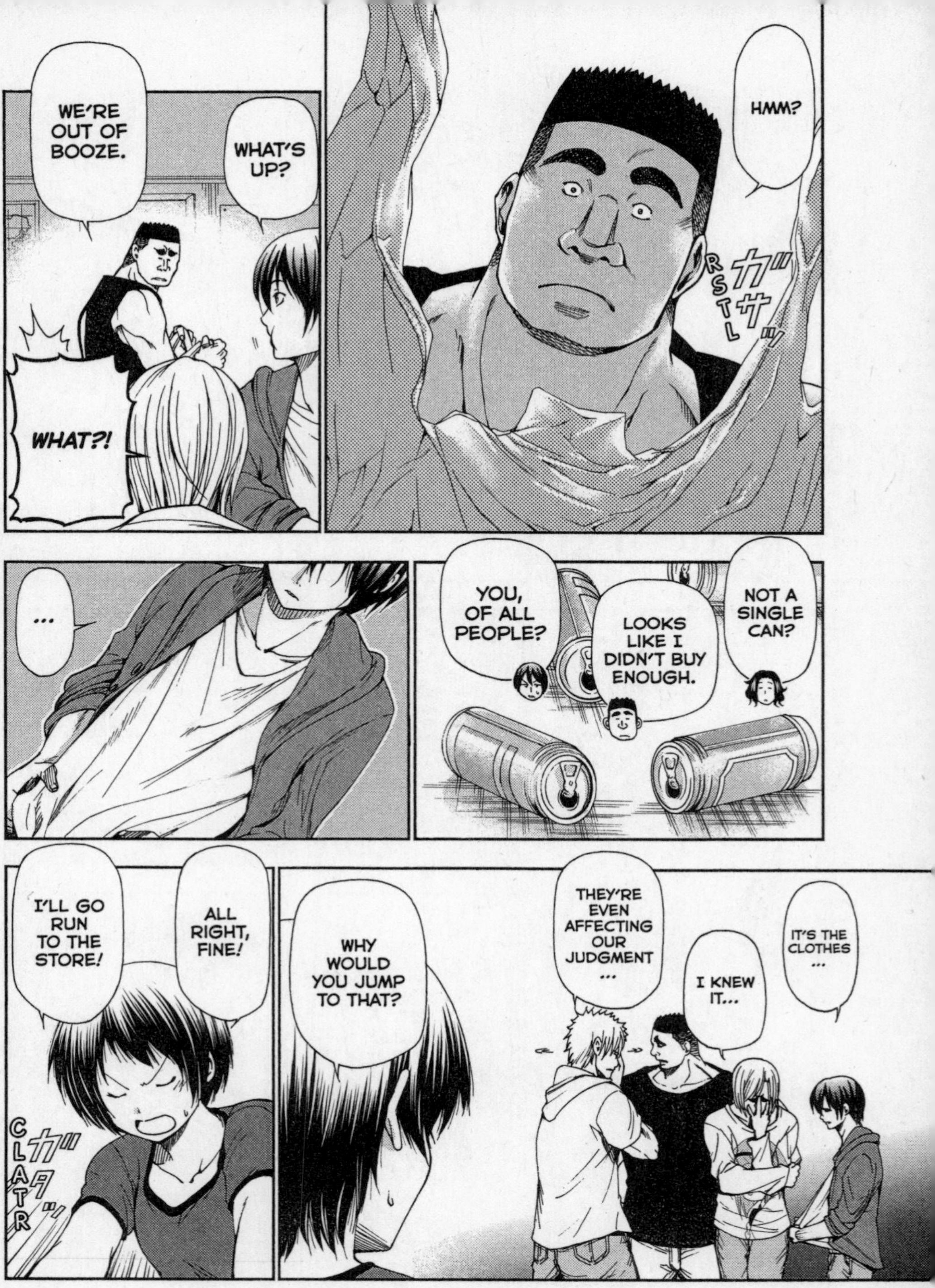
HMM?
RSTL
ガサッ
WHAT'S UP?
WE'RE OUT OF BOOZE.
WHAT?!
NOT A SINGLE CAN?
LOOKS LIKE I DIDN'T BUY ENOUGH.
YOU, OF ALL PEOPLE?
...
IT'S THE CLOTHES ...
I KNEW IT...
THEY'RE EVEN AFFECTING OUR JUDGMENT ...
WHY WOULD YOU JUMP TO THAT?
ALL RIGHT, FINE!
I'LL GO RUN TO THE STORE!
CLATR
ガタッ

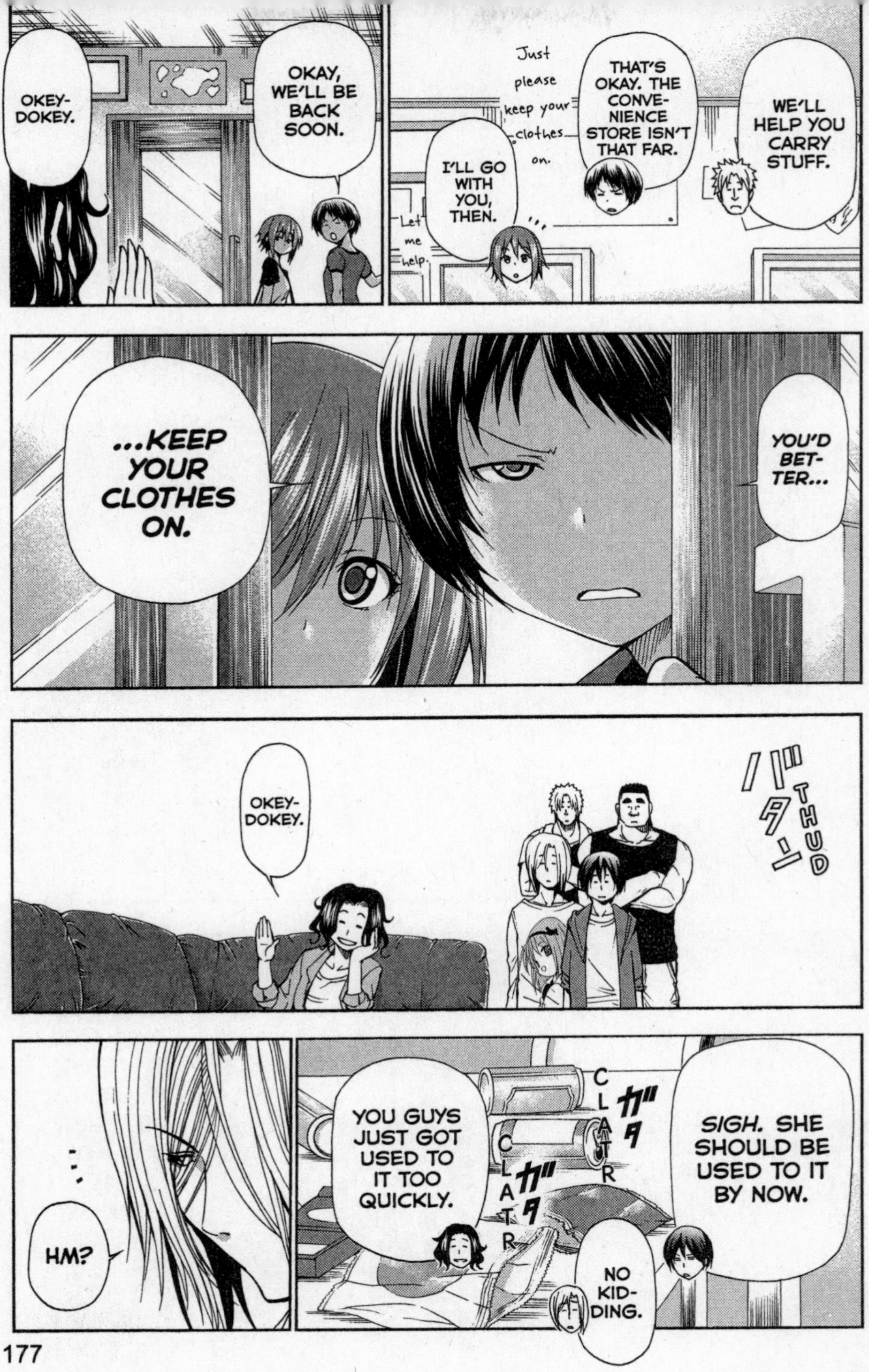
WE'LL HELP YOU CARRY STUFF.
THAT'S OKAY. THE CONVE-NIENCE STORE ISN'T THAT FAR.
Just please keep your clothes on.
I'LL GO WITH YOU, THEN.
Let me help.
OKAY, WE'LL BE BACK SOON.
OKEY-DOKEY.
YOU'D BET-TER...
...KEEP YOUR CLOTHES ON.
THUD
OKEY-DOKEY.
SIGH. SHE SHOULD BE USED TO IT BY NOW.
CLATR
CLATR
NO KID-DING.
YOU GUYS JUST GOT USED TO IT TOO QUICKLY.
...
HM?

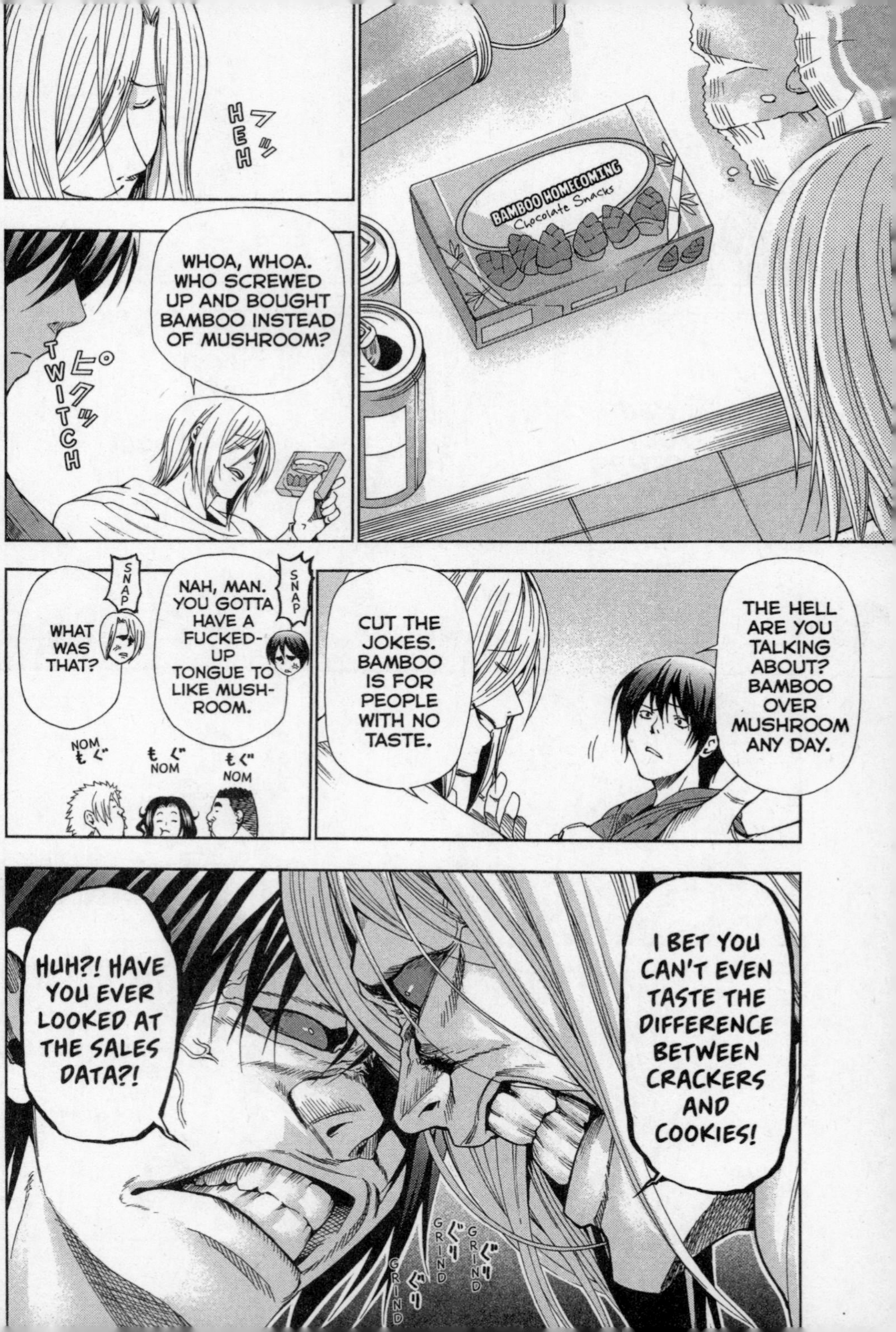
BAMBOO HOMECOMING
Chocolate Snacks
HEH
フッ
WHOA, WHOA. WHO SCREWED UP AND BOUGHT BAMBOO INSTEAD OF MUSHROOM?
TWITCH
ピクッ
THE HELL ARE YOU TALKING ABOUT? BAMBOO OVER MUSHROOM ANY DAY.
CUT THE JOKES. BAMBOO IS FOR PEOPLE WITH NO TASTE.
SNAP
NAH, MAN. YOU GOTTA HAVE A FUCKED-UP TONGUE TO LIKE MUSH-ROOM.
SNAP
WHAT WAS THAT?
もぐ NOM
もぐ NOM
NOM もぐ
I BET YOU CAN'T EVEN TASTE THE DIFFERENCE BETWEEN CRACKERS AND COOKIES!
HUH?! HAVE YOU EVER LOOKED AT THE SALES DATA?!
GRIND ぐり
GRIND ぐり
GRIND ぐり

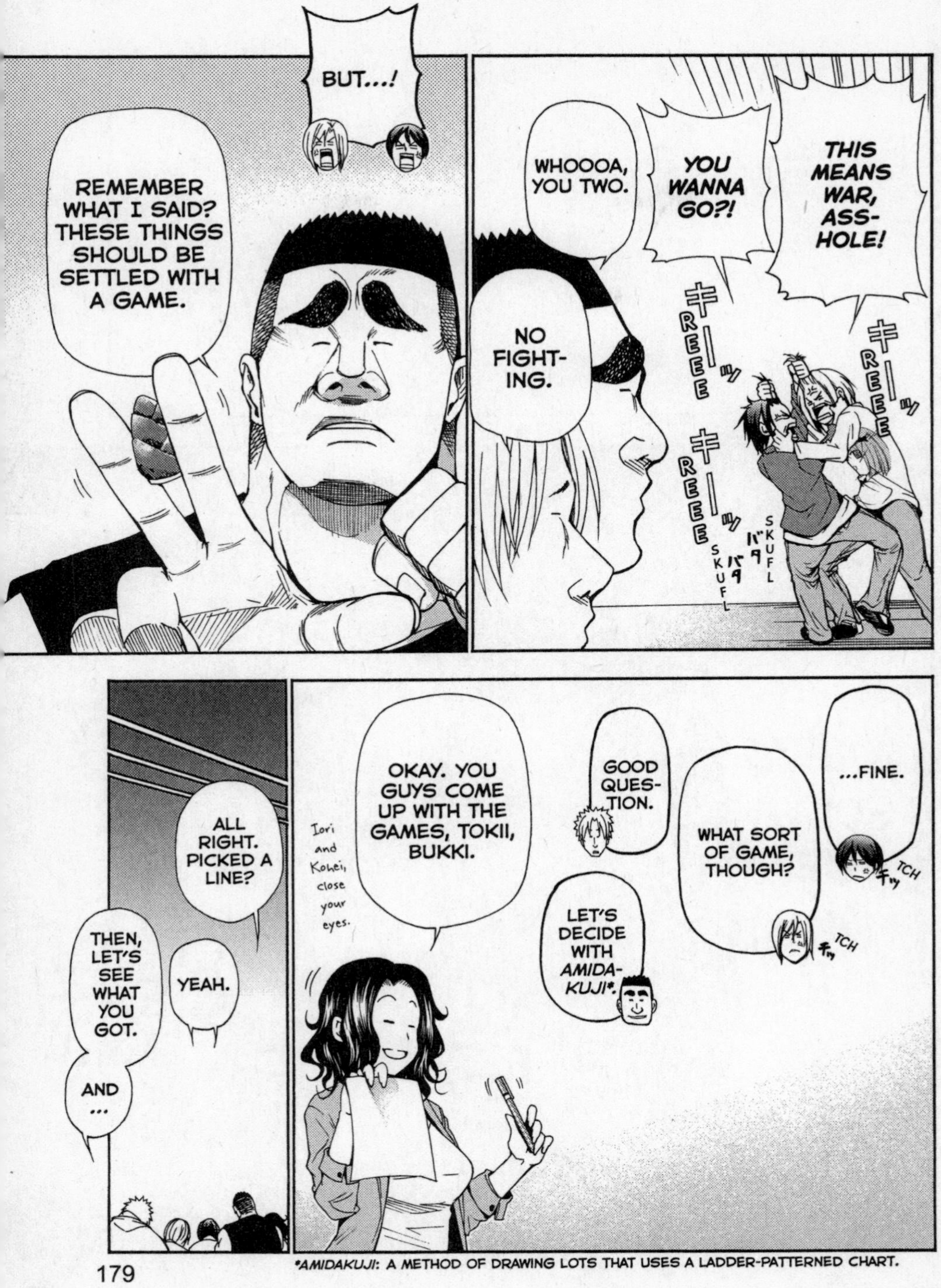
THIS MEANS WAR, ASS-HOLE!
YOU WANNA GO?!
WHOOOA, YOU TWO.
NO FIGHT-ING.
キーーッ REEE
キーーッ REEE
キーーッ REEE
バタバタ SKUFL SKUFL
BUT...!
REMEMBER WHAT I SAID? THESE THINGS SHOULD BE SETTLED WITH A GAME.
...FINE.
チッ TCH
WHAT SORT OF GAME, THOUGH?
チッ TCH
GOOD QUES-TION.
LET'S DECIDE WITH AMIDA-KUJI*.
OKAY. YOU GUYS COME UP WITH THE GAMES, TOKII, BUKKI.
Iori and Kohei, close your eyes.
ALL RIGHT. PICKED A LINE?
YEAH.
THEN, LET'S SEE WHAT YOU GOT.
AND ...

**AMIDAKUJI*: A METHOD OF DRAWING LOTS THAT USES A LADDER-PATTERNED CHART.

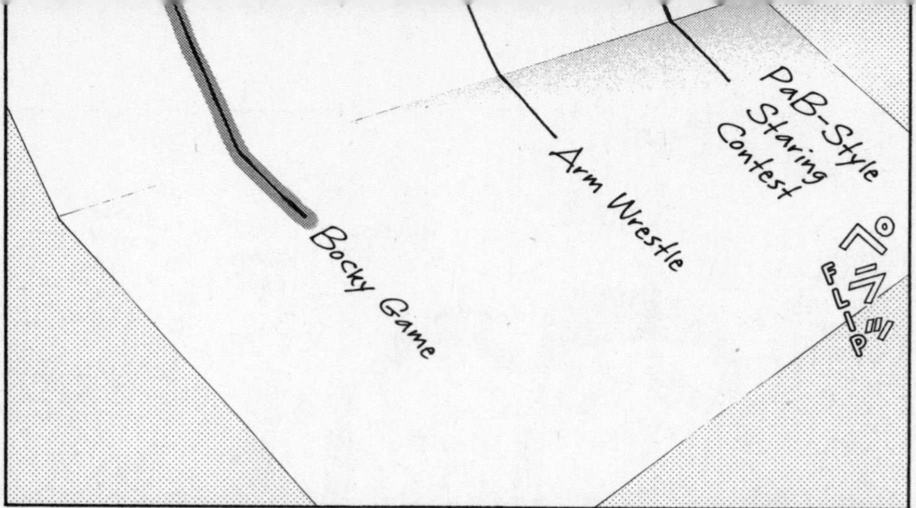
PaB-Style Staring Contest
FLIP
Arm Wrestle
Bocky Game

*Bocky Game: A parody of the Pocky Game, a game in which two people play chicken by eating from either end of a stick of Pocky and work towards the center until one person gives up, breaks off their end, or the two kiss.

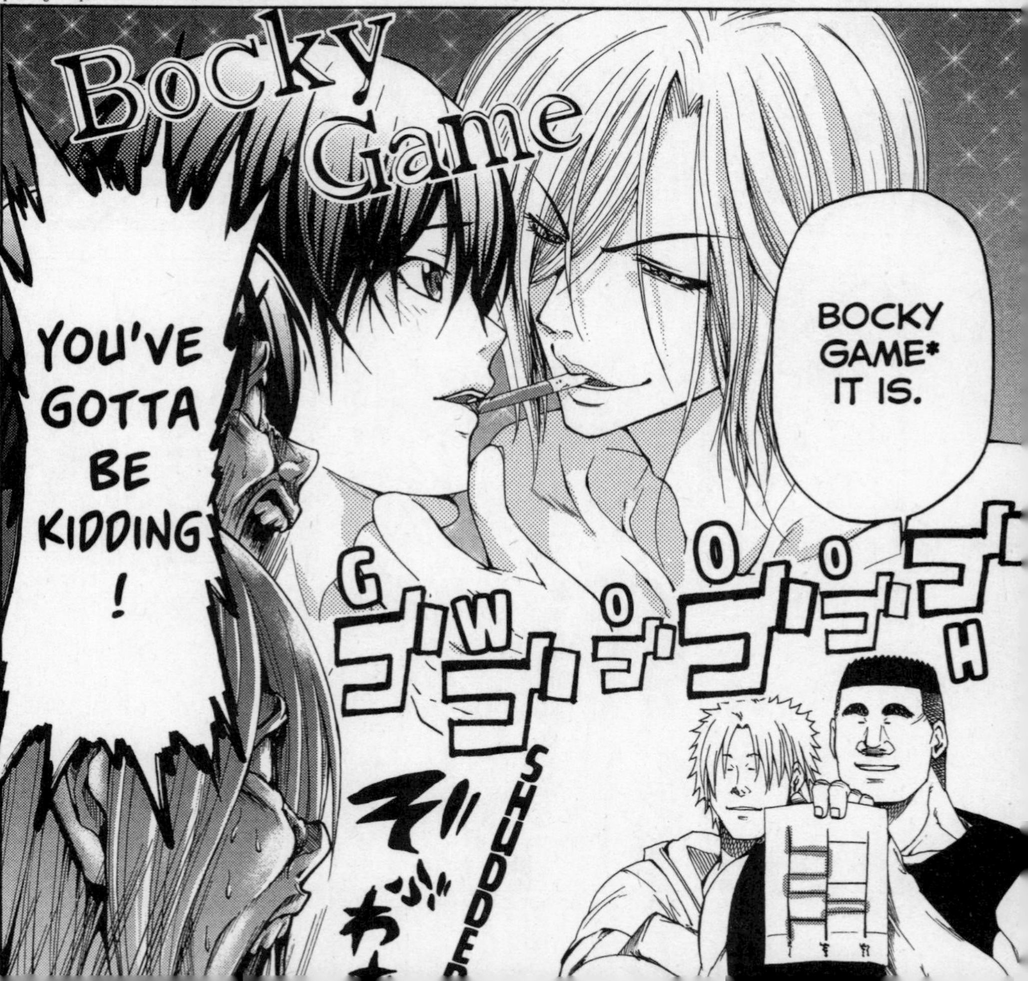
Bocky Game
BOCKY GAME* IT IS.
YOU'VE GOTTA BE KIDDING!
GWOOOOH
SHUDDER

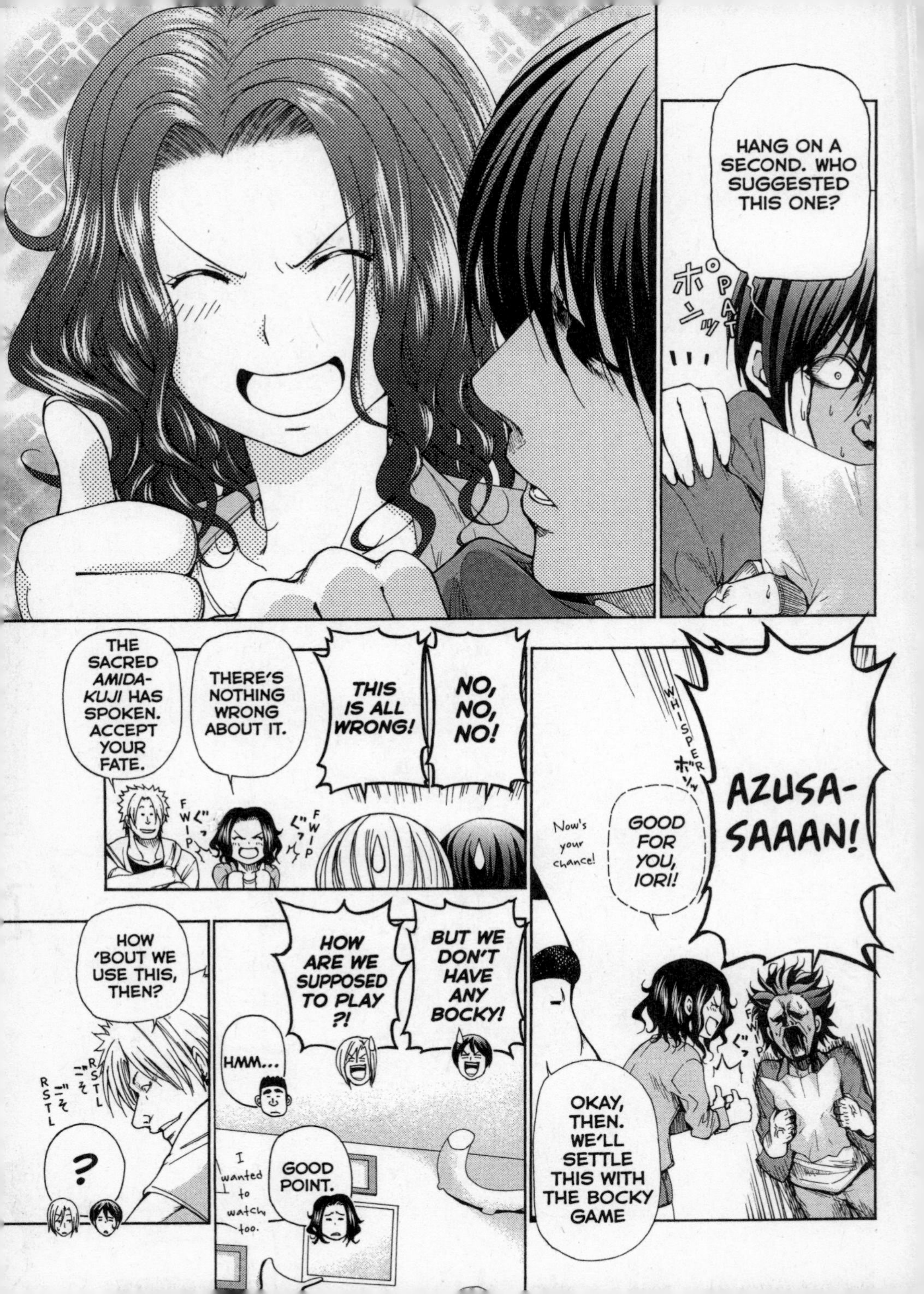
HANG ON A SECOND. WHO SUGGESTED THIS ONE?
PAT
AZUSA-SAAAN!
WHISPER
GOOD FOR YOU, IORI!
Now's your chance!
FWIP
OKAY, THEN. WE'LL SETTLE THIS WITH THE BOCKY GAME
NO, NO, NO!
THIS IS ALL WRONG!
THERE'S NOTHING WRONG ABOUT IT.
THE SACRED *AMIDA-KUJI* HAS SPOKEN. ACCEPT YOUR FATE.
FWIP
FWIP
BUT WE DON'T HAVE ANY BOCKY!
HOW ARE WE SUPPOSED TO PLAY ?!
HMM...
GOOD POINT.
I wanted to watch too.
HOW 'BOUT WE USE THIS, THEN?
RSTL
RSTL
?

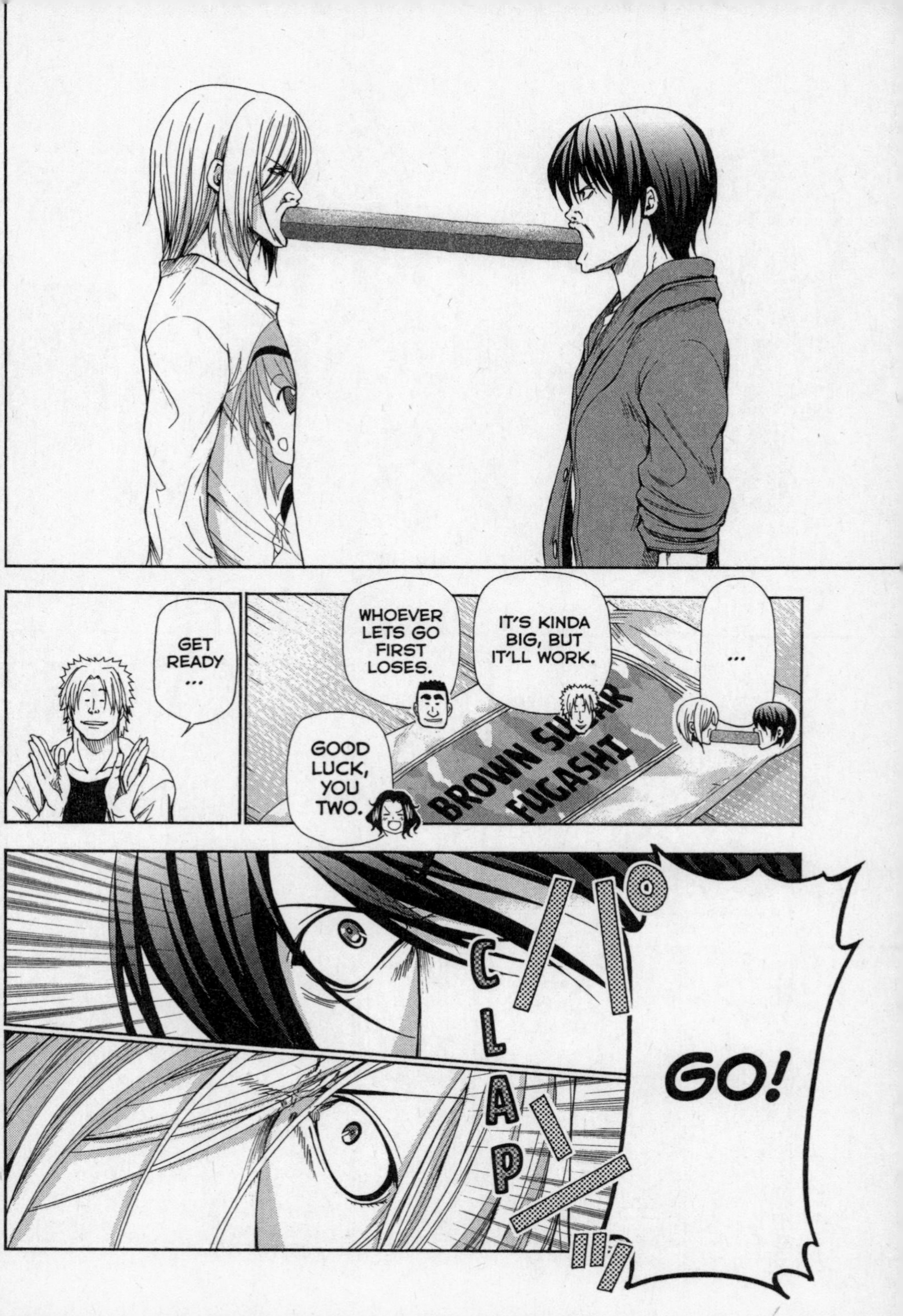
...
IT'S KINDA BIG, BUT IT'LL WORK.
WHOEVER LETS GO FIRST LOSES.
BROWN SUGAR FUGASHI
GOOD LUCK, YOU TWO.
GET READY ...
CLAP
GO!

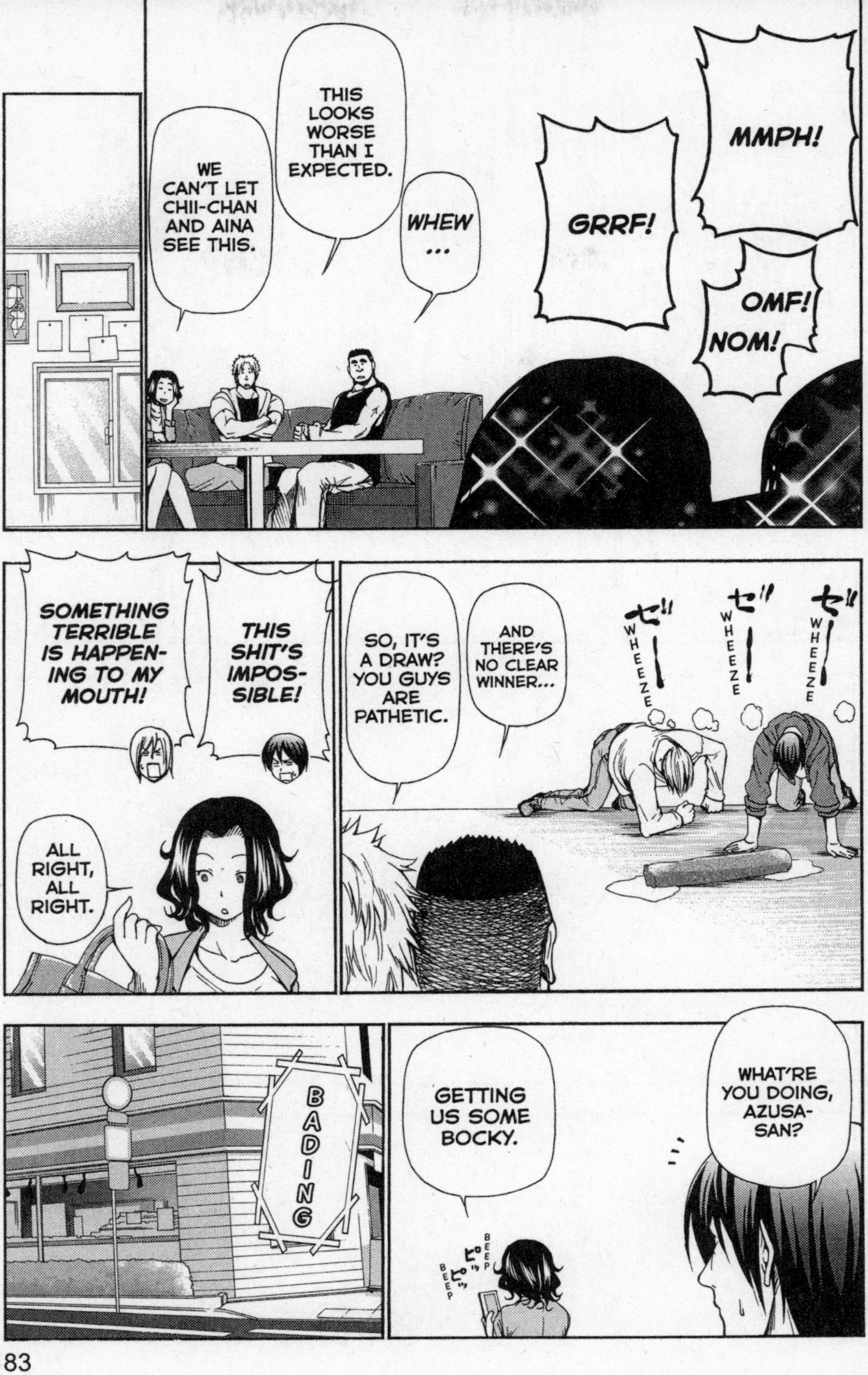
MMPH!
GRRF!
OMF! NOM!
WHEW ...
THIS LOOKS WORSE THAN I EXPECTED.
WE CAN'T LET CHII-CHAN AND AINA SEE THIS.
WHEEZE
WHEEZE
WHEEZE
AND THERE'S NO CLEAR WINNER...
SO, IT'S A DRAW? YOU GUYS ARE PATHETIC.
THIS SHIT'S IMPOSSIBLE!
SOMETHING TERRIBLE IS HAPPENING TO MY MOUTH!
ALL RIGHT, ALL RIGHT.
WHAT'RE YOU DOING, AZUSA-SAN?
GETTING US SOME BOCKY.
BEEP
BEEP
BADING

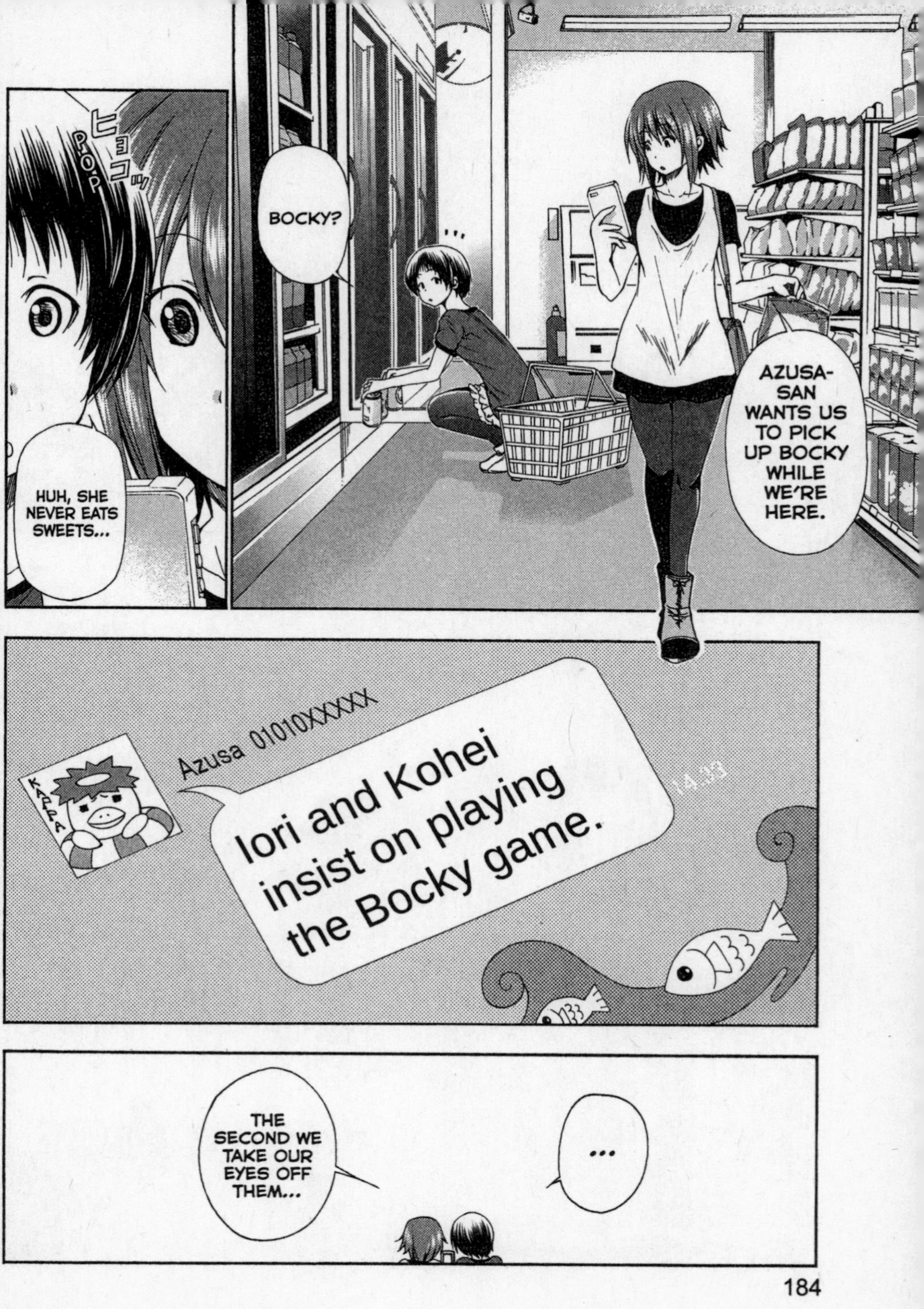
AZUSA-SAN WANTS US TO PICK UP BOCKY WHILE WE'RE HERE.
BOCKY?
ヒョコッ
POP
HUH, SHE NEVER EATS SWEETS...
Azusa 01010XXXX
KAPPA
Iori and Kohei insist on playing the Bocky game.
...
THE SECOND WE TAKE OUR EYES OFF THEM...

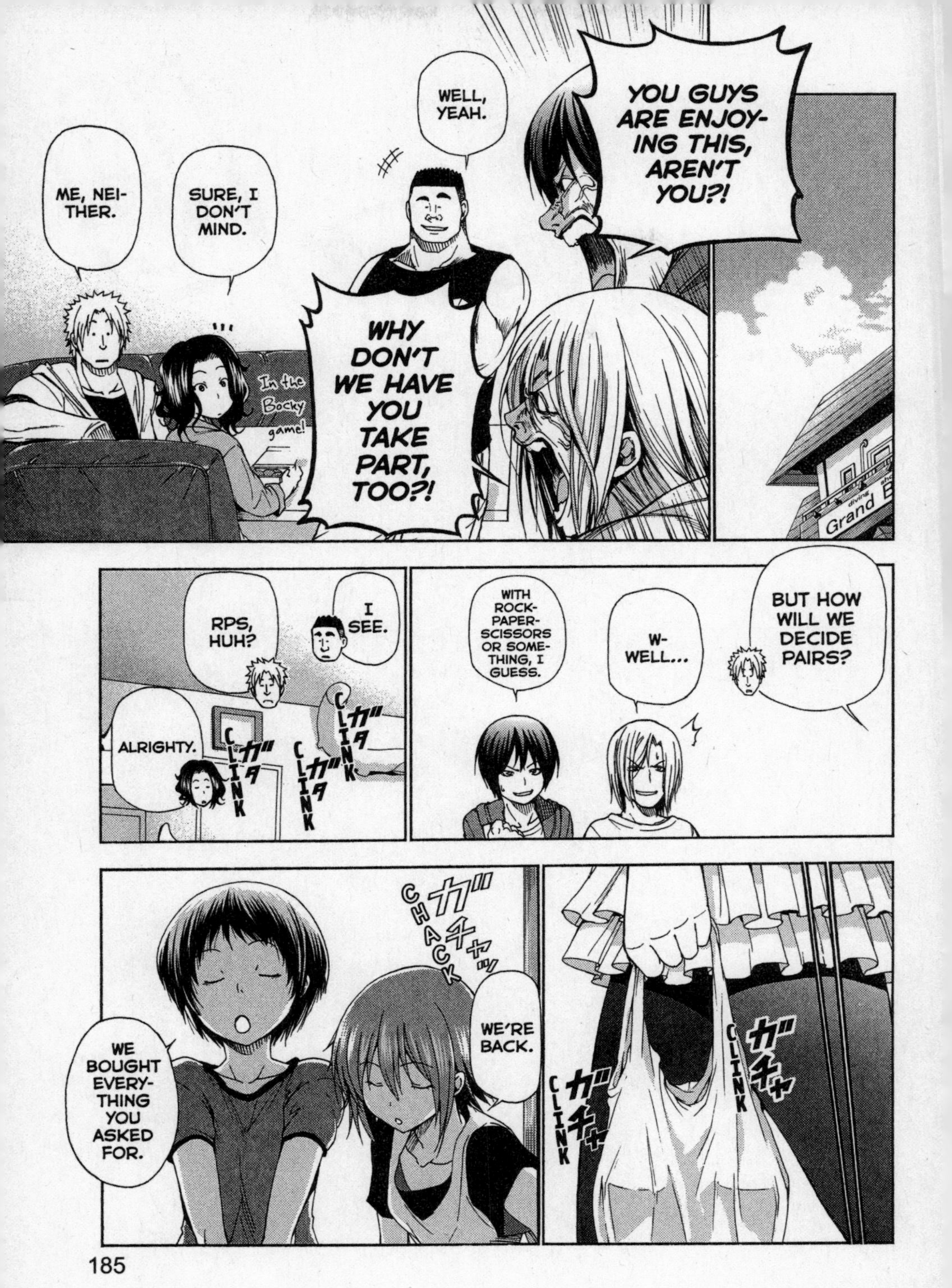
YOU GUYS ARE ENJOYING THIS, AREN'T YOU?!
WHY DON'T WE HAVE YOU TAKE PART, TOO?!
WELL, YEAH.
SURE, I DON'T MIND.
ME, NEITHER.
In the Bocky game!
BUT HOW WILL WE DECIDE PAIRS?
W-WELL...
WITH ROCK-PAPER-SCISSORS OR SOMETHING, I GUESS.
I SEE.
RPS, HUH?
CLINK ガタ
CLINK ガタ
ALRIGHTY.
CLINK ガタ
CLINK ガチャ
CLINK ガチャ
CHACK ガチャッ
WE'RE BACK.
WE BOUGHT EVERYTHING YOU ASKED FOR.

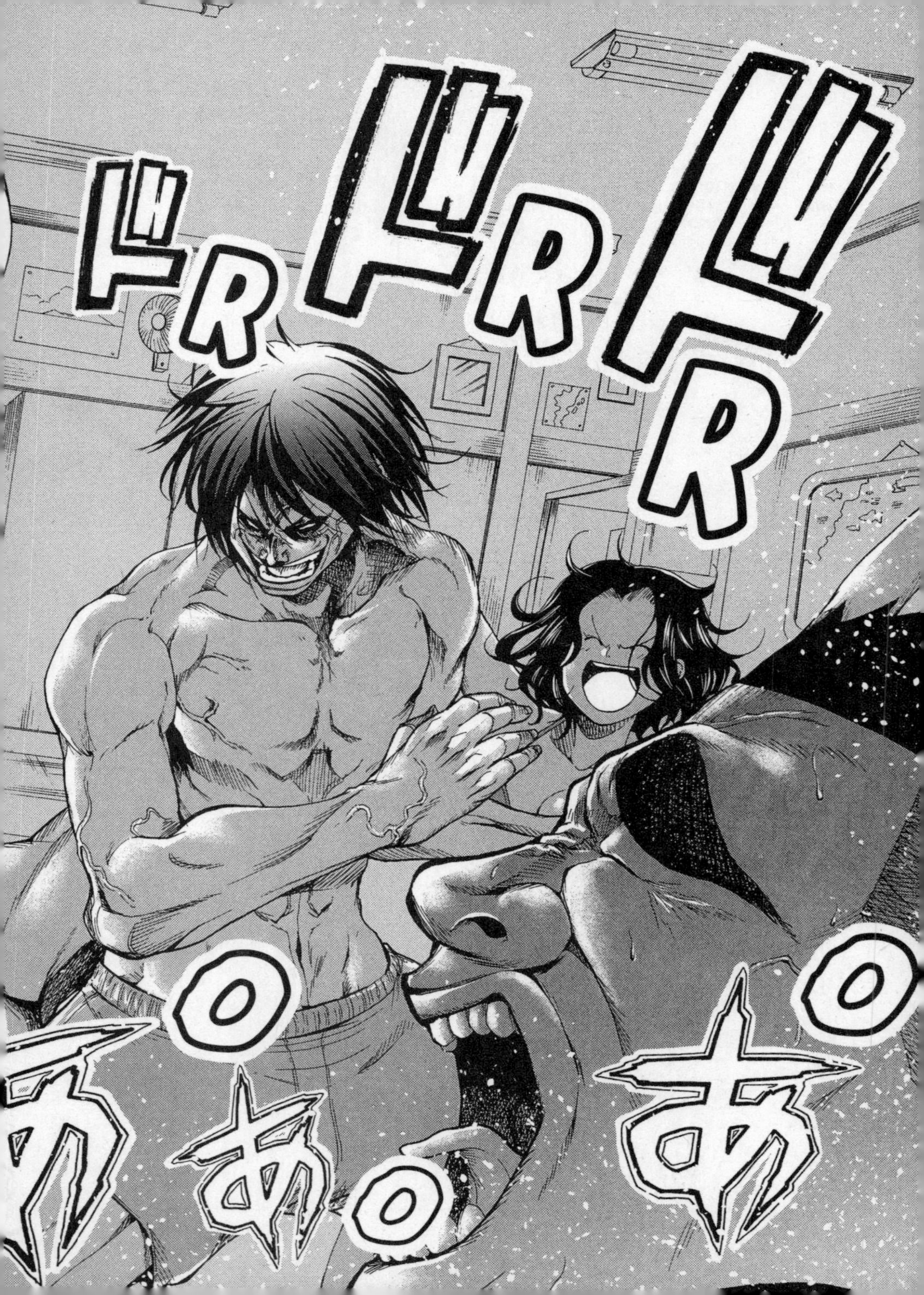

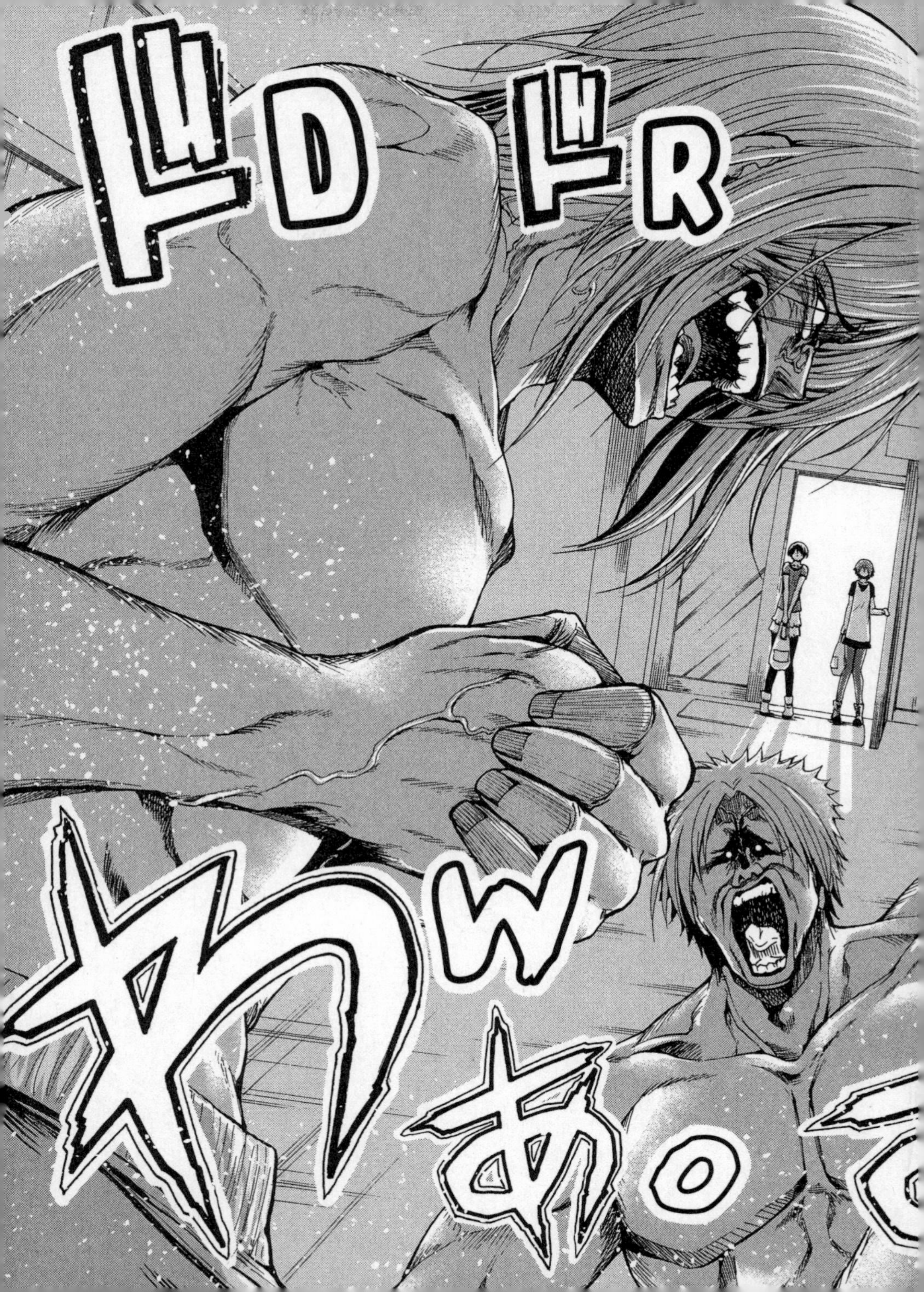

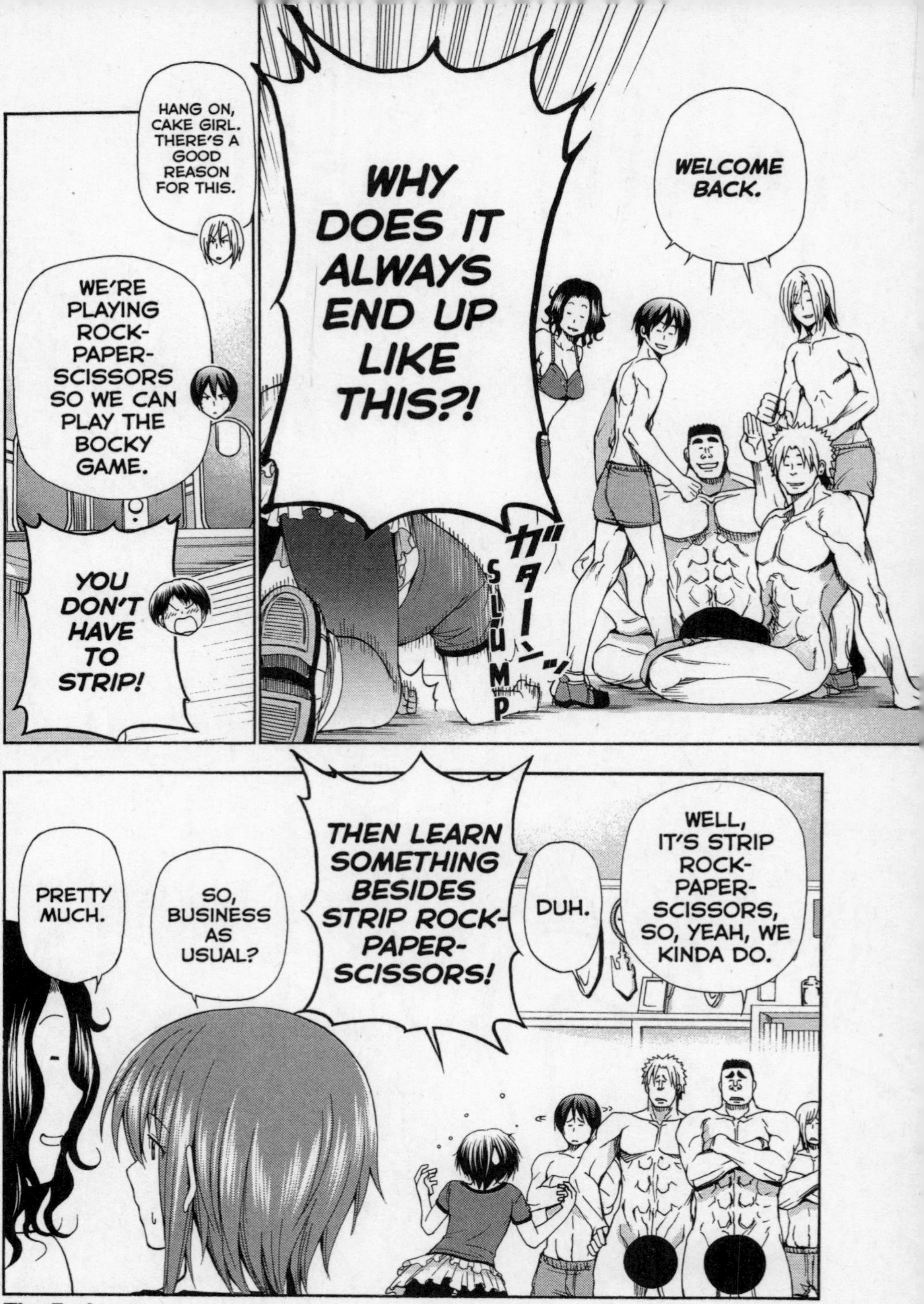
WELCOME BACK.
WHY DOES IT ALWAYS END UP LIKE THIS?!
ガターン
SLUMP
HANG ON, CAKE GIRL. THERE'S A GOOD REASON FOR THIS.
WE'RE PLAYING ROCK-PAPER-SCISSORS SO WE CAN PLAY THE BOCKY GAME.
YOU DON'T HAVE TO STRIP!
WELL, IT'S STRIP ROCK-PAPER-SCISSORS, SO, YEAH, WE KINDA DO.
DUH.
THEN LEARN SOMETHING BESIDES STRIP ROCK-PAPER-SCISSORS!
SO, BUSINESS AS USUAL?
PRETTY MUCH.

The End

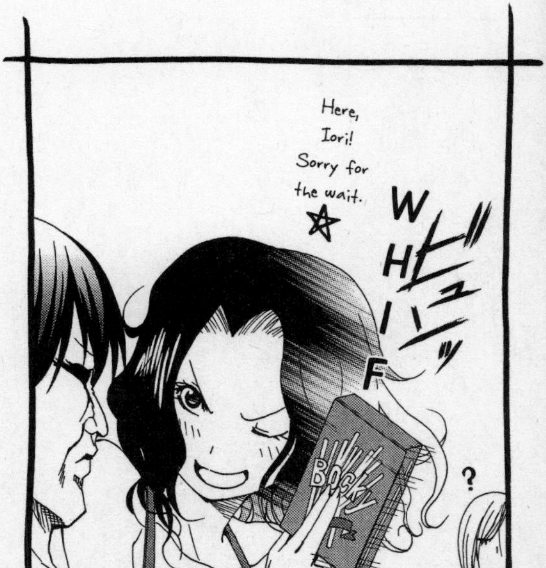
Here, Iori! Sorry for the wait. ☆
WHIFF
?

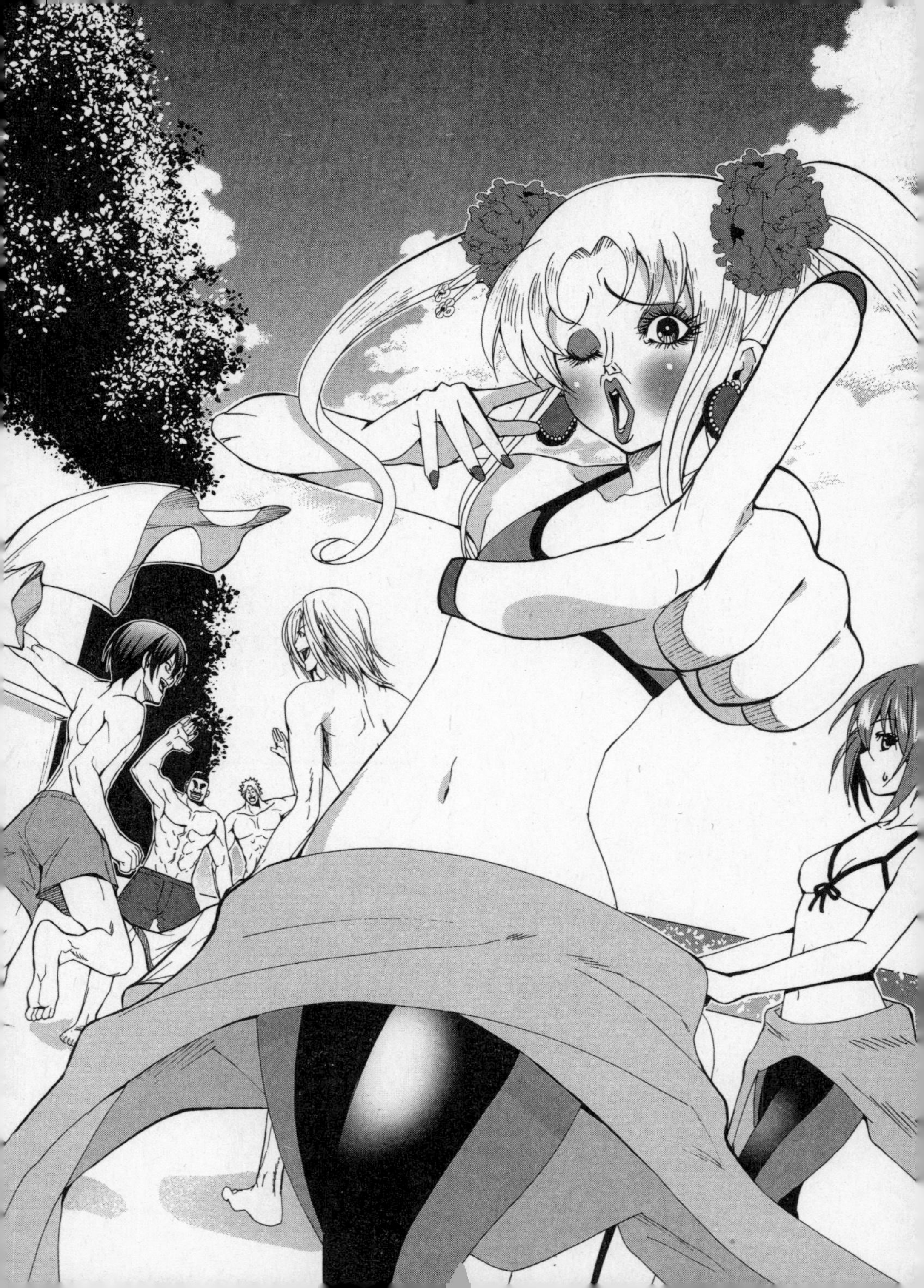

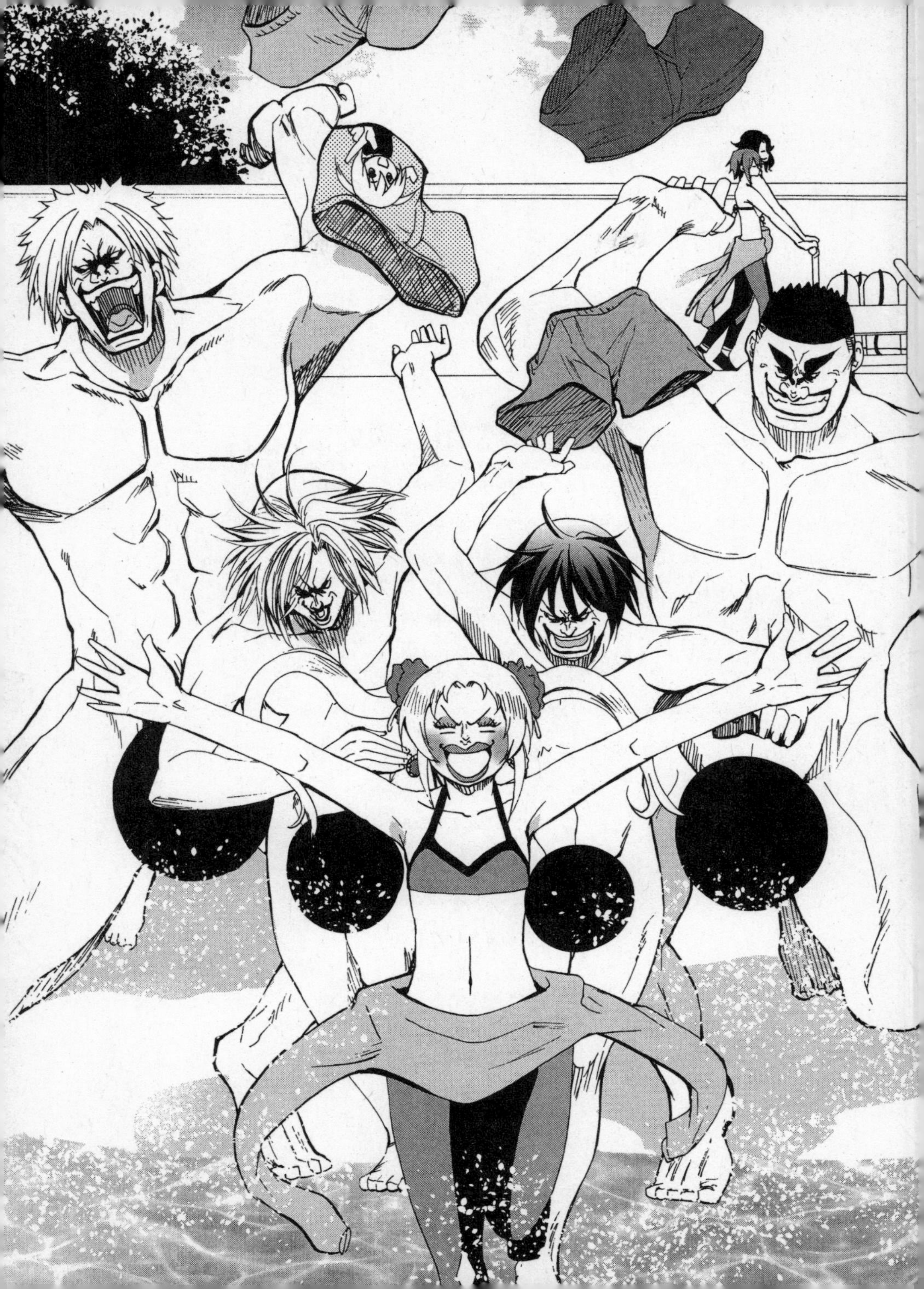

A Kodansha Comics Trade Paperback Original.

Grand Blue Dreaming volume 3 copyright © 2015 Kenji Inoue/Kimitake Yoshioka
English translation copyright © 2018 Kenji Inoue/Kimitake Yoshioka

Published in the United States by Kodansha Comics,
an imprint of Kodansha USA Publishing, LLC, New York.

Publication rights for this English edition arranged through Kodansha Ltd., Tokyo.

First published in Japan in 2015 by Kodansha Ltd., Tokyo.

Cover Design: YUKI YOSHIDA (futaba)

ISBN 978-1-63236-668-9

Printed in the United States of America.

www.kodanshacomics.com

9 8 7 6 5 4 3 2 1

Translation: Adam Hirsch
Lettering: Jan Lan Ivan Concepcion
Editing: Sarah Tilson and Paul Starr
Editorial Assistance: YKS Services LLC/SKY Japan, INC.
Kodansha Comics Edition Cover Design: Phil Balsman